ALSO BY JEFFREY BROWN

LITTLE THINGS
INCREDIBLE CHANGE-BOTS
CAT GETTING OUT OF A BAG
I AM GOING TO BE SMALL
EVERY GIRL IS THE END OF THE WORLD FOR ME
AEIOU: ANY EASY INTIMACY
BIGHEAD
UNLIKELY
CLUMSY

FUNNY MISSHAPEN BODY

JEFFREY BROWN

A TOUCHSTONE BOOK
PUBLISHED BY SIMON & SCHUSTER
NEW YORK · LONDON · TORONTO · SYDNEY

Touchstone
A Division of Simon & Schuster, Inc.
1230 Avenue of the Americas
New York, NY 10020

First Touchstone Trade paperback edition April 2009

TOUCHSTONE and colophon are registered trademarks of Simon & Schuster, Inc.

For information about special discounts for bulk purchases, please contact Simon & Schuster Special Sales at 1-800-456-6798 or business@simonandschuster.com

Manufactured in the United States of America

10 9 8 7 6 5 4 3 2 1

Library of Congress Cataloging-in-Publication Data is available.

ISBN-13: 978-1-4165-4947-5
ISBN-10:   1-4165-4947-1

FUNNY
MISSHAPEN
BODY

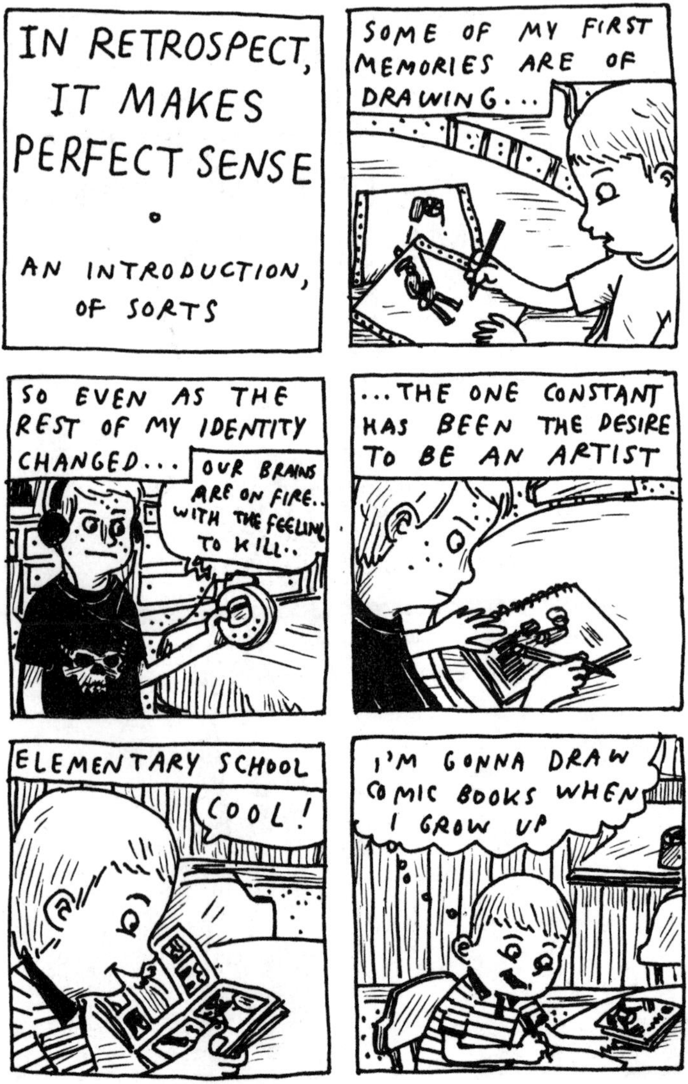
IN RETROSPECT, IT MAKES PERFECT SENSE
AN INTRODUCTION, OF SORTS
SOME OF MY FIRST MEMORIES ARE OF DRAWING...
SO EVEN AS THE REST OF MY IDENTITY CHANGED...
OUR BRAINS ARE ON FIRE.. WITH THE FEELING TO KILL..
...THE ONE CONSTANT HAS BEEN THE DESIRE TO BE AN ARTIST
ELEMENTARY SCHOOL
COOL!
I'M GONNA DRAW COMIC BOOKS WHEN I GROW UP

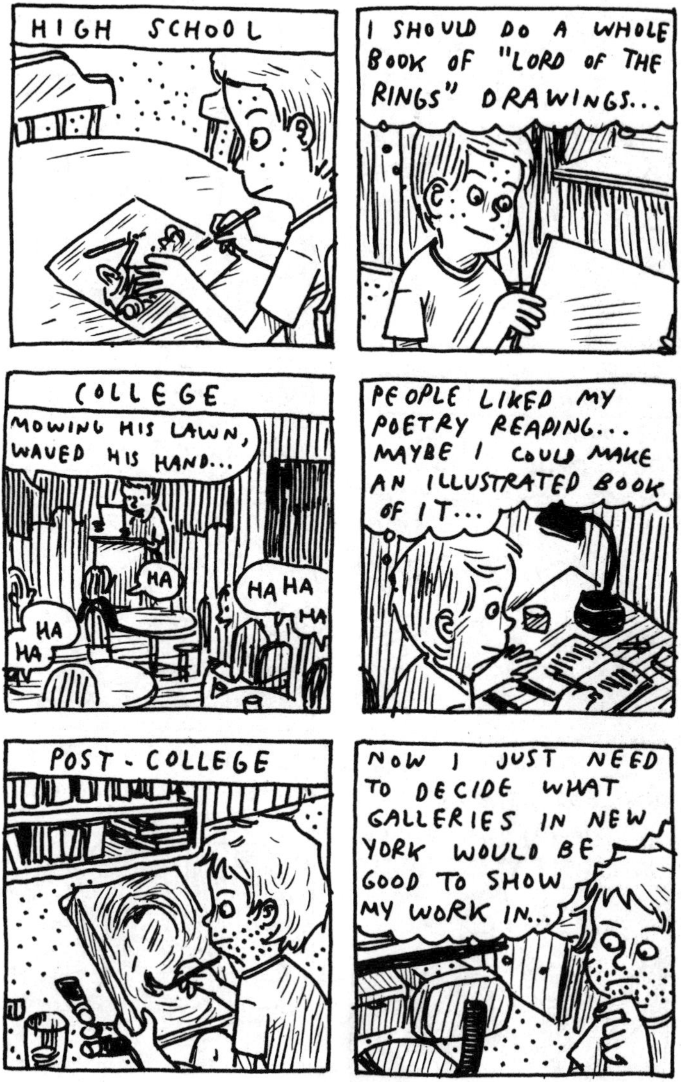
HIGH SCHOOL
I SHOULD DO A WHOLE BOOK OF "LORD OF THE RINGS" DRAWINGS...
COLLEGE
MOWING HIS LAWN, WAVED HIS HAND...
HA
HA HA
HA
HA
HA
PEOPLE LIKED MY POETRY READING... MAYBE I COULD MAKE AN ILLUSTRATED BOOK OF IT...
POST-COLLEGE
NOW I JUST NEED TO DECIDE WHAT GALLERIES IN NEW YORK WOULD BE GOOD TO SHOW MY WORK IN...

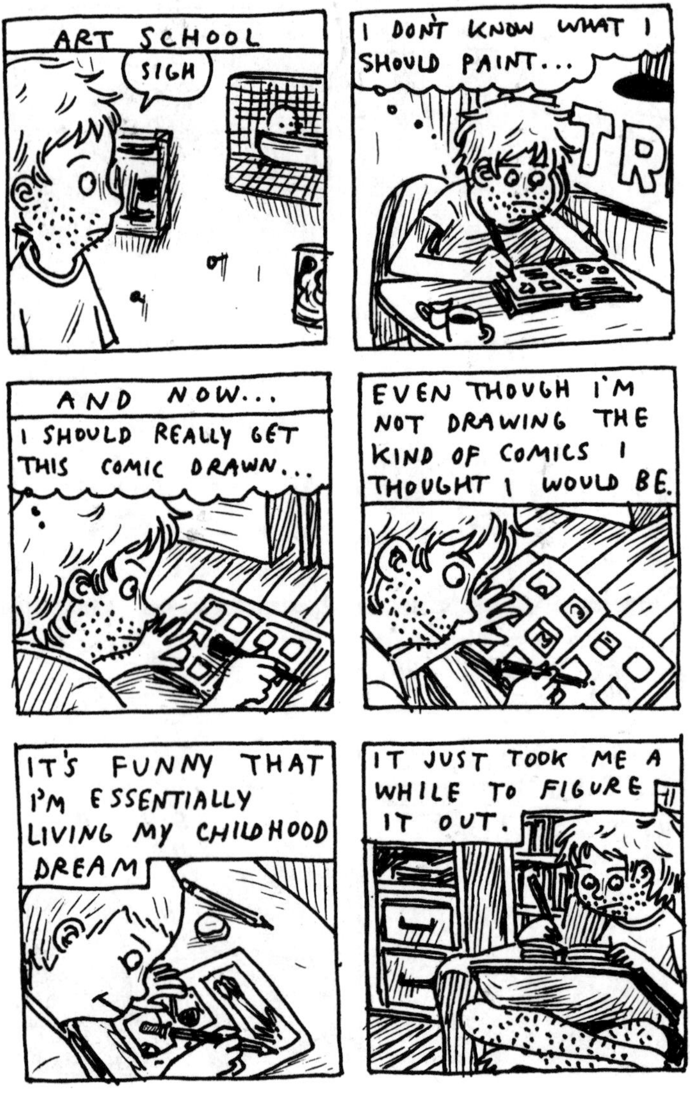
ART SCHOOL
SIGH
I DON'T KNOW WHAT I SHOULD PAINT...
TR
AND NOW...
I SHOULD REALLY GET THIS COMIC DRAWN...
EVEN THOUGH I'M NOT DRAWING THE KIND OF COMICS I THOUGHT I WOULD BE.
IT'S FUNNY THAT I'M ESSENTIALLY LIVING MY CHILDHOOD DREAM
IT JUST TOOK ME A WHILE TO FIGURE IT OUT.

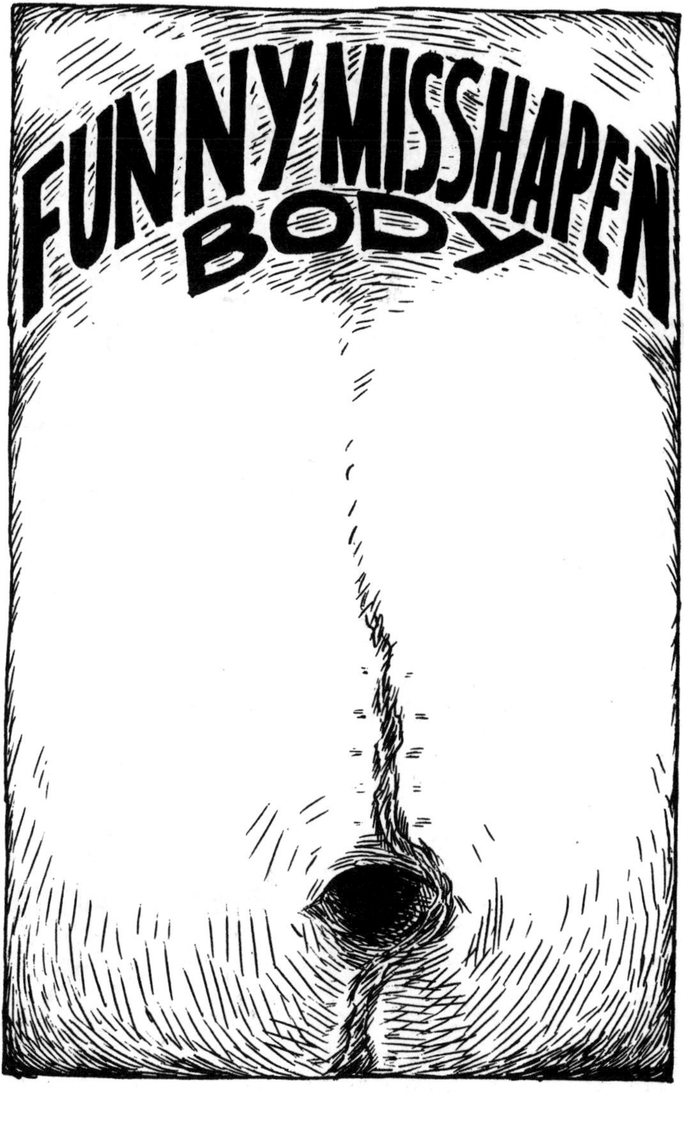
FUNNY MISSHAPEN
BODY

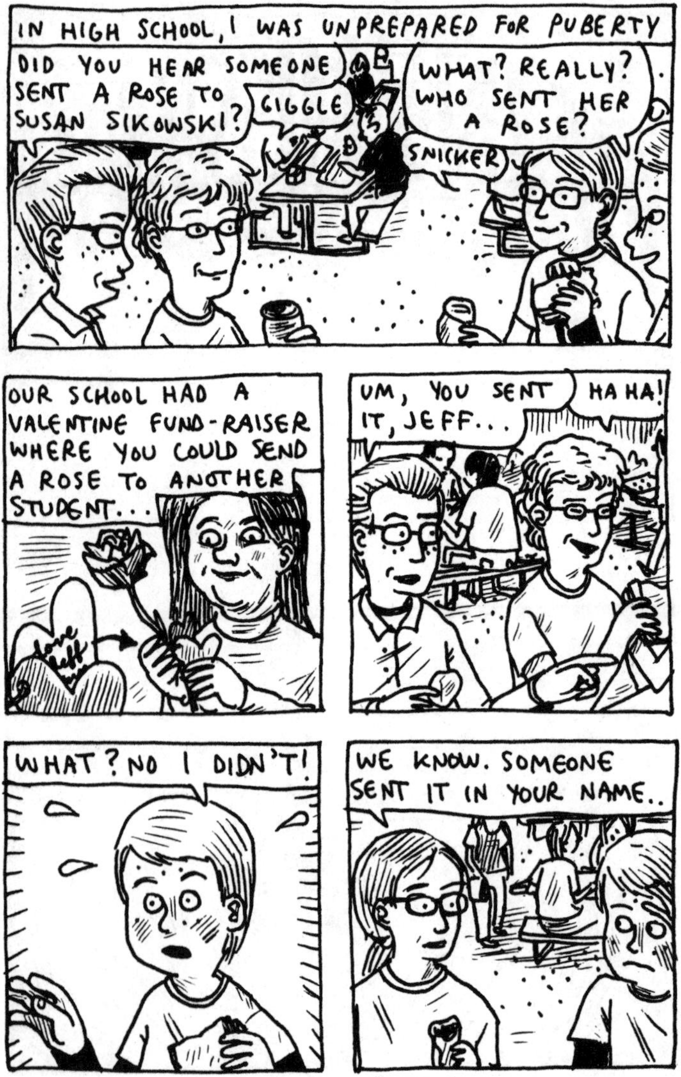
IN HIGH SCHOOL, I WAS UNPREPARED FOR PUBERTY
DID YOU HEAR SOMEONE SENT A ROSE TO SUSAN SIKOWSKI?
GIGGLE
WHAT? REALLY? WHO SENT HER A ROSE?
SNICKER
OUR SCHOOL HAD A VALENTINE FUND-RAISER WHERE YOU COULD SEND A ROSE TO ANOTHER STUDENT...
love Jeff
UM, YOU SENT IT, JEFF...
HA HA!
WHAT? NO I DIDN'T!
WE KNOW. SOMEONE SENT IT IN YOUR NAME..

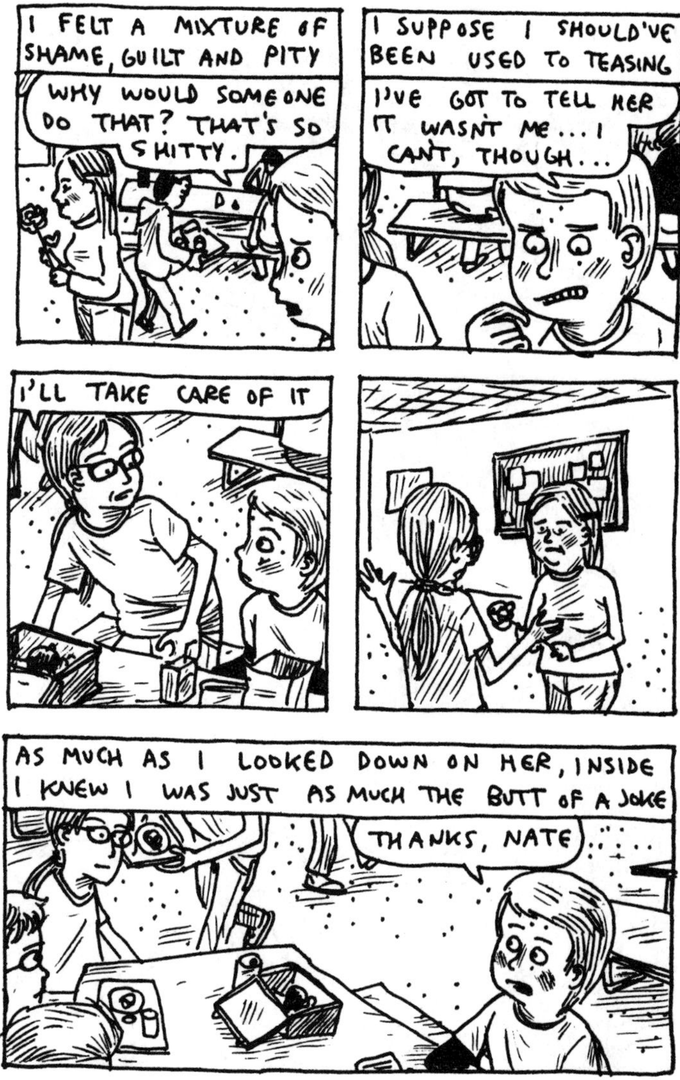
I FELT A MIXTURE OF SHAME, GUILT AND PITY
WHY WOULD SOMEONE DO THAT? THAT'S SO SHITTY.
I SUPPOSE I SHOULD'VE BEEN USED TO TEASING
I'VE GOT TO TELL HER IT WASN'T ME... I CAN'T, THOUGH...
I'LL TAKE CARE OF IT
AS MUCH AS I LOOKED DOWN ON HER, INSIDE I KNEW I WAS JUST AS MUCH THE BUTT OF A JOKE
THANKS, NATE

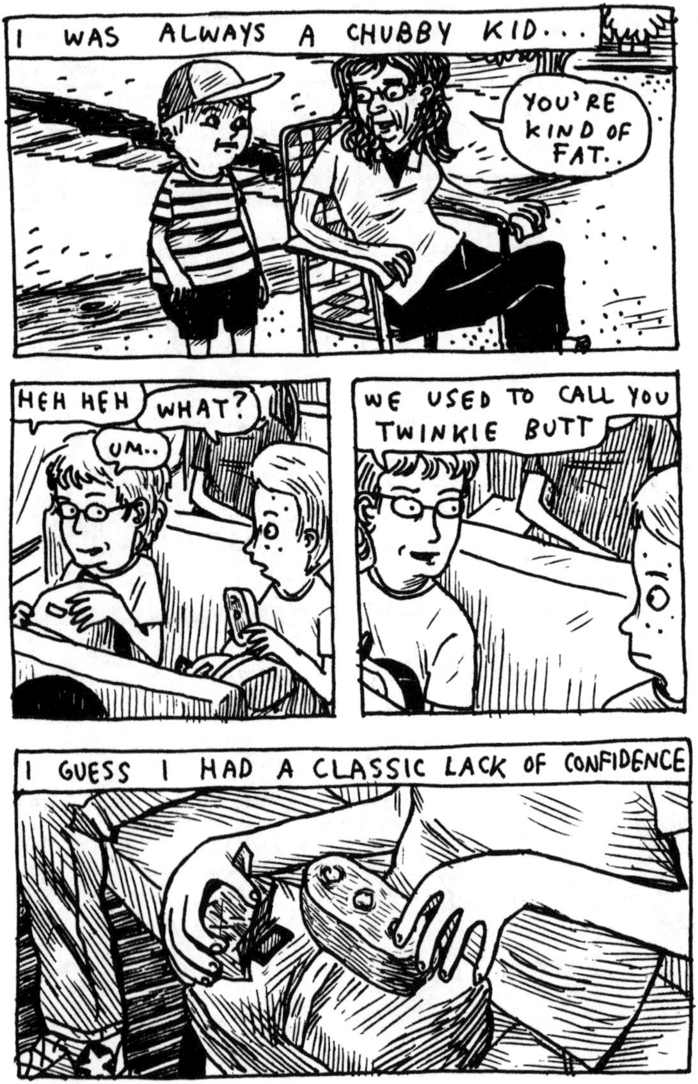
I WAS ALWAYS A CHUBBY KID...
YOU'RE KIND OF FAT.
HEH HEH
WHAT?
UM..
WE USED TO CALL YOU TWINKIE BUTT
I GUESS I HAD A CLASSIC LACK OF CONFIDENCE

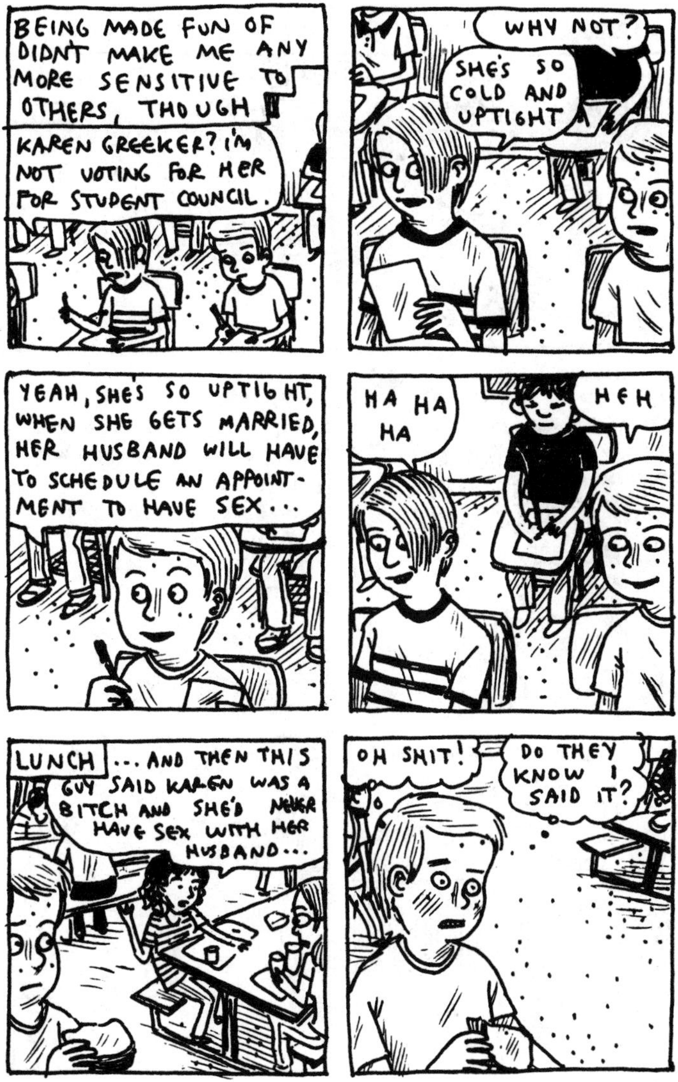
BEING MADE FUN OF DIDN'T MAKE ME ANY MORE SENSITIVE TO OTHERS, THOUGH
KAREN GREEKER? I'M NOT VOTING FOR HER FOR STUDENT COUNCIL.
WHY NOT?
SHE'S SO COLD AND UPTIGHT
YEAH, SHE'S SO UPTIGHT, WHEN SHE GETS MARRIED, HER HUSBAND WILL HAVE TO SCHEDULE AN APPOINTMENT TO HAVE SEX...
HA HA HA
HEH
LUNCH
... AND THEN THIS GUY SAID KAREN WAS A BITCH AND SHE'D NEVER HAVE SEX WITH HER HUSBAND...
OH SHIT!
DO THEY KNOW I SAID IT?

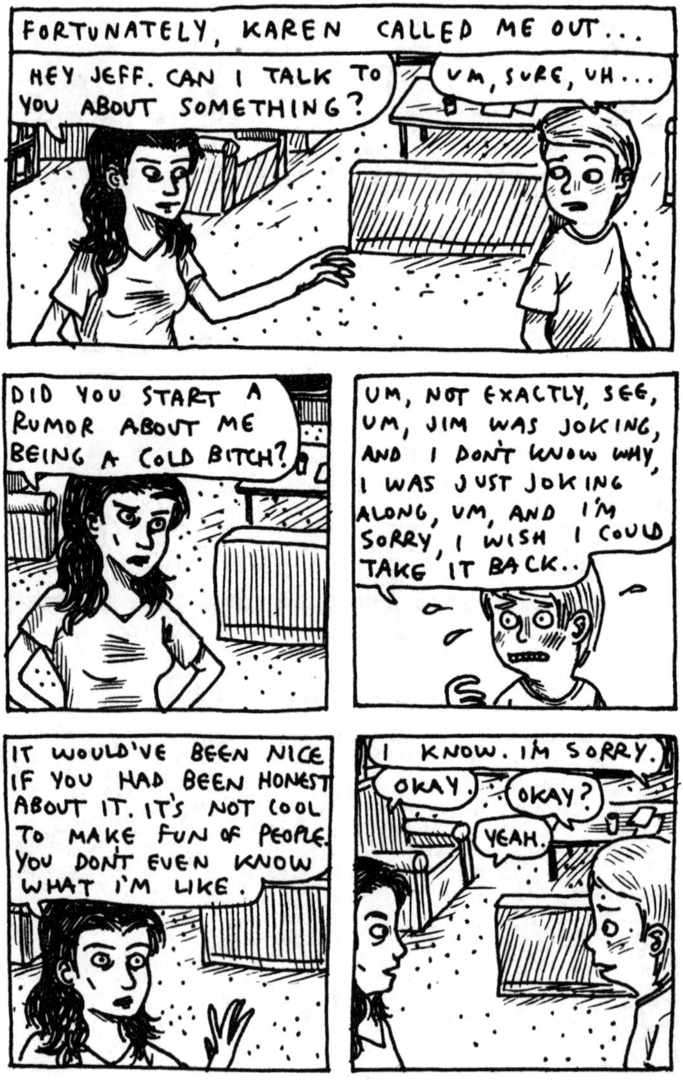
FORTUNATELY, KAREN CALLED ME OUT...
HEY JEFF. CAN I TALK TO YOU ABOUT SOMETHING?
UM, SURE, UH...
DID YOU START A RUMOR ABOUT ME BEING A COLD BITCH?
UM, NOT EXACTLY, SEE, UM, JIM WAS JOKING, AND I DON'T KNOW WHY, I WAS JUST JOKING ALONG, UM, AND I'M SORRY, I WISH I COULD TAKE IT BACK..
IT WOULD'VE BEEN NICE IF YOU HAD BEEN HONEST ABOUT IT. IT'S NOT COOL TO MAKE FUN OF PEOPLE. YOU DON'T EVEN KNOW WHAT I'M LIKE.
I KNOW. I'M SORRY.
OKAY.
OKAY?
YEAH.

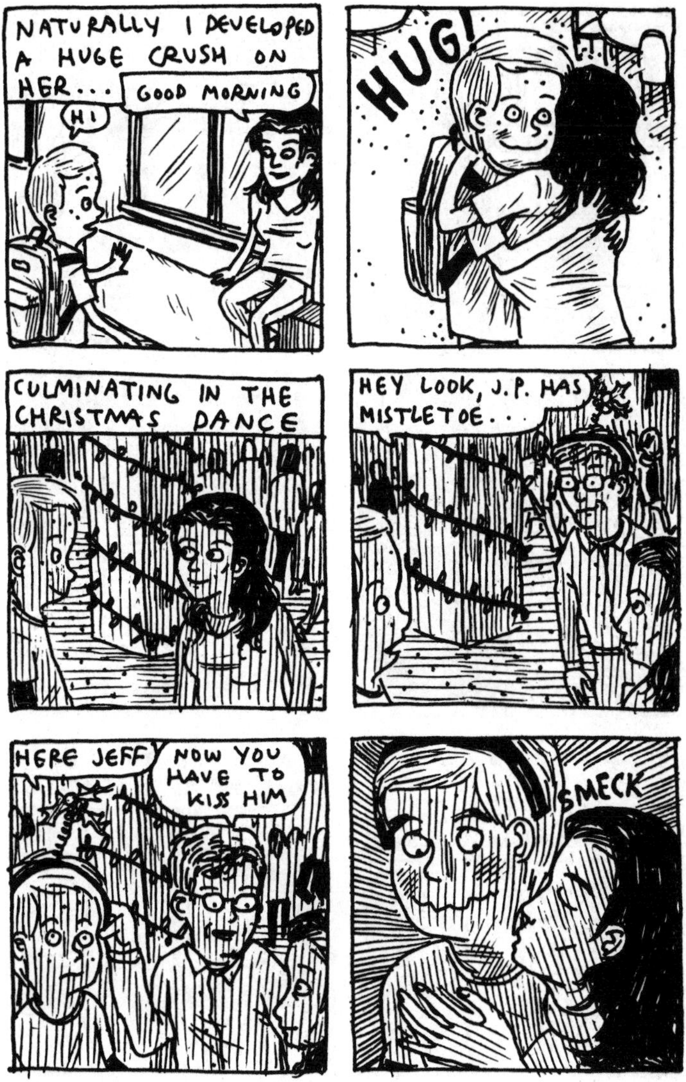
NATURALLY I DEVELOPED A HUGE CRUSH ON HER...
HI
GOOD MORNING
HUG!
CULMINATING IN THE CHRISTMAS DANCE
HEY LOOK, J.P. HAS MISTLETOE...
HERE JEFF
NOW YOU HAVE TO KISS HIM
SMECK

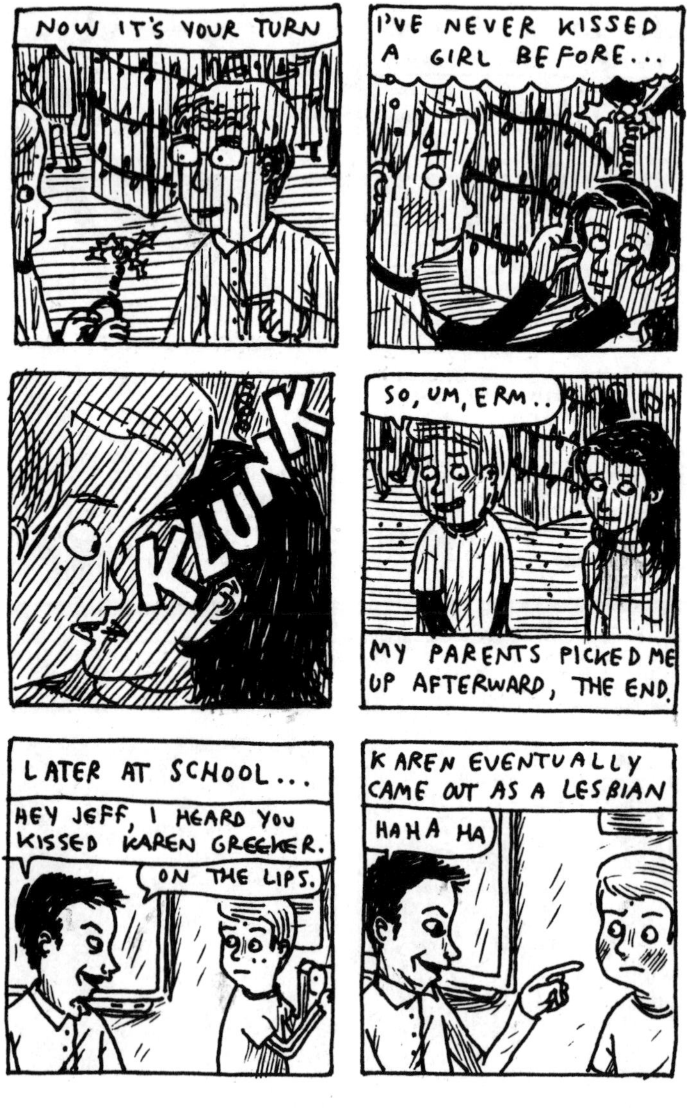

NOW IT'S YOUR TURN
I'VE NEVER KISSED A GIRL BEFORE...
KLUNK
SO, UM, ERM..
MY PARENTS PICKED ME UP AFTERWARD, THE END.
LATER AT SCHOOL...
HEY JEFF, I HEARD YOU KISSED KAREN GREEKER.
ON THE LIPS.
KAREN EVENTUALLY CAME OUT AS A LESBIAN
HAHA HA

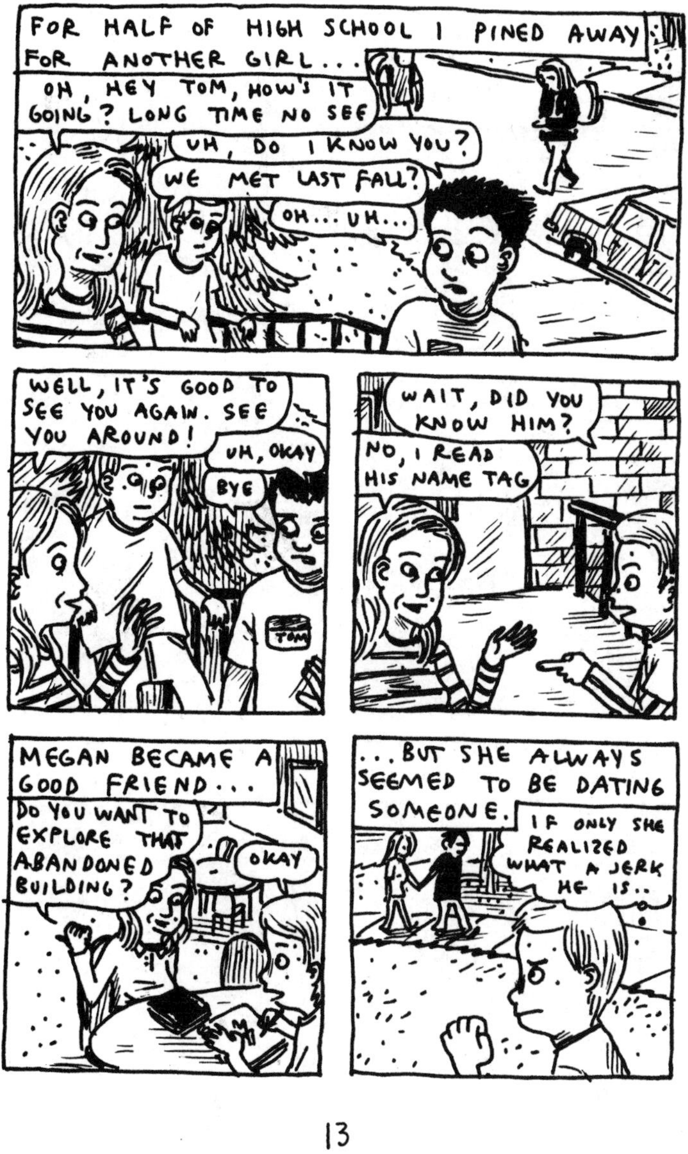

FOR HALF OF HIGH SCHOOL I PINED AWAY FOR ANOTHER GIRL...
OH, HEY TOM, HOW'S IT GOING? LONG TIME NO SEE
UH, DO I KNOW YOU?
WE MET LAST FALL?
OH... UH...
WELL, IT'S GOOD TO SEE YOU AGAIN. SEE YOU AROUND!
UH, OKAY
BYE
TOM
WAIT, DID YOU KNOW HIM?
NO, I READ HIS NAME TAG
MEGAN BECAME A GOOD FRIEND...
DO YOU WANT TO EXPLORE THAT ABANDONED BUILDING?
OKAY
...BUT SHE ALWAYS SEEMED TO BE DATING SOMEONE.
IF ONLY SHE REALIZED WHAT A JERK HE IS..

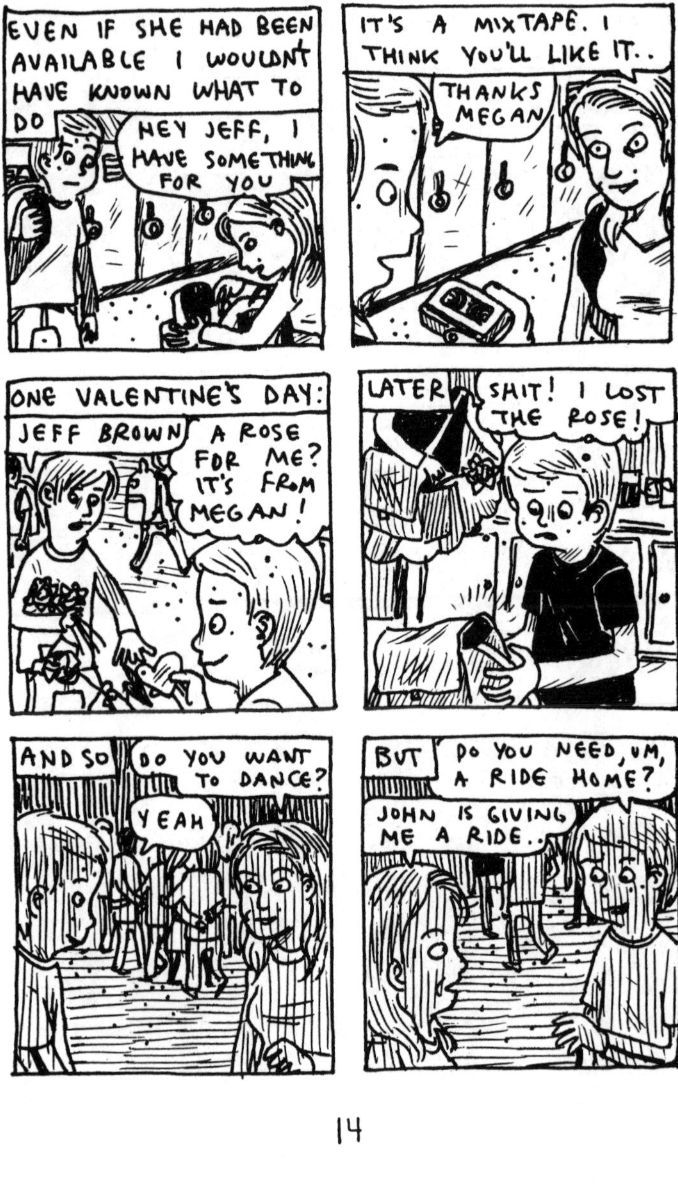
EVEN IF SHE HAD BEEN AVAILABLE I WOULDN'T HAVE KNOWN WHAT TO DO
HEY JEFF, I HAVE SOMETHING FOR YOU
IT'S A MIXTAPE. I THINK YOU'LL LIKE IT..
THANKS MEGAN
ONE VALENTINE'S DAY:
JEFF BROWN
A ROSE FOR ME? IT'S FROM MEGAN!
LATER
SHIT! I LOST THE ROSE!
AND SO
DO YOU WANT TO DANCE?
YEAH
BUT
DO YOU NEED, UM, A RIDE HOME?
JOHN IS GIVING ME A RIDE..

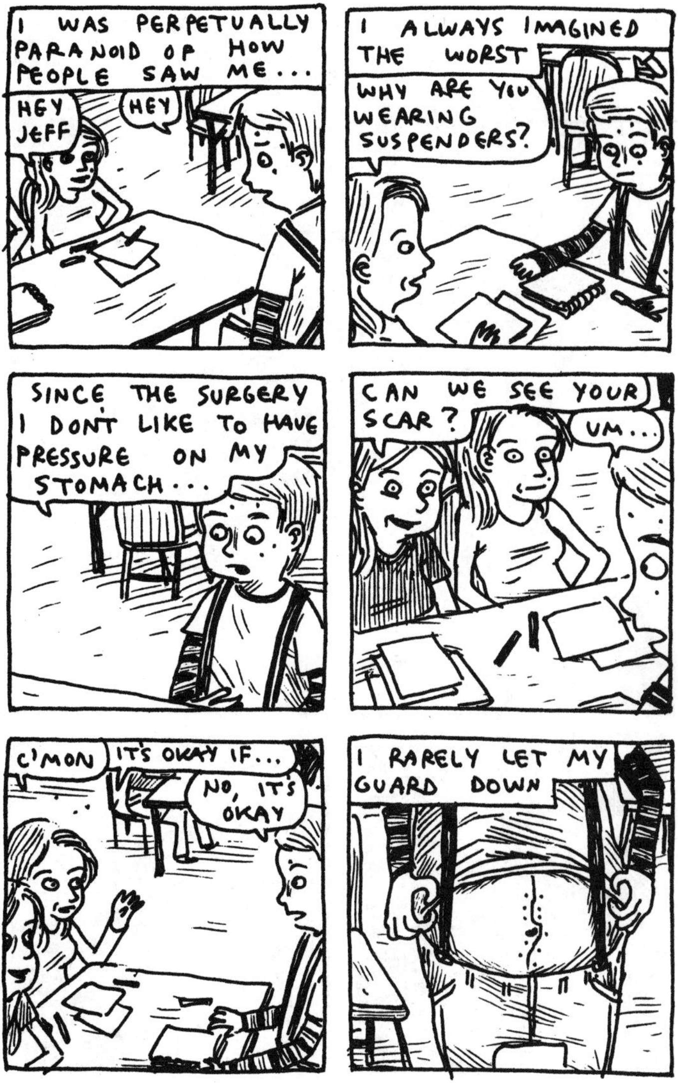
I WAS PERPETUALLY PARANOID OF HOW PEOPLE SAW ME...
HEY JEFF
HEY
I ALWAYS IMAGINED THE WORST
WHY ARE YOU WEARING SUSPENDERS?
SINCE THE SURGERY I DONT LIKE TO HAVE PRESSURE ON MY STOMACH...
CAN WE SEE YOUR SCAR?
UM...
C'MON
IT'S OKAY IF...
NO, IT'S OKAY
I RARELY LET MY GUARD DOWN

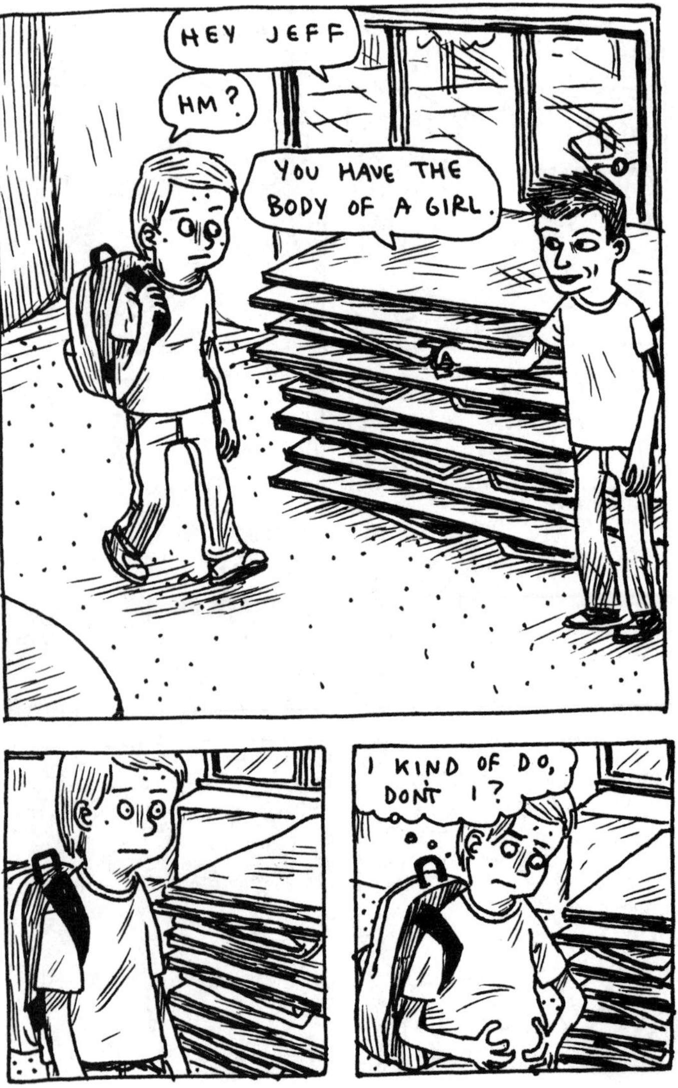
HEY JEFF
HM?
YOU HAVE THE BODY OF A GIRL.
I KIND OF DO, DONT I?

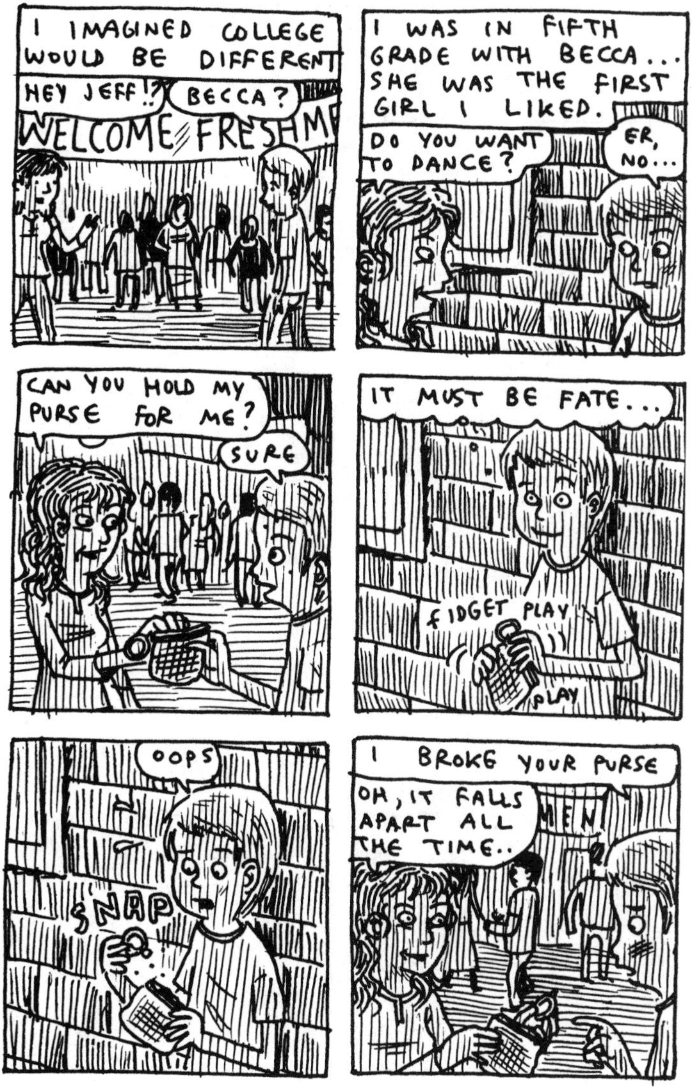
I IMAGINED COLLEGE WOULD BE DIFFERENT
HEY JEFF!?
BECCA?
WELCOME FRESHM
I WAS IN FIFTH GRADE WITH BECCA... SHE WAS THE FIRST GIRL I LIKED.
DO YOU WANT TO DANCE?
ER, NO...
CAN YOU HOLD MY PURSE FOR ME?
SURE
IT MUST BE FATE...
FIDGET PLAY
PLAY
OOPS
SNAP
I BROKE YOUR PURSE
OH, IT FALLS APART ALL THE TIME..
MEN

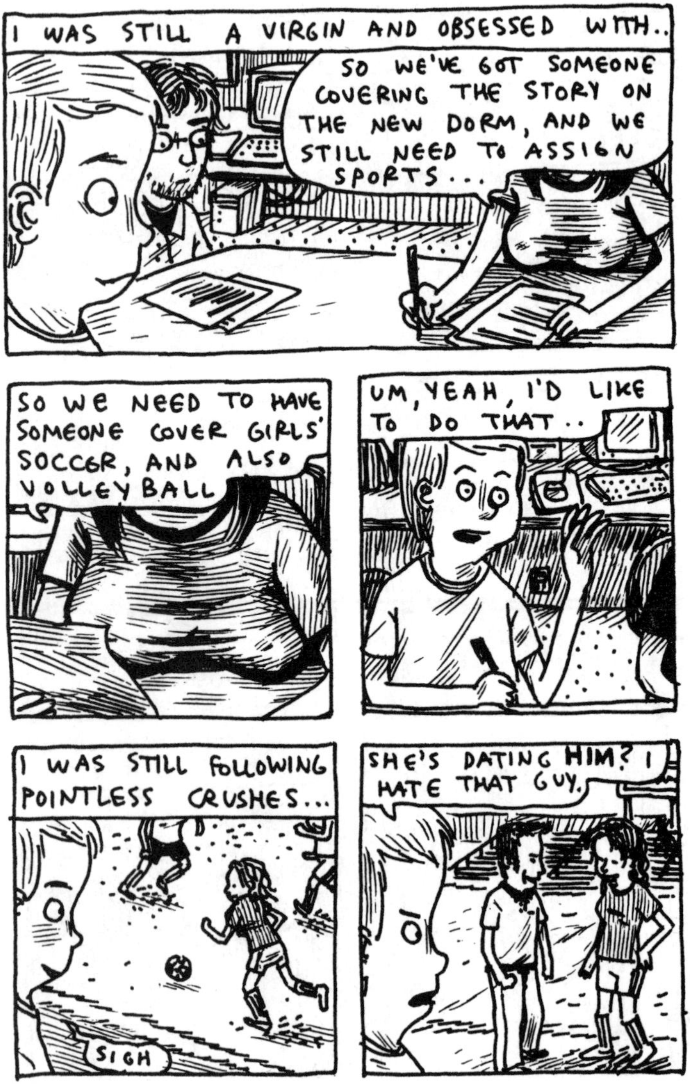

I WAS STILL A VIRGIN AND OBSESSED WITH..
SO WE'VE GOT SOMEONE COVERING THE STORY ON THE NEW DORM, AND WE STILL NEED TO ASSIGN SPORTS...
SO WE NEED TO HAVE SOMEONE COVER GIRLS' SOCCER, AND ALSO VOLLEYBALL
UM, YEAH, I'D LIKE TO DO THAT..
I WAS STILL FOLLOWING POINTLESS CRUSHES...
SIGH
SHE'S DATING HIM? I HATE THAT GUY.

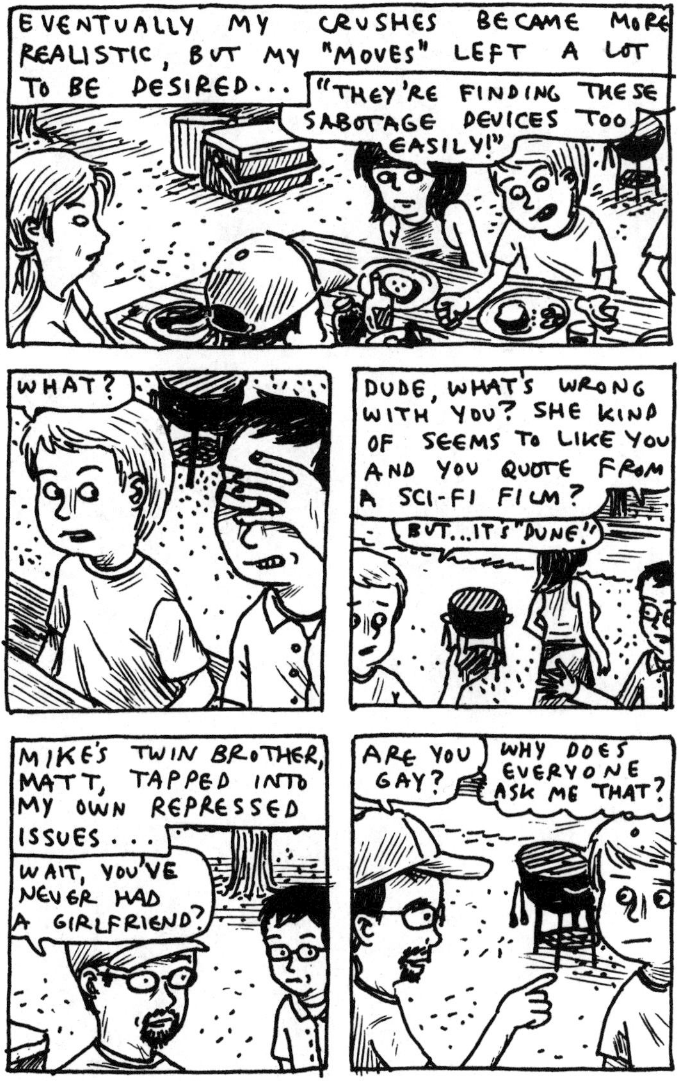
EVENTUALLY MY CRUSHES BECAME MORE REALISTIC, BUT MY "MOVES" LEFT A LOT TO BE DESIRED...
"THEY'RE FINDING THESE SABOTAGE DEVICES TOO EASILY!"
WHAT?
DUDE, WHAT'S WRONG WITH YOU? SHE KIND OF SEEMS TO LIKE YOU AND YOU QUOTE FROM A SCI-FI FILM?
BUT...IT'S "DUNE"!
MIKE'S TWIN BROTHER, MATT, TAPPED INTO MY OWN REPRESSED ISSUES...
WAIT, YOU'VE NEVER HAD A GIRLFRIEND?
ARE YOU GAY?
WHY DOES EVERYONE ASK ME THAT?

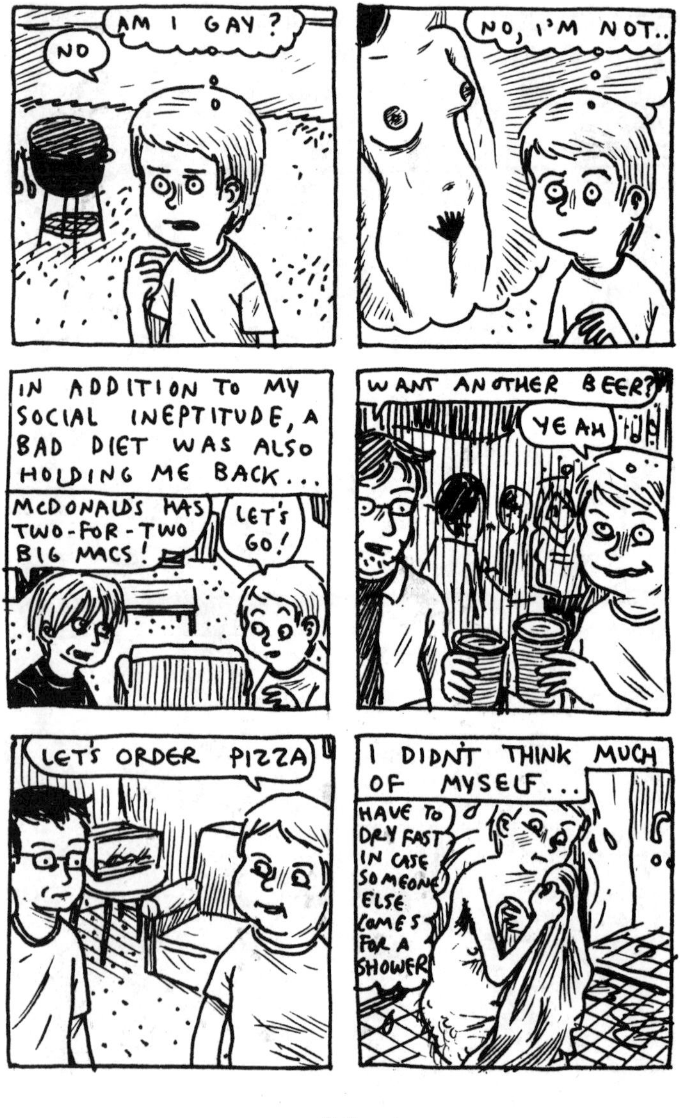
AM I GAY?
NO
NO, I'M NOT..
IN ADDITION TO MY SOCIAL INEPTITUDE, A BAD DIET WAS ALSO HOLDING ME BACK...
MCDONALD'S HAS TWO-FOR-TWO BIG MACS!
LET'S GO!
WANT ANOTHER BEER?
YEAH
LET'S ORDER PIZZA
I DIDN'T THINK MUCH OF MYSELF...
HAVE TO DRY FAST IN CASE SOMEONE ELSE COMES FOR A SHOWER

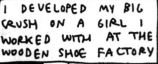
I DEVELOPED MY BIG CRUSH ON A GIRL I WORKED WITH AT THE WOODEN SHOE FACTORY

SHE WAS ONE OF THE EXTRA WORKERS HIRED FOR THE BUSY "TULIP TIME" CELEBRATION

I'LL BE BACK IN A MINUTE...

GOING TO SEE YOUR LITTLE GIRL-FRIEND?

I CONSTANTLY FLIRTED WITH HER

THE PHRASE "PUPPY DOG" COMES TO MIND FOR SOME REASON.

BUT SCHOOL WAS OVER FOR THE SUMMER

BYE

SEE YOU NEXT FALL

I MUST WIN HER HEART!

21

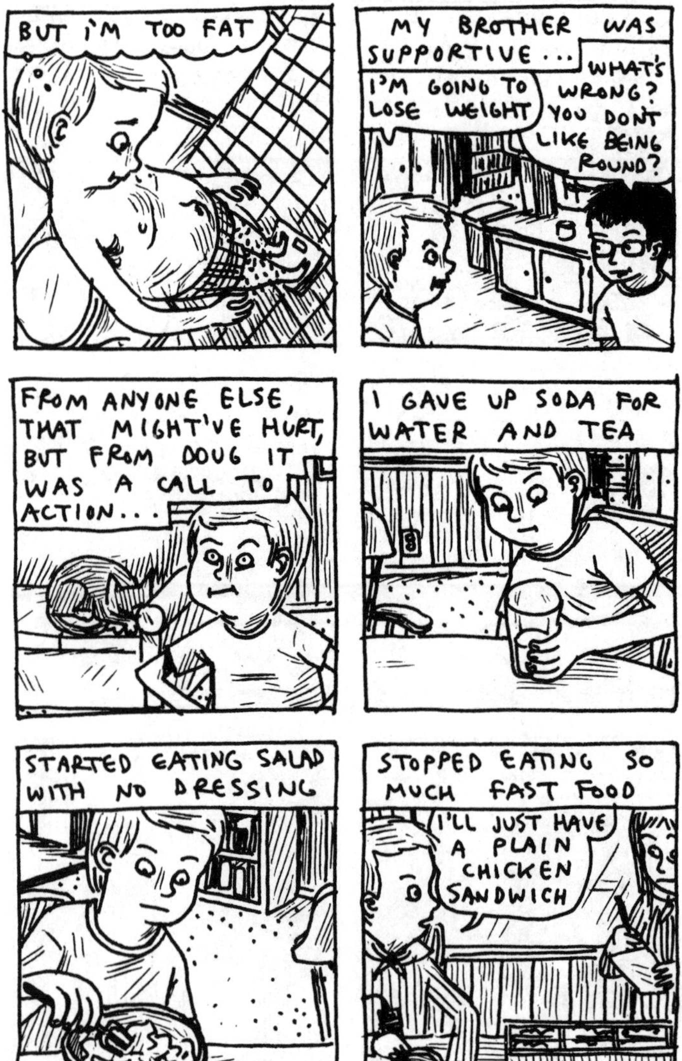
BUT I'M TOO FAT
MY BROTHER WAS SUPPORTIVE...
I'M GOING TO LOSE WEIGHT
WHAT'S WRONG? YOU DON'T LIKE BEING ROUND?
FROM ANYONE ELSE, THAT MIGHT'VE HURT, BUT FROM DOUG IT WAS A CALL TO ACTION...
I GAVE UP SODA FOR WATER AND TEA
STARTED EATING SALAD WITH NO DRESSING
STOPPED EATING SO MUCH FAST FOOD
I'LL JUST HAVE A PLAIN CHICKEN SANDWICH

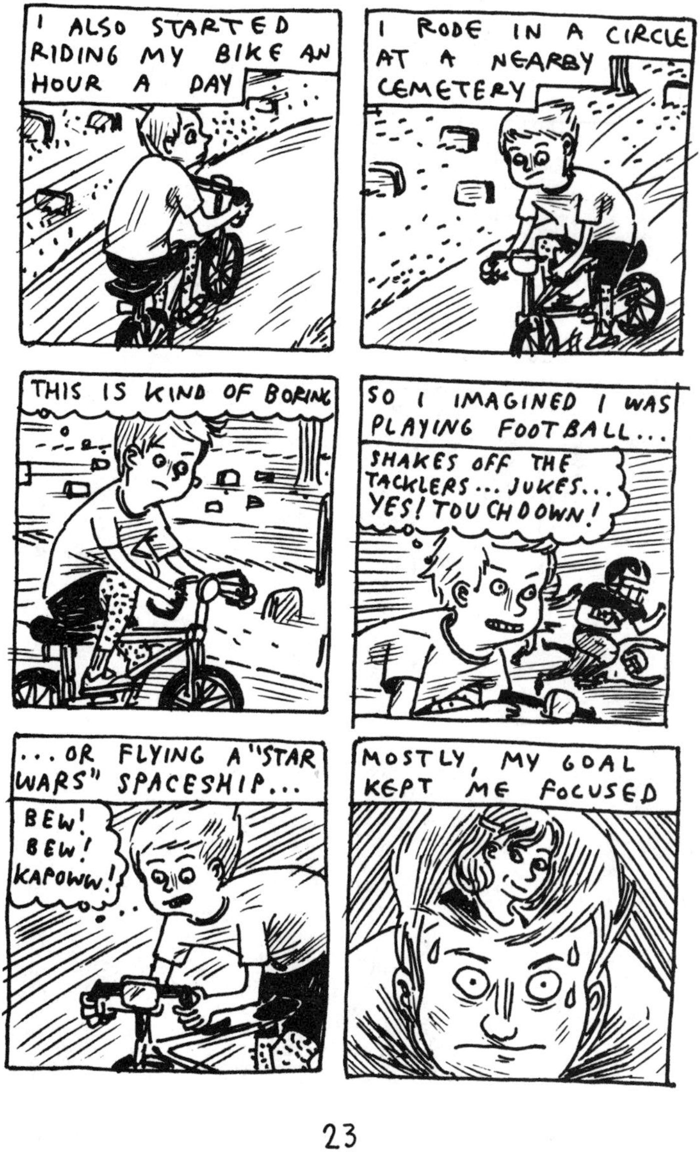
I ALSO STARTED RIDING MY BIKE AN HOUR A DAY
I RODE IN A CIRCLE AT A NEARBY CEMETERY
THIS IS KIND OF BORING
SO I IMAGINED I WAS PLAYING FOOTBALL...
SHAKES OFF THE TACKLERS... JUKES... YES! TOUCHDOWN!
...OR FLYING A "STAR WARS" SPACESHIP...
BEW! BEW! KAPOWW!
MOSTLY, MY GOAL KEPT ME FOCUSED

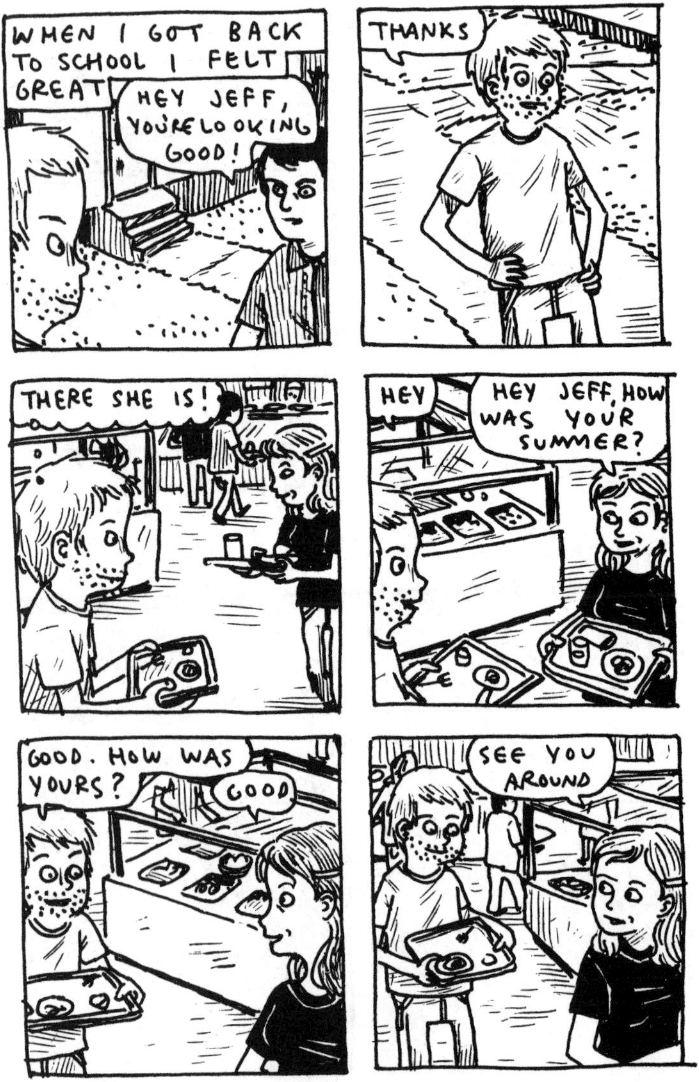
WHEN I GOT BACK TO SCHOOL I FELT GREAT
HEY JEFF, YOU'RE LOOKING GOOD!
THANKS
THERE SHE IS!
HEY
HEY JEFF, HOW WAS YOUR SUMMER?
GOOD. HOW WAS YOURS?
GOOD
SEE YOU AROUND

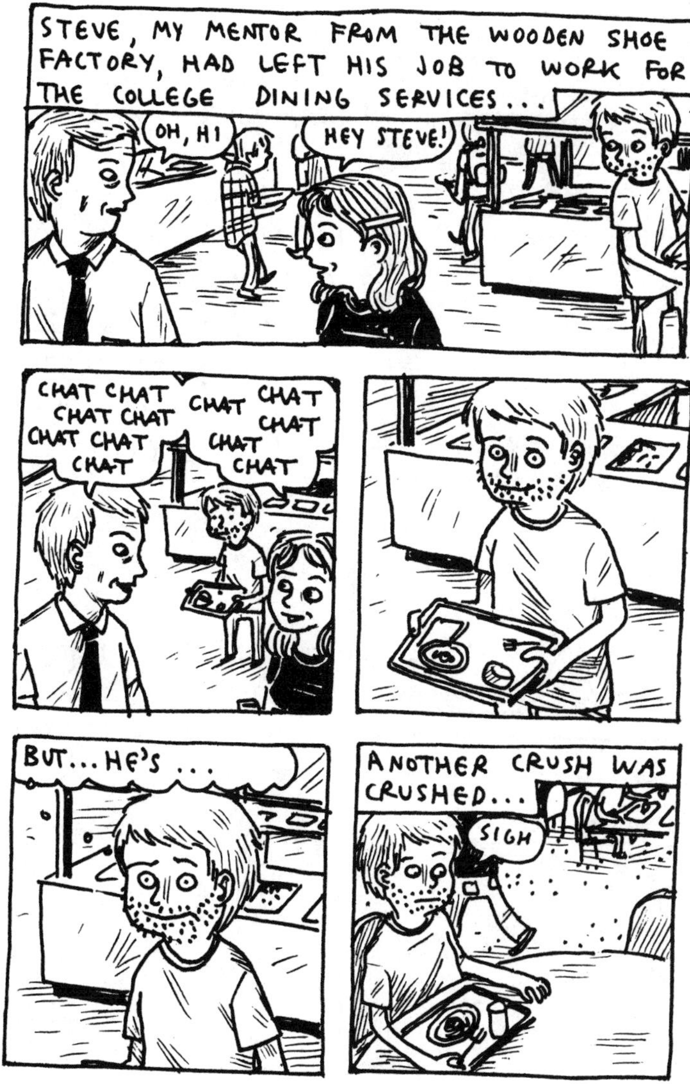
STEVE, MY MENTOR FROM THE WOODEN SHOE FACTORY, HAD LEFT HIS JOB TO WORK FOR THE COLLEGE DINING SERVICES...
OH, HI
HEY STEVE!
CHAT CHAT CHAT CHAT CHAT CHAT CHAT
CHAT CHAT CHAT CHAT CHAT
BUT...HE'S ...
ANOTHER CRUSH WAS CRUSHED...
SIGH

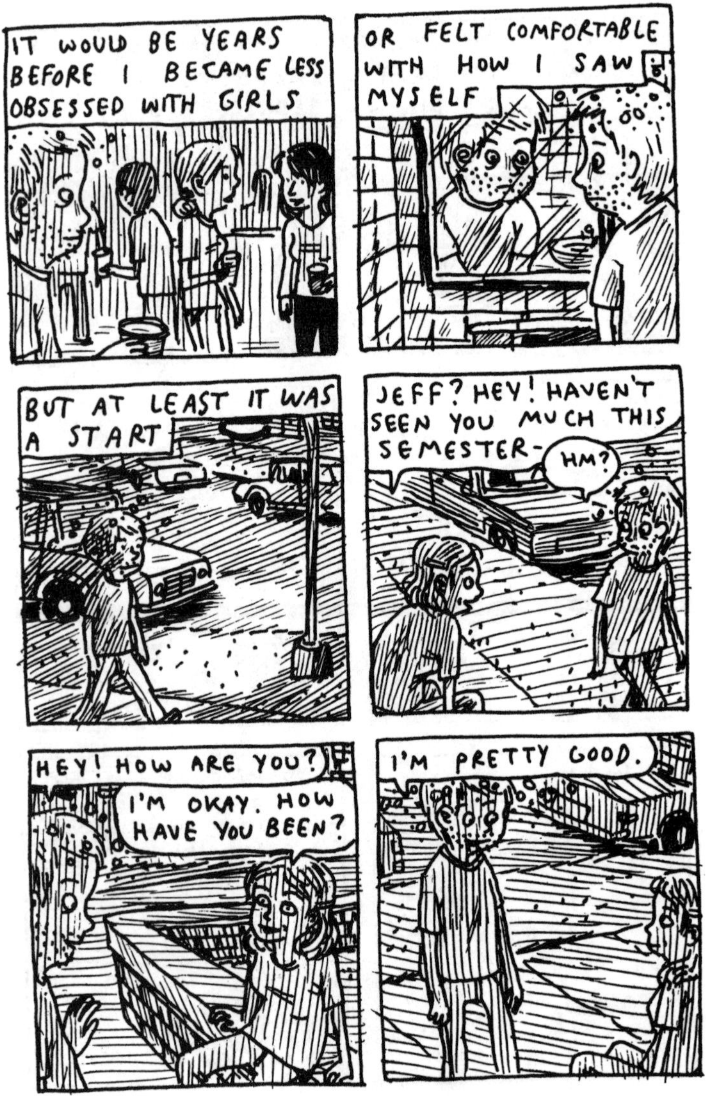
IT WOULD BE YEARS BEFORE I BECAME LESS OBSESSED WITH GIRLS
OR FELT COMFORTABLE WITH HOW I SAW MYSELF
BUT AT LEAST IT WAS A START
JEFF? HEY! HAVEN'T SEEN YOU MUCH THIS SEMESTER-
HM?
HEY! HOW ARE YOU?
I'M OKAY. HOW HAVE YOU BEEN?
I'M PRETTY GOOD.

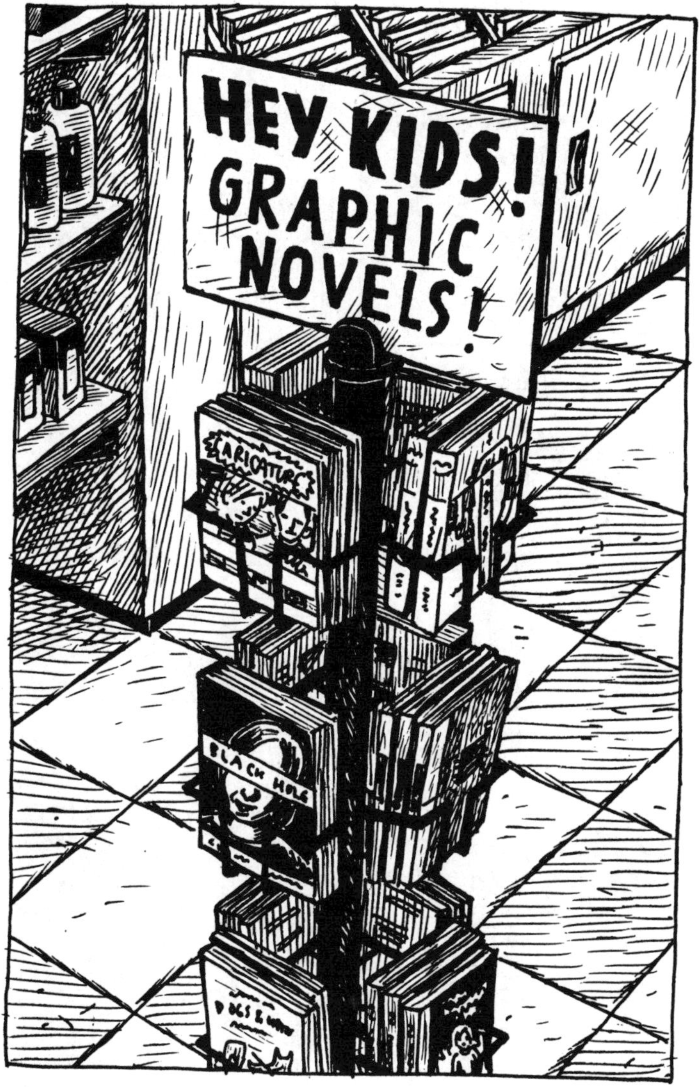
HEY KIDS!
GRAPHIC NOVELS!
CARICATURE
BLACK HOLE

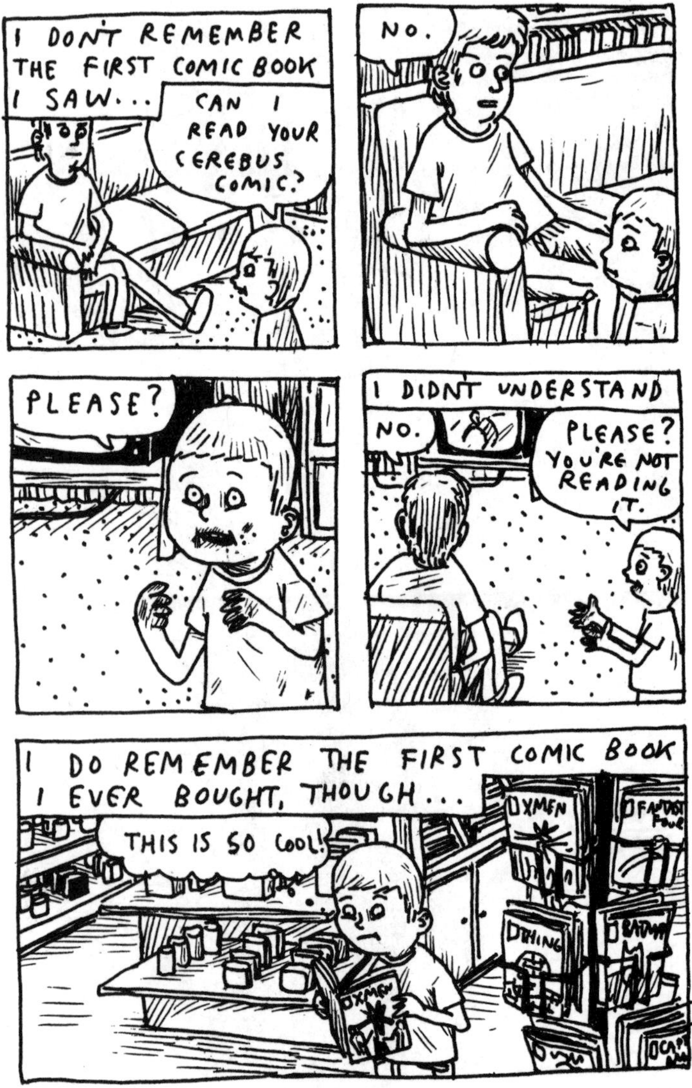
I DON'T REMEMBER THE FIRST COMIC BOOK I SAW...
CAN I READ YOUR CEREBUS COMIC?
NO.
PLEASE?
I DIDN'T UNDERSTAND
NO.
PLEASE? YOU'RE NOT READING IT.
I DO REMEMBER THE FIRST COMIC BOOK I EVER BOUGHT, THOUGH...
THIS IS SO COOL!
XMEN
FANTASTIC FOUR
THING
BATMAN
XMEN

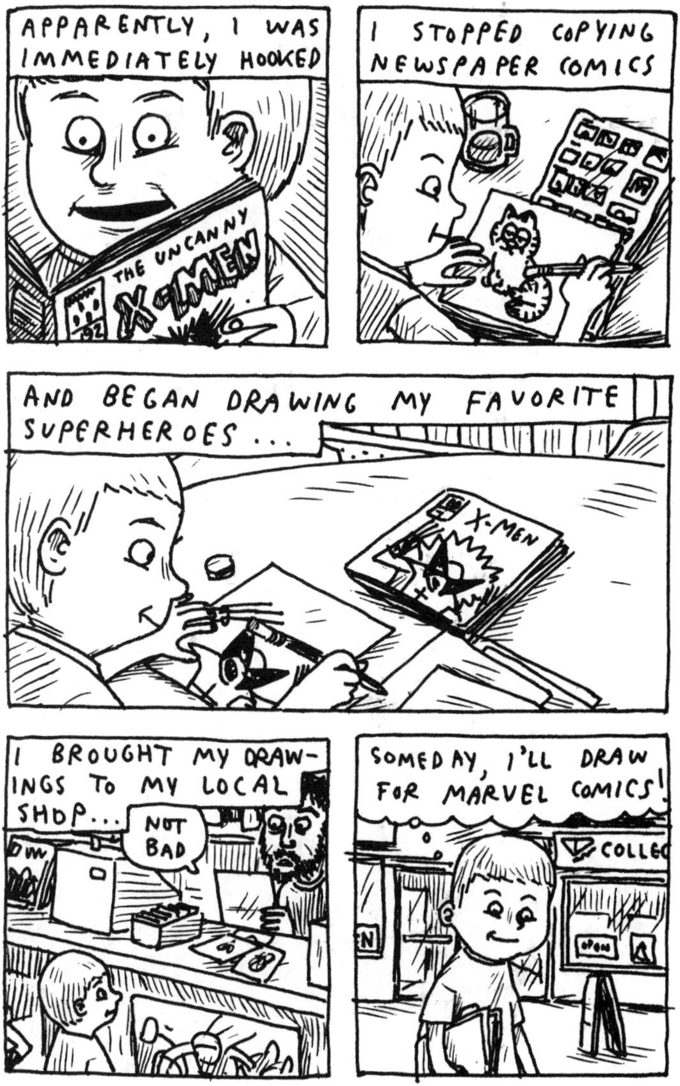
APPARENTLY, I WAS IMMEDIATELY HOOKED
THE UNCANNY X-MEN
I STOPPED COPYING NEWSPAPER COMICS
AND BEGAN DRAWING MY FAVORITE SUPERHEROES ...
X-MEN
I BROUGHT MY DRAWINGS TO MY LOCAL SHOP...
NOT BAD
SOMEDAY, I'LL DRAW FOR MARVEL COMICS!
COLLE
OPEN

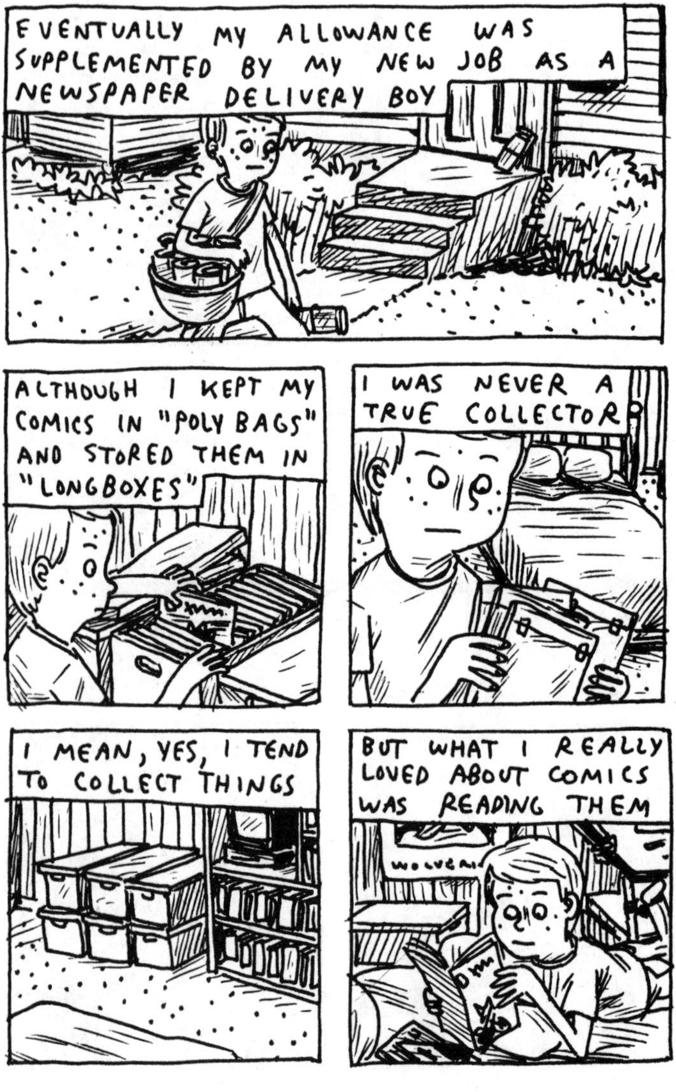
EVENTUALLY MY ALLOWANCE WAS SUPPLEMENTED BY MY NEW JOB AS A NEWSPAPER DELIVERY BOY
ALTHOUGH I KEPT MY COMICS IN "POLY BAGS" AND STORED THEM IN "LONGBOXES"
I WAS NEVER A TRUE COLLECTOR
I MEAN, YES, I TEND TO COLLECT THINGS
BUT WHAT I REALLY LOVED ABOUT COMICS WAS READING THEM

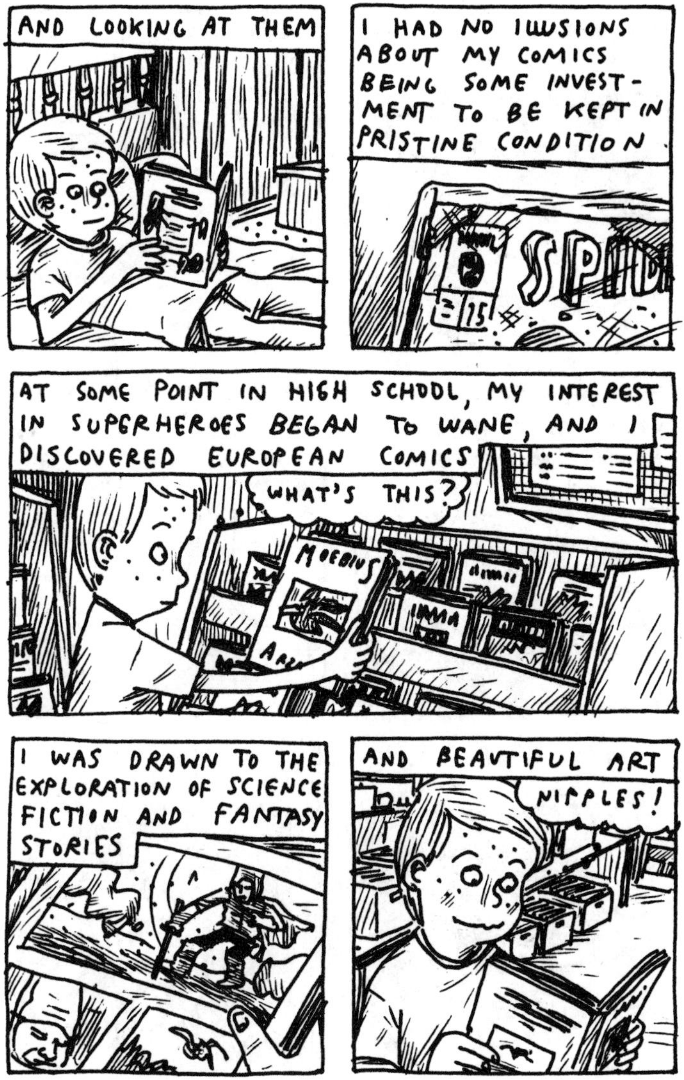
AND LOOKING AT THEM
I HAD NO ILLUSIONS ABOUT MY COMICS BEING SOME INVESTMENT TO BE KEPT IN PRISTINE CONDITION.
AT SOME POINT IN HIGH SCHOOL, MY INTEREST IN SUPERHEROES BEGAN TO WANE, AND I DISCOVERED EUROPEAN COMICS
WHAT'S THIS?
MOEBIUS
I WAS DRAWN TO THE EXPLORATION OF SCIENCE FICTION AND FANTASY STORIES
AND BEAUTIFUL ART
NIPPLES!

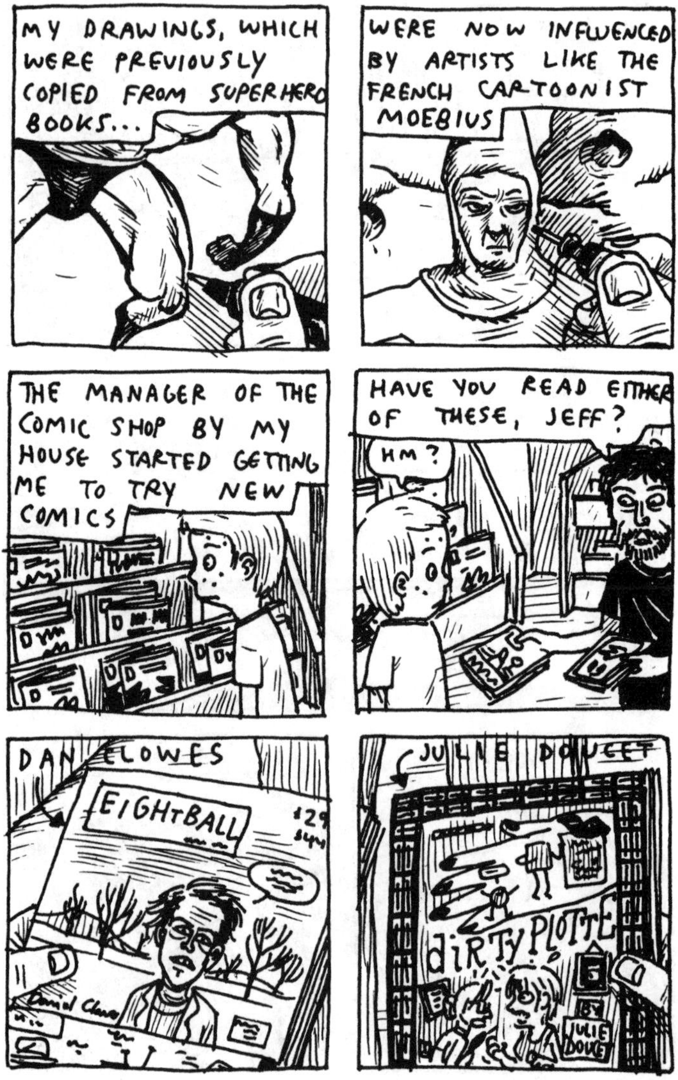
MY DRAWINGS, WHICH WERE PREVIOUSLY COPIED FROM SUPERHERO BOOKS...
WERE NOW INFLUENCED BY ARTISTS LIKE THE FRENCH CARTOONIST MOEBIUS
THE MANAGER OF THE COMIC SHOP BY MY HOUSE STARTED GETTING ME TO TRY NEW COMICS
HAVE YOU READ EITHER OF THESE, JEFF?
HM?
DAN CLOWES
EIGHTBALL
JULIE DOUCET
DIRTY PLOTTE
BY

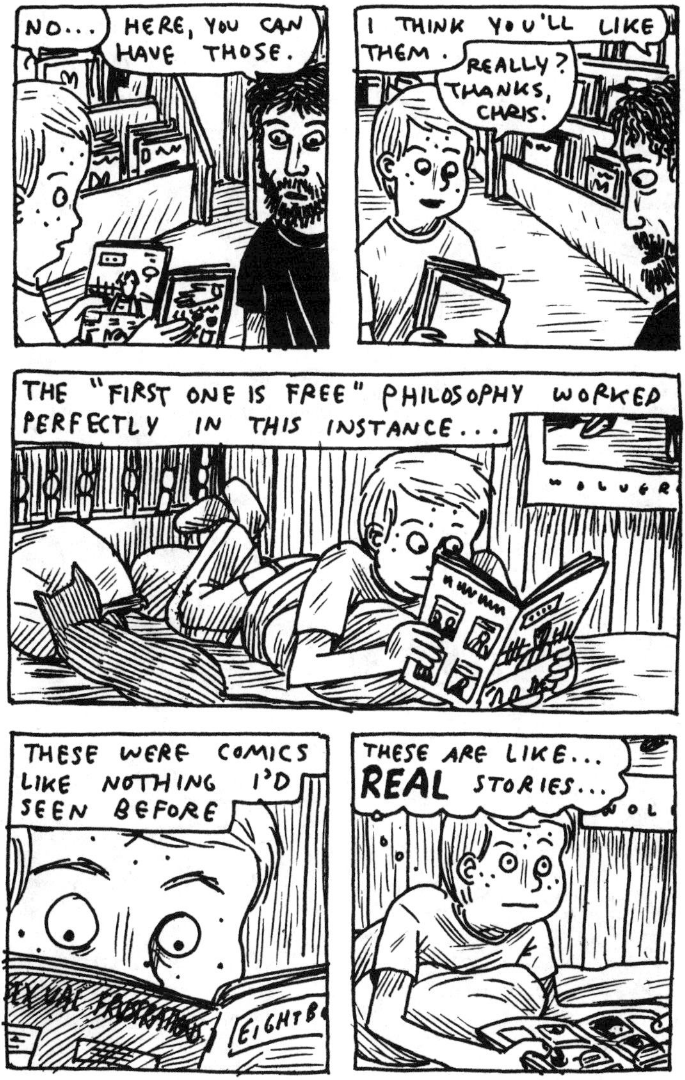
NO...
HERE, YOU CAN HAVE THOSE.
I THINK YOU'LL LIKE THEM.
REALLY? THANKS, CHRIS.
THE "FIRST ONE IS FREE" PHILOSOPHY WORKED PERFECTLY IN THIS INSTANCE...
THESE WERE COMICS LIKE NOTHING I'D SEEN BEFORE
EIGHTB
THESE ARE LIKE... **REAL** STORIES...

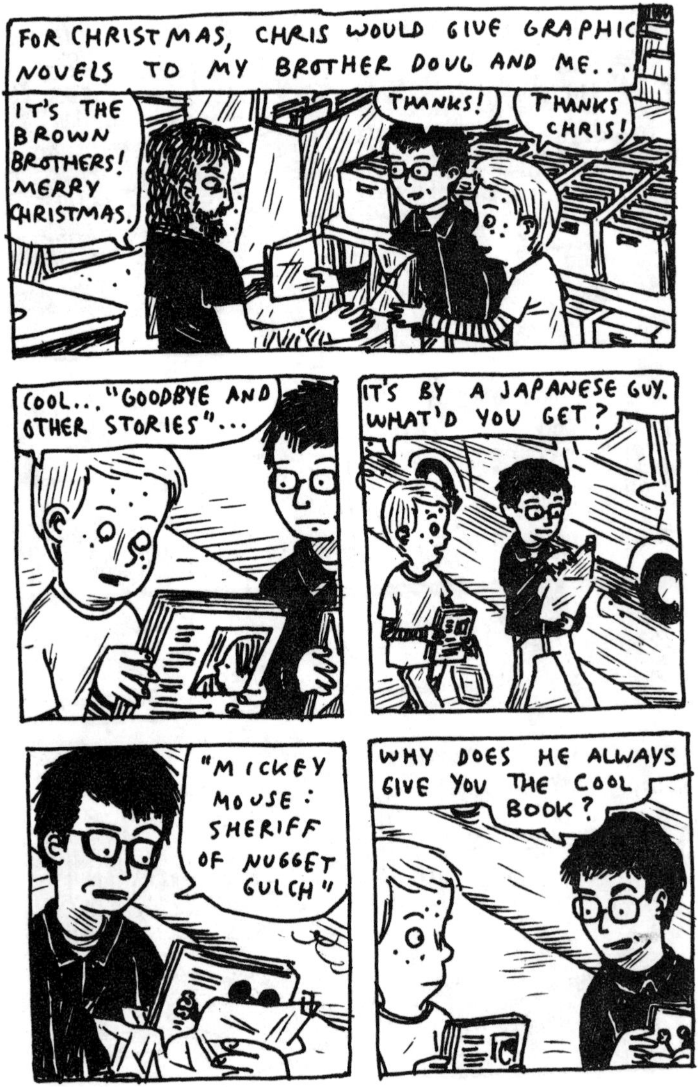
FOR CHRISTMAS, CHRIS WOULD GIVE GRAPHIC NOVELS TO MY BROTHER DOUG AND ME...
IT'S THE BROWN BROTHERS! MERRY CHRISTMAS.
THANKS!
THANKS CHRIS!
COOL... "GOODBYE AND OTHER STORIES"...
IT'S BY A JAPANESE GUY. WHAT'D YOU GET?
"MICKEY MOUSE: SHERIFF OF NUGGET GULCH"
WHY DOES HE ALWAYS GIVE YOU THE COOL BOOK?

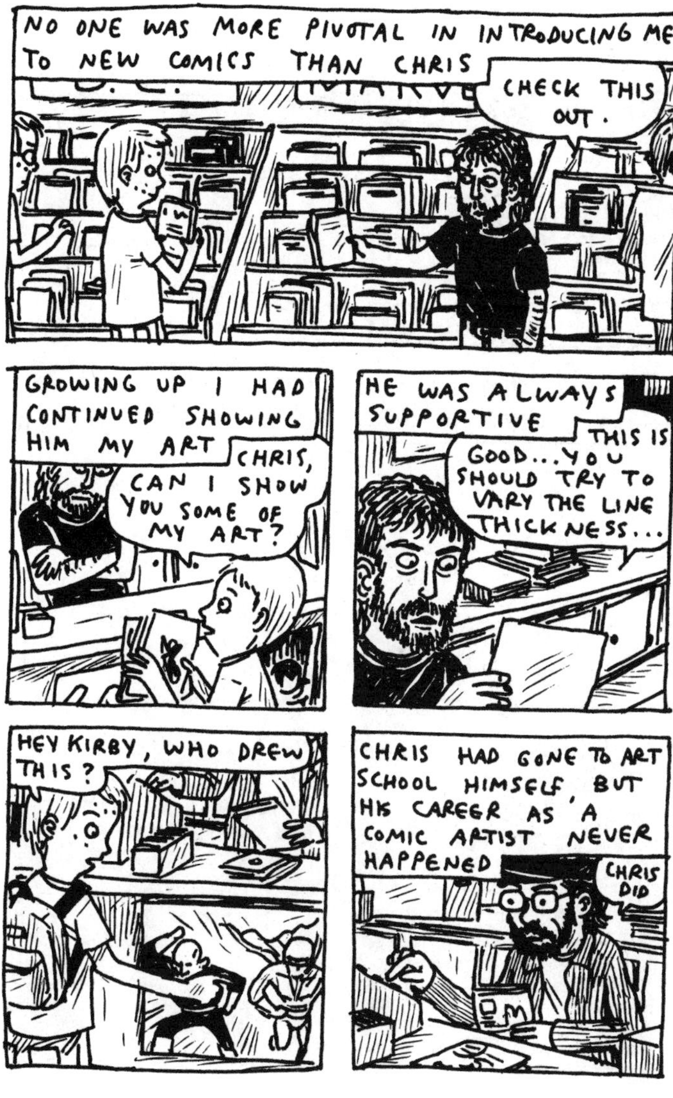
NO ONE WAS MORE PIVOTAL IN INTRODUCING ME TO NEW COMICS THAN CHRIS
CHECK THIS OUT.
GROWING UP I HAD CONTINUED SHOWING HIM MY ART
CHRIS, CAN I SHOW YOU SOME OF MY ART?
HE WAS ALWAYS SUPPORTIVE
THIS IS GOOD... YOU SHOULD TRY TO VARY THE LINE THICKNESS...
HEY KIRBY, WHO DREW THIS?
CHRIS HAD GONE TO ART SCHOOL HIMSELF, BUT HIS CAREER AS A COMIC ARTIST NEVER HAPPENED
CHRIS DID

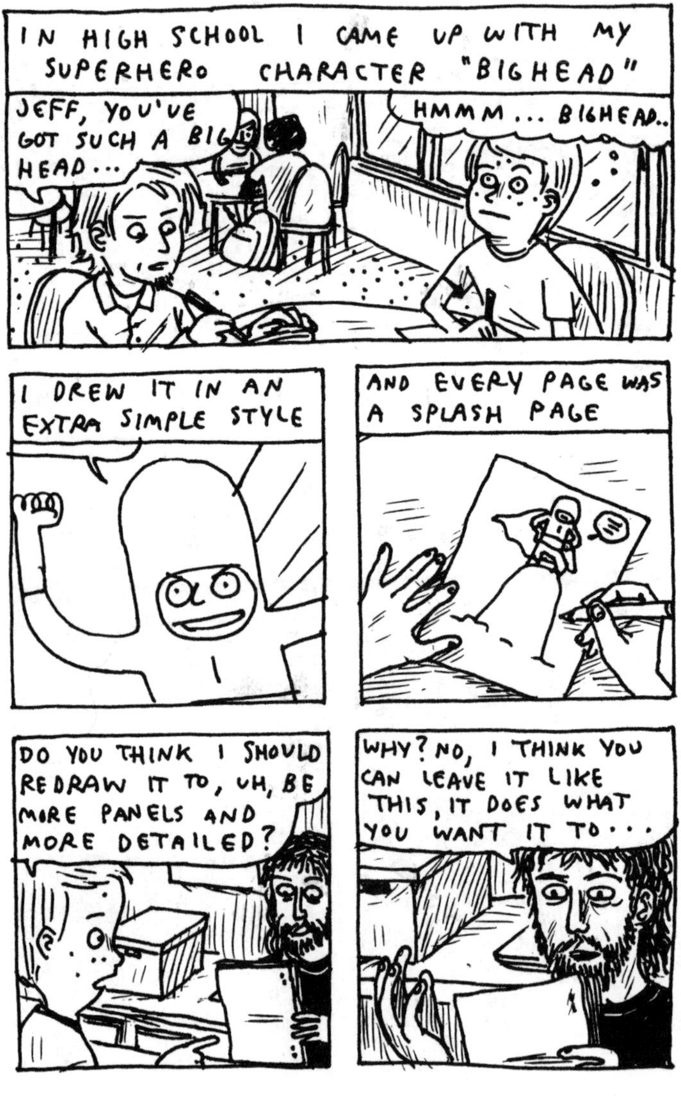
IN HIGH SCHOOL I CAME UP WITH MY SUPERHERO CHARACTER "BIGHEAD"
JEFF, YOU'VE GOT SUCH A BIG HEAD...
HMMM... BIGHEAD..
I DREW IT IN AN EXTRA SIMPLE STYLE
AND EVERY PAGE WAS A SPLASH PAGE
DO YOU THINK I SHOULD REDRAW IT TO, UH, BE MORE PANELS AND MORE DETAILED?
WHY? NO, I THINK YOU CAN LEAVE IT LIKE THIS, IT DOES WHAT YOU WANT IT TO...

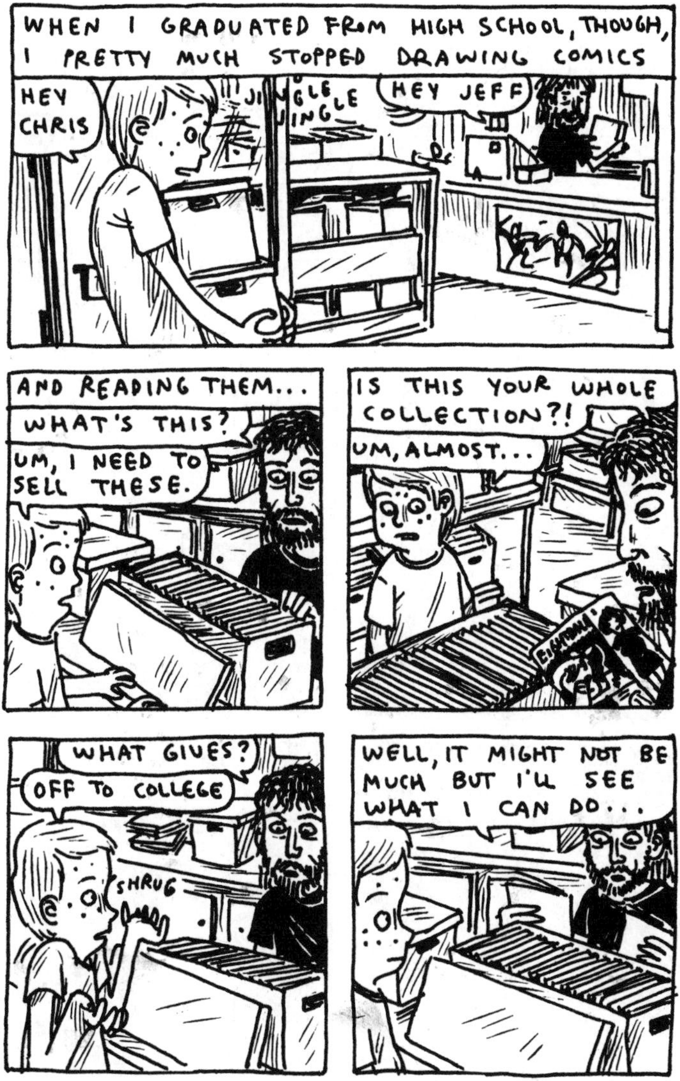
WHEN I GRADUATED FROM HIGH SCHOOL, THOUGH, I PRETTY MUCH STOPPED DRAWING COMICS
HEY CHRIS
JINGLE JINGLE
HEY JEFF
AND READING THEM...
WHAT'S THIS?
UM, I NEED TO SELL THESE.
IS THIS YOUR WHOLE COLLECTION?!
UM, ALMOST...
WHAT GIVES?
OFF TO COLLEGE
SHRUG
WELL, IT MIGHT NOT BE MUCH BUT I'LL SEE WHAT I CAN DO...

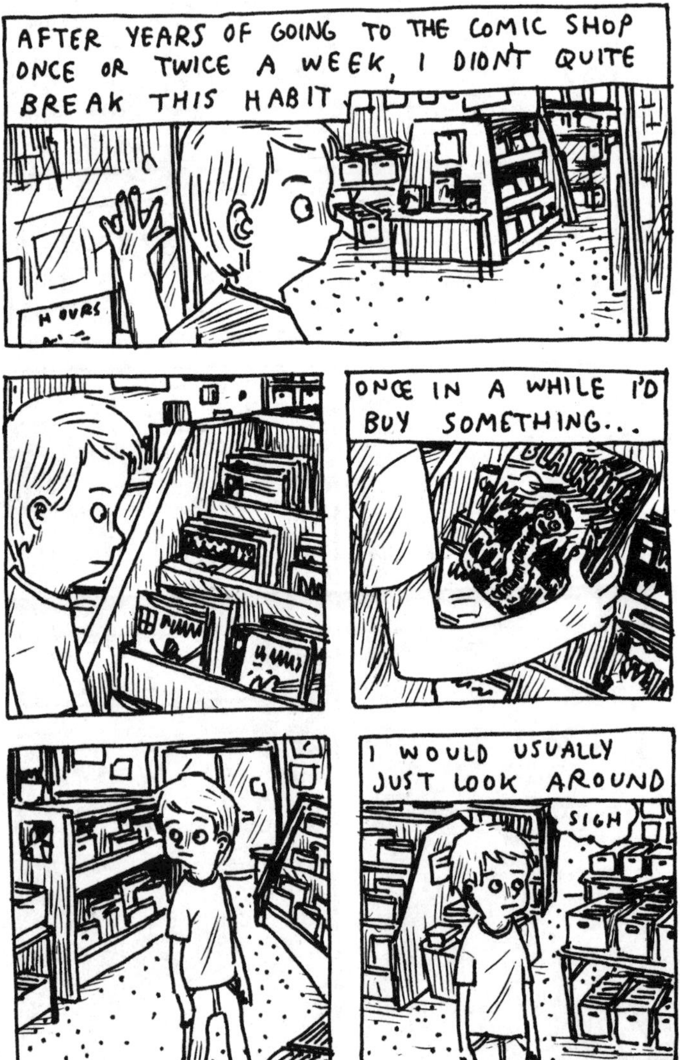
AFTER YEARS OF GOING TO THE COMIC SHOP ONCE OR TWICE A WEEK, I DIDN'T QUITE BREAK THIS HABIT
HOURS
ONCE IN A WHILE I'D BUY SOMETHING...
I WOULD USUALLY JUST LOOK AROUND
SIGH

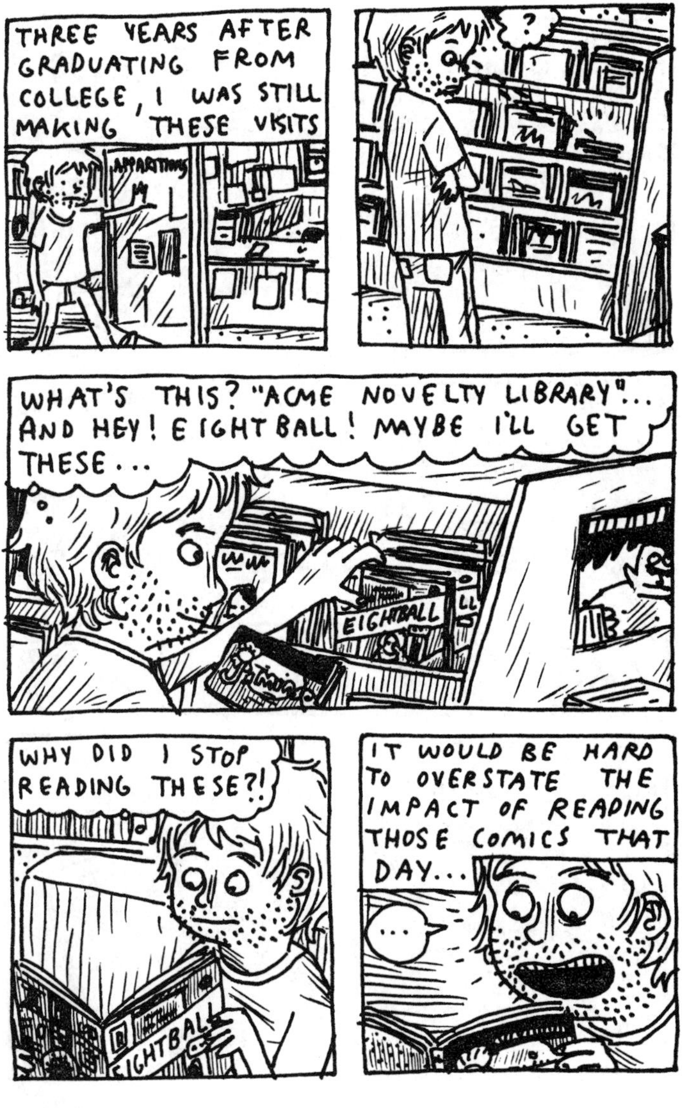
THREE YEARS AFTER GRADUATING FROM COLLEGE, I WAS STILL MAKING THESE VISITS
APPARITIONS
?
WHAT'S THIS? "ACME NOVELTY LIBRARY"... AND HEY! EIGHTBALL! MAYBE I'LL GET THESE...
EIGHTBALL
WHY DID I STOP READING THESE?!
EIGHTBALL
IT WOULD BE HARD TO OVERSTATE THE IMPACT OF READING THOSE COMICS THAT DAY...
...

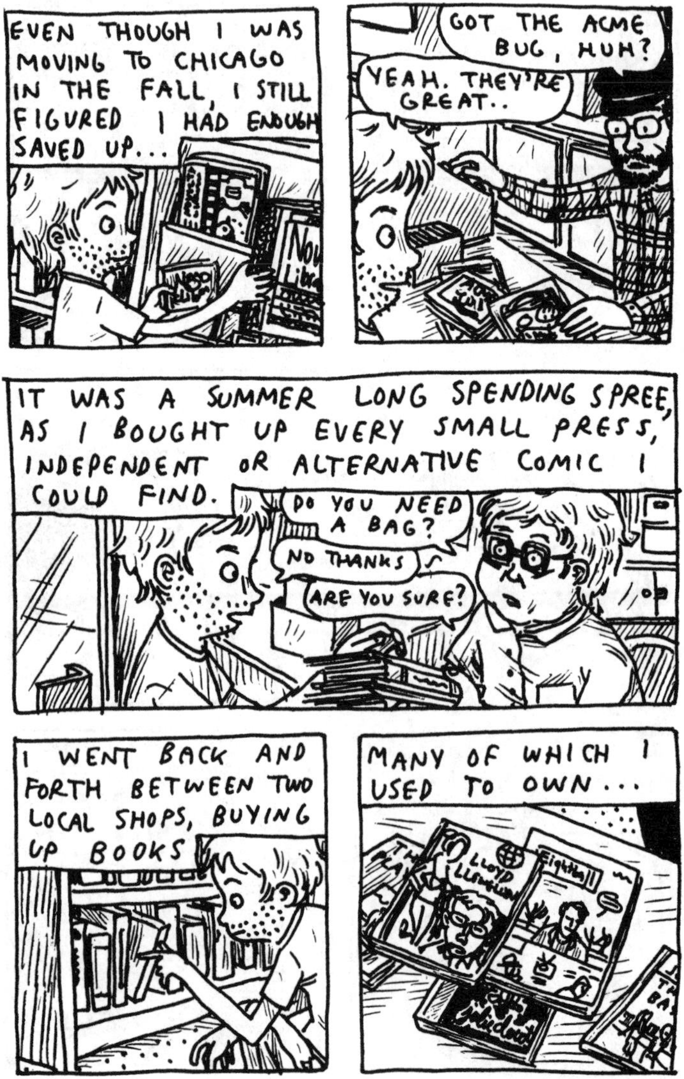
EVEN THOUGH I WAS MOVING TO CHICAGO IN THE FALL, I STILL FIGURED I HAD ENOUGH SAVED UP...
GOT THE ACME BUG, HUH?
YEAH. THEY'RE GREAT..
IT WAS A SUMMER LONG SPENDING SPREE, AS I BOUGHT UP EVERY SMALL PRESS, INDEPENDENT OR ALTERNATIVE COMIC I COULD FIND.
DO YOU NEED A BAG?
NO THANKS
ARE YOU SURE?
I WENT BACK AND FORTH BETWEEN TWO LOCAL SHOPS, BUYING UP BOOKS
MANY OF WHICH I USED TO OWN...

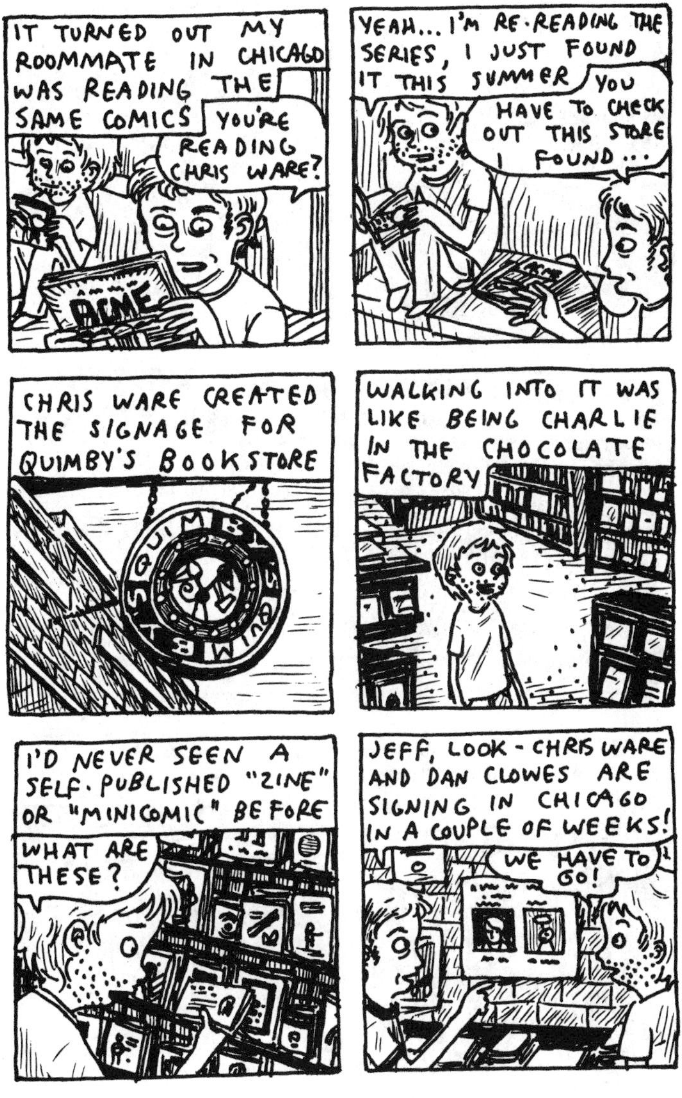
IT TURNED OUT MY ROOMMATE IN CHICAGO WAS READING THE SAME COMICS
YOU'RE READING CHRIS WARE?
ACME
YEAH... I'M RE-READING THE SERIES, I JUST FOUND IT THIS SUMMER
YOU HAVE TO CHECK OUT THIS STORE I FOUND...
CHRIS WARE CREATED THE SIGNAGE FOR QUIMBY'S BOOKSTORE
QUIMBYS
WALKING INTO IT WAS LIKE BEING CHARLIE IN THE CHOCOLATE FACTORY
I'D NEVER SEEN A SELF-PUBLISHED "ZINE" OR "MINICOMIC" BEFORE
WHAT ARE THESE?
JEFF, LOOK - CHRIS WARE AND DAN CLOWES ARE SIGNING IN CHICAGO IN A COUPLE OF WEEKS!
WE HAVE TO GO!

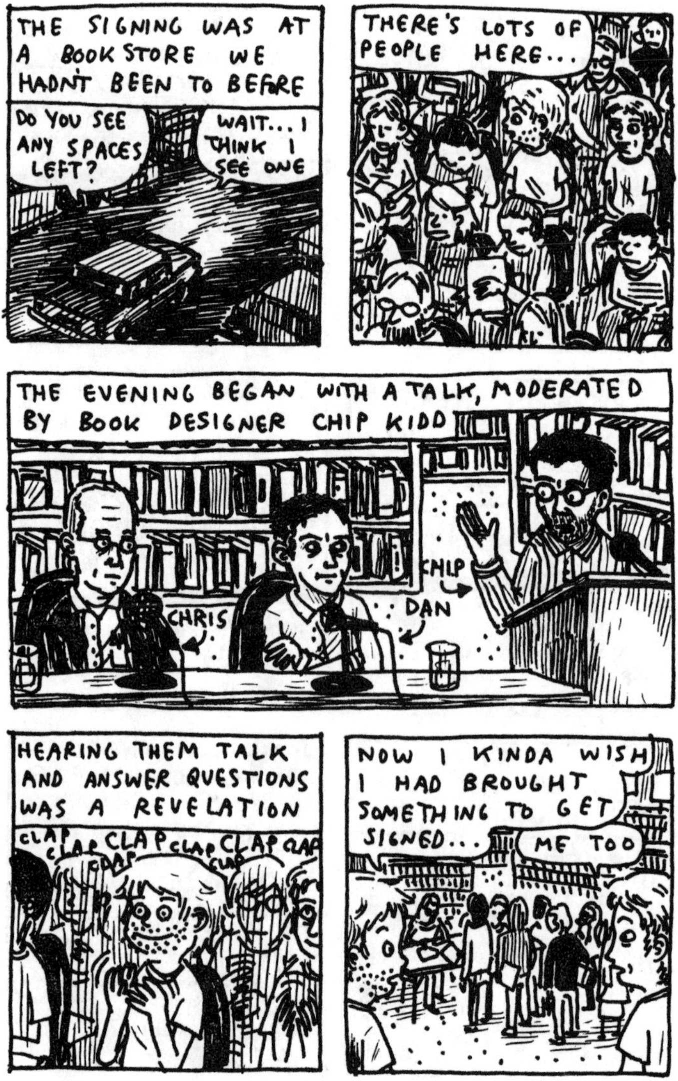
THE SIGNING WAS AT A BOOK STORE WE HADN'T BEEN TO BEFORE
DO YOU SEE ANY SPACES LEFT?
WAIT... I THINK I SEE ONE
THERE'S LOTS OF PEOPLE HERE...
THE EVENING BEGAN WITH A TALK, MODERATED BY BOOK DESIGNER CHIP KIDD
CHIP
DAN
CHRIS
HEARING THEM TALK AND ANSWER QUESTIONS WAS A REVELATION
CLAP CLAP CLAP CLAP CLAP CLAP CLAP CLAP
NOW I KINDA WISH I HAD BROUGHT SOMETHING TO GET SIGNED...
ME TOO

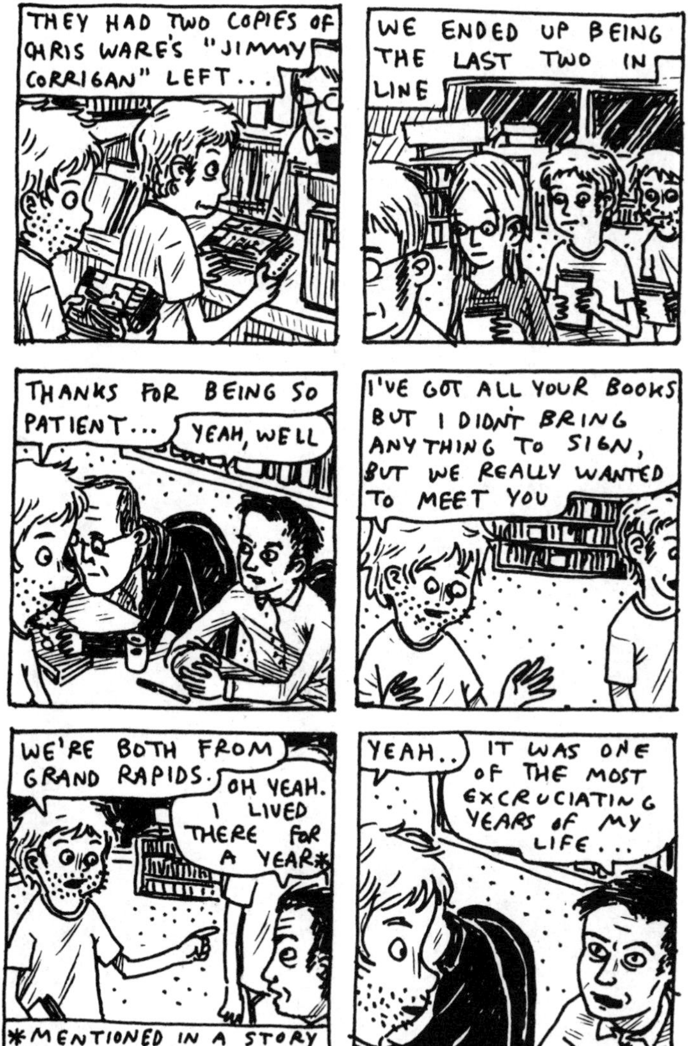
THEY HAD TWO COPIES OF CHRIS WARE'S "JIMMY CORRIGAN" LEFT...
WE ENDED UP BEING THE LAST TWO IN LINE
THANKS FOR BEING SO PATIENT...
YEAH, WELL
I'VE GOT ALL YOUR BOOKS BUT I DIDN'T BRING ANYTHING TO SIGN, BUT WE REALLY WANTED TO MEET YOU
WE'RE BOTH FROM GRAND RAPIDS.
OH YEAH. I LIVED THERE FOR A YEAR*
*MENTIONED IN A STORY FROM EIGHTBALL, ISSUE 11
YEAH..
IT WAS ONE OF THE MOST EXCRUCIATING YEARS OF MY LIFE...

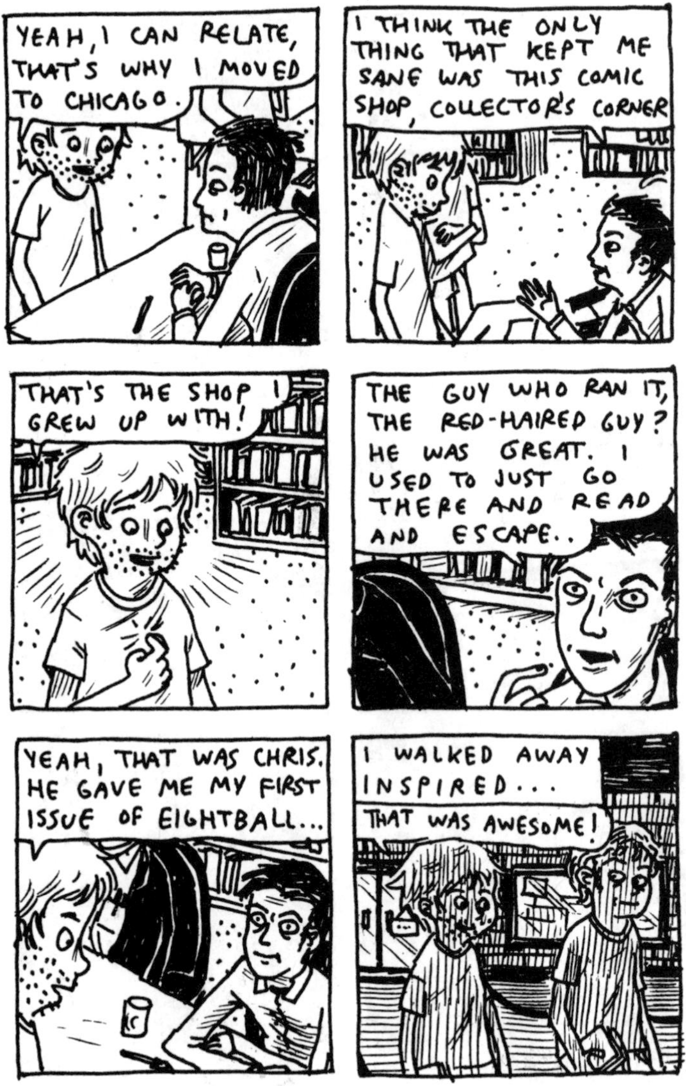
YEAH, I CAN RELATE, THAT'S WHY I MOVED TO CHICAGO.
I THINK THE ONLY THING THAT KEPT ME SANE WAS THIS COMIC SHOP, COLLECTOR'S CORNER
THAT'S THE SHOP I GREW UP WITH!
THE GUY WHO RAN IT, THE RED-HAIRED GUY? HE WAS GREAT. I USED TO JUST GO THERE AND READ AND ESCAPE..
YEAH, THAT WAS CHRIS. HE GAVE ME MY FIRST ISSUE OF EIGHTBALL...
I WALKED AWAY INSPIRED...
THAT WAS AWESOME!

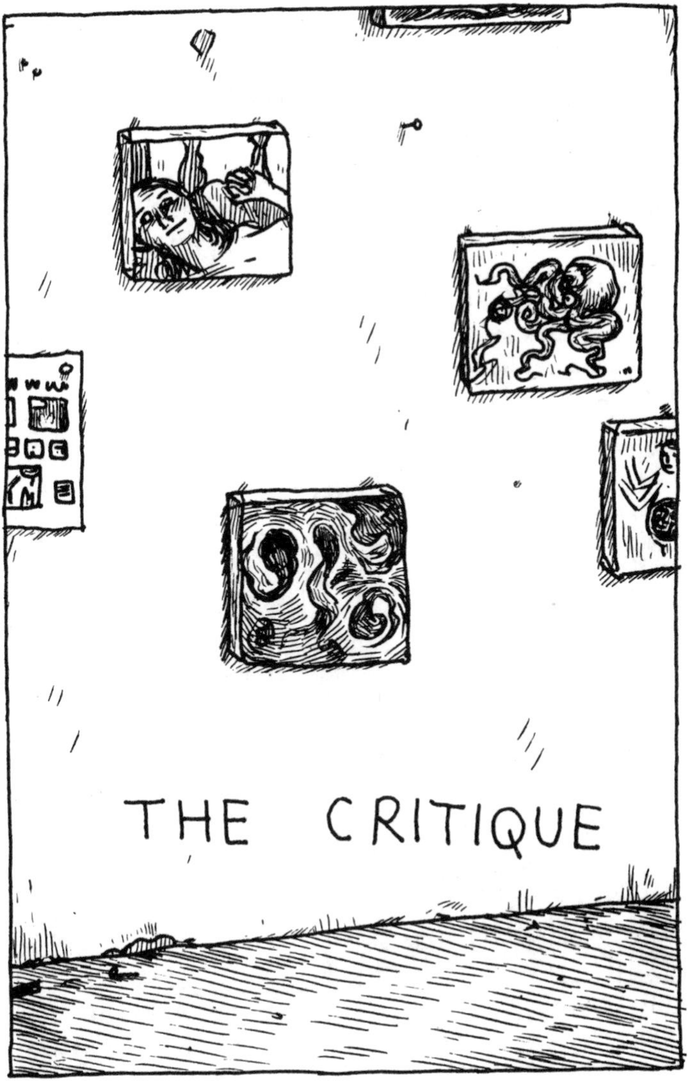
THE CRITIQUE

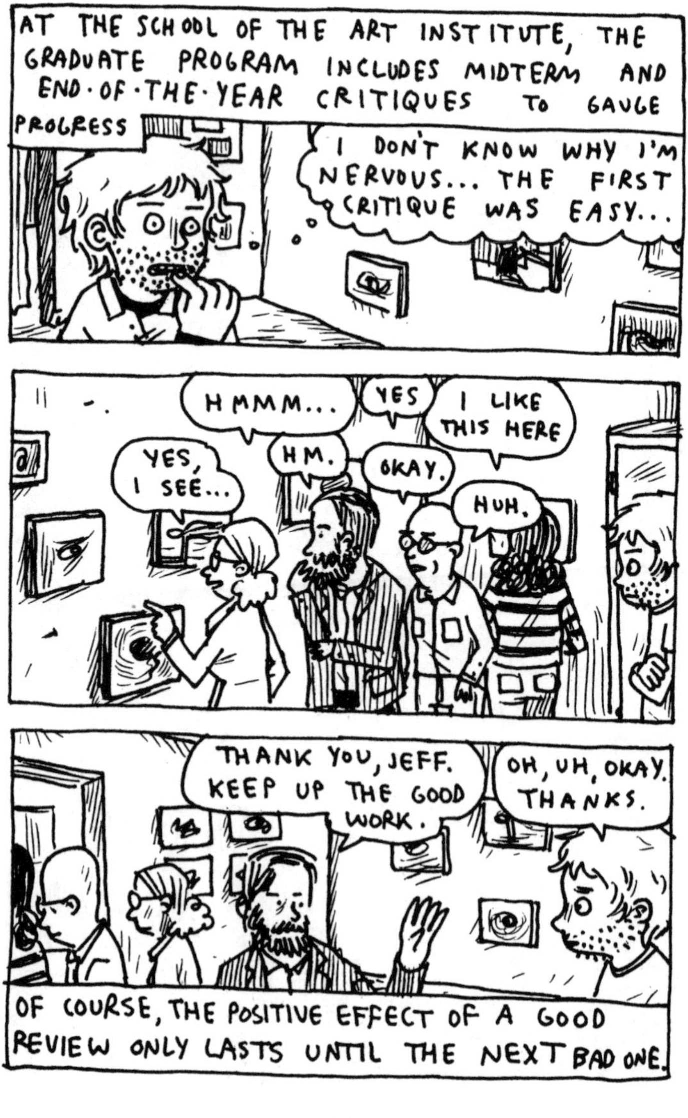
AT THE SCHOOL OF THE ART INSTITUTE, THE GRADUATE PROGRAM INCLUDES MIDTERM AND END-OF-THE-YEAR CRITIQUES TO GAUGE PROGRESS
I DON'T KNOW WHY I'M NERVOUS... THE FIRST CRITIQUE WAS EASY...
HMMM...
YES
I LIKE THIS HERE
YES, I SEE...
HM.
OKAY.
HUH.
THANK YOU, JEFF. KEEP UP THE GOOD WORK.
OH, UH, OKAY. THANKS.
OF COURSE, THE POSITIVE EFFECT OF A GOOD REVIEW ONLY LASTS UNTIL THE NEXT BAD ONE.

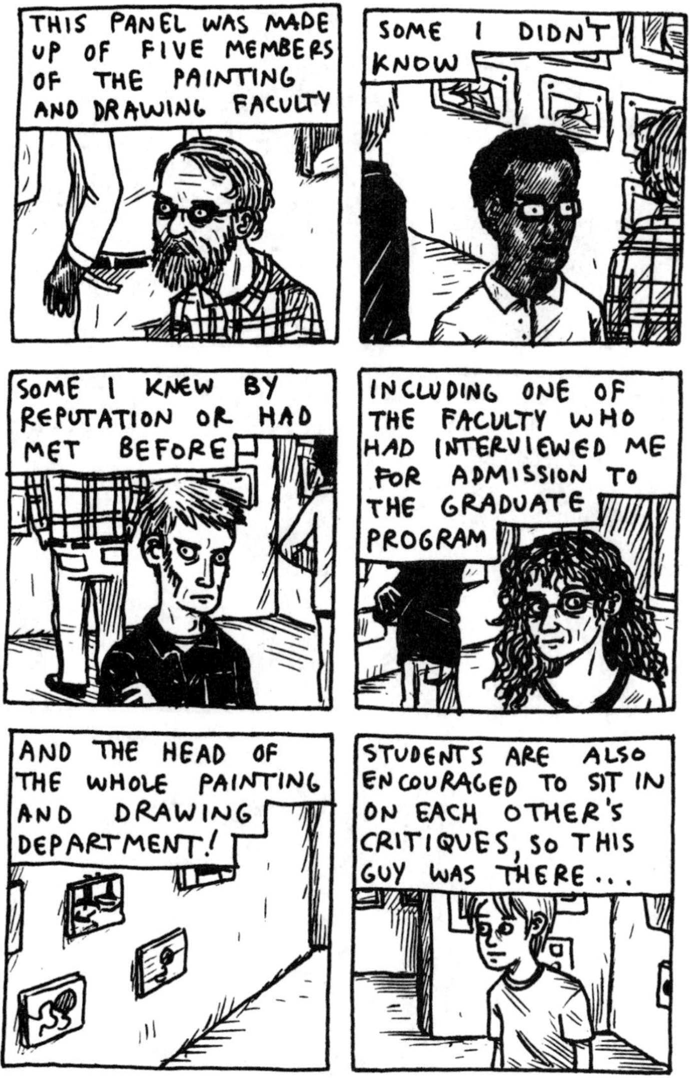
THIS PANEL WAS MADE UP OF FIVE MEMBERS OF THE PAINTING AND DRAWING FACULTY
SOME I DIDN'T KNOW
SOME I KNEW BY REPUTATION OR HAD MET BEFORE
INCLUDING ONE OF THE FACULTY WHO HAD INTERVIEWED ME FOR ADMISSION TO THE GRADUATE PROGRAM
AND THE HEAD OF THE WHOLE PAINTING AND DRAWING DEPARTMENT!
STUDENTS ARE ALSO ENCOURAGED TO SIT IN ON EACH OTHER'S CRITIQUES, SO THIS GUY WAS THERE...

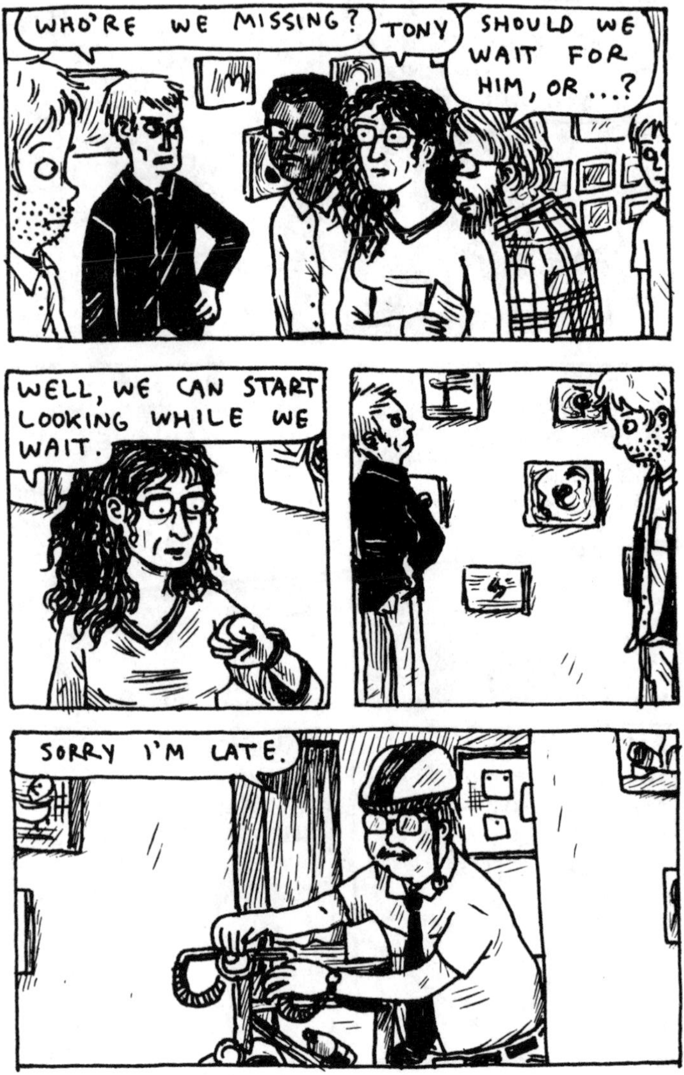
WHO'RE WE MISSING?
TONY
SHOULD WE WAIT FOR HIM, OR ...?
WELL, WE CAN START LOOKING WHILE WE WAIT.
SORRY I'M LATE.

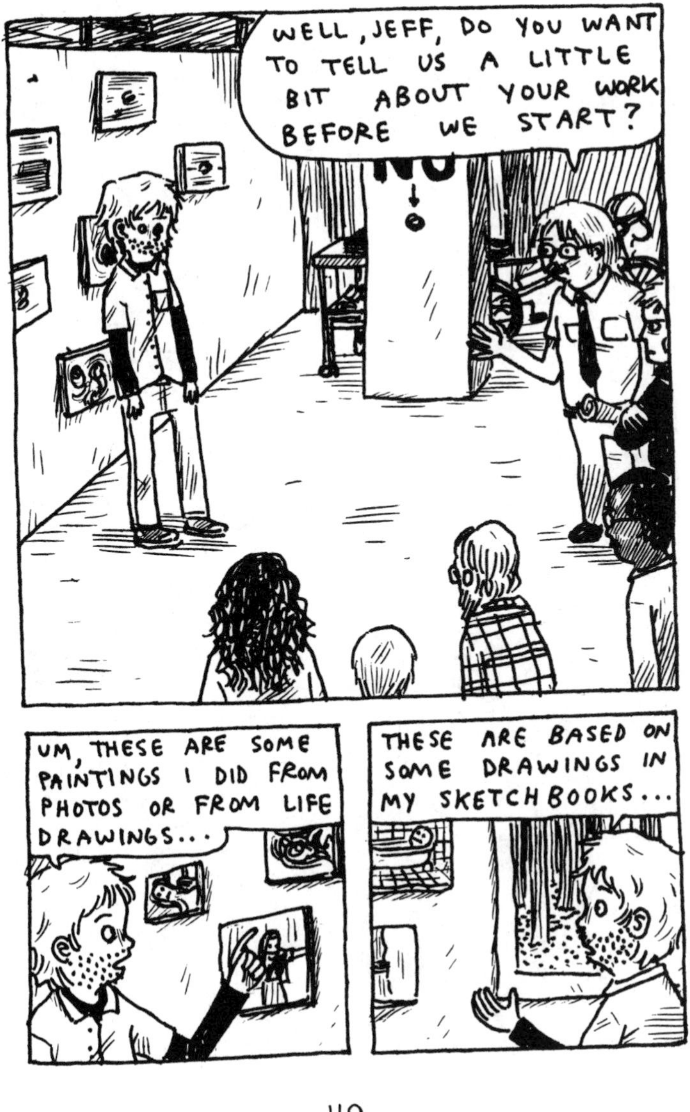
WELL, JEFF, DO YOU WANT TO TELL US A LITTLE BIT ABOUT YOUR WORK BEFORE WE START?
UM, THESE ARE SOME PAINTINGS I DID FROM PHOTOS OR FROM LIFE DRAWINGS...
THESE ARE BASED ON SOME DRAWINGS IN MY SKETCHBOOKS...

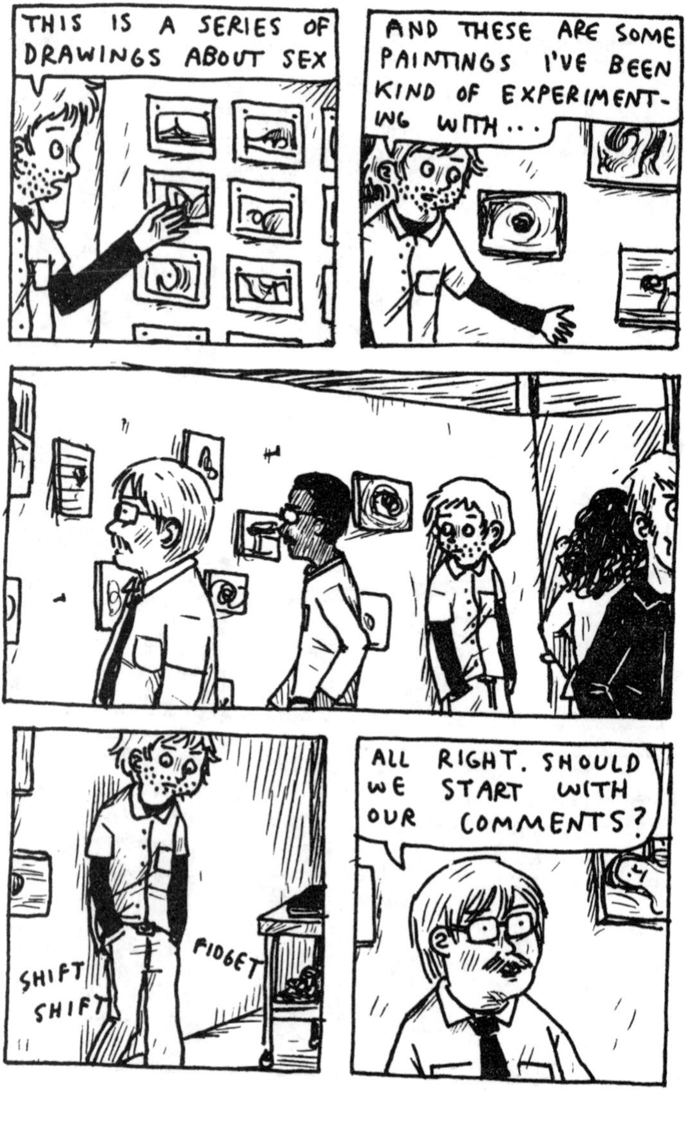
THIS IS A SERIES OF DRAWINGS ABOUT SEX
AND THESE ARE SOME PAINTINGS I'VE BEEN KIND OF EXPERIMENT-ING WITH...
SHIFT
SHIFT
FIDGET
ALL RIGHT. SHOULD WE START WITH OUR COMMENTS?

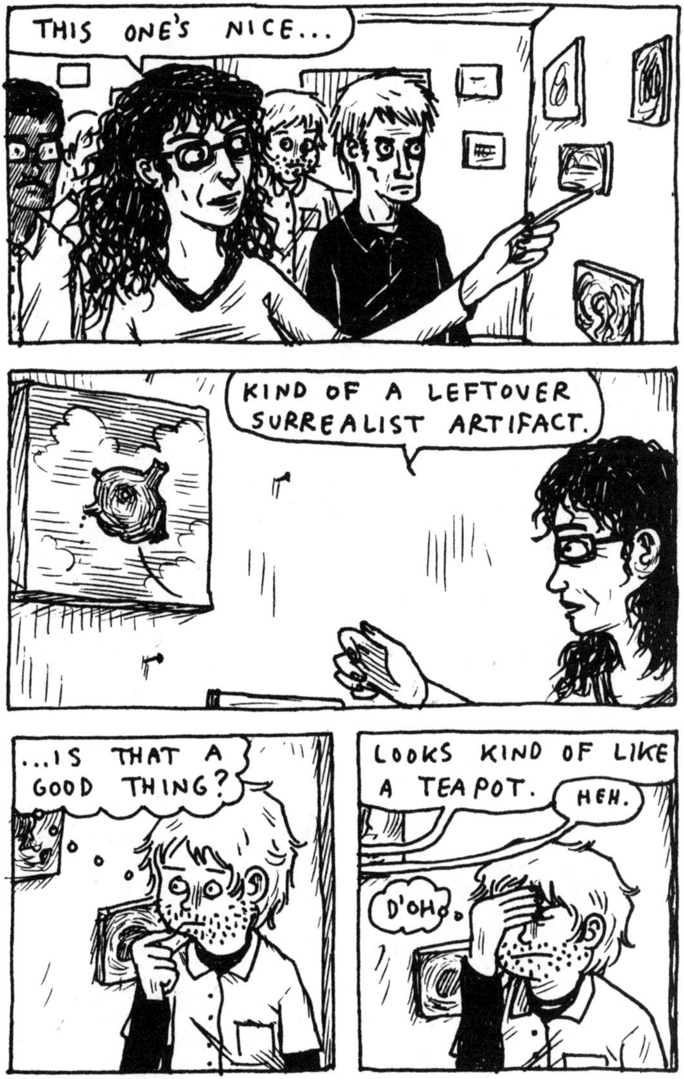
THIS ONE'S NICE...
KIND OF A LEFTOVER SURREALIST ARTIFACT.
...IS THAT A GOOD THING?
LOOKS KIND OF LIKE A TEAPOT.
HEH.
D'OH.

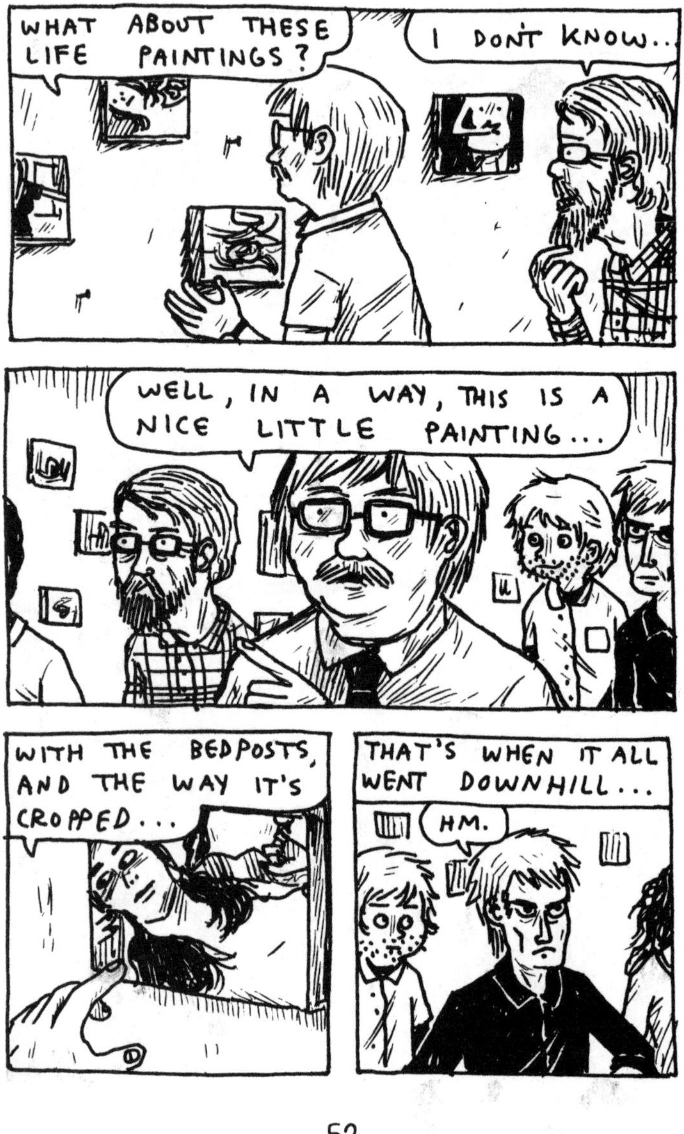
WHAT ABOUT THESE LIFE PAINTINGS?
I DON'T KNOW...
WELL, IN A WAY, THIS IS A NICE LITTLE PAINTING...
WITH THE BEDPOSTS, AND THE WAY IT'S CROPPED...
THAT'S WHEN IT ALL WENT DOWNHILL...
HM.

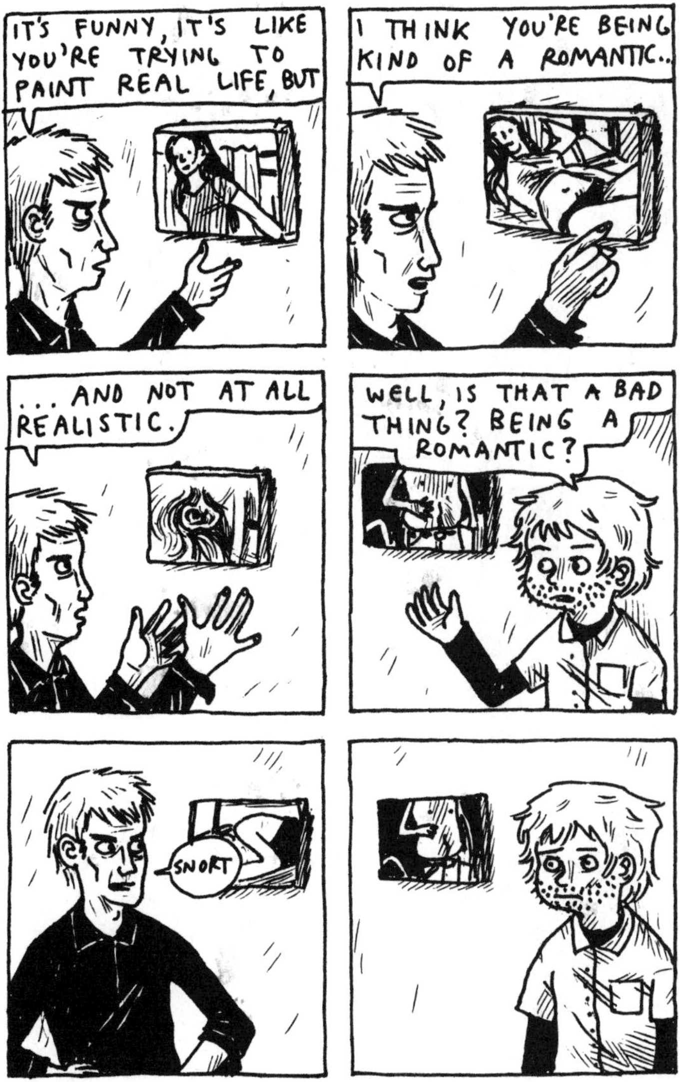
IT'S FUNNY, IT'S LIKE YOU'RE TRYING TO PAINT REAL LIFE, BUT
I THINK YOU'RE BEING KIND OF A ROMANTIC..
... AND NOT AT ALL REALISTIC.
WELL, IS THAT A BAD THING? BEING A ROMANTIC?
SNORT

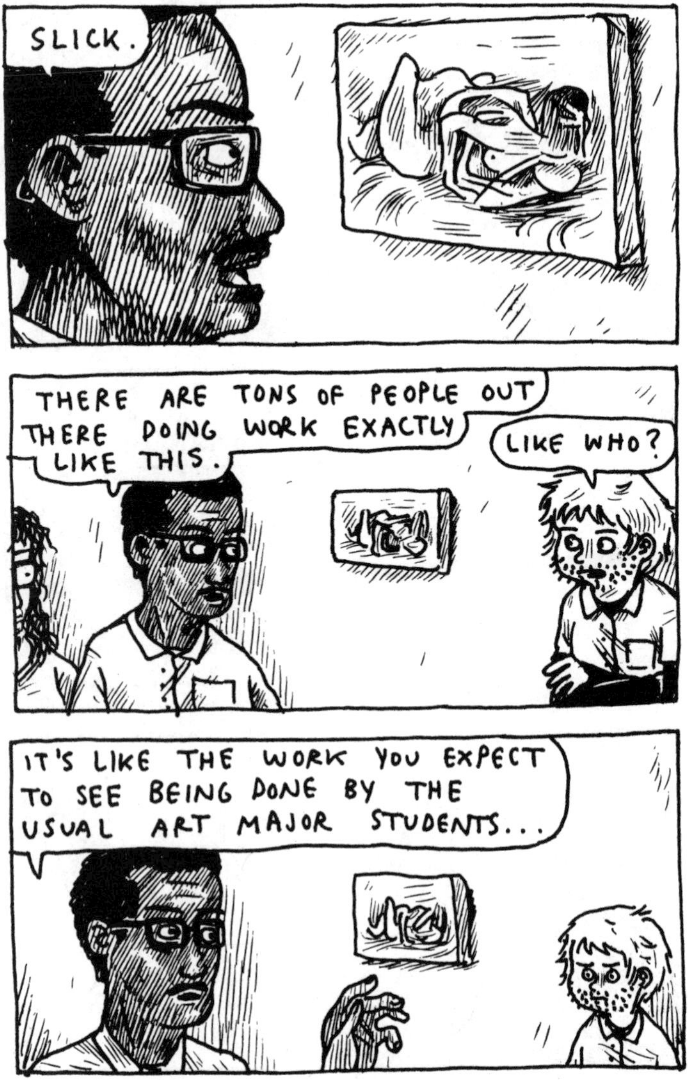
SLICK.
THERE ARE TONS OF PEOPLE OUT THERE DOING WORK EXACTLY LIKE THIS.
LIKE WHO?
IT'S LIKE THE WORK YOU EXPECT TO SEE BEING DONE BY THE USUAL ART MAJOR STUDENTS...

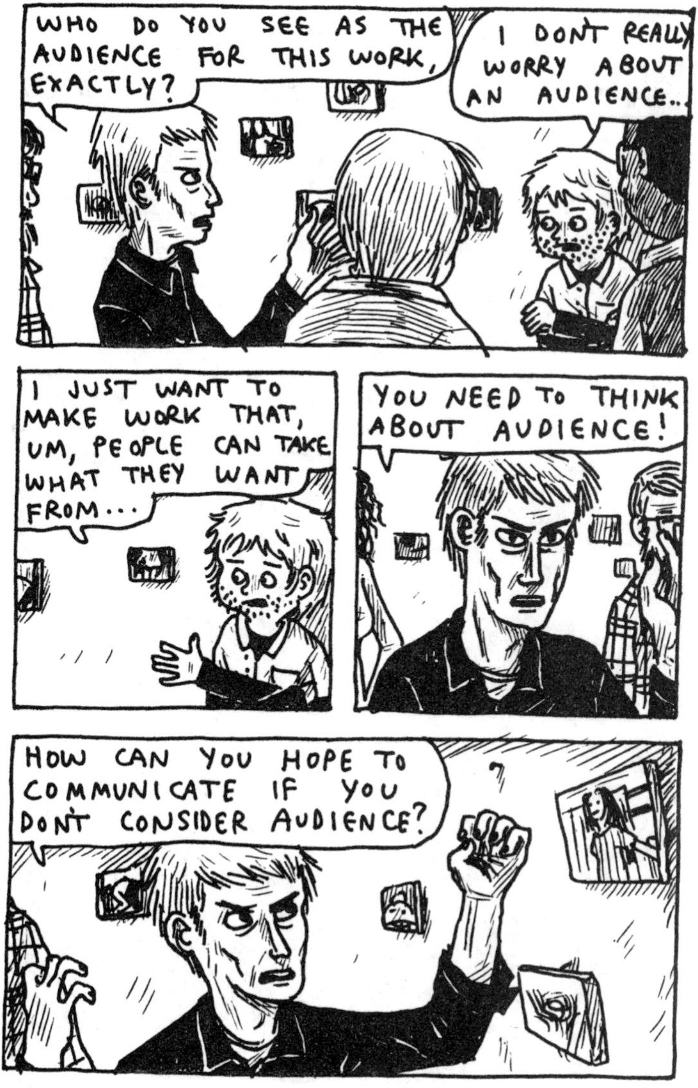
WHO DO YOU SEE AS THE AUDIENCE FOR THIS WORK, EXACTLY?
I DONT REALLY WORRY ABOUT AN AUDIENCE..
I JUST WANT TO MAKE WORK THAT, UM, PEOPLE CAN TAKE WHAT THEY WANT FROM...
YOU NEED TO THINK ABOUT AUDIENCE!
HOW CAN YOU HOPE TO COMMUNICATE IF YOU DON'T CONSIDER AUDIENCE?

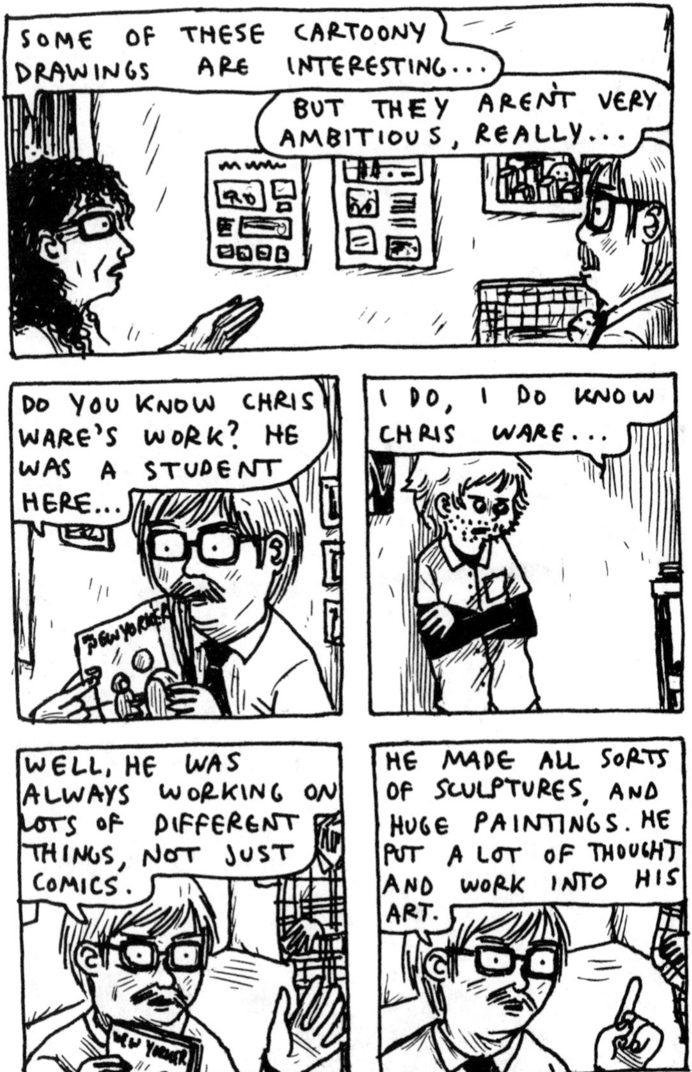
SOME OF THESE CARTOONY DRAWINGS ARE INTERESTING...
BUT THEY AREN'T VERY AMBITIOUS, REALLY...
DO YOU KNOW CHRIS WARE'S WORK? HE WAS A STUDENT HERE...
NEW YORKER
I DO, I DO KNOW CHRIS WARE...
WELL, HE WAS ALWAYS WORKING ON LOTS OF DIFFERENT THINGS, NOT JUST COMICS.
NEW YORKER
HE MADE ALL SORTS OF SCULPTURES, AND HUGE PAINTINGS. HE PUT A LOT OF THOUGHT AND WORK INTO HIS ART.

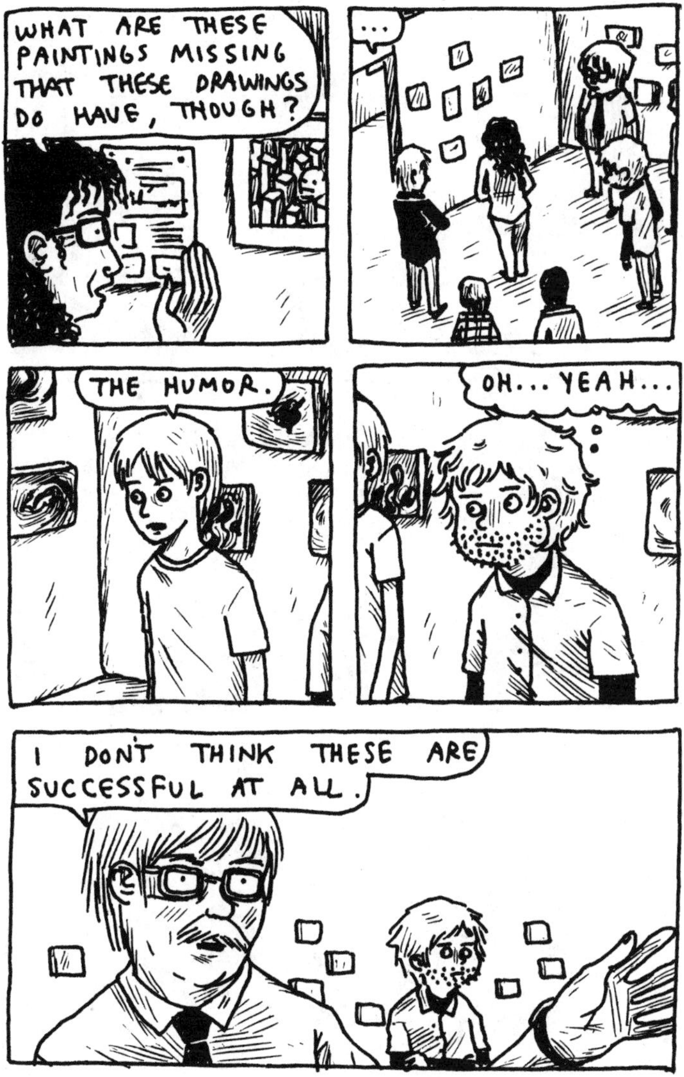
WHAT ARE THESE PAINTINGS MISSING THAT THESE DRAWINGS DO HAVE, THOUGH?
...
THE HUMOR.
OH... YEAH...
I DON'T THINK THESE ARE SUCCESSFUL AT ALL.

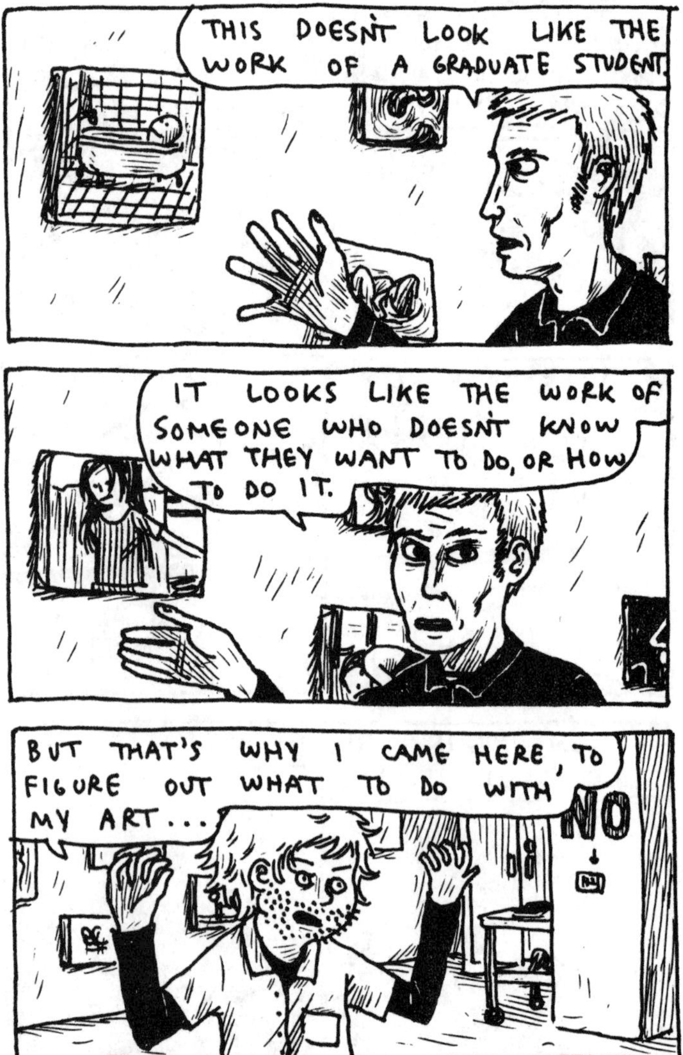
THIS DOESN'T LOOK LIKE THE WORK OF A GRADUATE STUDENT.
IT LOOKS LIKE THE WORK OF SOMEONE WHO DOESN'T KNOW WHAT THEY WANT TO DO, OR HOW TO DO IT.
BUT THAT'S WHY I CAME HERE, TO FIGURE OUT WHAT TO DO WITH MY ART...
NO

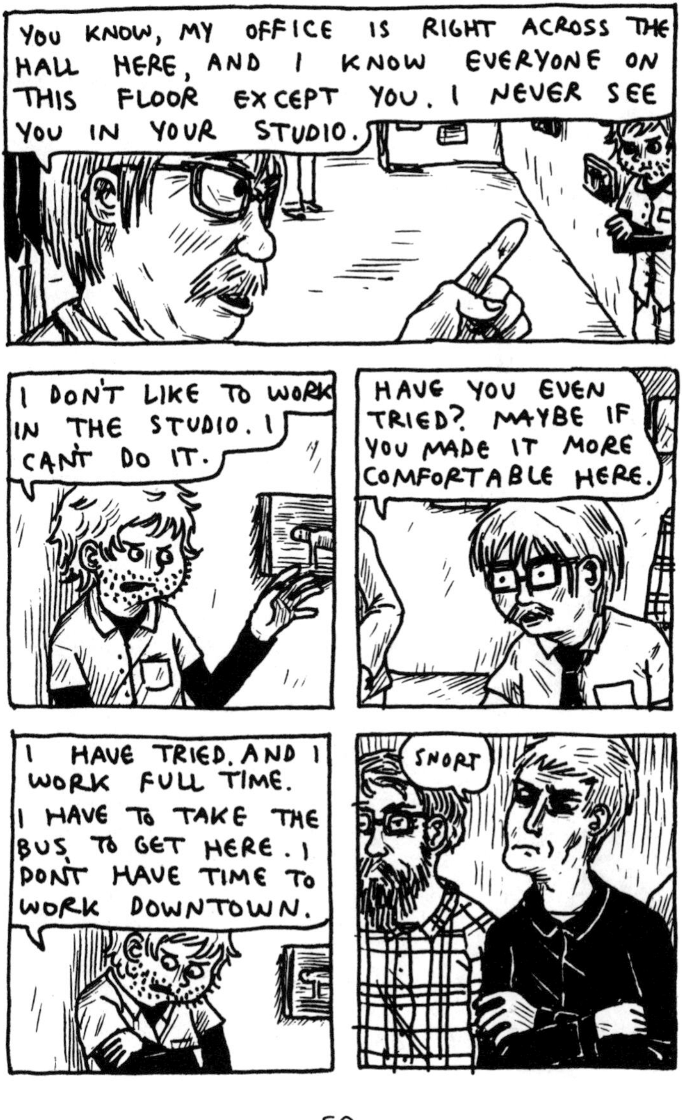
YOU KNOW, MY OFFICE IS RIGHT ACROSS THE HALL HERE, AND I KNOW EVERYONE ON THIS FLOOR EXCEPT YOU. I NEVER SEE YOU IN YOUR STUDIO.
I DON'T LIKE TO WORK IN THE STUDIO. I CAN'T DO IT.
HAVE YOU EVEN TRIED? MAYBE IF YOU MADE IT MORE COMFORTABLE HERE.
I HAVE TRIED. AND I WORK FULL TIME.
I HAVE TO TAKE THE BUS TO GET HERE. I DON'T HAVE TIME TO WORK DOWNTOWN.
SNORT

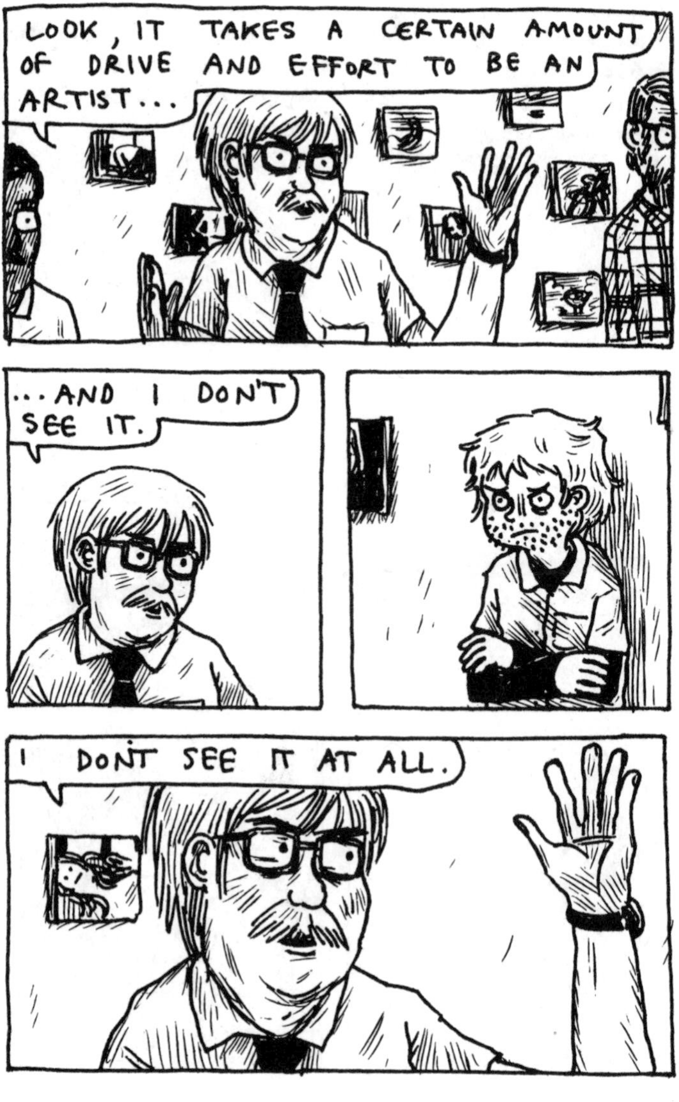

LOOK, IT TAKES A CERTAIN AMOUNT OF DRIVE AND EFFORT TO BE AN ARTIST...
...AND I DON'T SEE IT.
I DON'T SEE IT AT ALL.

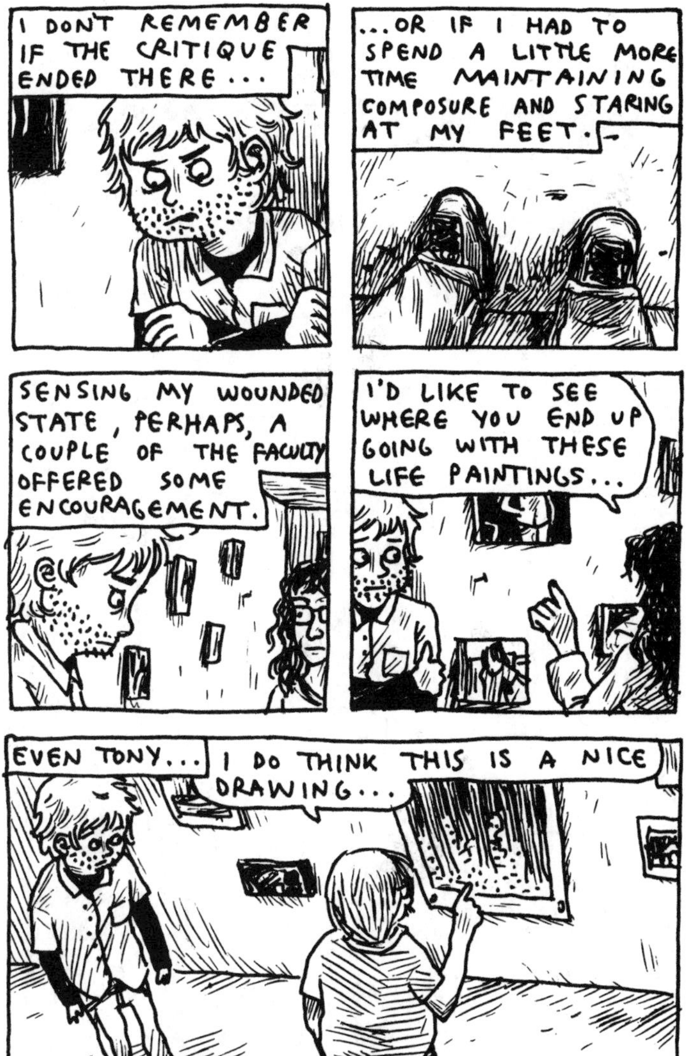
I DON'T REMEMBER IF THE CRITIQUE ENDED THERE...
...OR IF I HAD TO SPEND A LITTLE MORE TIME MAINTAINING COMPOSURE AND STARING AT MY FEET.
SENSING MY WOUNDED STATE, PERHAPS, A COUPLE OF THE FACULTY OFFERED SOME ENCOURAGEMENT.
I'D LIKE TO SEE WHERE YOU END UP GOING WITH THESE LIFE PAINTINGS...
EVEN TONY...
I DO THINK THIS IS A NICE DRAWING...

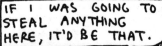

IF I WAS GOING TO STEAL ANYTHING HERE, IT'D BE THAT.

(IRONICALLY, WHEN I MOVED OUT OF MY STUDIO A YEAR LATER, THAT DRAWING HAD DISAPPEARED)

AWKWARD ELEVATOR RIDE AFTERWARD

I THOUGHT THEY WERE A LITTLE HARSH. I LIKE YOUR DRAWINGS.

THANKS.

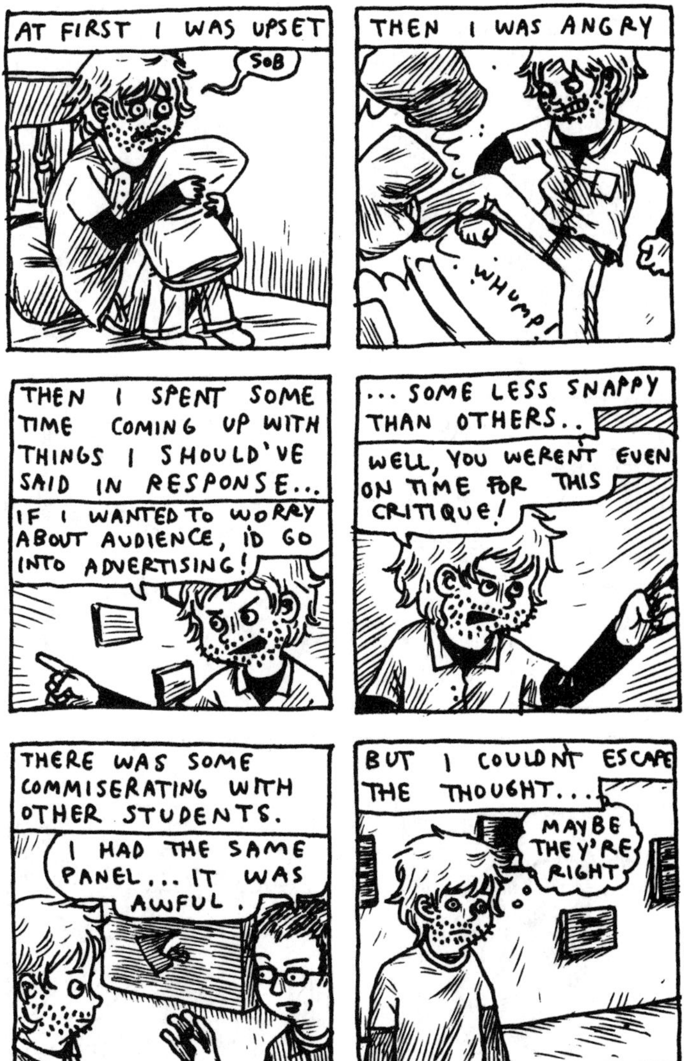
AT FIRST I WAS UPSET
SOB
THEN I WAS ANGRY
WHUMP!
THEN I SPENT SOME TIME COMING UP WITH THINGS I SHOULD'VE SAID IN RESPONSE...
IF I WANTED TO WORRY ABOUT AUDIENCE, I'D GO INTO ADVERTISING!
...SOME LESS SNAPPY THAN OTHERS..
WELL, YOU WEREN'T EVEN ON TIME FOR THIS CRITIQUE!
THERE WAS SOME COMMISERATING WITH OTHER STUDENTS.
I HAD THE SAME PANEL... IT WAS AWFUL.
BUT I COULDN'T ESCAPE THE THOUGHT...
MAYBE THEY'RE RIGHT

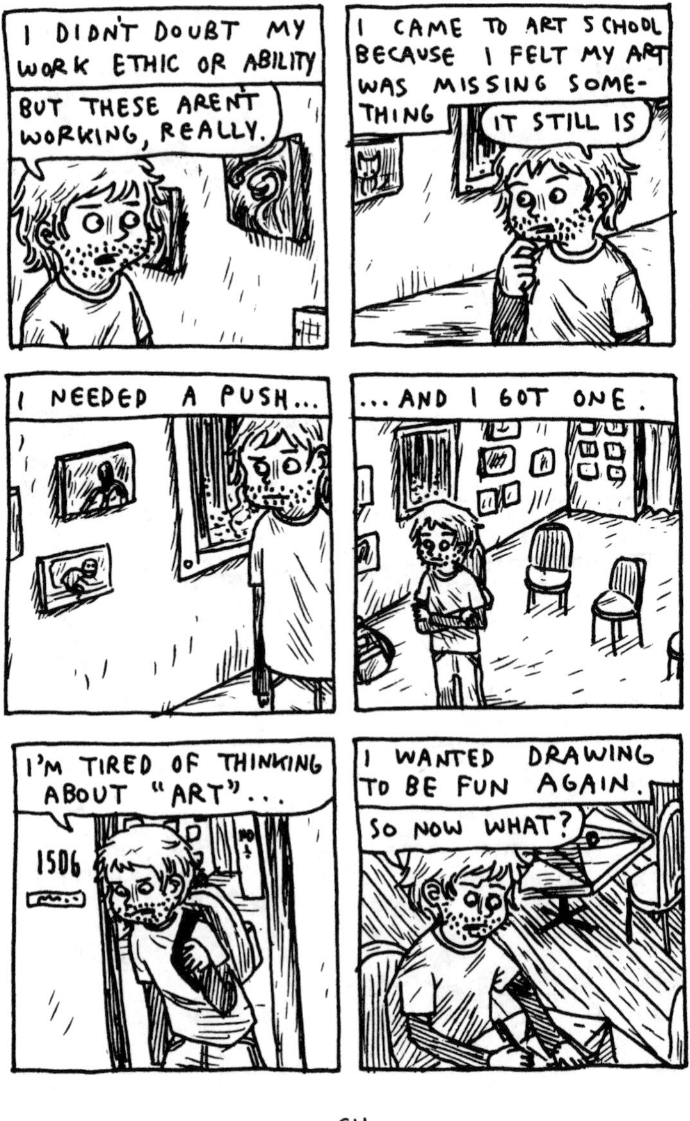
I DIDN'T DOUBT MY WORK ETHIC OR ABILITY
BUT THESE AREN'T WORKING, REALLY.
I CAME TO ART SCHOOL BECAUSE I FELT MY ART WAS MISSING SOME-THING
IT STILL IS
I NEEDED A PUSH...
...AND I GOT ONE.
I'M TIRED OF THINKING ABOUT "ART"...
1506
I WANTED DRAWING TO BE FUN AGAIN.
SO NOW WHAT?

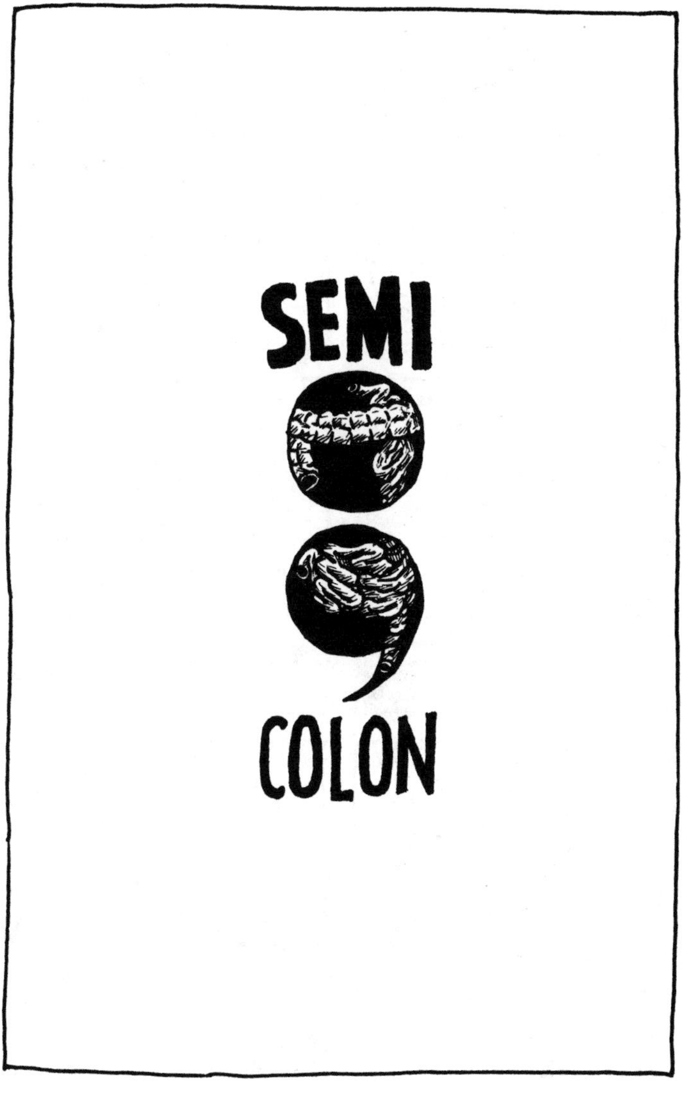
SEMI
COLON

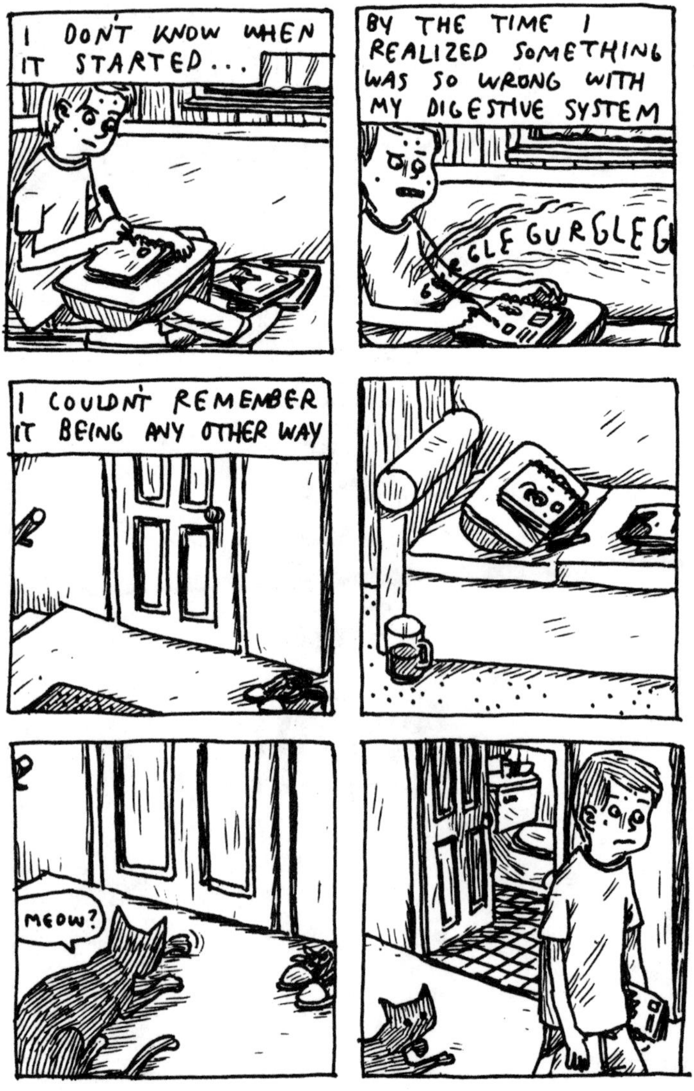
I DON'T KNOW WHEN IT STARTED...
BY THE TIME I REALIZED SOMETHING WAS SO WRONG WITH MY DIGESTIVE SYSTEM
GLEGURGLEG
I COULDN'T REMEMBER IT BEING ANY OTHER WAY
MEOW?

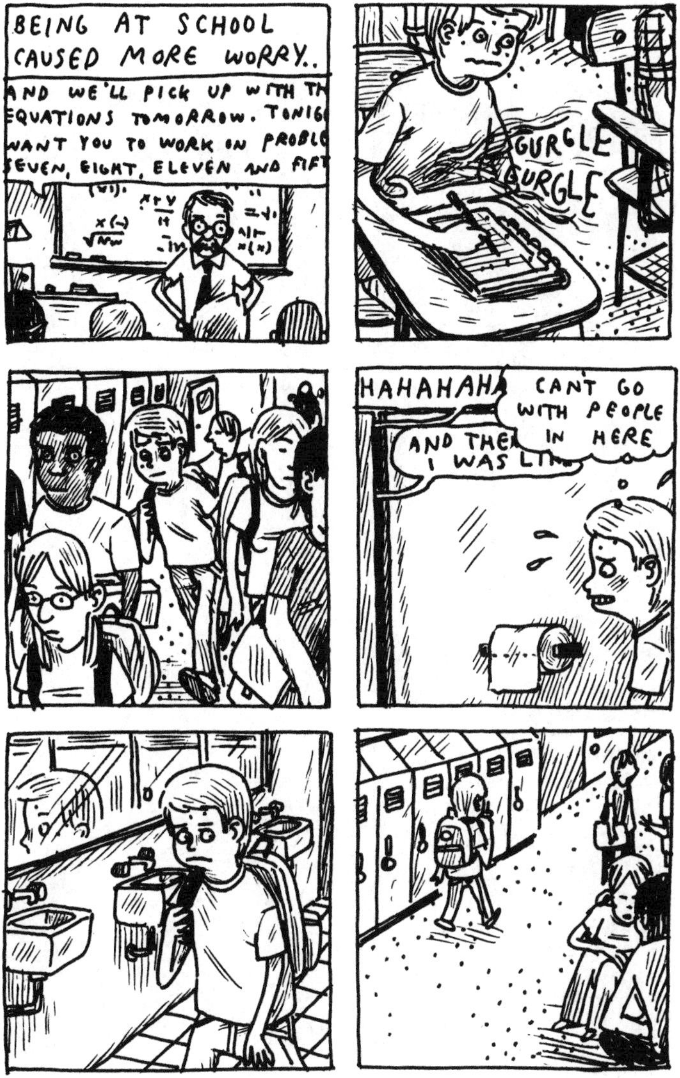
BEING AT SCHOOL CAUSED MORE WORRY..
AND WE'LL PICK UP WITH TH
EQUATIONS TOMORROW. TONIG
WANT YOU TO WORK ON PROBL
SEVEN, EIGHT, ELEVEN AND FIFT
GURGLE
GURGLE
HAHAHAHA
AND THE
I WAS LI
CAN'T GO WITH PEOPLE IN HERE

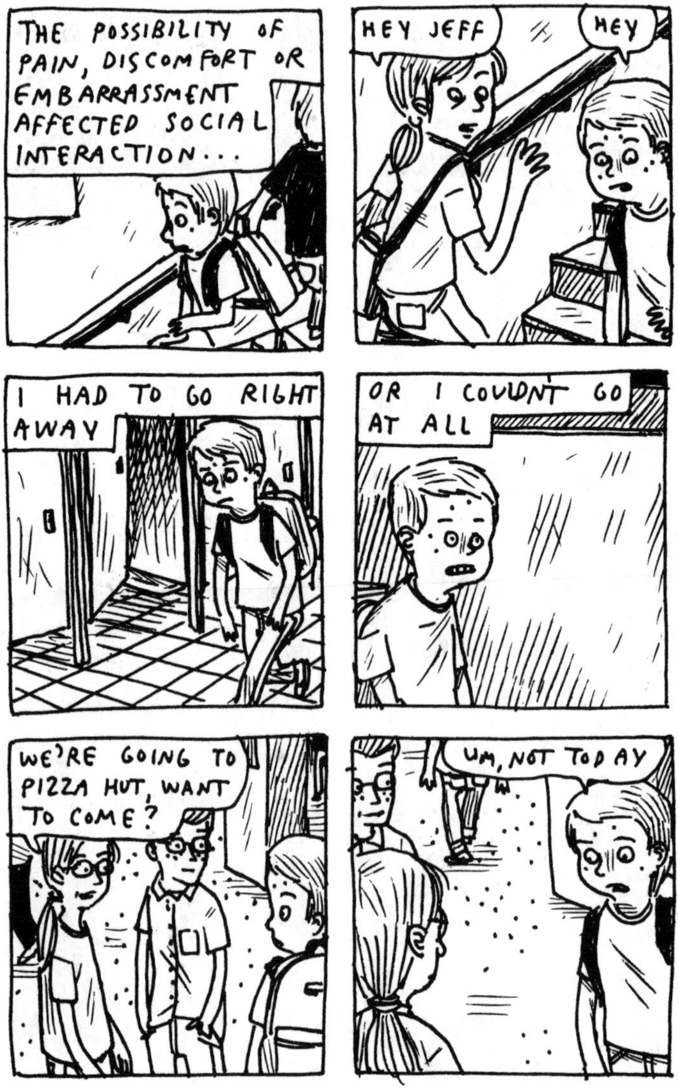
THE POSSIBILITY OF PAIN, DISCOMFORT OR EMBARRASSMENT AFFECTED SOCIAL INTERACTION...
HEY JEFF
HEY
I HAD TO GO RIGHT AWAY
OR I COULDN'T GO AT ALL
WE'RE GOING TO PIZZA HUT, WANT TO COME?
UM, NOT TODAY

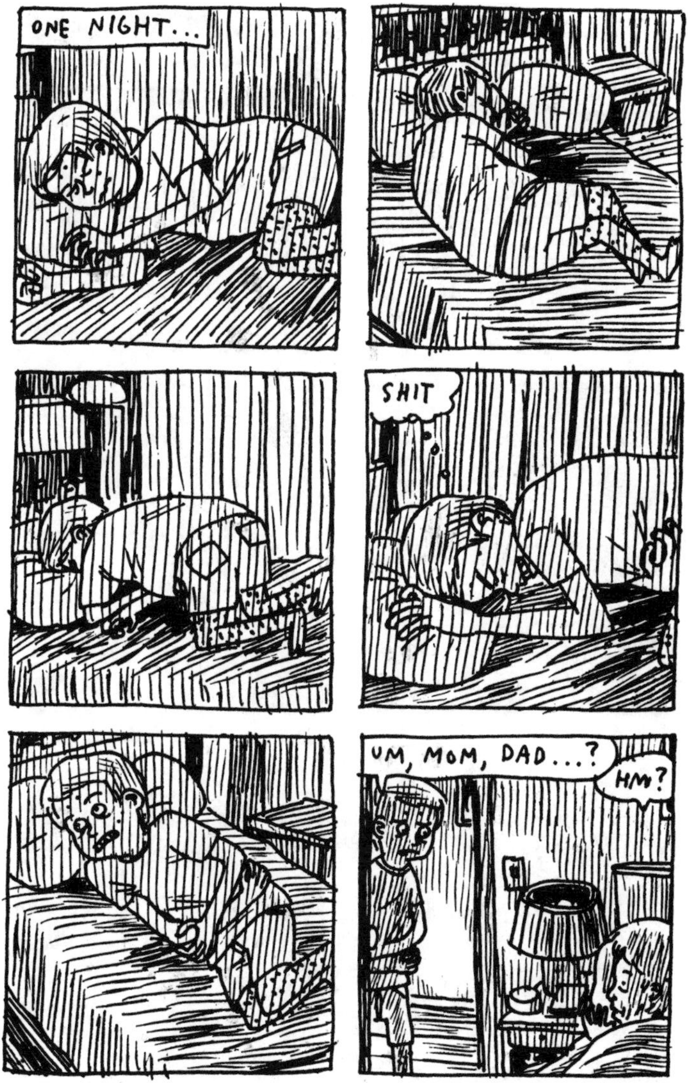
ONE NIGHT...
SHIT
UM, MOM, DAD...?
HM?

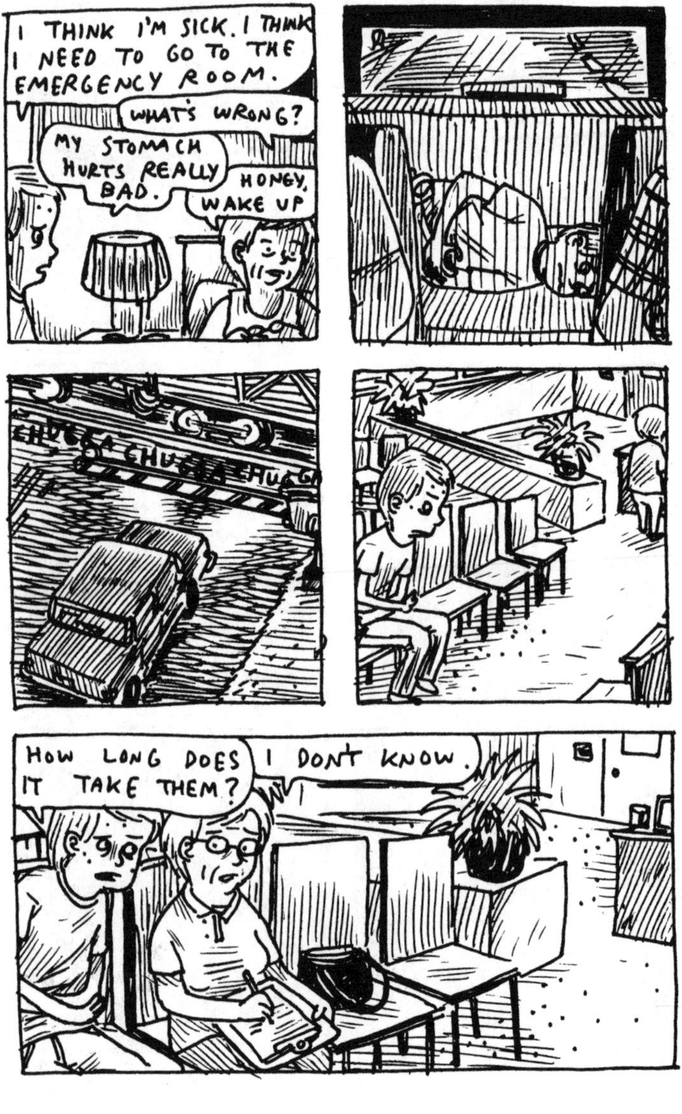
I THINK I'M SICK. I THINK I NEED TO GO TO THE EMERGENCY ROOM.
WHAT'S WRONG?
MY STOMACH HURTS REALLY BAD.
HONEY, WAKE UP
CHUGGA CHUGGA CHUGGA
HOW LONG DOES IT TAKE THEM?
I DON'T KNOW.

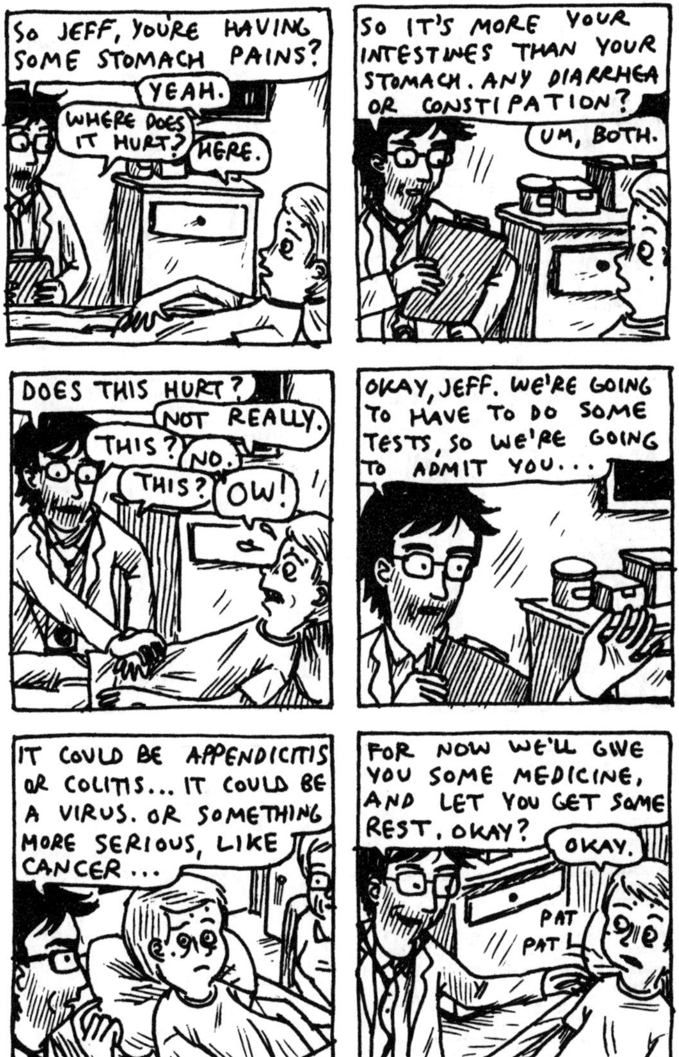
SO JEFF, YOU'RE HAVING SOME STOMACH PAINS?
YEAH.
WHERE DOES IT HURT?
HERE.
SO IT'S MORE YOUR INTESTINES THAN YOUR STOMACH. ANY DIARRHEA OR CONSTIPATION?
UM, BOTH.
DOES THIS HURT?
NOT REALLY.
THIS?
NO.
THIS?
OW!
OKAY, JEFF. WE'RE GOING TO HAVE TO DO SOME TESTS, SO WE'RE GOING TO ADMIT YOU...
IT COULD BE APPENDICITIS OR COLITIS... IT COULD BE A VIRUS. OR SOMETHING MORE SERIOUS, LIKE CANCER...
FOR NOW WE'LL GIVE YOU SOME MEDICINE, AND LET YOU GET SOME REST. OKAY?
OKAY.
PAT
PAT

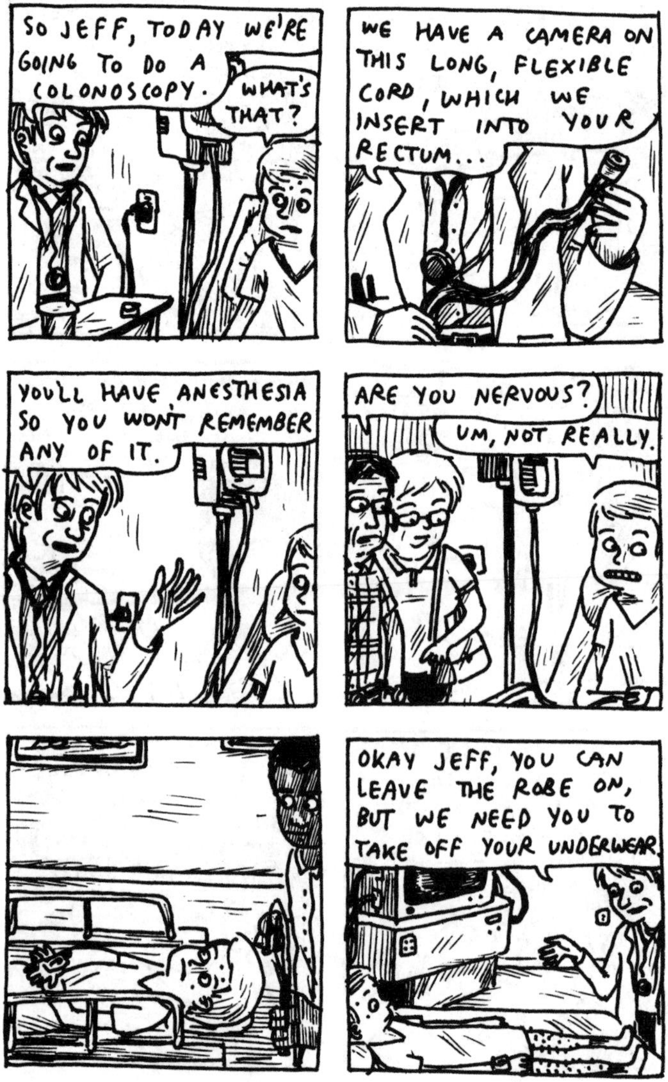
SO JEFF, TODAY WE'RE GOING TO DO A COLONOSCOPY.
WHAT'S THAT?
WE HAVE A CAMERA ON THIS LONG, FLEXIBLE CORD, WHICH WE INSERT INTO YOUR RECTUM...
YOU'LL HAVE ANESTHESIA SO YOU WON'T REMEMBER ANY OF IT.
ARE YOU NERVOUS?
UM, NOT REALLY.
OKAY JEFF, YOU CAN LEAVE THE ROBE ON, BUT WE NEED YOU TO TAKE OFF YOUR UNDERWEAR.

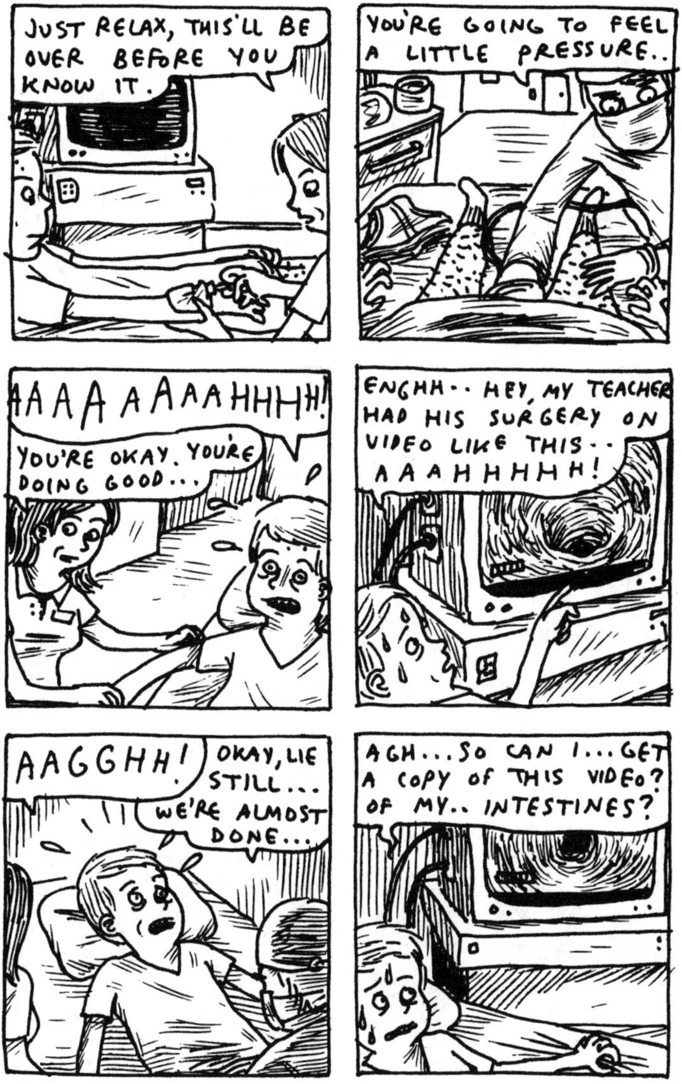
JUST RELAX, THIS'LL BE OVER BEFORE YOU KNOW IT.
YOU'RE GOING TO FEEL A LITTLE PRESSURE..
AAAAAAAAHHHH!
YOU'RE OKAY. YOU'RE DOING GOOD...
ENGHH.. HEY, MY TEACHER HAD HIS SURGERY ON VIDEO LIKE THIS.. AAAHHHHH!
AAGGHH!
OKAY, LIE STILL... WE'RE ALMOST DONE...
AGH...SO CAN I...GET A COPY OF THIS VIDEO? OF MY.. INTESTINES?

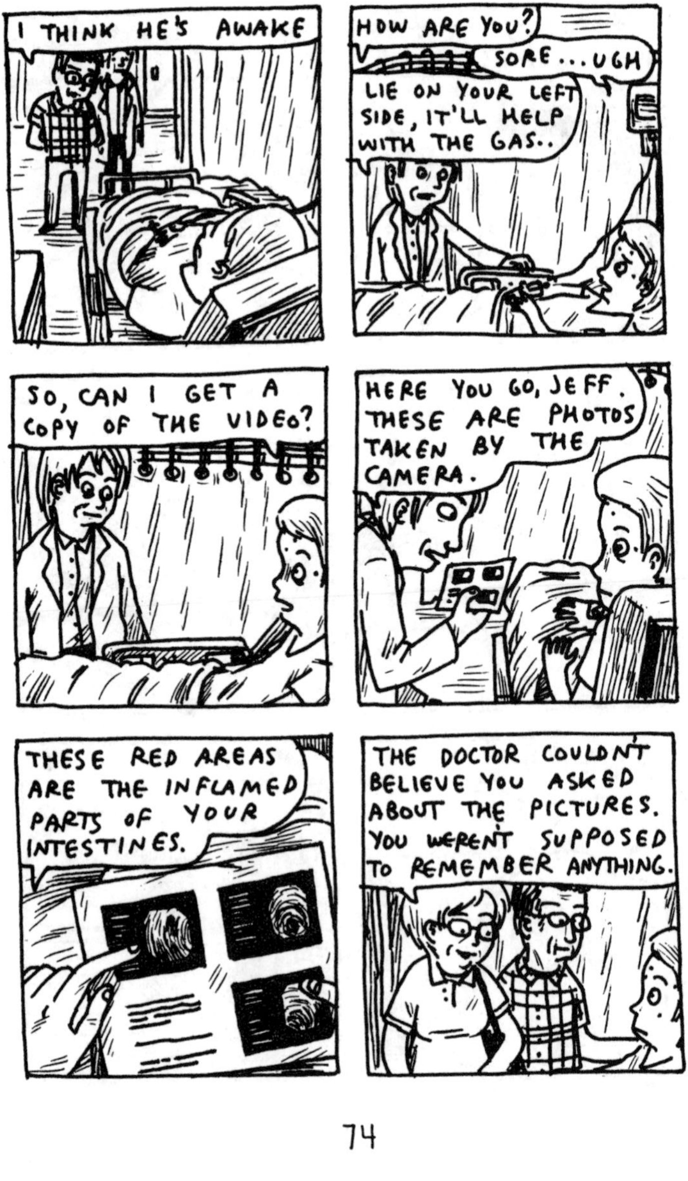
I THINK HE'S AWAKE
HOW ARE YOU?
SORE... UGH
LIE ON YOUR LEFT SIDE, IT'LL HELP WITH THE GAS..
SO, CAN I GET A COPY OF THE VIDEO?
HERE YOU GO, JEFF. THESE ARE PHOTOS TAKEN BY THE CAMERA.
THESE RED AREAS ARE THE INFLAMED PARTS OF YOUR INTESTINES.
THE DOCTOR COULDN'T BELIEVE YOU ASKED ABOUT THE PICTURES. YOU WEREN'T SUPPOSED TO REMEMBER ANYTHING.

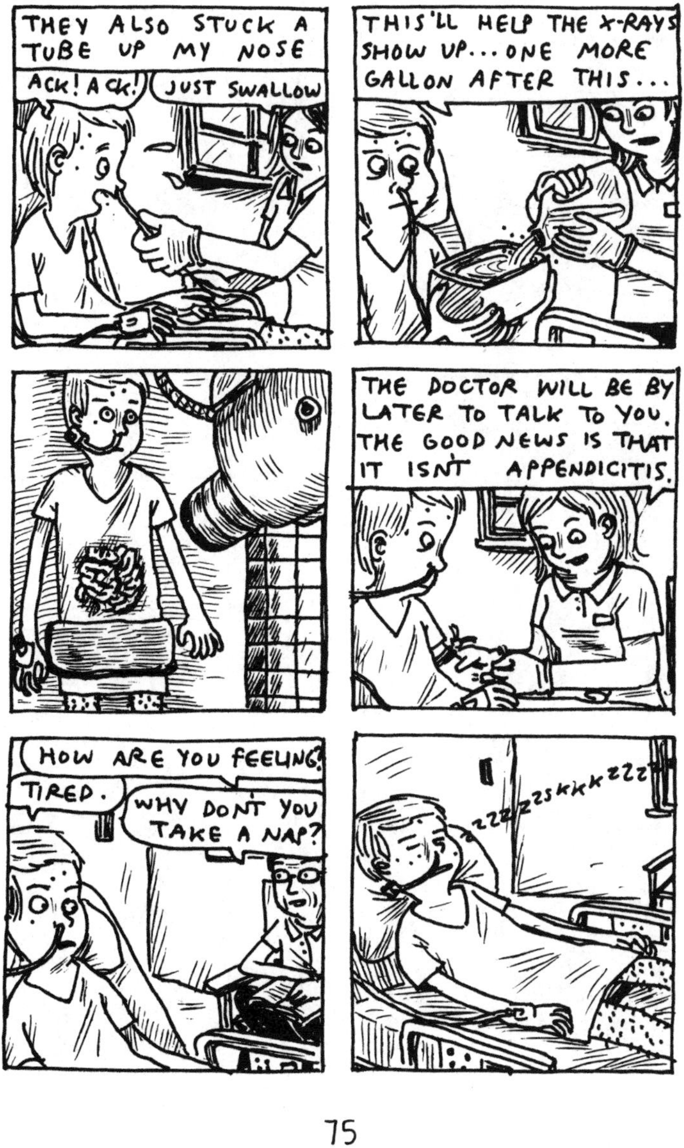
THEY ALSO STUCK A TUBE UP MY NOSE
ACK! ACK!
JUST SWALLOW
THIS'LL HELP THE X-RAYS SHOW UP... ONE MORE GALLON AFTER THIS...
THE DOCTOR WILL BE BY LATER TO TALK TO YOU. THE GOOD NEWS IS THAT IT ISN'T APPENDICITIS.
HOW ARE YOU FEELING?
TIRED.
WHY DON'T YOU TAKE A NAP?
ZZZZZSKKKZZZ

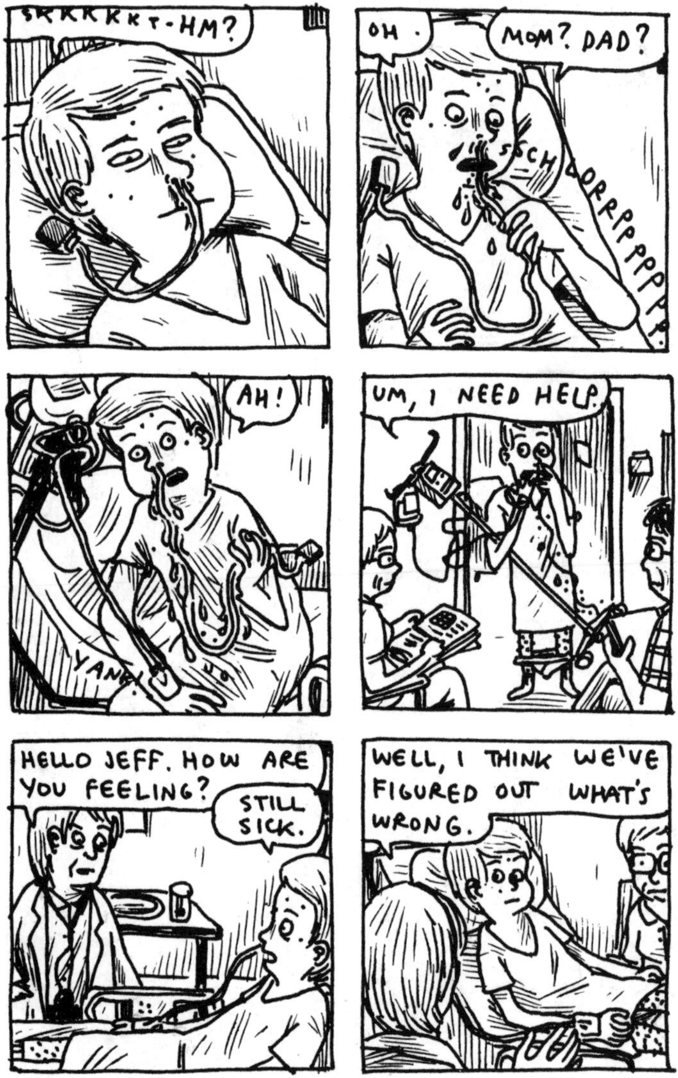
SKKKKKT-HM?
OH.
MOM? DAD?
SSCHLORRRPPPPPPP
AH!
YANK
UM, I NEED HELP.
HELLO JEFF. HOW ARE YOU FEELING?
STILL SICK.
WELL, I THINK WE'VE FIGURED OUT WHAT'S WRONG.

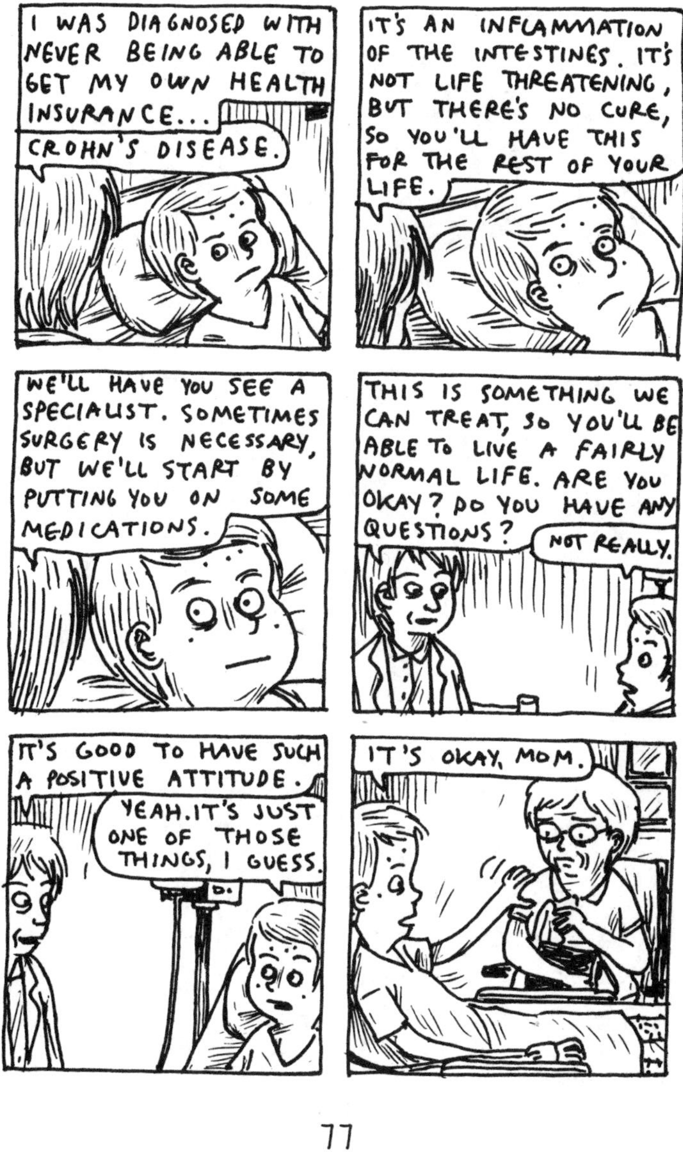
I WAS DIAGNOSED WITH NEVER BEING ABLE TO GET MY OWN HEALTH INSURANCE...
CROHN'S DISEASE.
IT'S AN INFLAMMATION OF THE INTESTINES. IT'S NOT LIFE THREATENING, BUT THERE'S NO CURE, SO YOU'LL HAVE THIS FOR THE REST OF YOUR LIFE.
WE'LL HAVE YOU SEE A SPECIALIST. SOMETIMES SURGERY IS NECESSARY, BUT WE'LL START BY PUTTING YOU ON SOME MEDICATIONS.
THIS IS SOMETHING WE CAN TREAT, SO YOU'LL BE ABLE TO LIVE A FAIRLY NORMAL LIFE. ARE YOU OKAY? DO YOU HAVE ANY QUESTIONS?
NOT REALLY.
IT'S GOOD TO HAVE SUCH A POSITIVE ATTITUDE.
YEAH. IT'S JUST ONE OF THOSE THINGS, I GUESS.
IT'S OKAY, MOM.

I BEGAN TAKING FIVE PILLS A DAY...

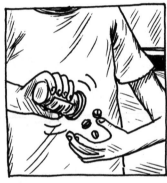

MUSCLE RELAXANT

PREDNISONE

VITAMIN

FIBER SUPPLEMENT

(REPEAT)

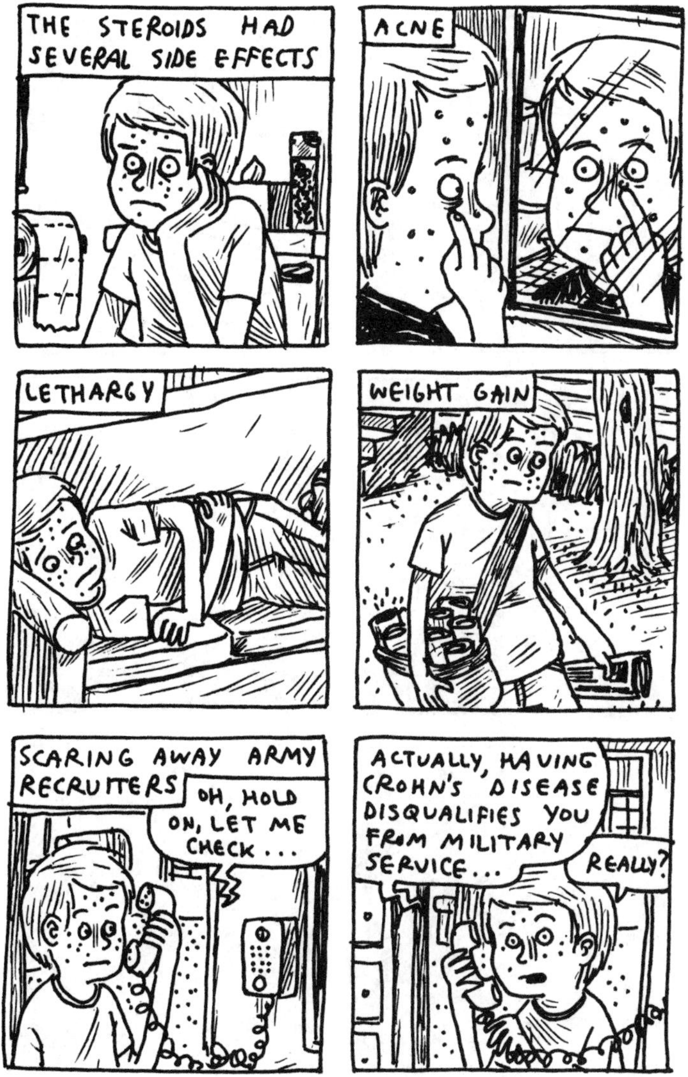
THE STEROIDS HAD SEVERAL SIDE EFFECTS
ACNE
LETHARGY
WEIGHT GAIN
SCARING AWAY ARMY RECRUITERS
OH, HOLD ON, LET ME CHECK...
ACTUALLY, HAVING CROHN'S DISEASE DISQUALIFIES YOU FROM MILITARY SERVICE...
REALLY?

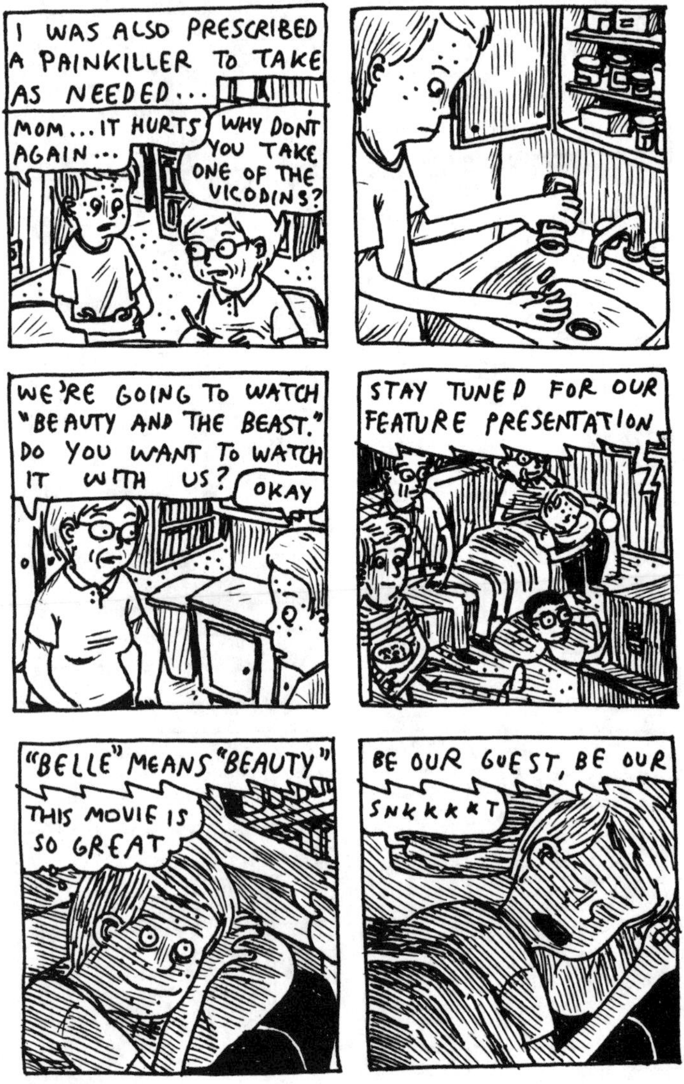
I WAS ALSO PRESCRIBED A PAINKILLER TO TAKE AS NEEDED...
MOM... IT HURTS AGAIN...
WHY DON'T YOU TAKE ONE OF THE VICODINS?
WE'RE GOING TO WATCH "BEAUTY AND THE BEAST." DO YOU WANT TO WATCH IT WITH US?
OKAY
STAY TUNED FOR OUR FEATURE PRESENTATION
"BELLE" MEANS "BEAUTY"
THIS MOVIE IS SO GREAT
BE OUR GUEST, BE OUR
SNKKKKT

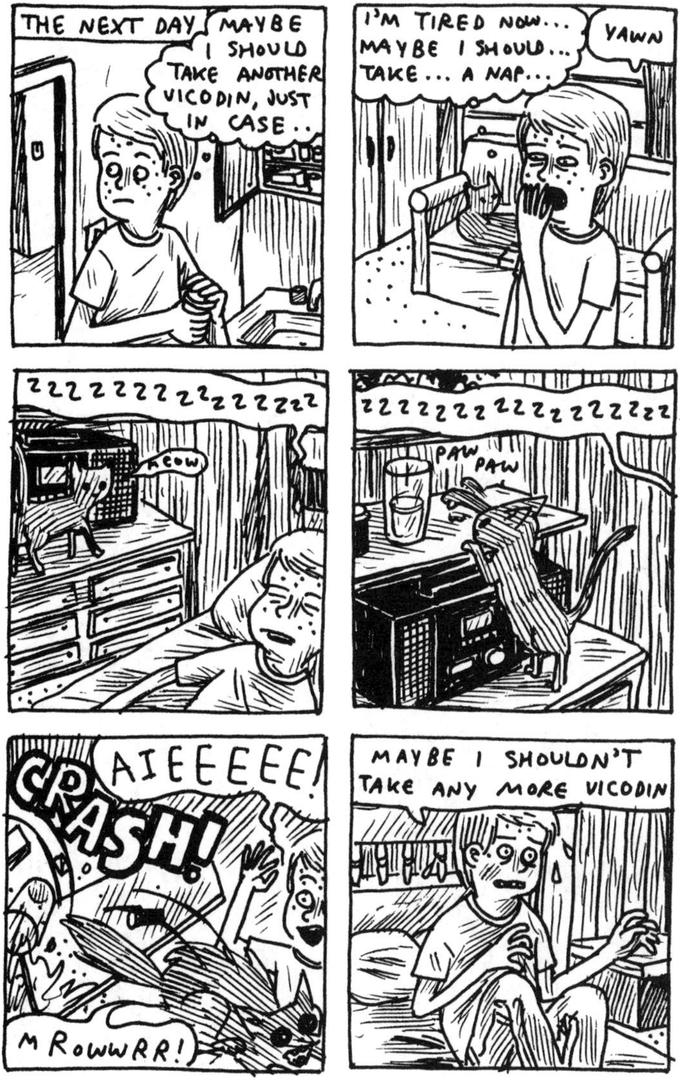
THE NEXT DAY
MAYBE I SHOULD TAKE ANOTHER VICODIN, JUST IN CASE..
I'M TIRED NOW... MAYBE I SHOULD... TAKE... A NAP...
YAWN
ZZZZZZZZZZZZZZZ
MEOW
ZZZZZZZZZZZZZZZZZZZ
PAW PAW
CRASH!
AIEEEEE!
MROWWRR!
MAYBE I SHOULDN'T TAKE ANY MORE VICODIN

AS SUMMER WENT ON, THEY OCCASIONALLY TRIED TO LOWER THE DOSAGES OF MEDICINE

GURGLE GURGLE

GURGLE
SQUIRM
SQUIRM

HURRY
HURRY
HURRY

FUMBLE
FUMBLE

GURGLE GURGLE

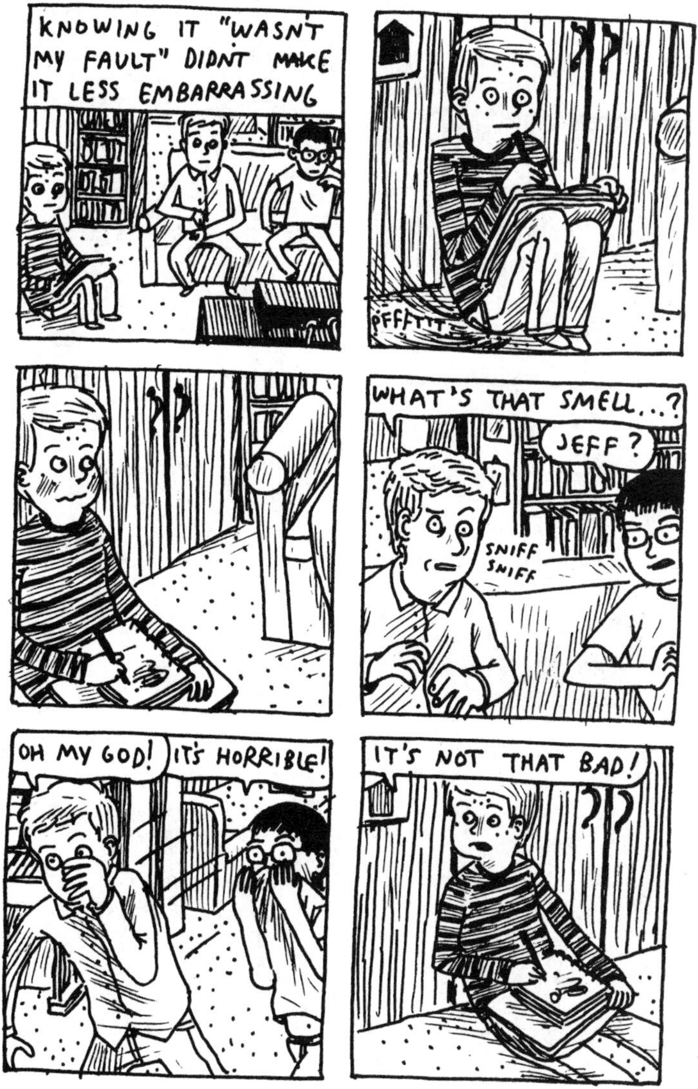
KNOWING IT "WASN'T MY FAULT" DIDN'T MAKE IT LESS EMBARRASSING
PFFFT'T
WHAT'S THAT SMELL...?
JEFF?
SNIFF SNIFF
OH MY GOD!
IT'S HORRIBLE!
IT'S NOT THAT BAD!

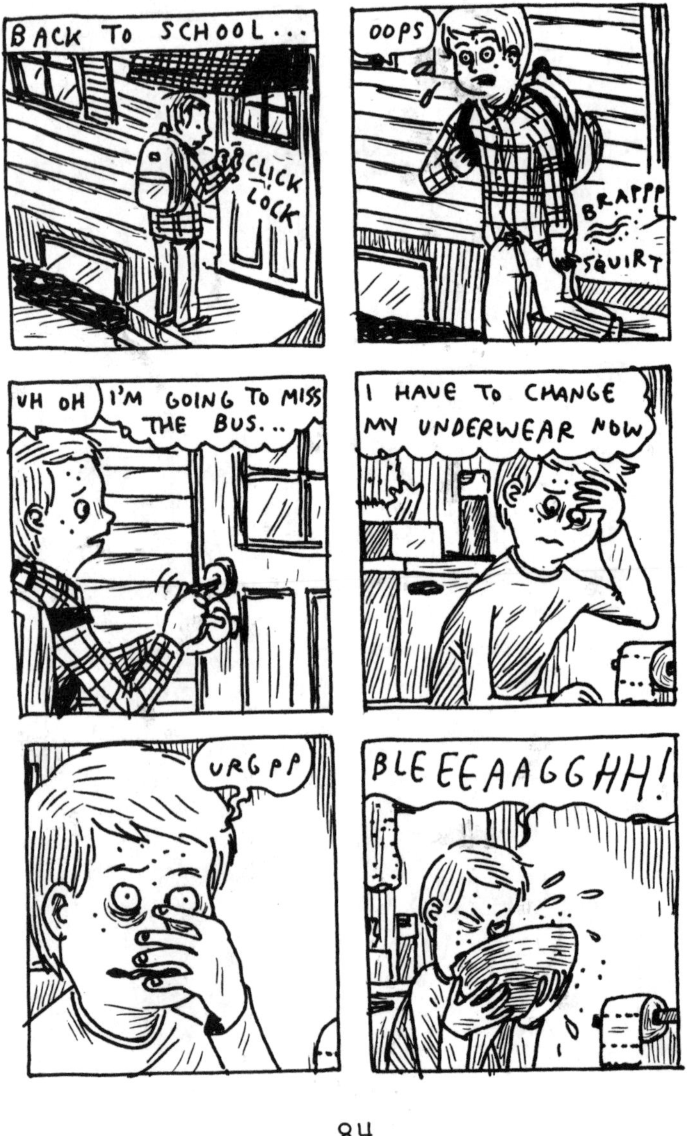
BACK TO SCHOOL...
CLICK
LOCK
OOPS
BRAPPP
SQUIRT
UH OH
I'M GOING TO MISS THE BUS...
I HAVE TO CHANGE MY UNDERWEAR NOW
URGPP
BLEEEAAGGHH!

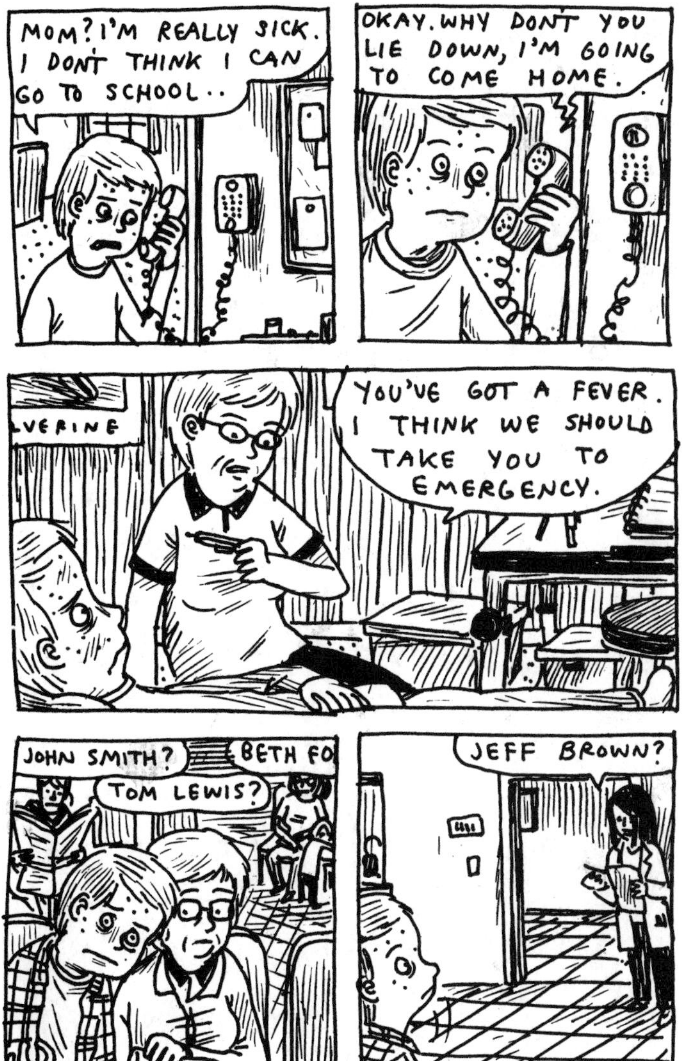
MOM? I'M REALLY SICK. I DON'T THINK I CAN GO TO SCHOOL..
OKAY. WHY DON'T YOU LIE DOWN, I'M GOING TO COME HOME.
LVERINE
YOU'VE GOT A FEVER. I THINK WE SHOULD TAKE YOU TO EMERGENCY.
JOHN SMITH?
BETH FO
TOM LEWIS?
JEFF BROWN?

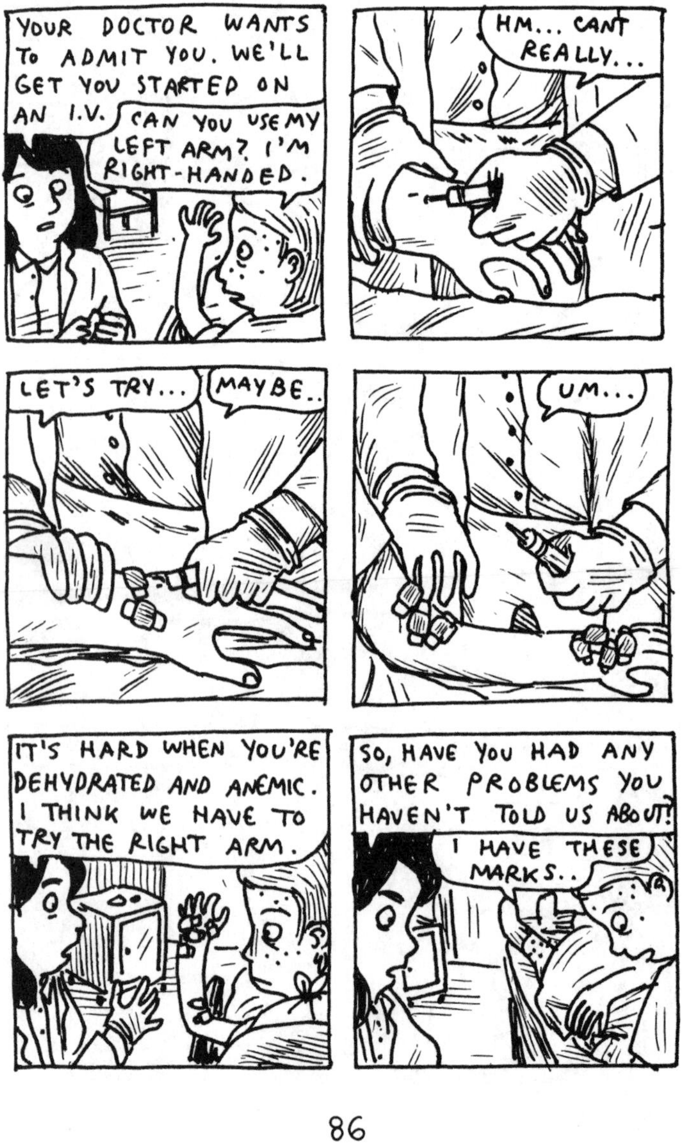
YOUR DOCTOR WANTS TO ADMIT YOU. WE'LL GET YOU STARTED ON AN I.V.
CAN YOU USE MY LEFT ARM? I'M RIGHT-HANDED.
HM... CANT REALLY...
LET'S TRY...
MAYBE..
UM...
IT'S HARD WHEN YOU'RE DEHYDRATED AND ANEMIC. I THINK WE HAVE TO TRY THE RIGHT ARM.
SO, HAVE YOU HAD ANY OTHER PROBLEMS YOU HAVEN'T TOLD US ABOUT?
I HAVE THESE MARKS..

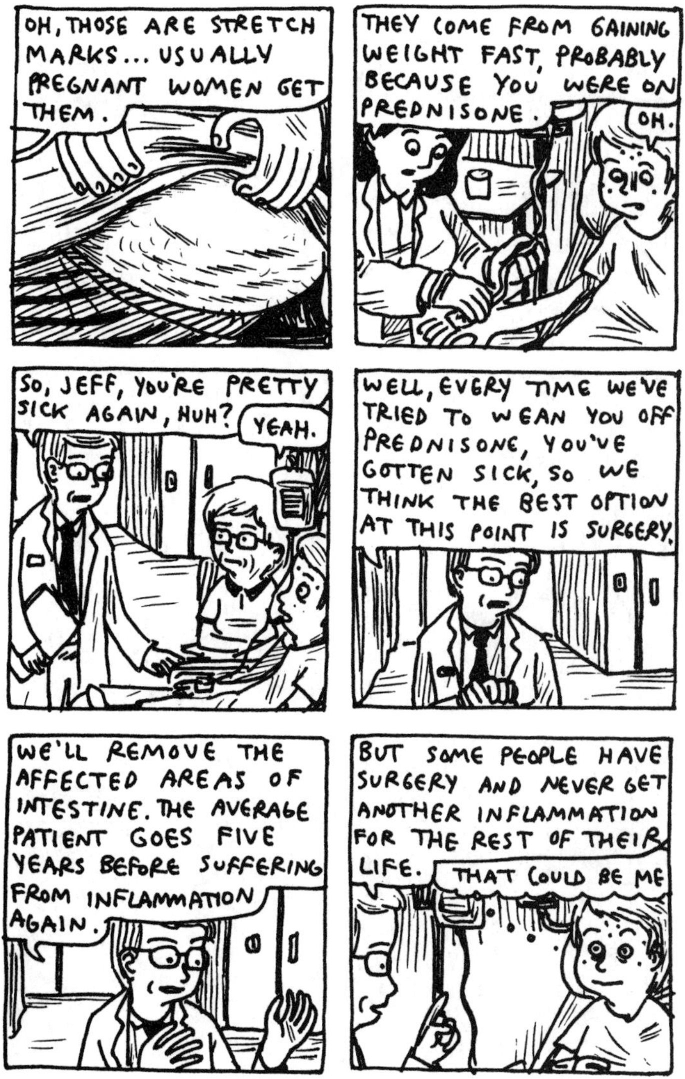
OH, THOSE ARE STRETCH MARKS... USUALLY PREGNANT WOMEN GET THEM.
THEY COME FROM GAINING WEIGHT FAST, PROBABLY BECAUSE YOU WERE ON PREDNISONE.
OH.
SO, JEFF, YOU'RE PRETTY SICK AGAIN, HUH?
YEAH.
WELL, EVERY TIME WE'VE TRIED TO WEAN YOU OFF PREDNISONE, YOU'VE GOTTEN SICK, SO WE THINK THE BEST OPTION AT THIS POINT IS SURGERY.
WE'LL REMOVE THE AFFECTED AREAS OF INTESTINE. THE AVERAGE PATIENT GOES FIVE YEARS BEFORE SUFFERING FROM INFLAMMATION AGAIN.
BUT SOME PEOPLE HAVE SURGERY AND NEVER GET ANOTHER INFLAMMATION FOR THE REST OF THEIR LIFE.
THAT COULD BE ME

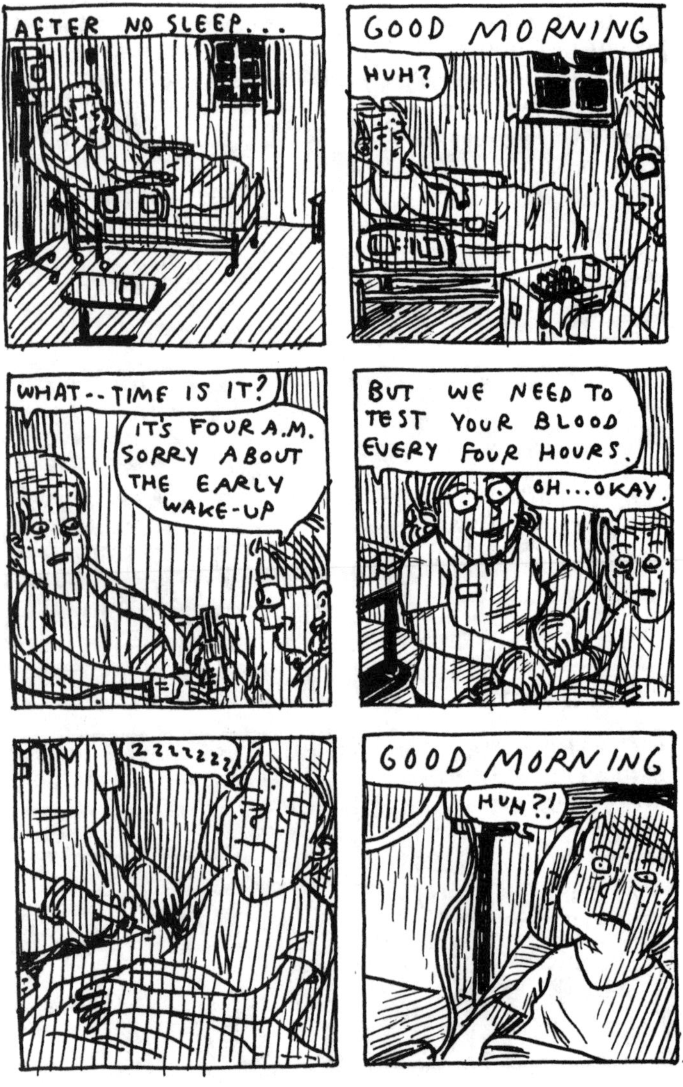
AFTER NO SLEEP...
GOOD MORNING
HUH?
WHAT--TIME IS IT?
IT'S FOUR A.M. SORRY ABOUT THE EARLY WAKE-UP
BUT WE NEED TO TEST YOUR BLOOD EVERY FOUR HOURS.
OH...OKAY.
ZZZZZZZ
GOOD MORNING
HUH?!

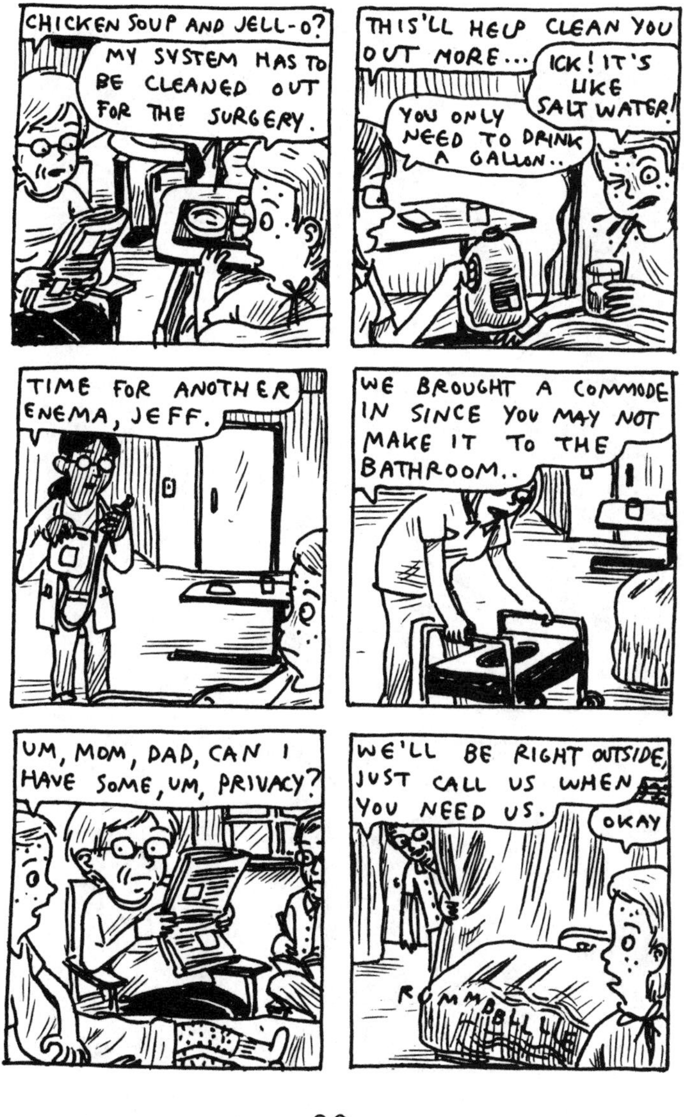
CHICKEN SOUP AND JELL-O?
MY SYSTEM HAS TO BE CLEANED OUT FOR THE SURGERY.
THIS'LL HELP CLEAN YOU OUT MORE...
YOU ONLY NEED TO DRINK A GALLON..
ICK! IT'S LIKE SALT WATER!
TIME FOR ANOTHER ENEMA, JEFF.
WE BROUGHT A COMMODE IN SINCE YOU MAY NOT MAKE IT TO THE BATHROOM..
UM, MOM, DAD, CAN I HAVE SOME, UM, PRIVACY?
WE'LL BE RIGHT OUTSIDE, JUST CALL US WHEN YOU NEED US.
OKAY
RUMMBBLLLE

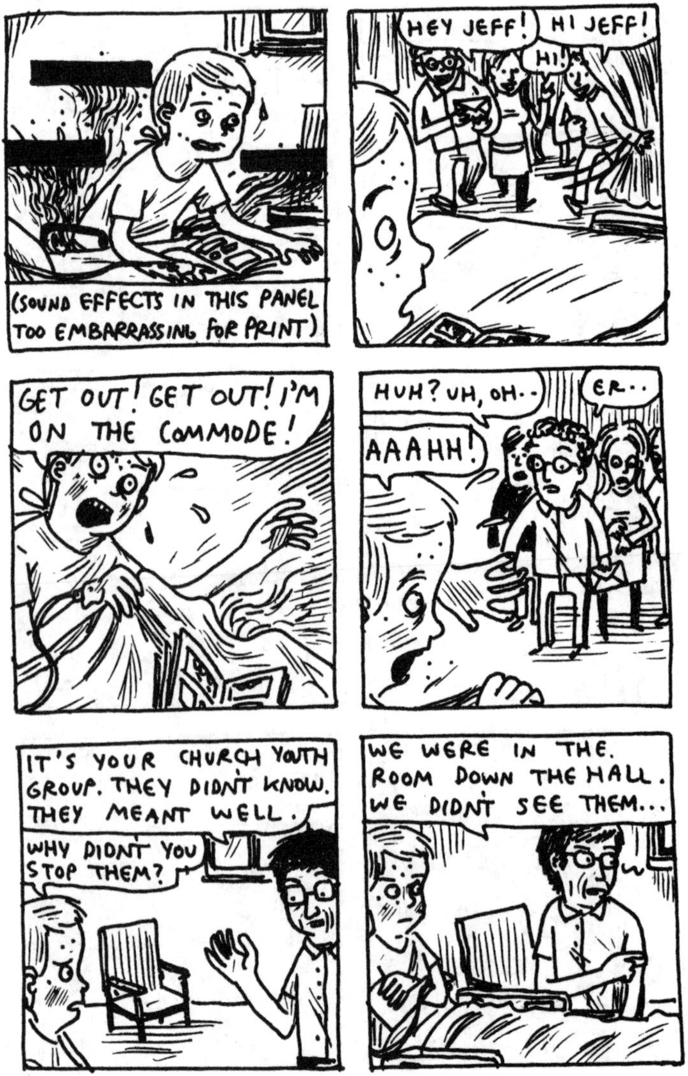
(SOUND EFFECTS IN THIS PANEL TOO EMBARRASSING FOR PRINT)
HEY JEFF!
HI JEFF!
HI!
GET OUT! GET OUT! I'M ON THE COMMODE!
HUH? UH, OH..
ER..
AAAHH!
IT'S YOUR CHURCH YOUTH GROUP. THEY DIDN'T KNOW. THEY MEANT WELL.
WHY DIDN'T YOU STOP THEM?
WE WERE IN THE ROOM DOWN THE HALL. WE DIDN'T SEE THEM...

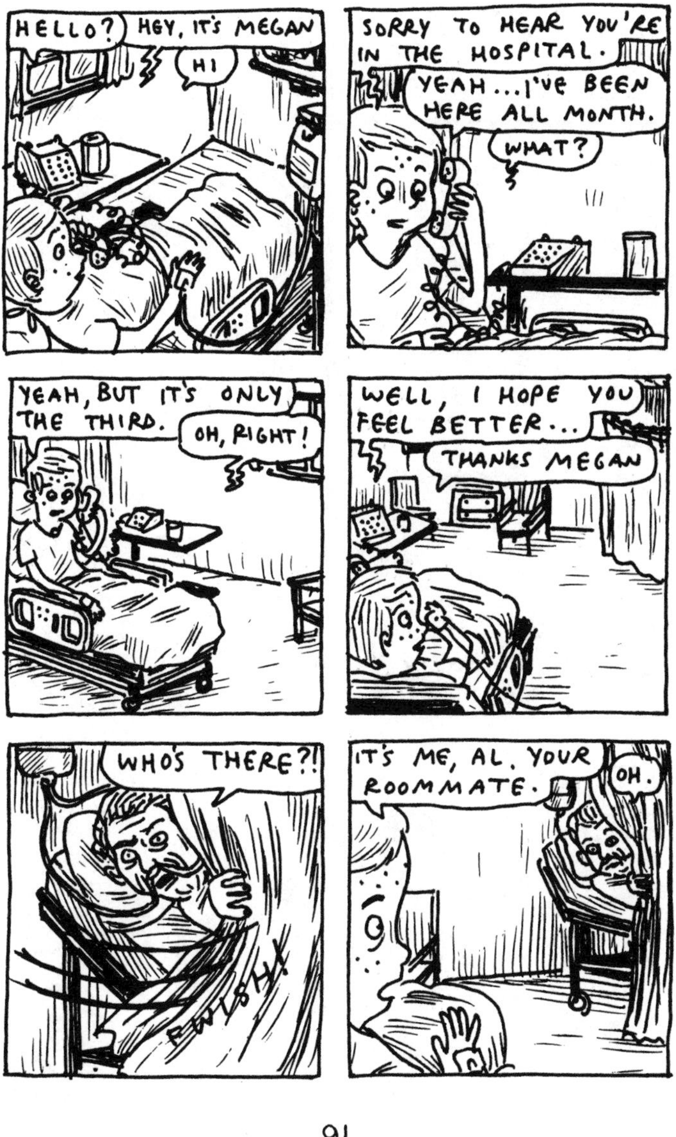
HELLO?
HEY, IT'S MEGAN
HI
SORRY TO HEAR YOU'RE IN THE HOSPITAL.
YEAH... I'VE BEEN HERE ALL MONTH.
WHAT?
YEAH, BUT IT'S ONLY THE THIRD.
OH, RIGHT!
WELL, I HOPE YOU FEEL BETTER...
THANKS MEGAN
WHO'S THERE?!
FWISH!
IT'S ME, AL. YOUR ROOMMATE.
OH.

AL SPENT A LOT OF THE TIME DISORIENTED...

WHERE'S MY TUBE?!

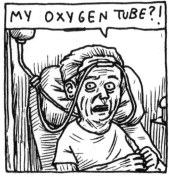

MY OXYGEN TUBE?!

IT'S ON YOUR HEAD, AL..

HERE

...BUT HE ALSO HAD MOMENTS OF CLARITY.

HERE, JEFF, TAKE MY JELL-O.

ARE YOU SURE, AL?

YEAH, YOU NEED TO BUILD UP YOUR STRENGTH

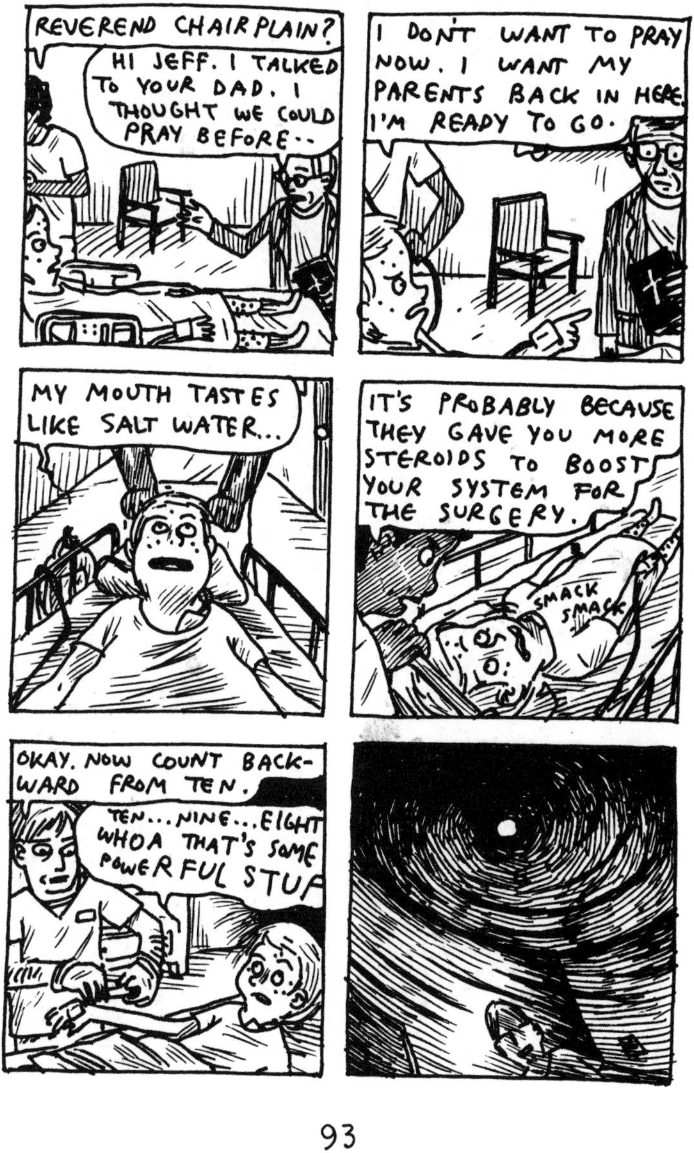
REVEREND CHAIRPLAIN?
HI JEFF. I TALKED TO YOUR DAD. I THOUGHT WE COULD PRAY BEFORE--
I DON'T WANT TO PRAY NOW. I WANT MY PARENTS BACK IN HERE. I'M READY TO GO.
MY MOUTH TASTES LIKE SALT WATER...
IT'S PROBABLY BECAUSE THEY GAVE YOU MORE STEROIDS TO BOOST YOUR SYSTEM FOR THE SURGERY.
SMACK SMACK
OKAY. NOW COUNT BACKWARD FROM TEN.
TEN...NINE...EIGHT WHOA THAT'S SOME POWERFUL STUF

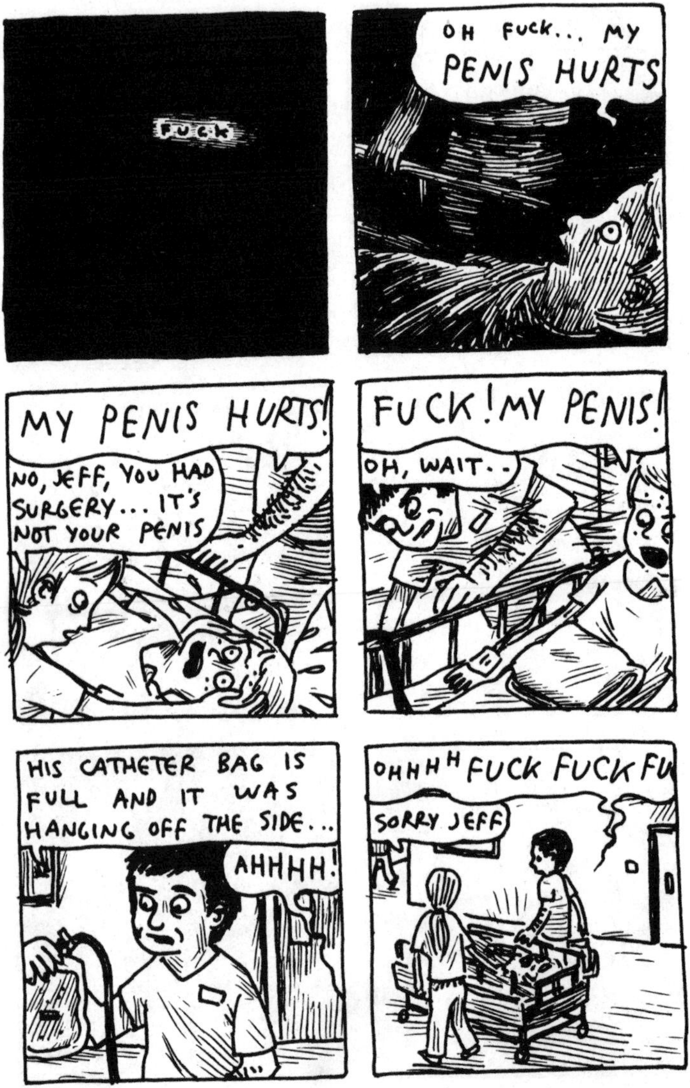
FUCK
OH FUCK... MY PENIS HURTS
MY PENIS HURTS!
NO, JEFF, YOU HAD SURGERY... IT'S NOT YOUR PENIS
FUCK! MY PENIS!
OH, WAIT..
HIS CATHETER BAG IS FULL AND IT WAS HANGING OFF THE SIDE...
AHHHH!
OHHHH FUCK FUCK FU
SORRY JEFF

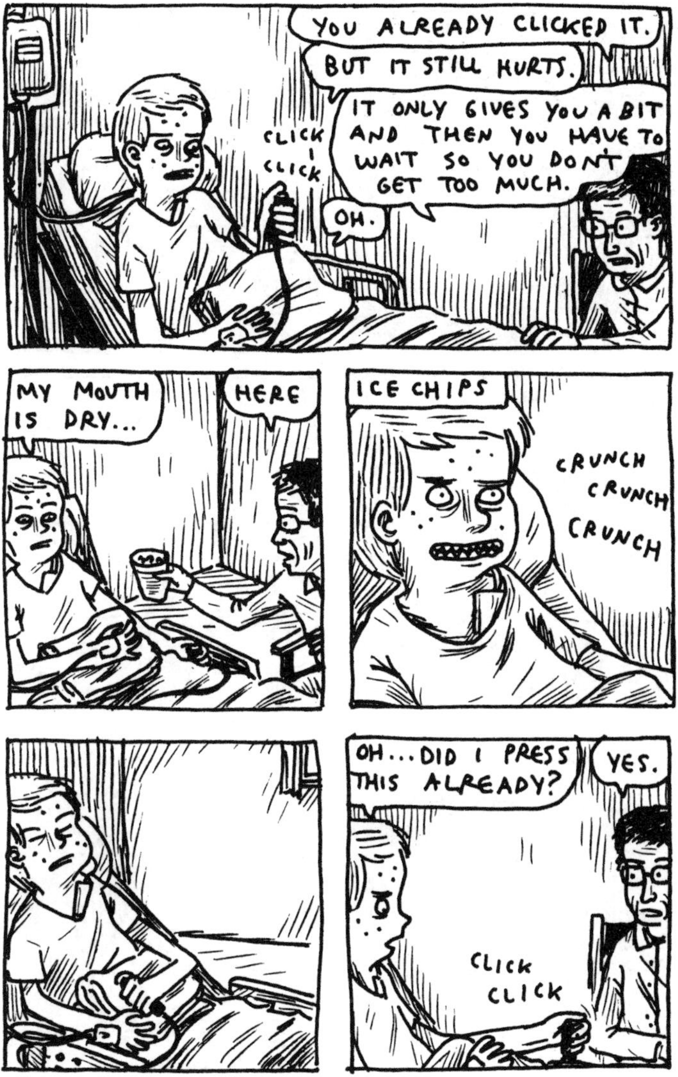
YOU ALREADY CLICKED IT.
BUT IT STILL HURTS.
IT ONLY GIVES YOU A BIT AND THEN YOU HAVE TO WAIT SO YOU DON'T GET TOO MUCH.
CLICK CLICK
OH.
MY MOUTH IS DRY...
HERE
ICE CHIPS
CRUNCH CRUNCH CRUNCH
OH... DID I PRESS THIS ALREADY?
YES.
CLICK CLICK

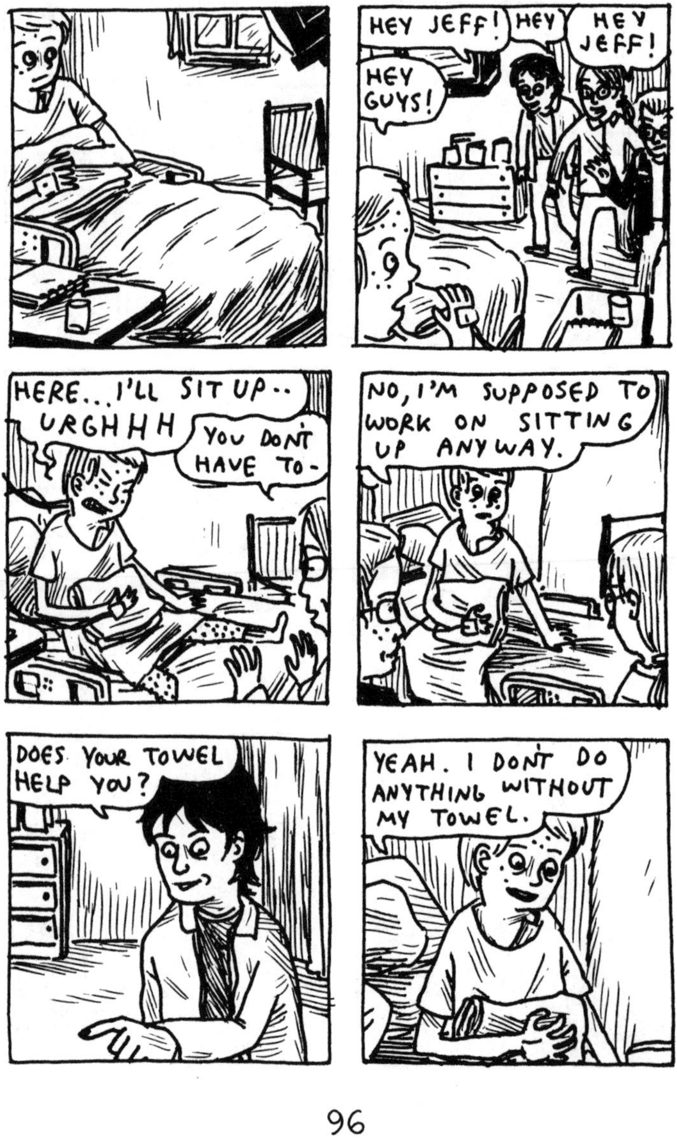
HEY JEFF!
HEY
HEY JEFF!
HEY GUYS!
HERE... I'LL SIT UP.. URGHHH
YOU DON'T HAVE TO-
NO, I'M SUPPOSED TO WORK ON SITTING UP ANYWAY.
DOES YOUR TOWEL HELP YOU?
YEAH. I DON'T DO ANYTHING WITHOUT MY TOWEL.

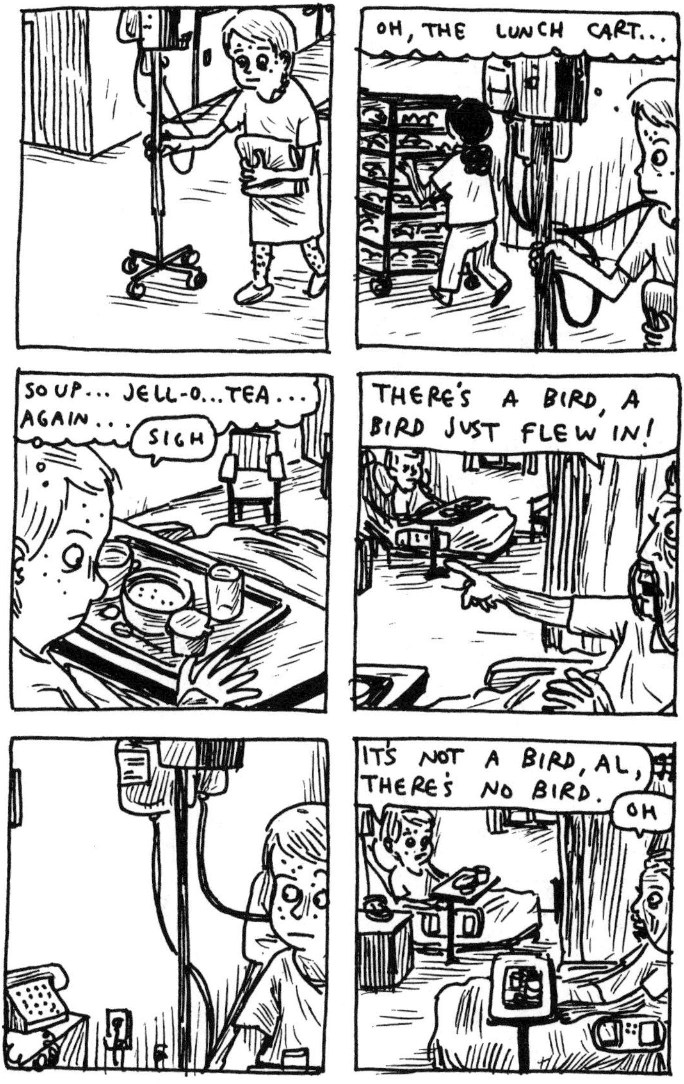
OH, THE LUNCH CART...
SOUP... JELL-O... TEA... AGAIN...
SIGH
THERE'S A BIRD, A BIRD JUST FLEW IN!
IT'S NOT A BIRD, AL, THERE'S NO BIRD.
OH

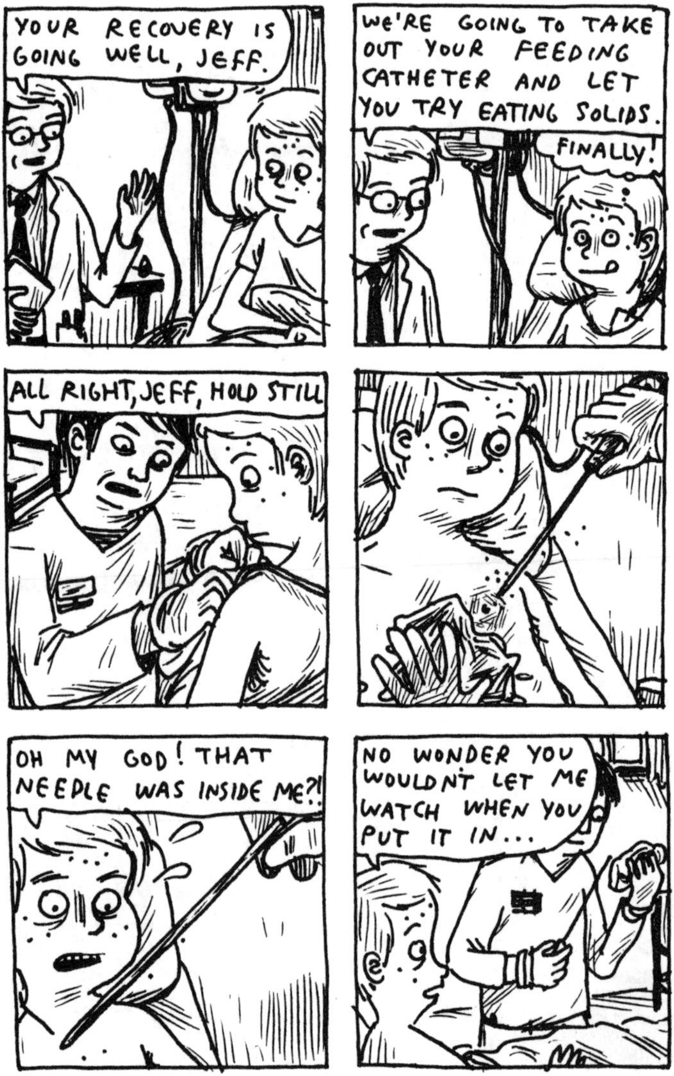
YOUR RECOVERY IS GOING WELL, JEFF.
WE'RE GOING TO TAKE OUT YOUR FEEDING CATHETER AND LET YOU TRY EATING SOLIDS.
FINALLY!
ALL RIGHT, JEFF, HOLD STILL
OH MY GOD! THAT NEEDLE WAS INSIDE ME?!
NO WONDER YOU WOULDN'T LET ME WATCH WHEN YOU PUT IT IN...

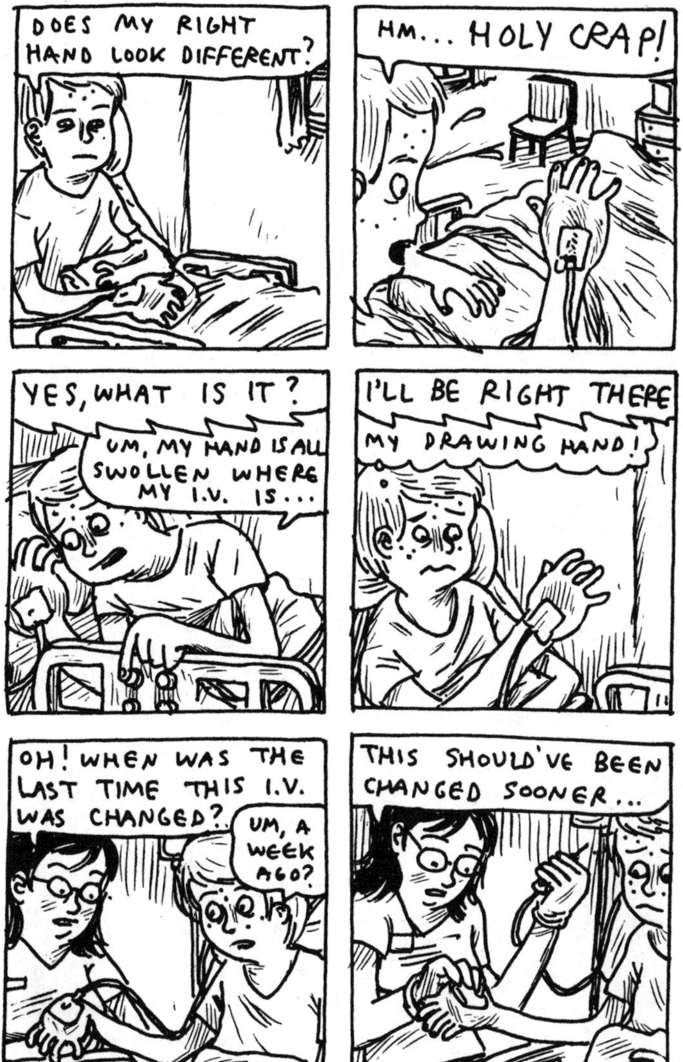
DOES MY RIGHT HAND LOOK DIFFERENT?
HM... HOLY CRAP!
YES, WHAT IS IT?
UM, MY HAND IS ALL SWOLLEN WHERE MY I.V. IS...
I'LL BE RIGHT THERE
MY DRAWING HAND!
OH! WHEN WAS THE LAST TIME THIS I.V. WAS CHANGED?
UM, A WEEK AGO?
THIS SHOULD'VE BEEN CHANGED SOONER...

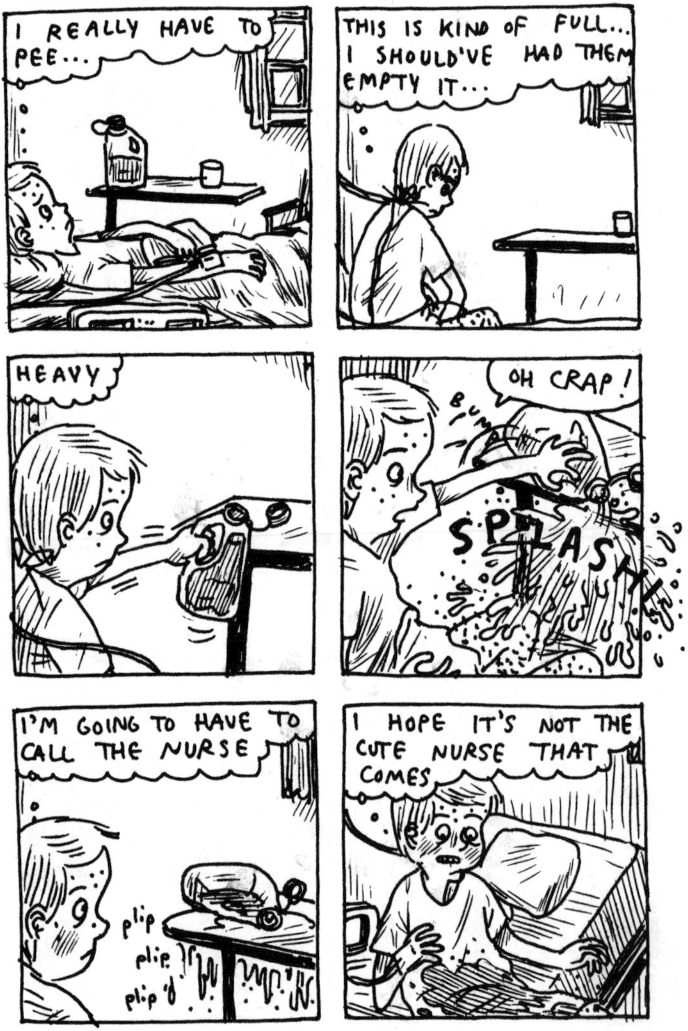
I REALLY HAVE TO PEE...
THIS IS KIND OF FULL... I SHOULD'VE HAD THEM EMPTY IT...
HEAVY
OH CRAP!
BUMP
SPLASH
I'M GOING TO HAVE TO CALL THE NURSE
plip
plip
plip
I HOPE IT'S NOT THE CUTE NURSE THAT COMES

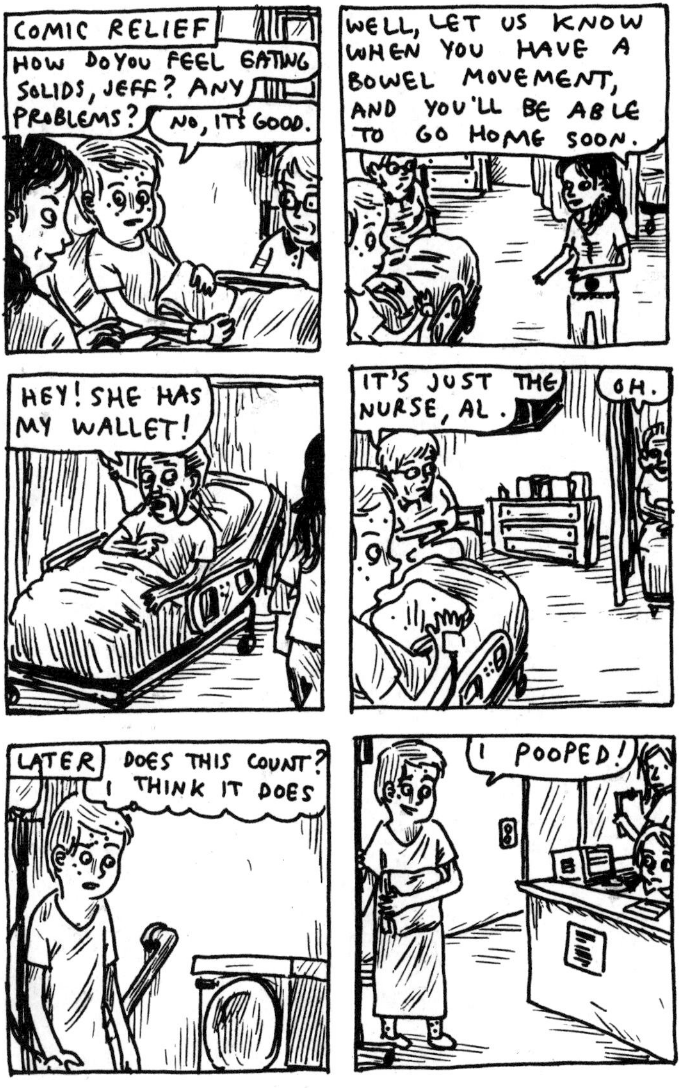
COMIC RELIEF
HOW DO YOU FEEL EATING SOLIDS, JEFF? ANY PROBLEMS?
NO, IT'S GOOD.
WELL, LET US KNOW WHEN YOU HAVE A BOWEL MOVEMENT, AND YOU'LL BE ABLE TO GO HOME SOON.
HEY! SHE HAS MY WALLET!
IT'S JUST THE NURSE, AL.
OH.
LATER
DOES THIS COUNT? I THINK IT DOES
I POOPED!

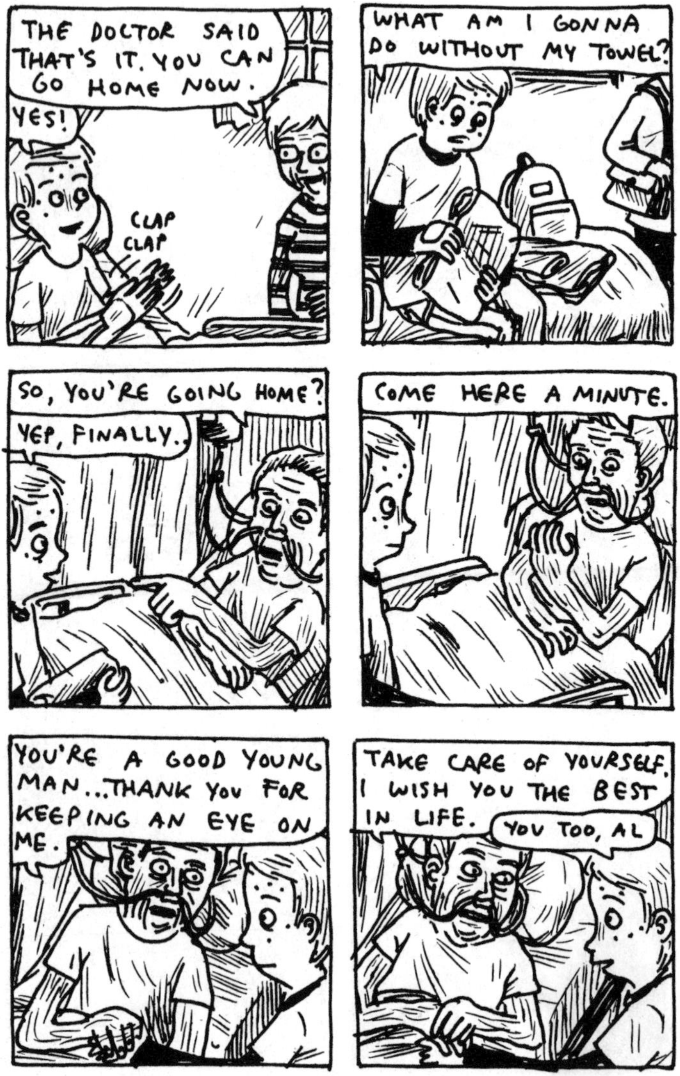
THE DOCTOR SAID THAT'S IT. YOU CAN GO HOME NOW.
YES!
CLAP CLAP
WHAT AM I GONNA DO WITHOUT MY TOWEL?
SO, YOU'RE GOING HOME?
YEP, FINALLY.
COME HERE A MINUTE.
YOU'RE A GOOD YOUNG MAN...THANK YOU FOR KEEPING AN EYE ON ME.
TAKE CARE OF YOURSELF. I WISH YOU THE BEST IN LIFE.
YOU TOO, AL

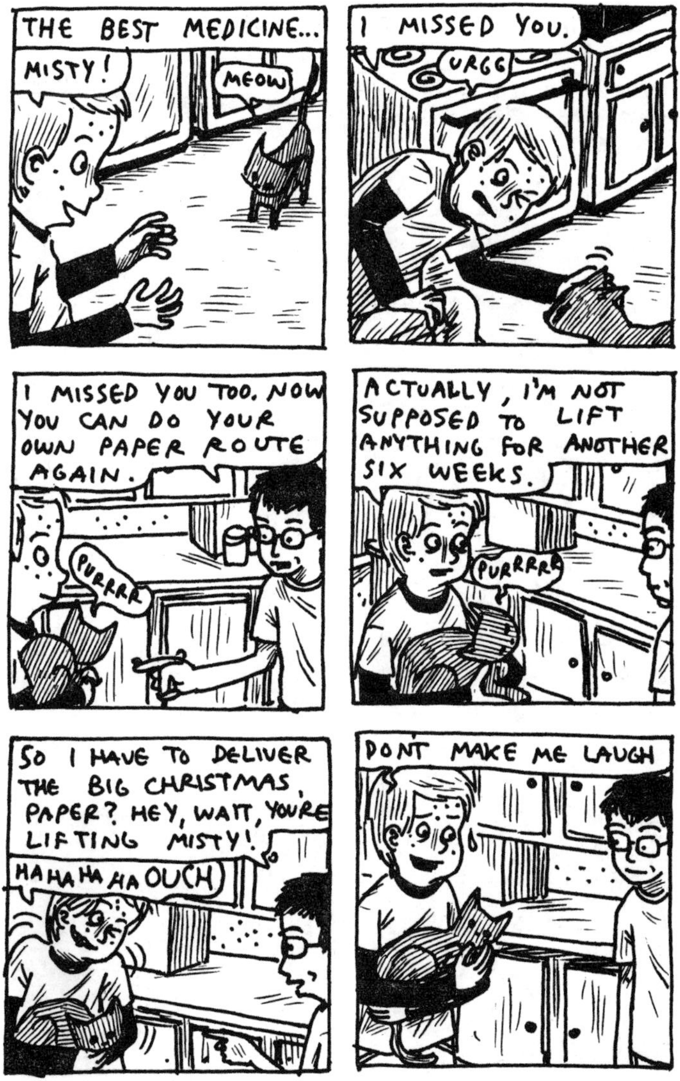
THE BEST MEDICINE...
MISTY!
MEOW
I MISSED YOU.
URGG
I MISSED YOU TOO. NOW YOU CAN DO YOUR OWN PAPER ROUTE AGAIN.
PURRRR
ACTUALLY, I'M NOT SUPPOSED TO LIFT ANYTHING FOR ANOTHER SIX WEEKS.
PURRRR
SO I HAVE TO DELIVER THE BIG CHRISTMAS PAPER? HEY, WAIT, YOU'RE LIFTING MISTY!
HAHAHA HA HA OUCH
DONT MAKE ME LAUGH

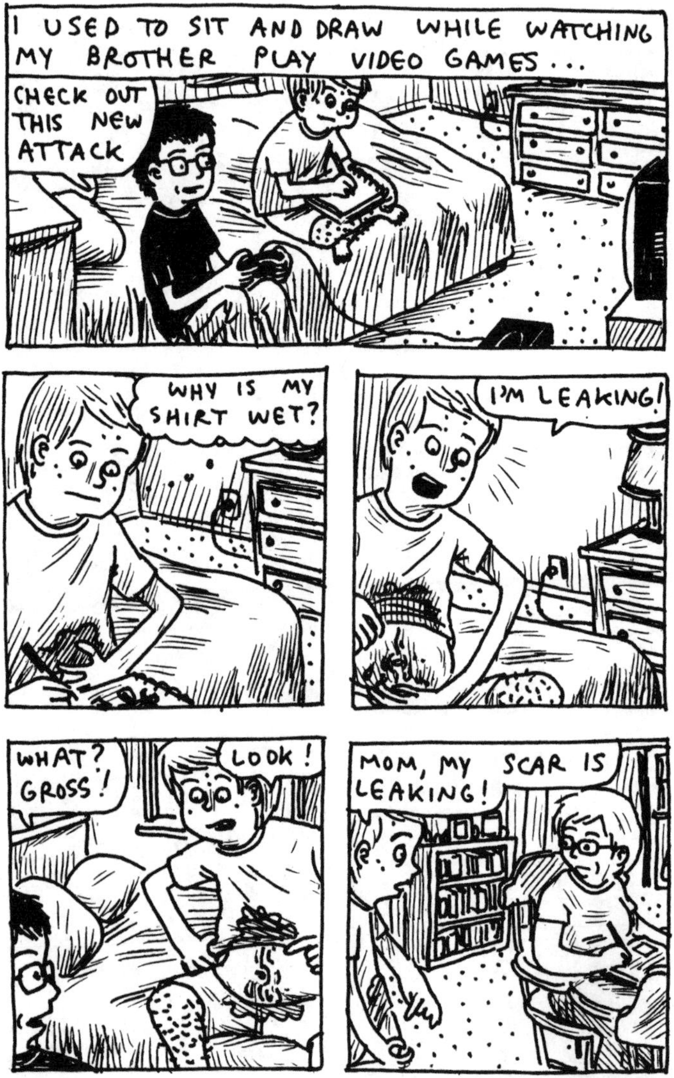
I USED TO SIT AND DRAW WHILE WATCHING MY BROTHER PLAY VIDEO GAMES...
CHECK OUT THIS NEW ATTACK
WHY IS MY SHIRT WET?
I'M LEAKING!
WHAT? GROSS!
LOOK!
MOM, MY SCAR IS LEAKING!

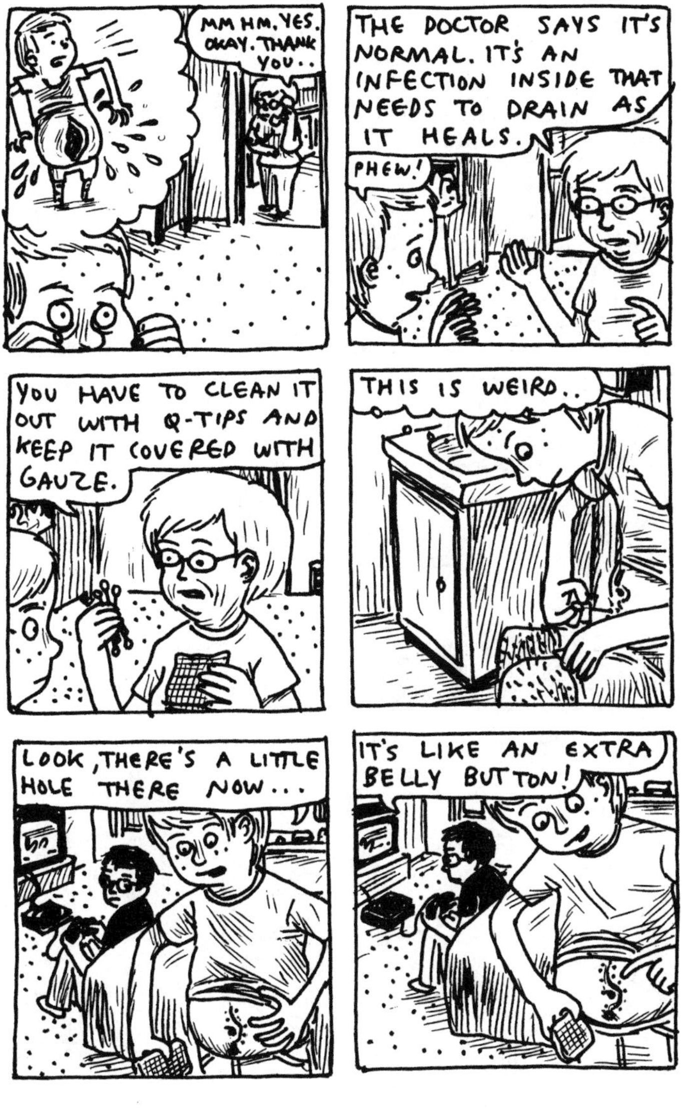
MM HM. YES. OKAY. THANK YOU..
THE DOCTOR SAYS IT'S NORMAL. IT'S AN INFECTION INSIDE THAT NEEDS TO DRAIN AS IT HEALS.
PHEW!
YOU HAVE TO CLEAN IT OUT WITH Q-TIPS AND KEEP IT COVERED WITH GAUZE.
THIS IS WEIRD..
LOOK, THERE'S A LITTLE HOLE THERE NOW...
IT'S LIKE AN EXTRA BELLY BUTTON!

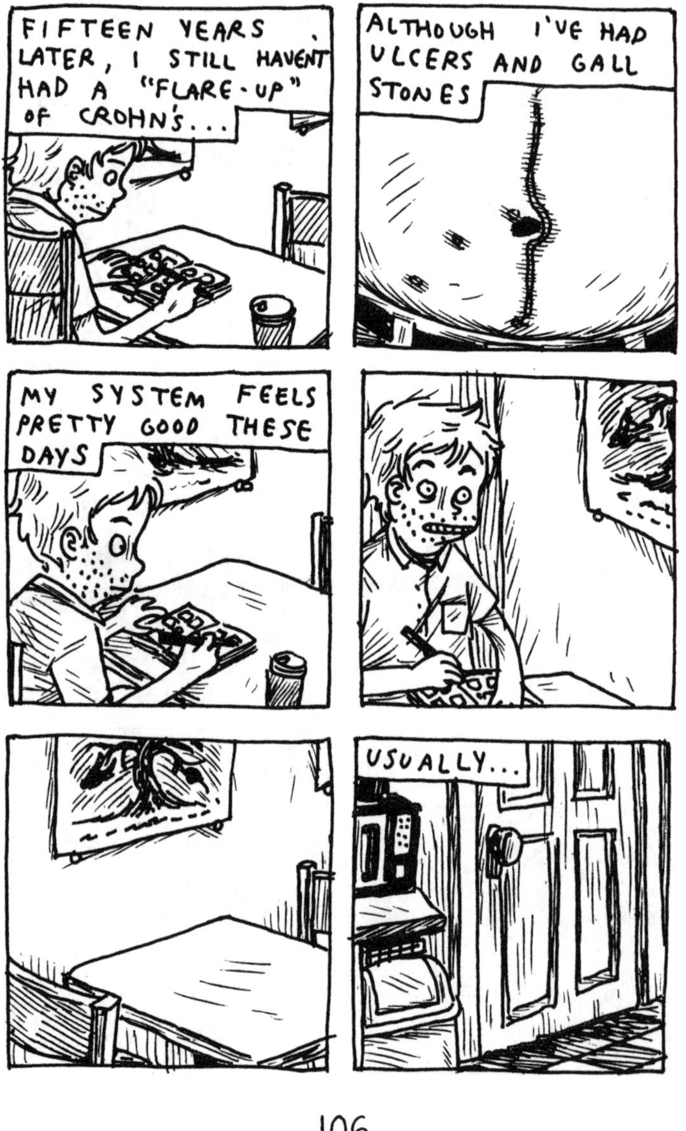
FIFTEEN YEARS LATER, I STILL HAVEN'T HAD A "FLARE-UP" OF CROHN'S...
ALTHOUGH I'VE HAD ULCERS AND GALL STONES
MY SYSTEM FEELS PRETTY GOOD THESE DAYS
USUALLY...

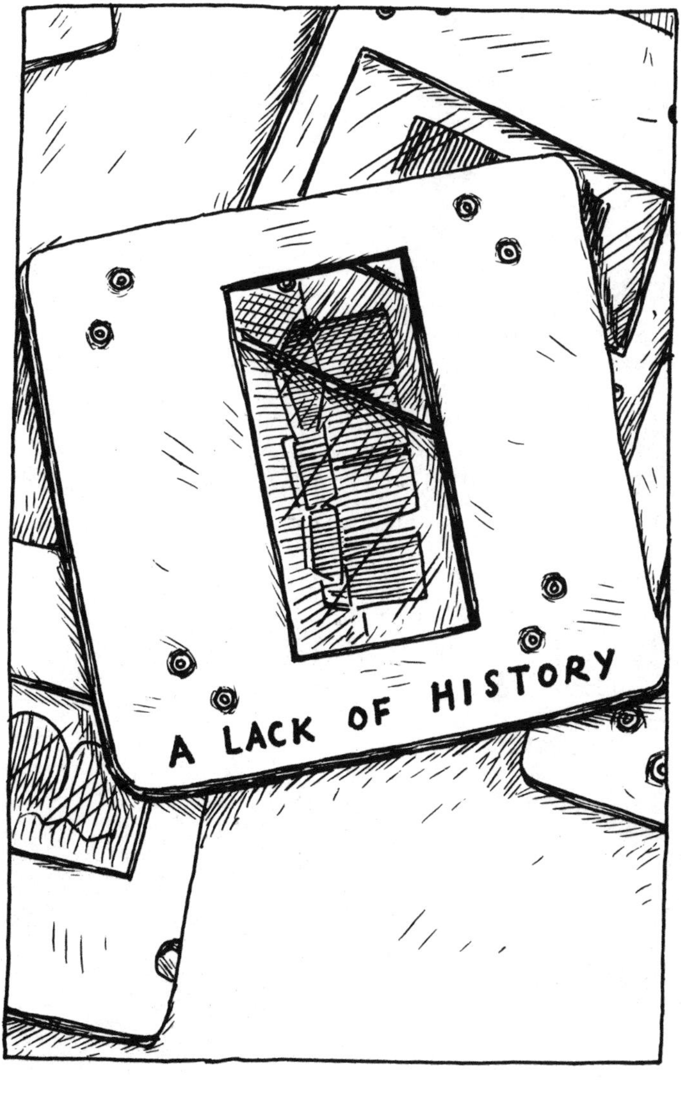
A LACK OF HISTORY

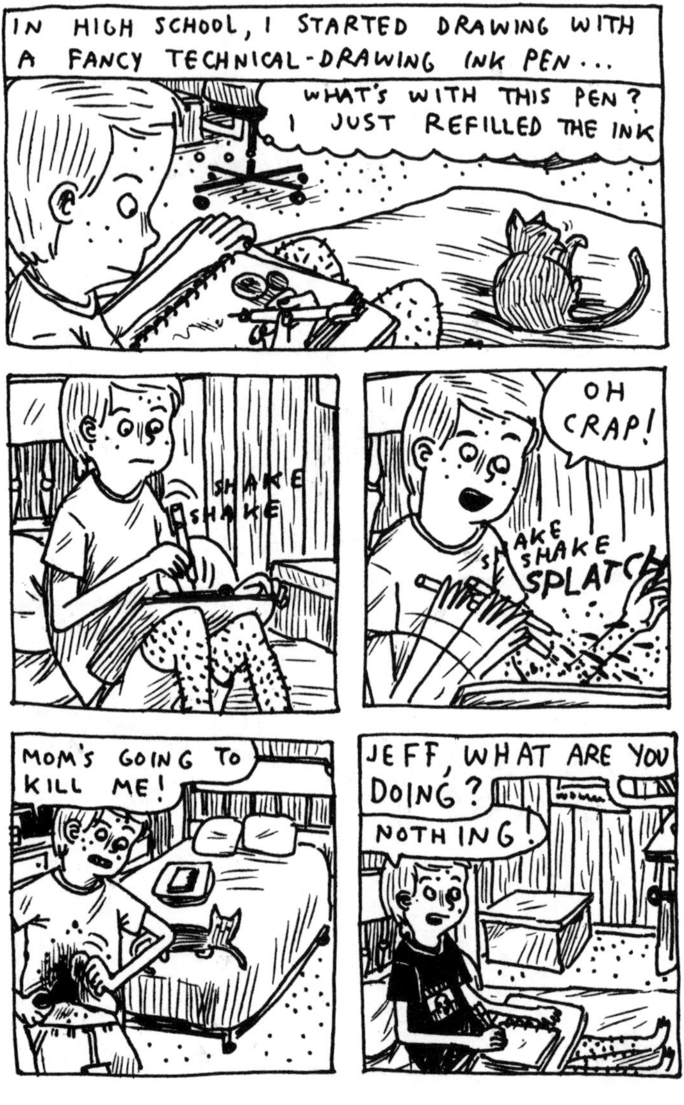
IN HIGH SCHOOL, I STARTED DRAWING WITH A FANCY TECHNICAL-DRAWING INK PEN...
WHAT'S WITH THIS PEN? I JUST REFILLED THE INK
SHAKE SHAKE
OH CRAP!
SHAKE SHAKE
SPLATCH
MOM'S GOING TO KILL ME!
JEFF, WHAT ARE YOU DOING?
NOTHING!

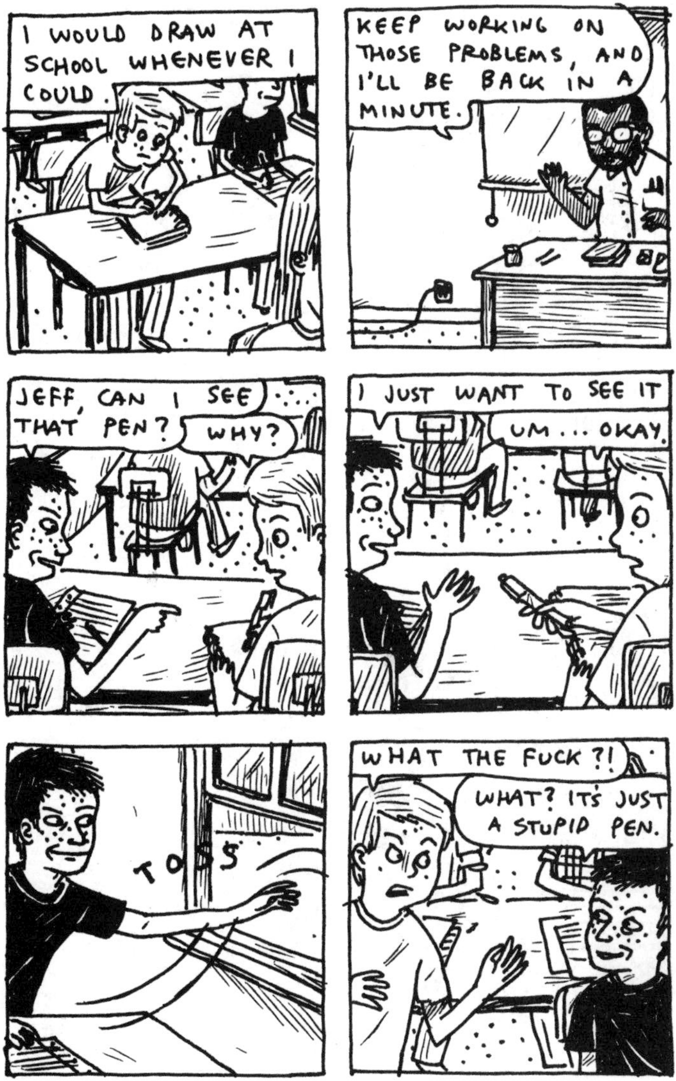
I WOULD DRAW AT SCHOOL WHENEVER I COULD.
KEEP WORKING ON THOSE PROBLEMS, AND I'LL BE BACK IN A MINUTE.
JEFF, CAN I SEE THAT PEN?
WHY?
I JUST WANT TO SEE IT
UM... OKAY.
TOSS
WHAT THE FUCK?!
WHAT? IT'S JUST A STUPID PEN.

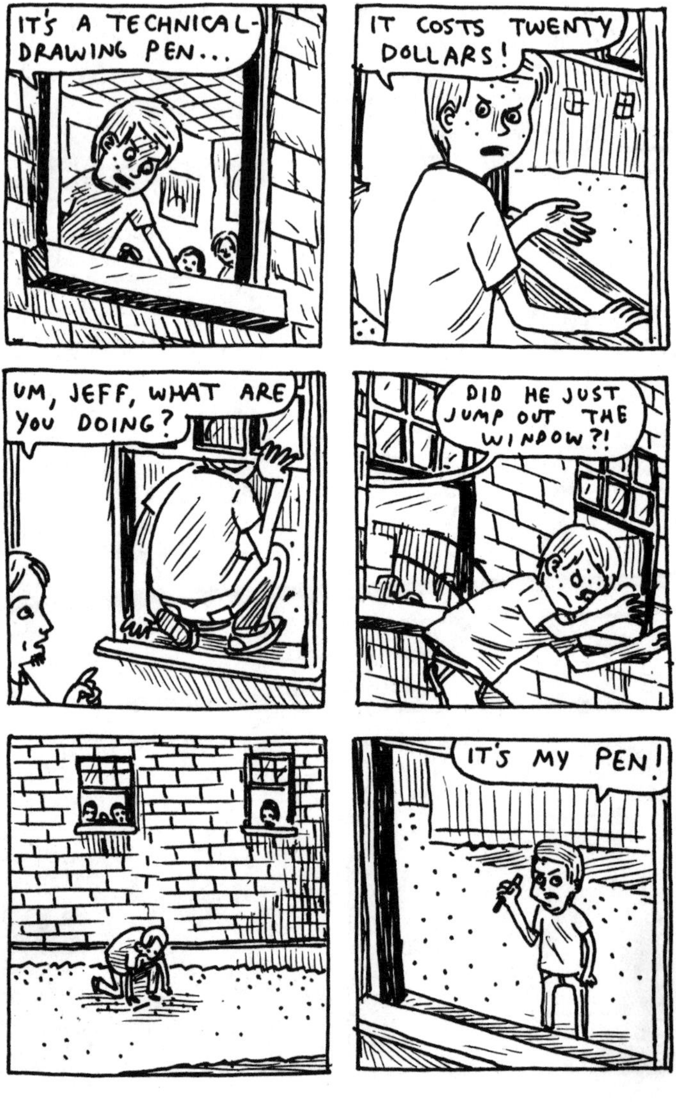
IT'S A TECHNICAL-DRAWING PEN...
IT COSTS TWENTY DOLLARS!
UM, JEFF, WHAT ARE YOU DOING?
DID HE JUST JUMP OUT THE WINDOW?!
IT'S MY PEN!

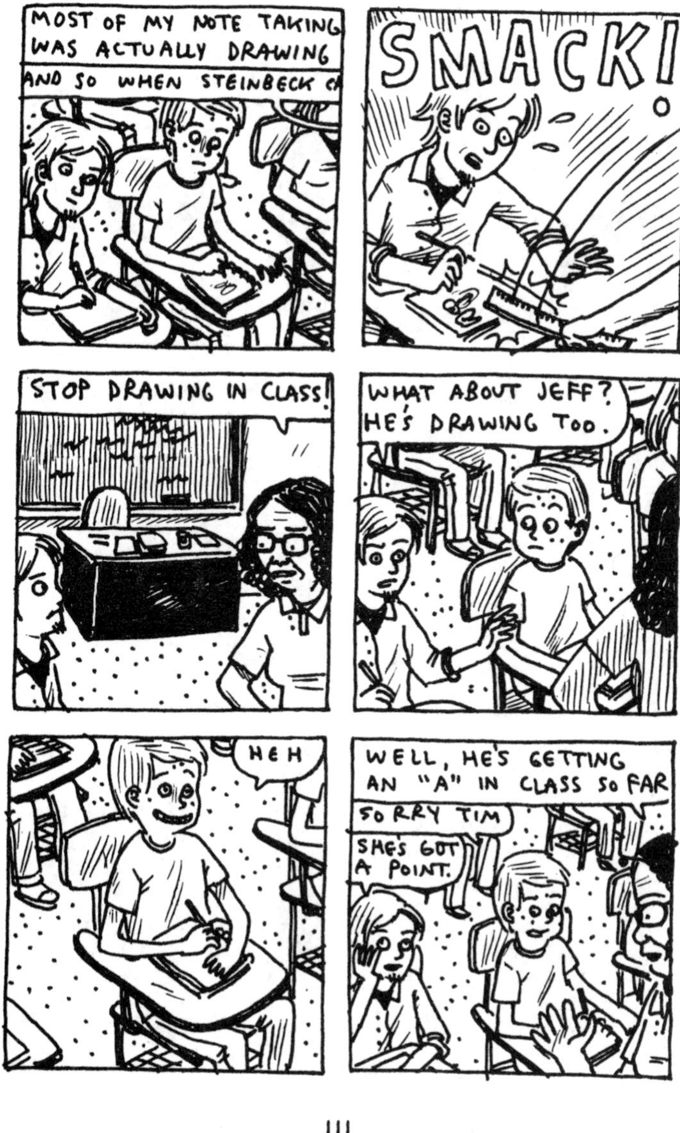
MOST OF MY NOTE TAKING WAS ACTUALLY DRAWING
AND SO WHEN STEINBECK CA
SMACK!
STOP DRAWING IN CLASS!
WHAT ABOUT JEFF? HE'S DRAWING TOO.
HEH
WELL, HE'S GETTING AN "A" IN CLASS SO FAR
SORRY TIM
SHE'S GOT A POINT.

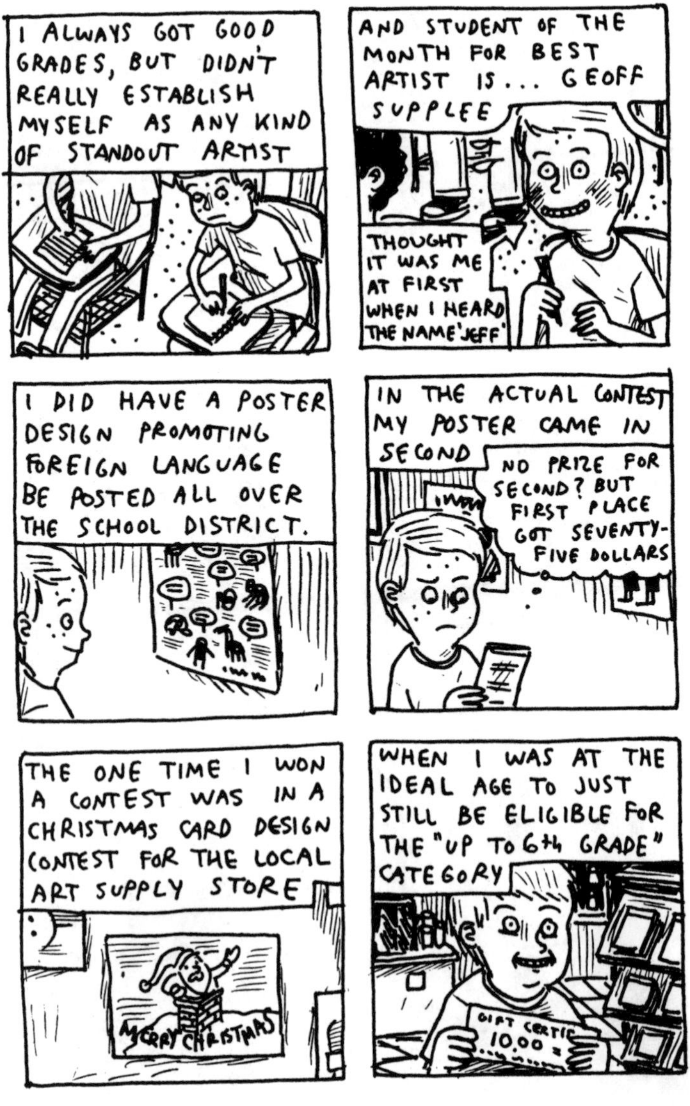
I ALWAYS GOT GOOD GRADES, BUT DIDN'T REALLY ESTABLISH MYSELF AS ANY KIND OF STANDOUT ARTIST
AND STUDENT OF THE MONTH FOR BEST ARTIST IS... GEOFF SUPPLEE
THOUGHT IT WAS ME AT FIRST WHEN I HEARD THE NAME 'JEFF'
I DID HAVE A POSTER DESIGN PROMOTING FOREIGN LANGUAGE BE POSTED ALL OVER THE SCHOOL DISTRICT.
IN THE ACTUAL CONTEST MY POSTER CAME IN SECOND
NO PRIZE FOR SECOND? BUT FIRST PLACE GOT SEVENTY-FIVE DOLLARS
THE ONE TIME I WON A CONTEST WAS IN A CHRISTMAS CARD DESIGN CONTEST FOR THE LOCAL ART SUPPLY STORE
MERRY CHRISTMAS
WHEN I WAS AT THE IDEAL AGE TO JUST STILL BE ELIGIBLE FOR THE "UP TO 6th GRADE" CATEGORY
10.00

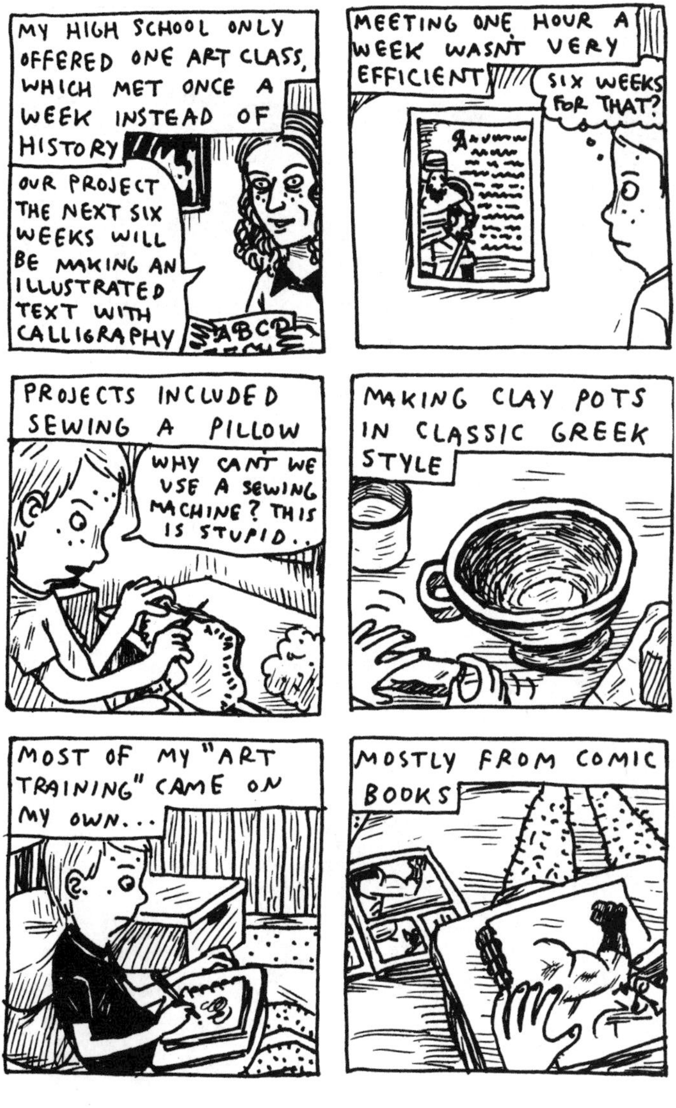
MY HIGH SCHOOL ONLY OFFERED ONE ART CLASS, WHICH MET ONCE A WEEK INSTEAD OF HISTORY
OUR PROJECT THE NEXT SIX WEEKS WILL BE MAKING AN ILLUSTRATED TEXT WITH CALLIGRAPHY
ABCD
MEETING ONE HOUR A WEEK WASN'T VERY EFFICIENT
SIX WEEKS FOR THAT?
PROJECTS INCLUDED SEWING A PILLOW
WHY CAN'T WE USE A SEWING MACHINE? THIS IS STUPID...
MAKING CLAY POTS IN CLASSIC GREEK STYLE
MOST OF MY "ART TRAINING" CAME ON MY OWN...
MOSTLY FROM COMIC BOOKS

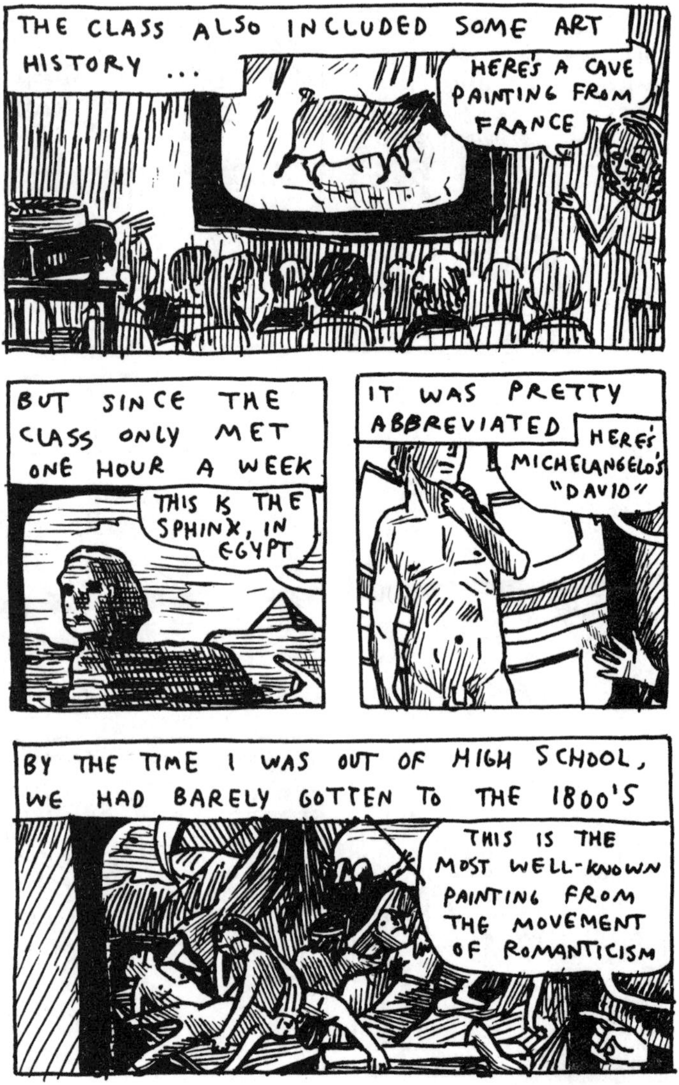
THE CLASS ALSO INCLUDED SOME ART HISTORY ...
HERE'S A CAVE PAINTING FROM FRANCE
BUT SINCE THE CLASS ONLY MET ONE HOUR A WEEK
THIS IS THE SPHINX, IN EGYPT
IT WAS PRETTY ABBREVIATED
HERE'S MICHELANGELO'S "DAVID"
BY THE TIME I WAS OUT OF HIGH SCHOOL, WE HAD BARELY GOTTEN TO THE 1800'S
THIS IS THE MOST WELL-KNOWN PAINTING FROM THE MOVEMENT OF ROMANTICISM

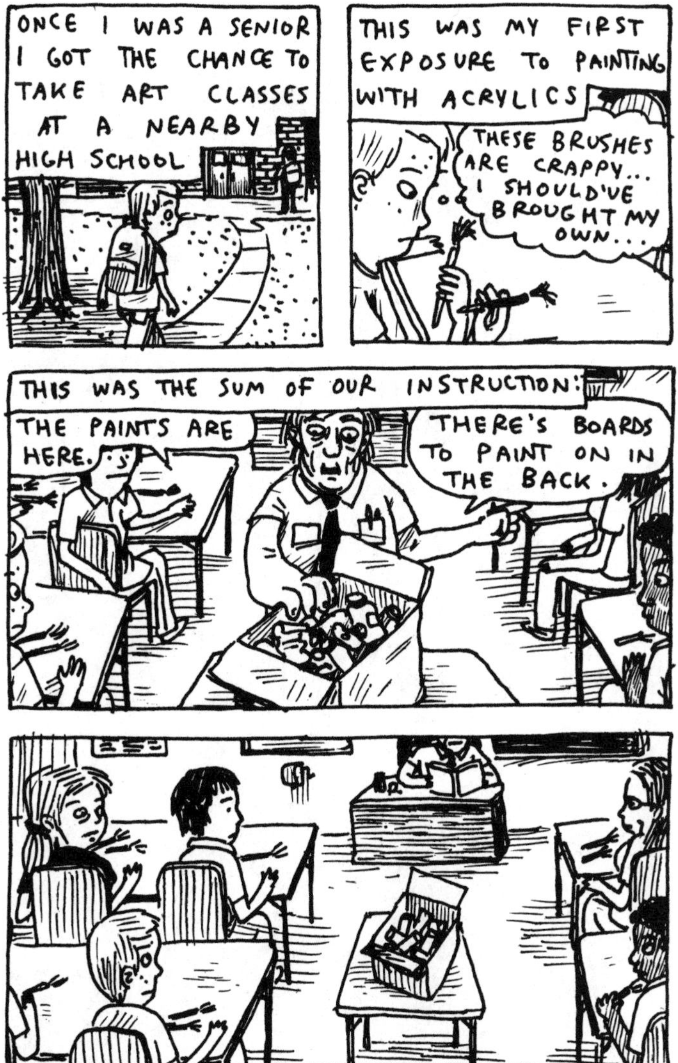
ONCE I WAS A SENIOR I GOT THE CHANCE TO TAKE ART CLASSES AT A NEARBY HIGH SCHOOL
THIS WAS MY FIRST EXPOSURE TO PAINTING WITH ACRYLICS
THESE BRUSHES ARE CRAPPY... I SHOULD'VE BROUGHT MY OWN...
THIS WAS THE SUM OF OUR INSTRUCTION:
THE PAINTS ARE HERE.
THERE'S BOARDS TO PAINT ON IN THE BACK.

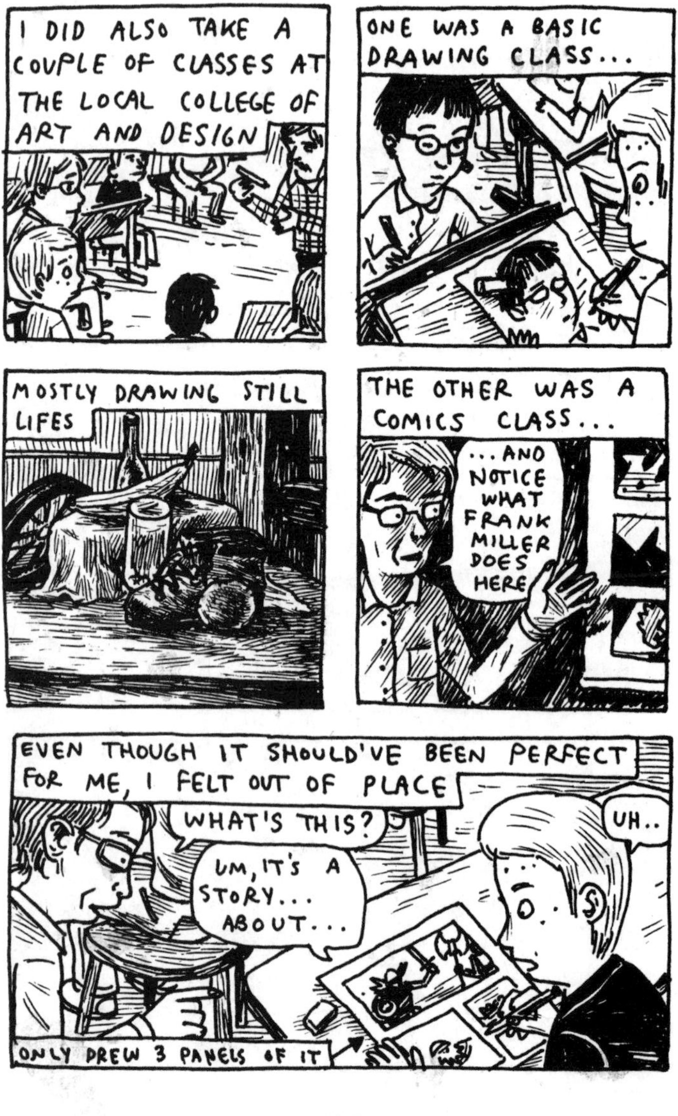
I DID ALSO TAKE A COUPLE OF CLASSES AT THE LOCAL COLLEGE OF ART AND DESIGN
ONE WAS A BASIC DRAWING CLASS...
MOSTLY DRAWING STILL LIFES
THE OTHER WAS A COMICS CLASS...
...AND NOTICE WHAT FRANK MILLER DOES HERE
EVEN THOUGH IT SHOULD'VE BEEN PERFECT FOR ME, I FELT OUT OF PLACE
WHAT'S THIS?
UH..
UM, IT'S A STORY... ABOUT...
ONLY DREW 3 PANELS OF IT

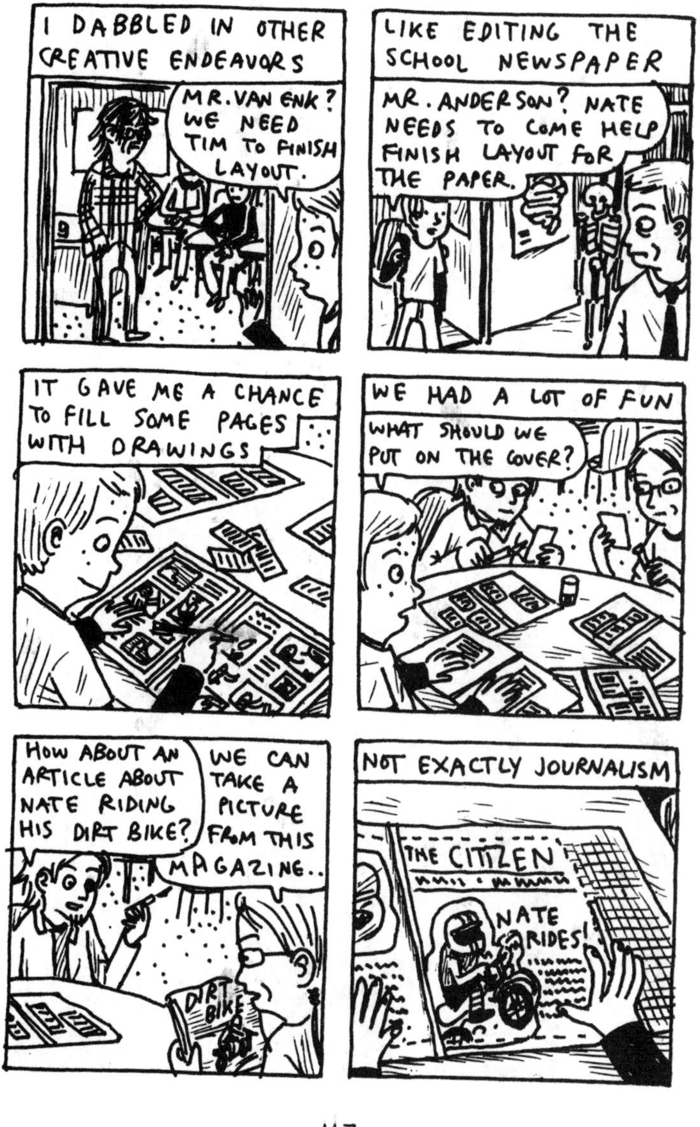
I DABBLED IN OTHER CREATIVE ENDEAVORS
MR. VAN ENK? WE NEED TIM TO FINISH LAYOUT.
LIKE EDITING THE SCHOOL NEWSPAPER
MR. ANDERSON? NATE NEEDS TO COME HELP FINISH LAYOUT FOR THE PAPER.
IT GAVE ME A CHANCE TO FILL SOME PAGES WITH DRAWINGS
WE HAD A LOT OF FUN
WHAT SHOULD WE PUT ON THE COVER?
HOW ABOUT AN ARTICLE ABOUT NATE RIDING HIS DIRT BIKE?
WE CAN TAKE A PICTURE FROM THIS MAGAZINE..
DIRT BIKE
NOT EXACTLY JOURNALISM
THE CITIZEN
NATE RIDES!

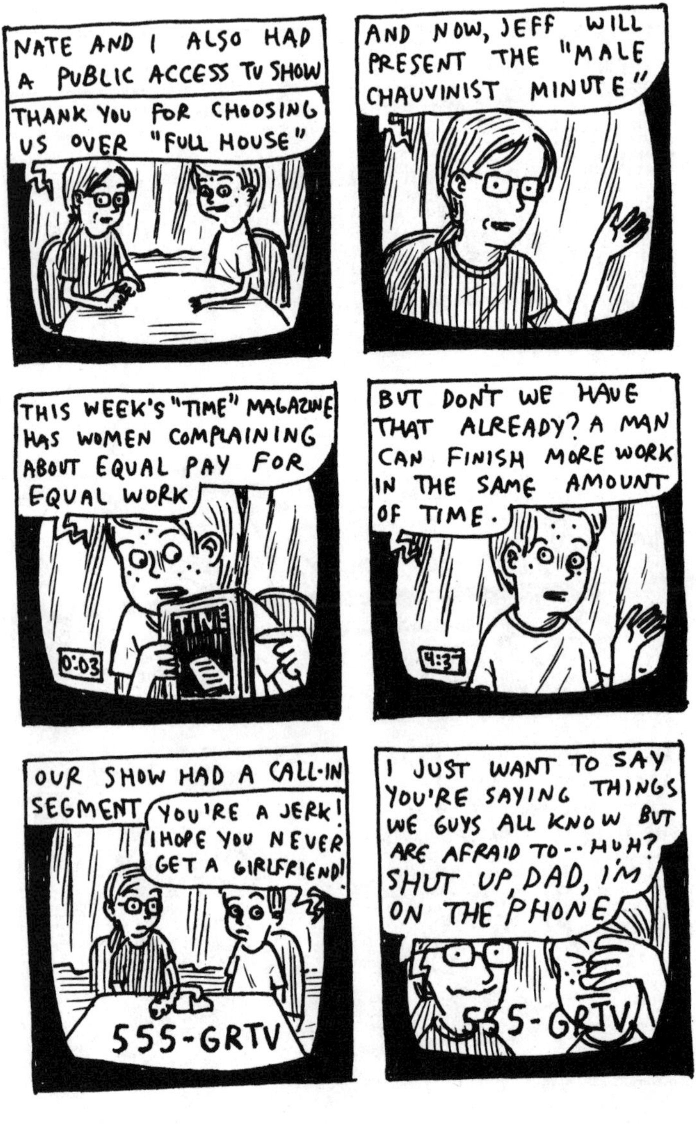
NATE AND I ALSO HAD A PUBLIC ACCESS TV SHOW
THANK YOU FOR CHOOSING US OVER "FULL HOUSE"
AND NOW, JEFF WILL PRESENT THE "MALE CHAUVINIST MINUTE"
THIS WEEK'S "TIME" MAGAZINE HAS WOMEN COMPLAINING ABOUT EQUAL PAY FOR EQUAL WORK
TIME
0:03
BUT DON'T WE HAVE THAT ALREADY? A MAN CAN FINISH MORE WORK IN THE SAME AMOUNT OF TIME.
4:37
OUR SHOW HAD A CALL-IN SEGMENT
YOU'RE A JERK! I HOPE YOU NEVER GET A GIRLFRIEND!
555-GRTV
I JUST WANT TO SAY YOU'RE SAYING THINGS WE GUYS ALL KNOW BUT ARE AFRAID TO-- HUH? SHUT UP, DAD, I'M ON THE PHONE
555-GRTV

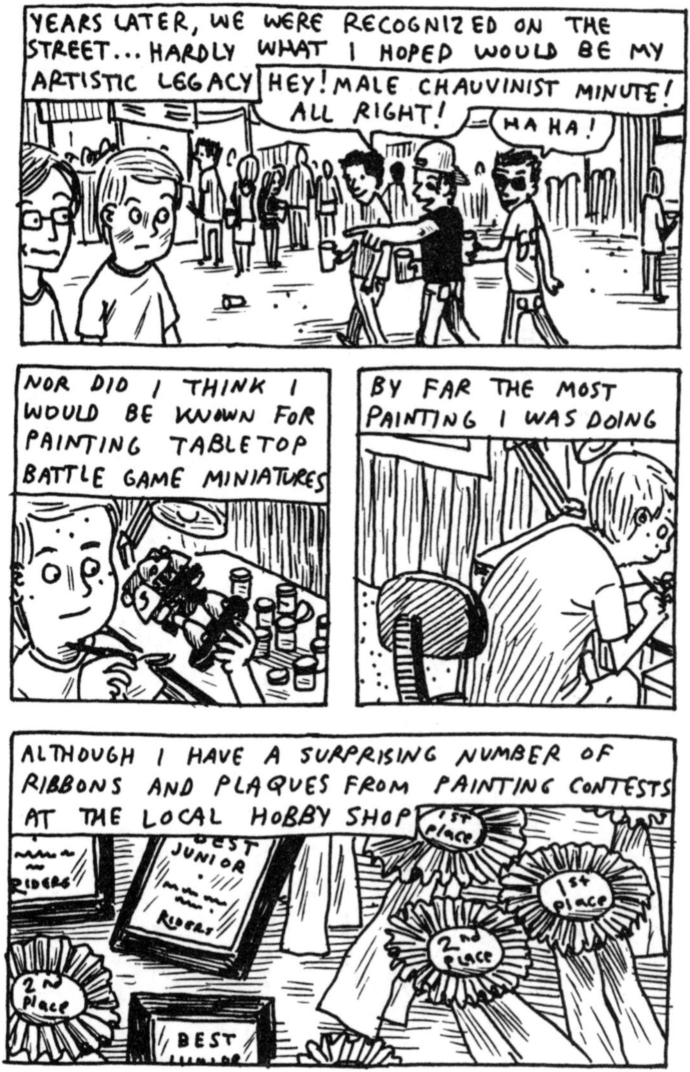
YEARS LATER, WE WERE RECOGNIZED ON THE STREET... HARDLY WHAT I HOPED WOULD BE MY ARTISTIC LEGACY
HEY! MALE CHAUVINIST MINUTE! ALL RIGHT!
HA HA!
NOR DID I THINK I WOULD BE KNOWN FOR PAINTING TABLETOP BATTLE GAME MINIATURES
BY FAR THE MOST PAINTING I WAS DOING
ALTHOUGH I HAVE A SURPRISING NUMBER OF RIBBONS AND PLAQUES FROM PAINTING CONTESTS AT THE LOCAL HOBBY SHOP
1st place
JUNIOR
RIDERS
RIDERS
1st place
2nd place
2nd place
BEST

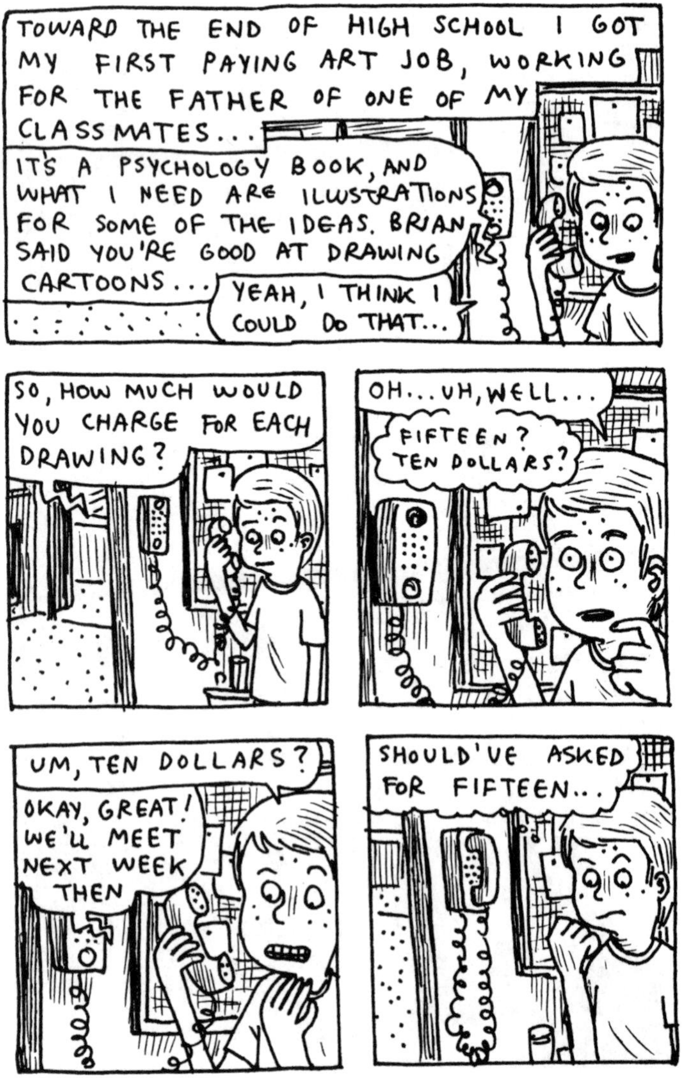
TOWARD THE END OF HIGH SCHOOL I GOT MY FIRST PAYING ART JOB, WORKING FOR THE FATHER OF ONE OF MY CLASSMATES...
IT'S A PSYCHOLOGY BOOK, AND WHAT I NEED ARE ILLUSTRATIONS FOR SOME OF THE IDEAS. BRIAN SAID YOU'RE GOOD AT DRAWING CARTOONS...
YEAH, I THINK I COULD DO THAT...
SO, HOW MUCH WOULD YOU CHARGE FOR EACH DRAWING?
OH...UH, WELL...
FIFTEEN? TEN DOLLARS?
UM, TEN DOLLARS?
OKAY, GREAT! WE'LL MEET NEXT WEEK THEN
SHOULD'VE ASKED FOR FIFTEEN...

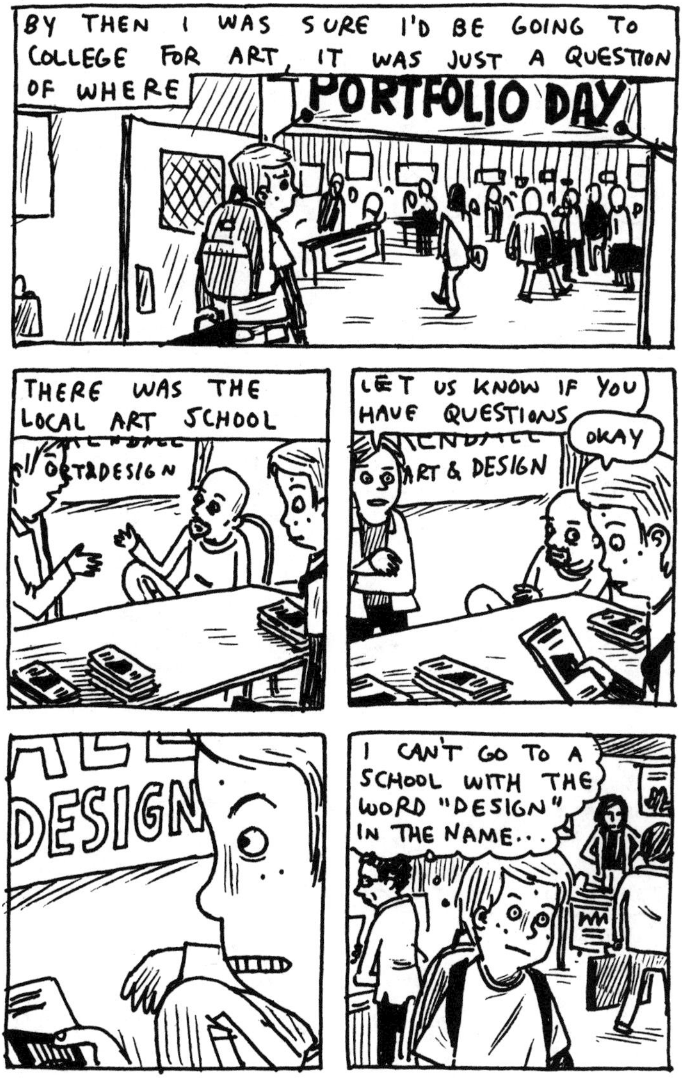
BY THEN I WAS SURE I'D BE GOING TO COLLEGE FOR ART, IT WAS JUST A QUESTION OF WHERE
PORTFOLIO DAY
THERE WAS THE LOCAL ART SCHOOL
ART&DESIGN
LET US KNOW IF YOU HAVE QUESTIONS
OKAY
ART & DESIGN
DESIGN
I CAN'T GO TO A SCHOOL WITH THE WORD "DESIGN" IN THE NAME...

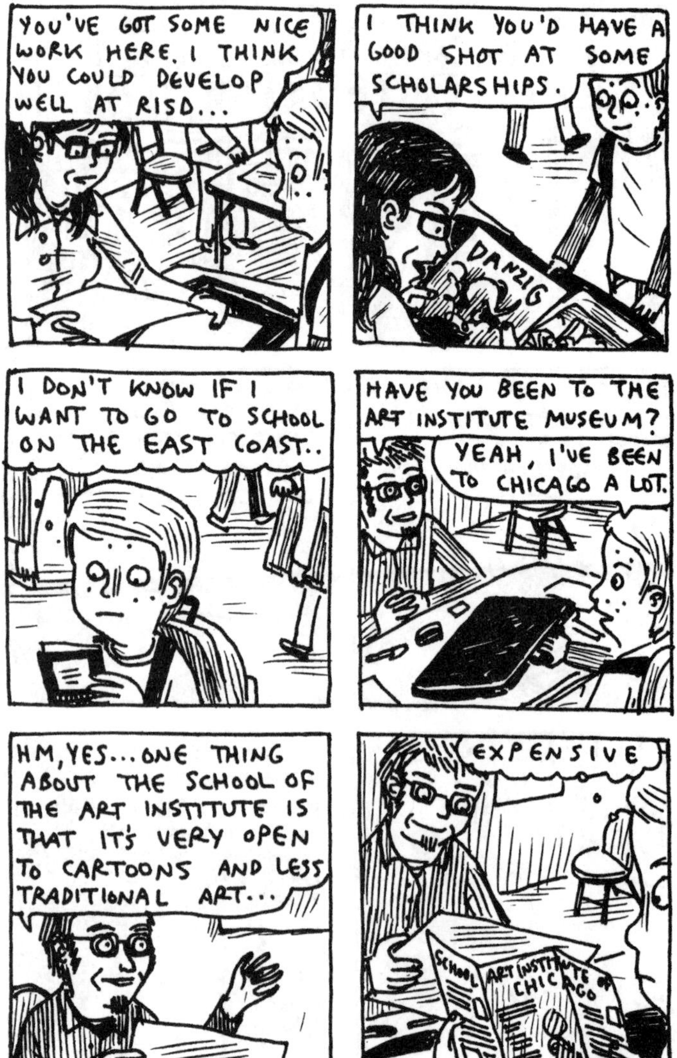
YOU'VE GOT SOME NICE WORK HERE. I THINK YOU COULD DEVELOP WELL AT RISD...
I THINK YOU'D HAVE A GOOD SHOT AT SOME SCHOLARSHIPS.
DANZIG
I DON'T KNOW IF I WANT TO GO TO SCHOOL ON THE EAST COAST..
HAVE YOU BEEN TO THE ART INSTITUTE MUSEUM?
YEAH, I'VE BEEN TO CHICAGO A LOT.
HM, YES... ONE THING ABOUT THE SCHOOL OF THE ART INSTITUTE IS THAT IT'S VERY OPEN TO CARTOONS AND LESS TRADITIONAL ART...
EXPENSIVE
SCHOOL ART INSTITUTE OF CHICAGO

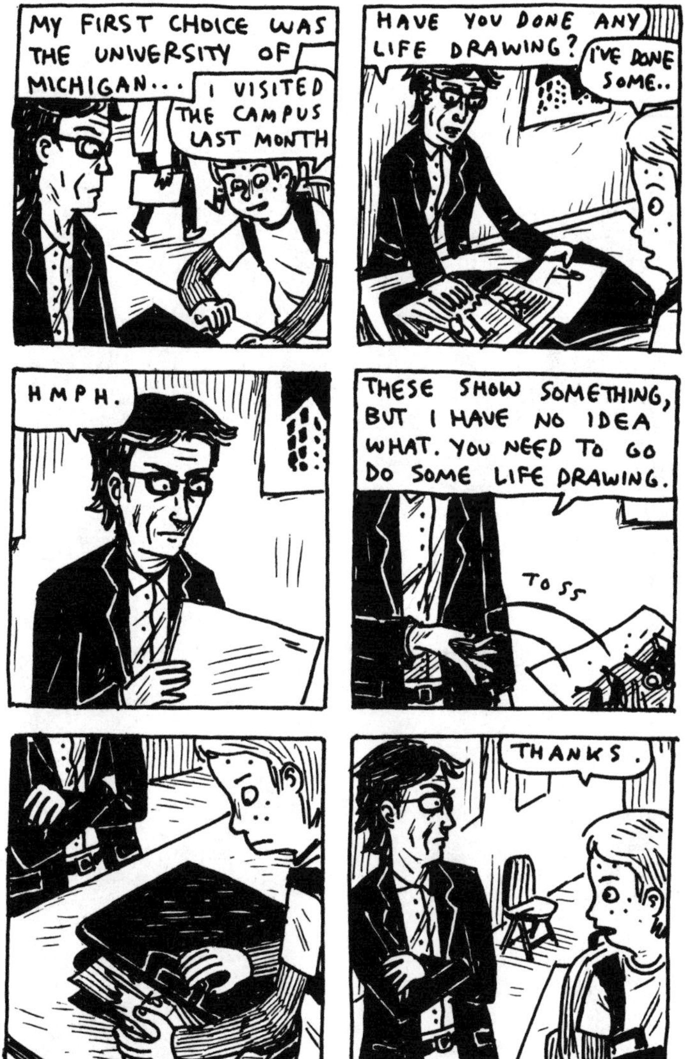
MY FIRST CHOICE WAS THE UNIVERSITY OF MICHIGAN...
I VISITED THE CAMPUS LAST MONTH
HAVE YOU DONE ANY LIFE DRAWING?
I'VE DONE SOME..
HMPH.
THESE SHOW SOMETHING, BUT I HAVE NO IDEA WHAT. YOU NEED TO GO DO SOME LIFE DRAWING.
TOSS
THANKS.

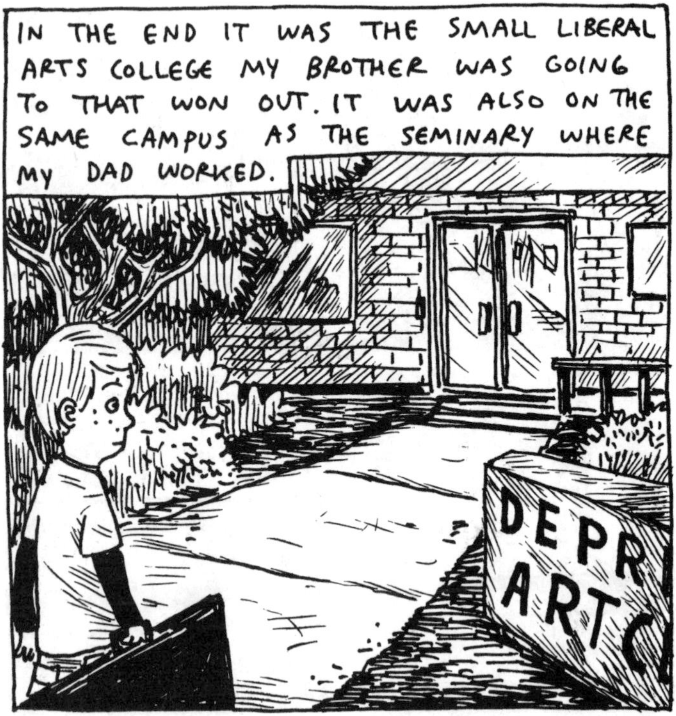
IN THE END IT WAS THE SMALL LIBERAL ARTS COLLEGE MY BROTHER WAS GOING TO THAT WON OUT. IT WAS ALSO ON THE SAME CAMPUS AS THE SEMINARY WHERE MY DAD WORKED.
DEPR
ARTC

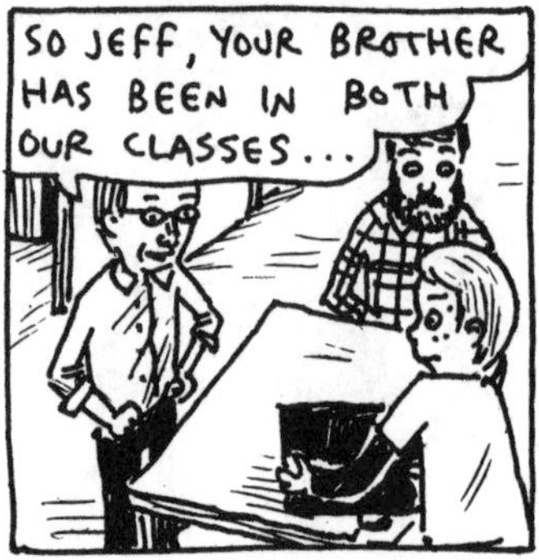
SO JEFF, YOUR BROTHER HAS BEEN IN BOTH OUR CLASSES...

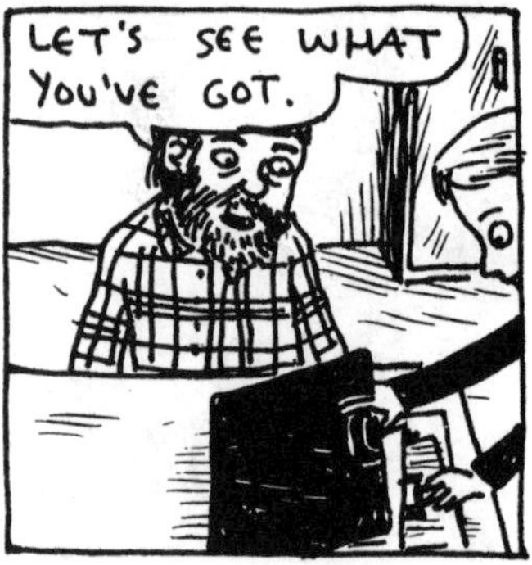
LET'S SEE WHAT YOU'VE GOT.

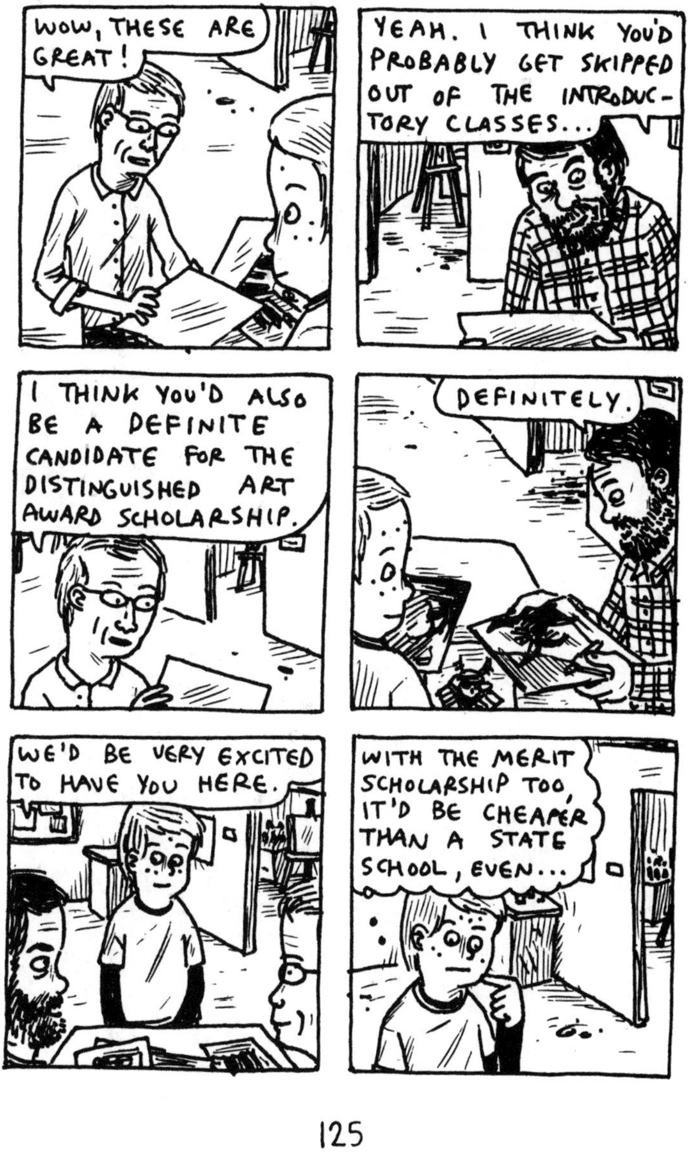
WOW, THESE ARE GREAT!
YEAH. I THINK YOU'D PROBABLY GET SKIPPED OUT OF THE INTRODUC-TORY CLASSES...
I THINK YOU'D ALSO BE A DEFINITE CANDIDATE FOR THE DISTINGUISHED ART AWARD SCHOLARSHIP.
DEFINITELY.
WE'D BE VERY EXCITED TO HAVE YOU HERE.
WITH THE MERIT SCHOLARSHIP TOO, IT'D BE CHEAPER THAN A STATE SCHOOL, EVEN...

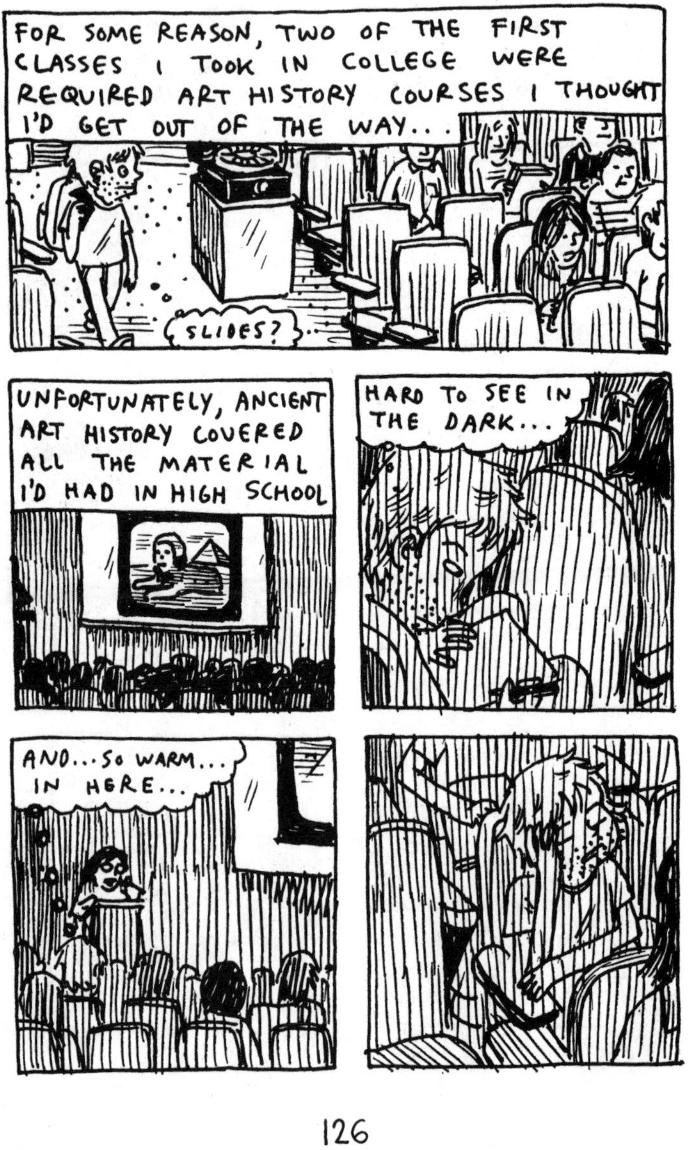
FOR SOME REASON, TWO OF THE FIRST CLASSES I TOOK IN COLLEGE WERE REQUIRED ART HISTORY COURSES I THOUGHT I'D GET OUT OF THE WAY...
SLIDES?
UNFORTUNATELY, ANCIENT ART HISTORY COVERED ALL THE MATERIAL I'D HAD IN HIGH SCHOOL
HARD TO SEE IN THE DARK...
AND...SO WARM... IN HERE...

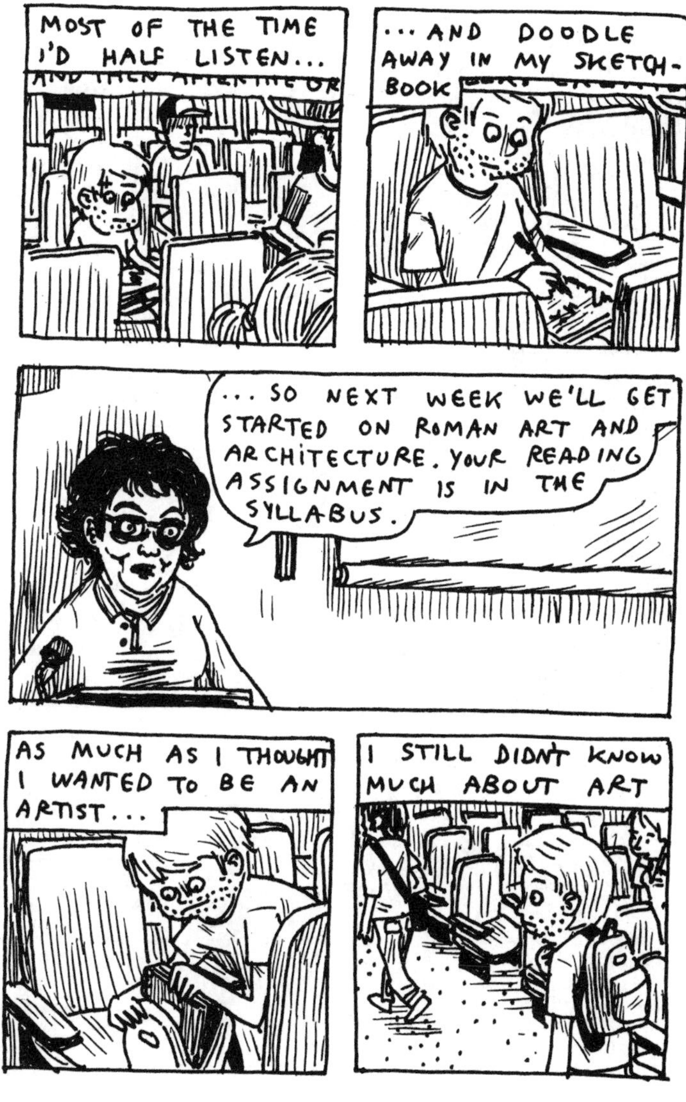
MOST OF THE TIME I'D HALF LISTEN...
...AND DOODLE AWAY IN MY SKETCH-BOOK
...SO NEXT WEEK WE'LL GET STARTED ON ROMAN ART AND ARCHITECTURE. YOUR READING ASSIGNMENT IS IN THE SYLLABUS.
AS MUCH AS I THOUGHT I WANTED TO BE AN ARTIST...
I STILL DIDN'T KNOW MUCH ABOUT ART

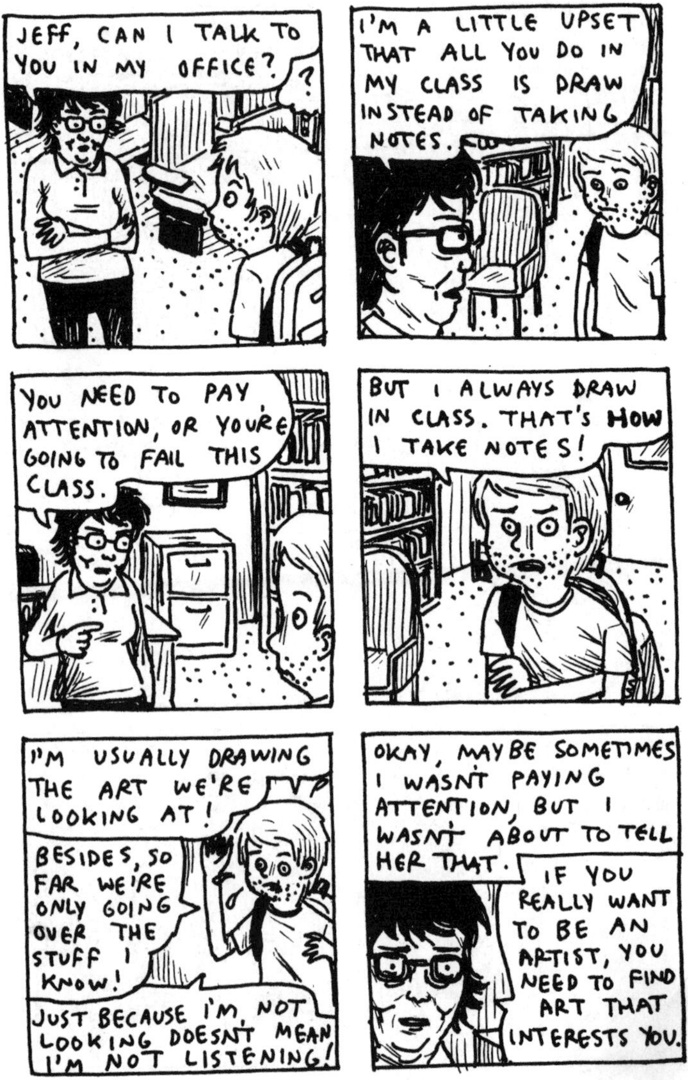
JEFF, CAN I TALK TO YOU IN MY OFFICE?
?
I'M A LITTLE UPSET THAT ALL YOU DO IN MY CLASS IS DRAW INSTEAD OF TAKING NOTES.
YOU NEED TO PAY ATTENTION, OR YOU'RE GOING TO FAIL THIS CLASS.
BUT I ALWAYS DRAW IN CLASS. THAT'S HOW I TAKE NOTES!
I'M USUALLY DRAWING THE ART WE'RE LOOKING AT!
BESIDES, SO FAR WE'RE ONLY GOING OVER THE STUFF I KNOW!
JUST BECAUSE I'M NOT LOOKING DOESN'T MEAN I'M NOT LISTENING!
OKAY, MAYBE SOMETIMES I WASN'T PAYING ATTENTION, BUT I WASN'T ABOUT TO TELL HER THAT.
IF YOU REALLY WANT TO BE AN ARTIST, YOU NEED TO FIND ART THAT INTERESTS YOU.

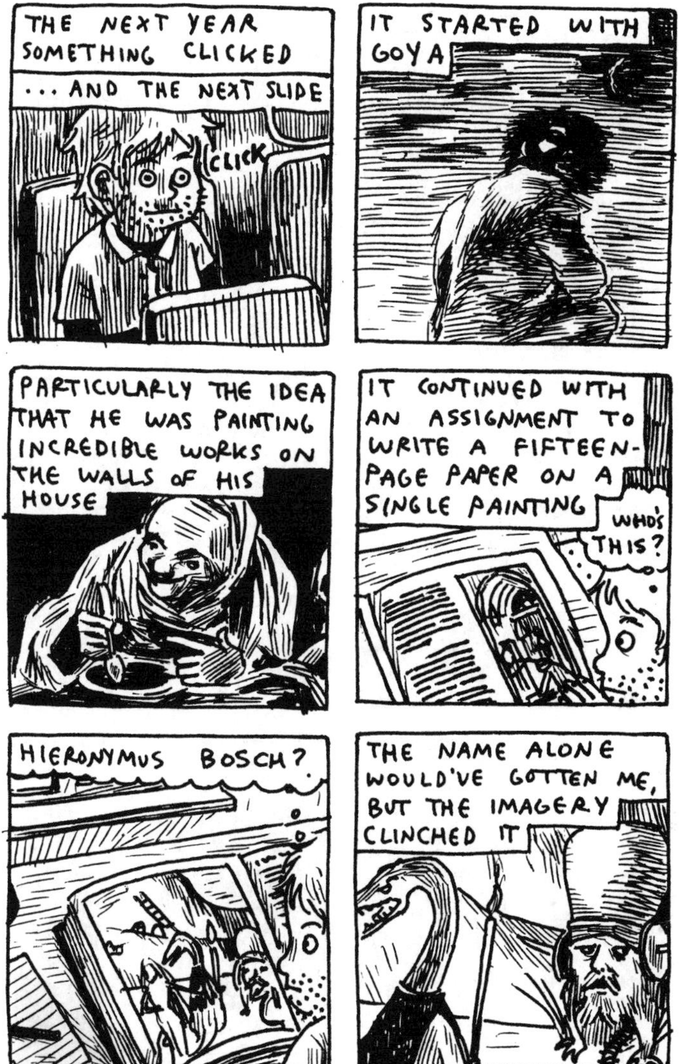
THE NEXT YEAR SOMETHING CLICKED
...AND THE NEXT SLIDE
CLICK
IT STARTED WITH GOYA
PARTICULARLY THE IDEA THAT HE WAS PAINTING INCREDIBLE WORKS ON THE WALLS OF HIS HOUSE
IT CONTINUED WITH AN ASSIGNMENT TO WRITE A FIFTEEN-PAGE PAPER ON A SINGLE PAINTING
WHO'S THIS?
HIERONYMUS BOSCH?
THE NAME ALONE WOULD'VE GOTTEN ME, BUT THE IMAGERY CLINCHED IT

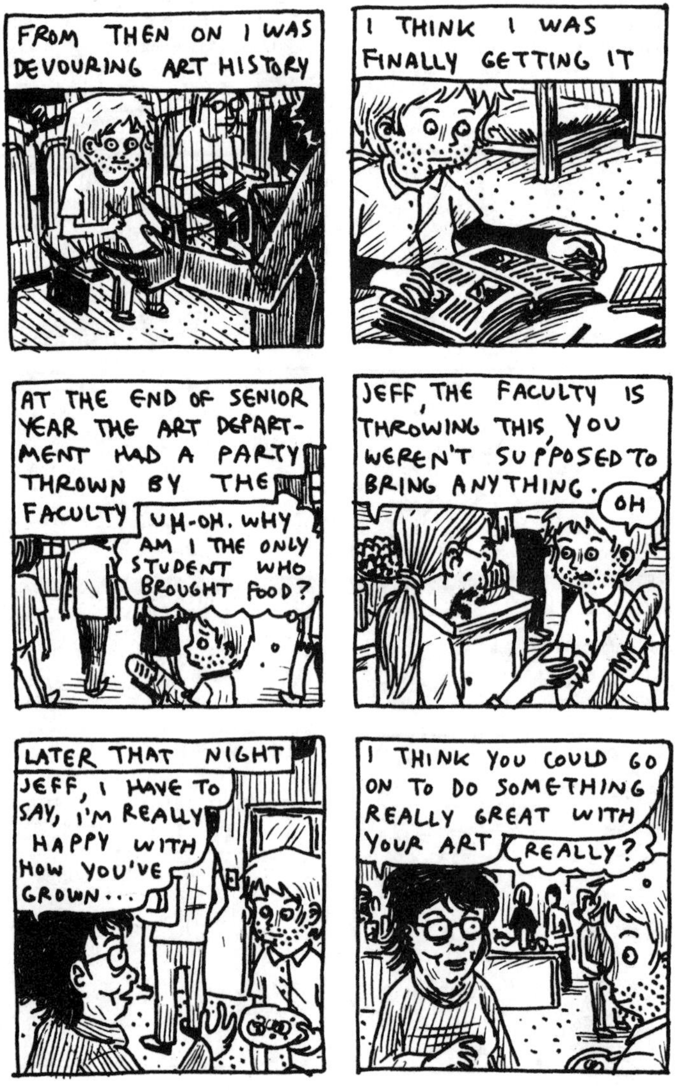

FROM THEN ON I WAS DEVOURING ART HISTORY
I THINK I WAS FINALLY GETTING IT
AT THE END OF SENIOR YEAR THE ART DEPARTMENT HAD A PARTY THROWN BY THE FACULTY
UH-OH. WHY AM I THE ONLY STUDENT WHO BROUGHT FOOD?
JEFF, THE FACULTY IS THROWING THIS, YOU WEREN'T SUPPOSED TO BRING ANYTHING.
OH
LATER THAT NIGHT
JEFF, I HAVE TO SAY, I'M REALLY HAPPY WITH HOW YOU'VE GROWN...
I THINK YOU COULD GO ON TO DO SOMETHING REALLY GREAT WITH YOUR ART
REALLY?

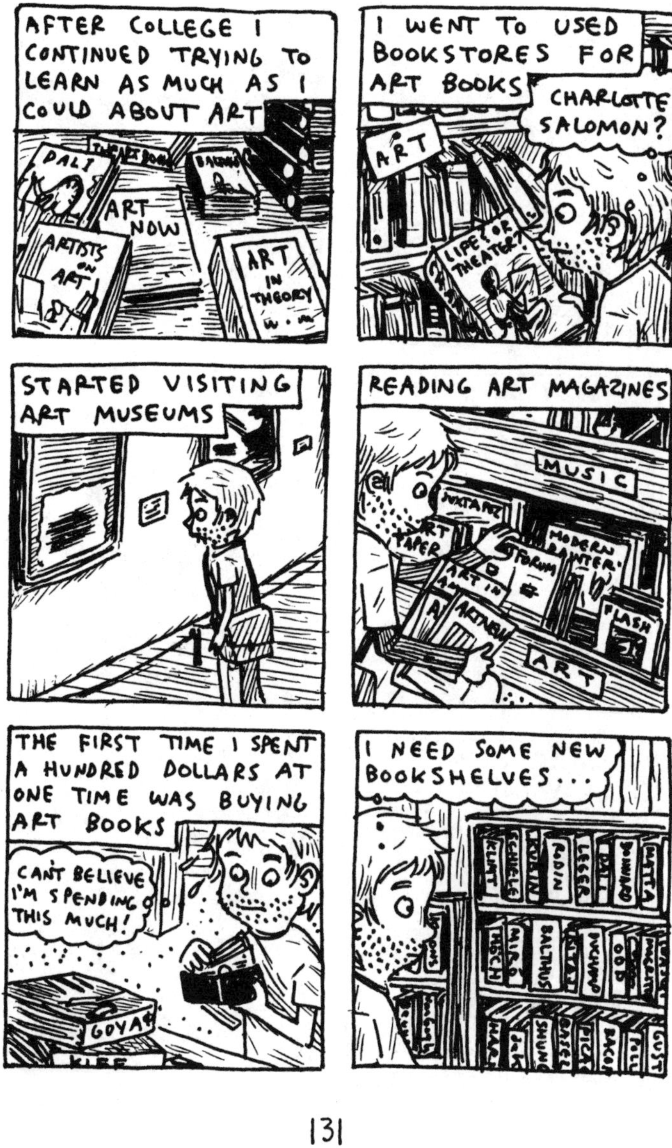
AFTER COLLEGE I CONTINUED TRYING TO LEARN AS MUCH AS I COULD ABOUT ART
DALI
ART NOW
ARTISTS ON ART
ART IN THEORY
I WENT TO USED BOOKSTORES FOR ART BOOKS
CHARLOTTE SALOMON?
ART
LIFE? OR THEATER?
STARTED VISITING ART MUSEUMS
READING ART MAGAZINES
MUSIC
JUXTAPOZ
ART PAPER
MODERN PAINTER
FORUM
ART IN
ARTNEWS
FLASH
ART
THE FIRST TIME I SPENT A HUNDRED DOLLARS AT ONE TIME WAS BUYING ART BOOKS
CAN'T BELIEVE I'M SPENDING THIS MUCH!
GOYA
I NEED SOME NEW BOOKSHELVES...
KLIMT
SCHIELE
RODIN
LEGER
BALTHUS
MIRO

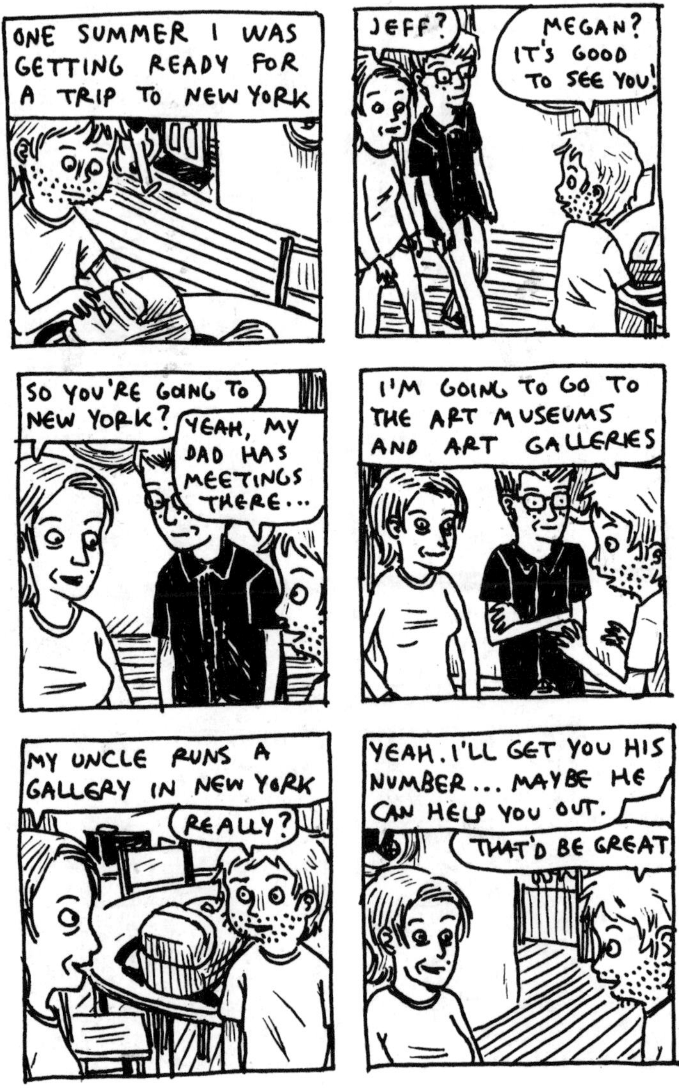
ONE SUMMER I WAS GETTING READY FOR A TRIP TO NEW YORK
JEFF?
MEGAN? IT'S GOOD TO SEE YOU!
SO YOU'RE GOING TO NEW YORK?
YEAH, MY DAD HAS MEETINGS THERE...
I'M GOING TO GO TO THE ART MUSEUMS AND ART GALLERIES
MY UNCLE RUNS A GALLERY IN NEW YORK
REALLY?
YEAH. I'LL GET YOU HIS NUMBER... MAYBE HE CAN HELP YOU OUT.
THAT'D BE GREAT

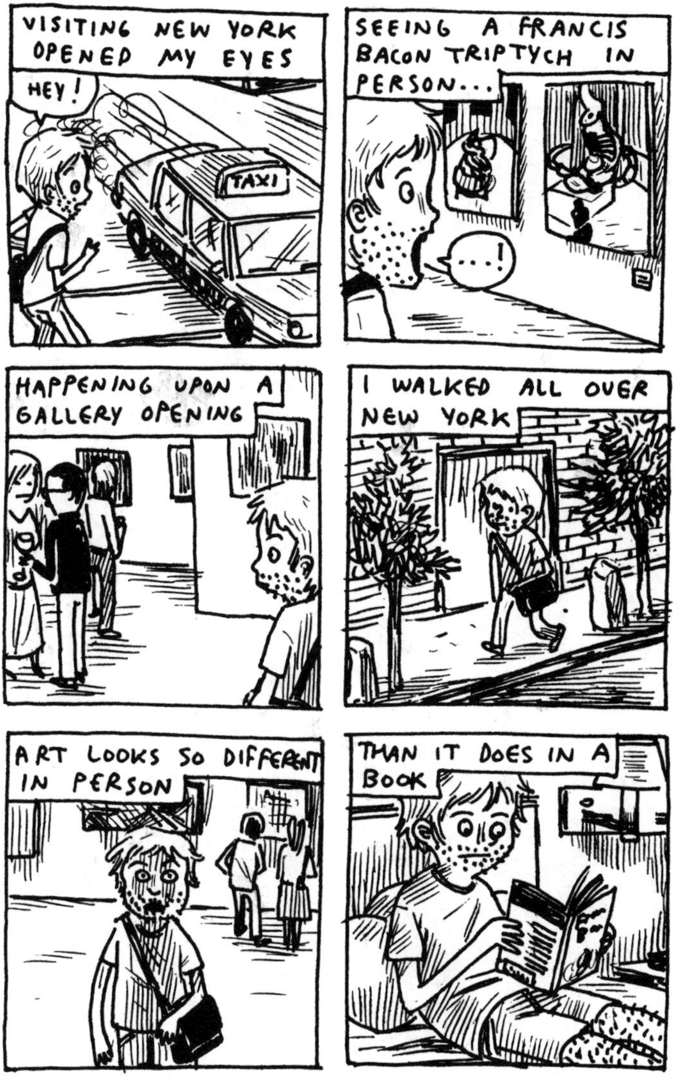
VISITING NEW YORK OPENED MY EYES
HEY!
TAXI
SEEING A FRANCIS BACON TRIPTYCH IN PERSON...
...!
HAPPENING UPON A GALLERY OPENING
I WALKED ALL OVER NEW YORK
ART LOOKS SO DIFFERENT IN PERSON
THAN IT DOES IN A BOOK

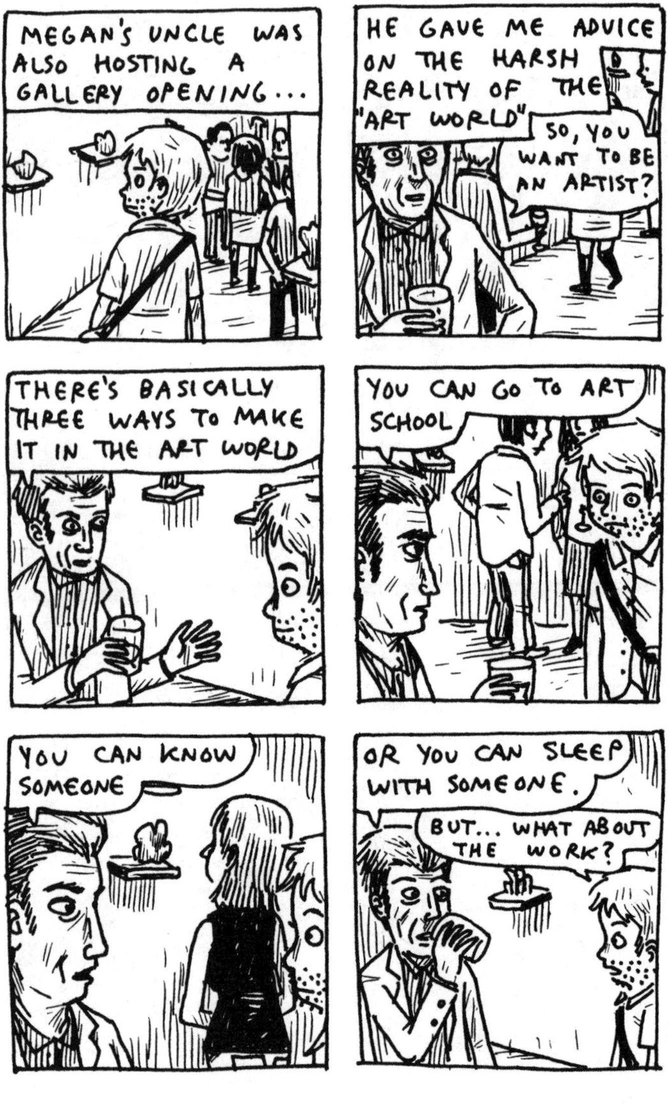
MEGAN'S UNCLE WAS ALSO HOSTING A GALLERY OPENING...
HE GAVE ME ADVICE ON THE HARSH REALITY OF THE "ART WORLD"
SO, YOU WANT TO BE AN ARTIST?
THERE'S BASICALLY THREE WAYS TO MAKE IT IN THE ART WORLD
YOU CAN GO TO ART SCHOOL
YOU CAN KNOW SOMEONE
OR YOU CAN SLEEP WITH SOMEONE.
BUT... WHAT ABOUT THE WORK?

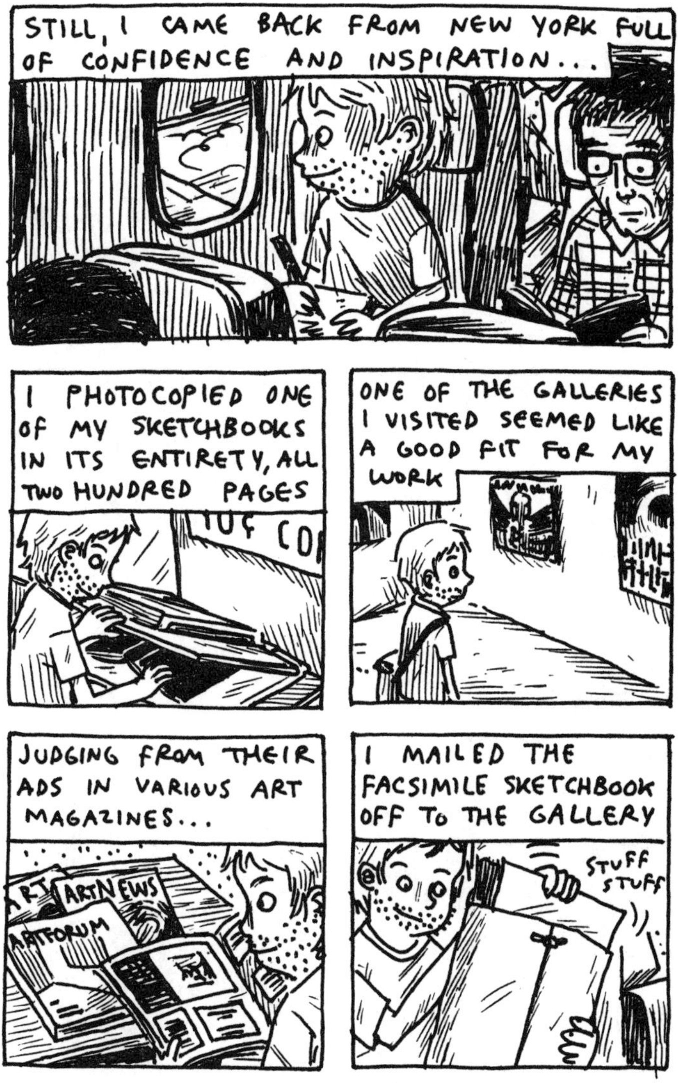
STILL, I CAME BACK FROM NEW YORK FULL OF CONFIDENCE AND INSPIRATION...
I PHOTOCOPIED ONE OF MY SKETCHBOOKS IN ITS ENTIRETY, ALL TWO HUNDRED PAGES
ONE OF THE GALLERIES I VISITED SEEMED LIKE A GOOD FIT FOR MY WORK
JUDGING FROM THEIR ADS IN VARIOUS ART MAGAZINES...
ARTNEWS
ARTFORUM
I MAILED THE FACSIMILE SKETCHBOOK OFF TO THE GALLERY
STUFF STUFF

BY THE TIME I GOT A RESPONSE, I'D ALMOST FORGOTTEN ABOUT IT...

THIS PACKAGE IS SO THICK - IT MUST BE BECAUSE—

—BECAUSE THEY SENT THE WHOLE SKETCHBOOK BACK TO ME?

GEORGE...
IIMI W W HM ST NY NY

why did you send this??

OH.

I SHOULD'VE KNOWN MY WORK NEEDED TO BE A LOT BETTER

SOMETIMES I'M A SLOW LEARNER.

AT LEAST THEY SENT IT BACK?

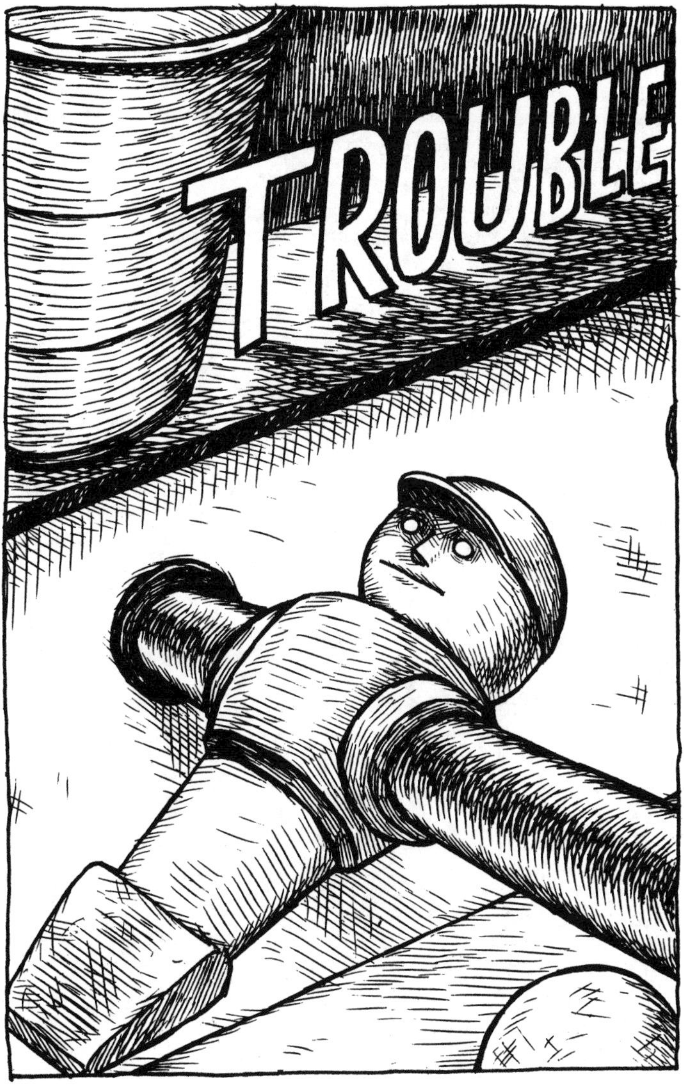
TROUBLE

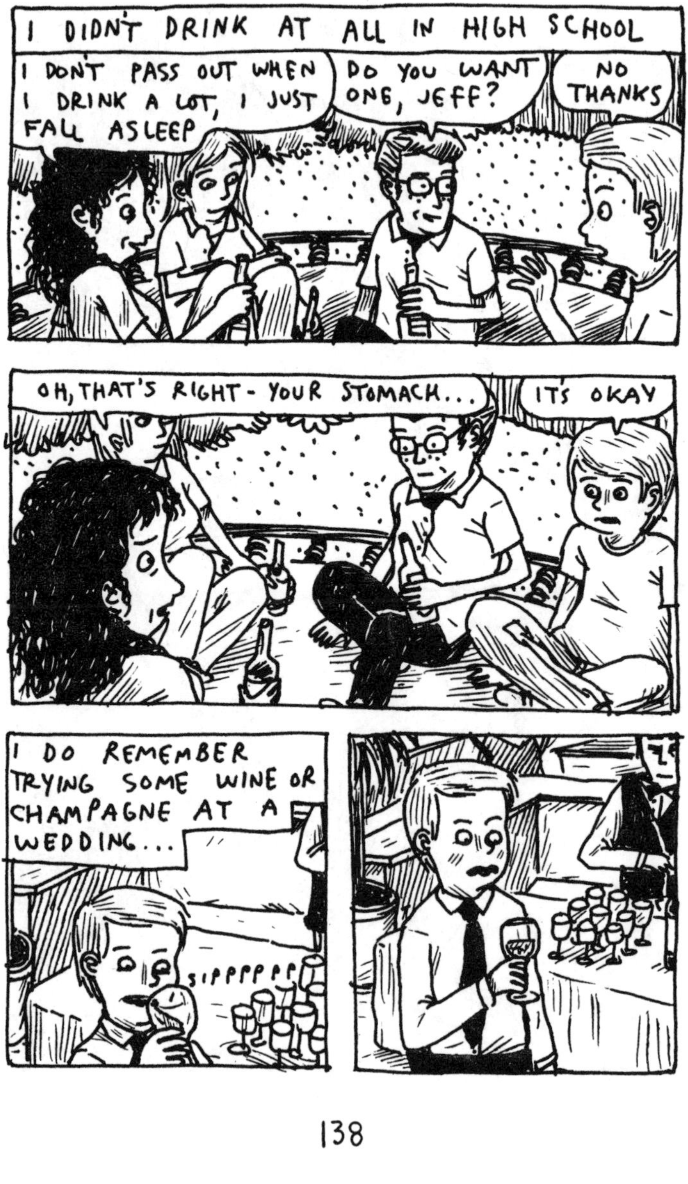

I DIDN'T DRINK AT ALL IN HIGH SCHOOL
I DON'T PASS OUT WHEN I DRINK A LOT, I JUST FALL ASLEEP
DO YOU WANT ONE, JEFF?
NO THANKS
OH, THAT'S RIGHT - YOUR STOMACH...
IT'S OKAY
I DO REMEMBER TRYING SOME WINE OR CHAMPAGNE AT A WEDDING...
SIPPPPPP

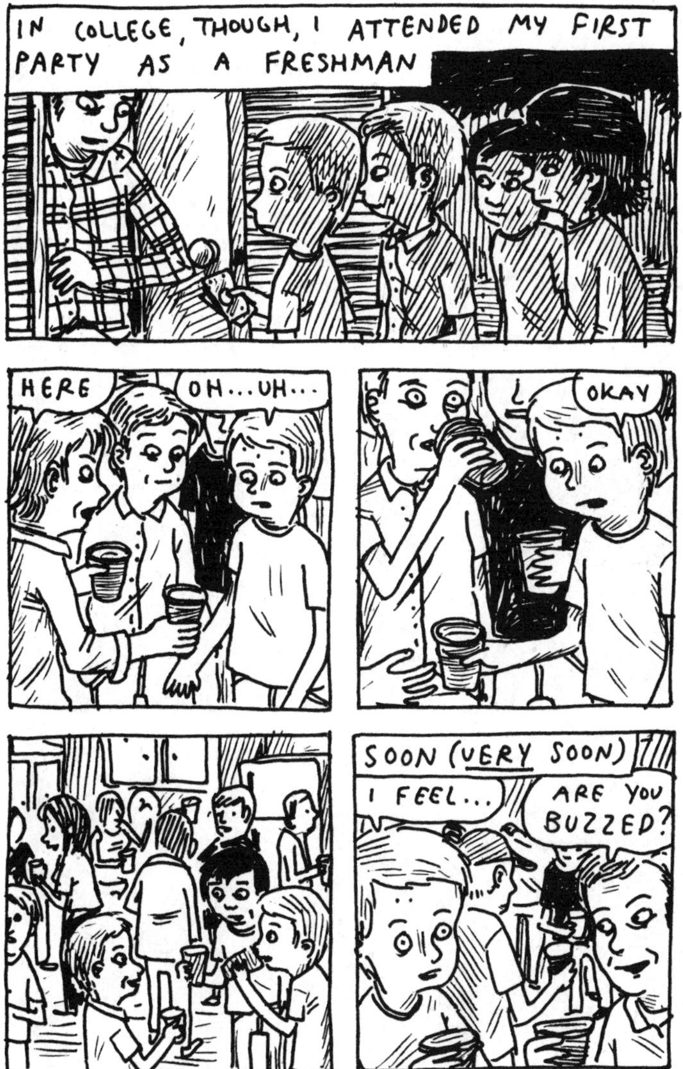
IN COLLEGE, THOUGH, I ATTENDED MY FIRST PARTY AS A FRESHMAN
HERE
OH...UH...
OKAY
SOON (VERY SOON)
I FEEL...
ARE YOU BUZZED?

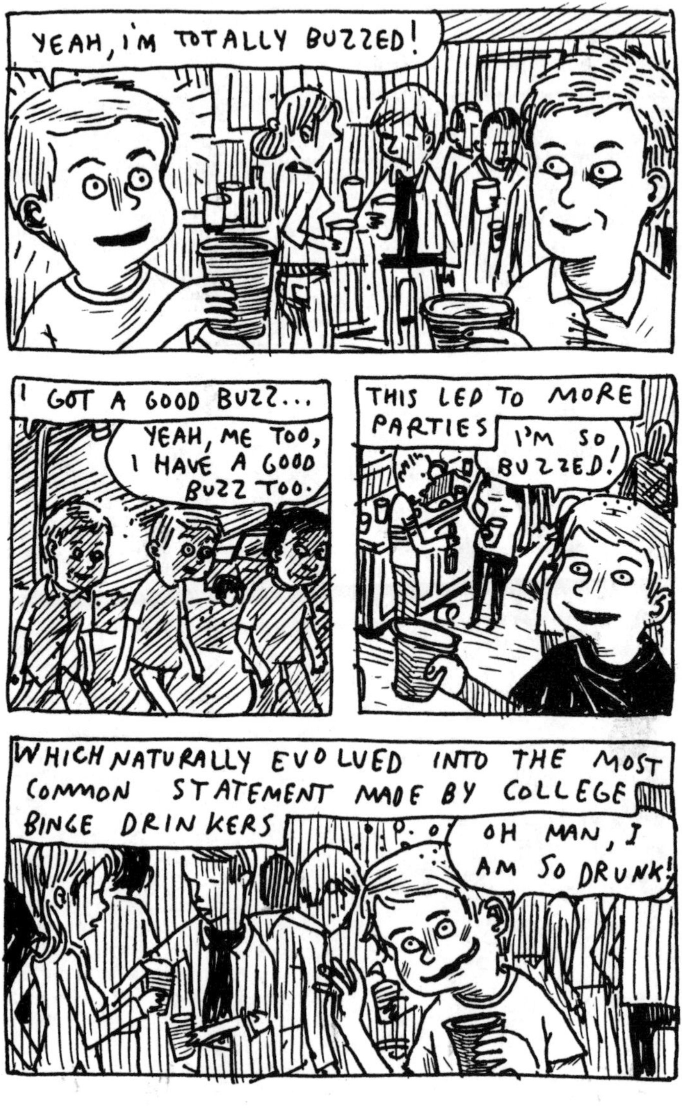
YEAH, I'M TOTALLY BUZZED!
I GOT A GOOD BUZZ...
YEAH, ME TOO, I HAVE A GOOD BUZZ TOO.
THIS LED TO MORE PARTIES
I'M SO BUZZED!
WHICH NATURALLY EVOLVED INTO THE MOST COMMON STATEMENT MADE BY COLLEGE BINGE DRINKERS
OH MAN, I AM SO DRUNK!

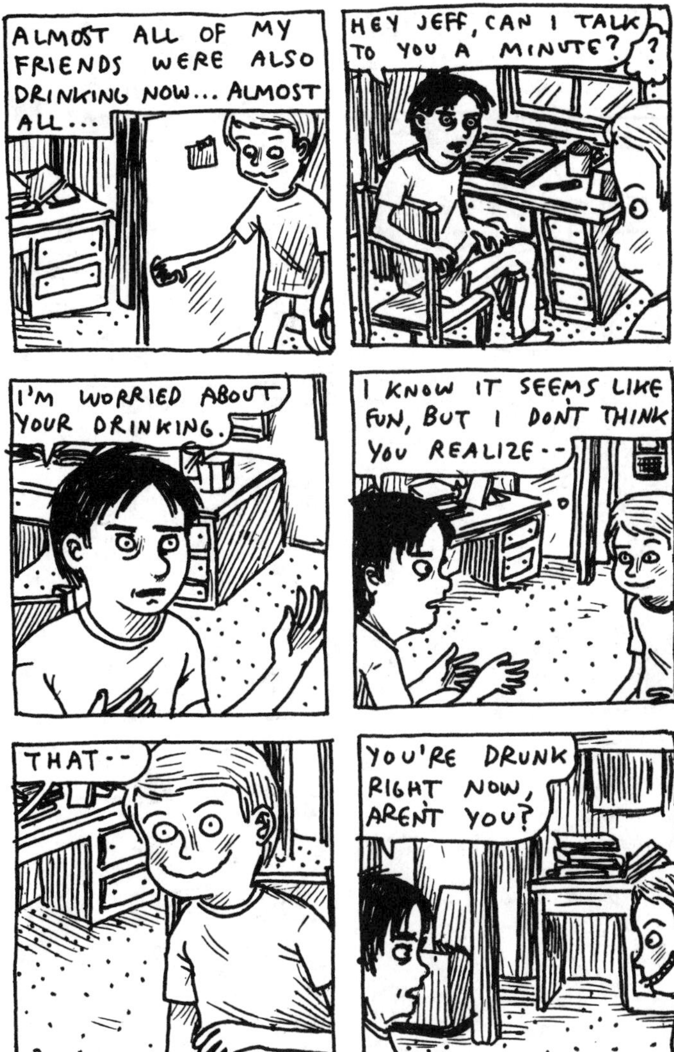
ALMOST ALL OF MY FRIENDS WERE ALSO DRINKING NOW... ALMOST ALL...
HEY JEFF, CAN I TALK TO YOU A MINUTE?
?
I'M WORRIED ABOUT YOUR DRINKING.
I KNOW IT SEEMS LIKE FUN, BUT I DON'T THINK YOU REALIZE--
THAT--
YOU'RE DRUNK RIGHT NOW, AREN'T YOU?

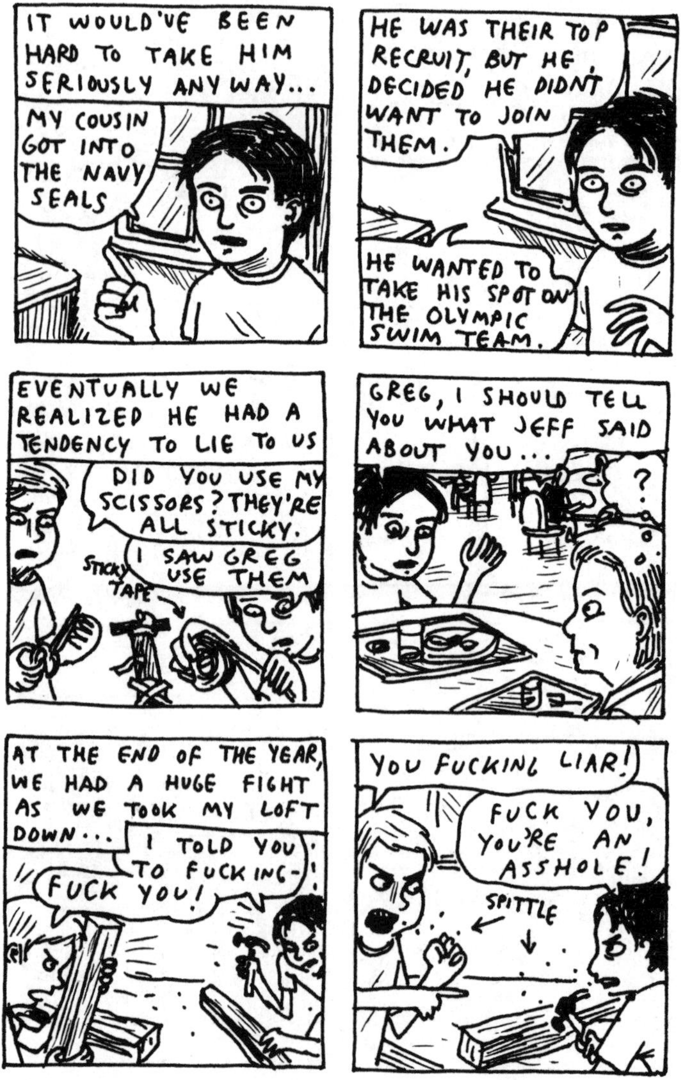
IT WOULD'VE BEEN HARD TO TAKE HIM SERIOUSLY ANYWAY...
MY COUSIN GOT INTO THE NAVY SEALS
HE WAS THEIR TOP RECRUIT, BUT HE DECIDED HE DIDN'T WANT TO JOIN THEM.
HE WANTED TO TAKE HIS SPOT ON THE OLYMPIC SWIM TEAM.
EVENTUALLY WE REALIZED HE HAD A TENDENCY TO LIE TO US
DID YOU USE MY SCISSORS? THEY'RE ALL STICKY.
I SAW GREG USE THEM
STICKY TAPE
GREG, I SHOULD TELL YOU WHAT JEFF SAID ABOUT YOU...
?
AT THE END OF THE YEAR, WE HAD A HUGE FIGHT AS WE TOOK MY LOFT DOWN...
I TOLD YOU TO FUCKING-
FUCK YOU!
YOU FUCKING LIAR!
FUCK YOU, YOU'RE AN ASSHOLE!
SPITTLE

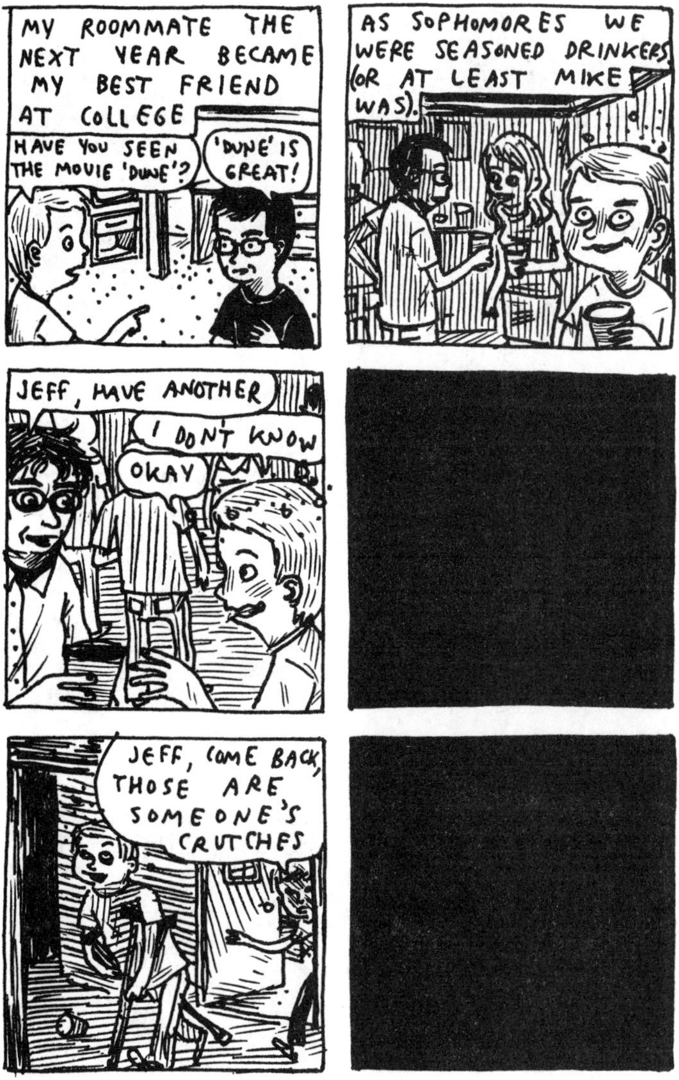
MY ROOMMATE THE NEXT YEAR BECAME MY BEST FRIEND AT COLLEGE
HAVE YOU SEEN THE MOVIE 'DUNE'?
'DUNE' IS GREAT!
AS SOPHOMORES WE WERE SEASONED DRINKERS (OR AT LEAST MIKE WAS).
JEFF, HAVE ANOTHER
I DON'T KNOW
OKAY
JEFF, COME BACK, THOSE ARE SOMEONE'S CRUTCHES

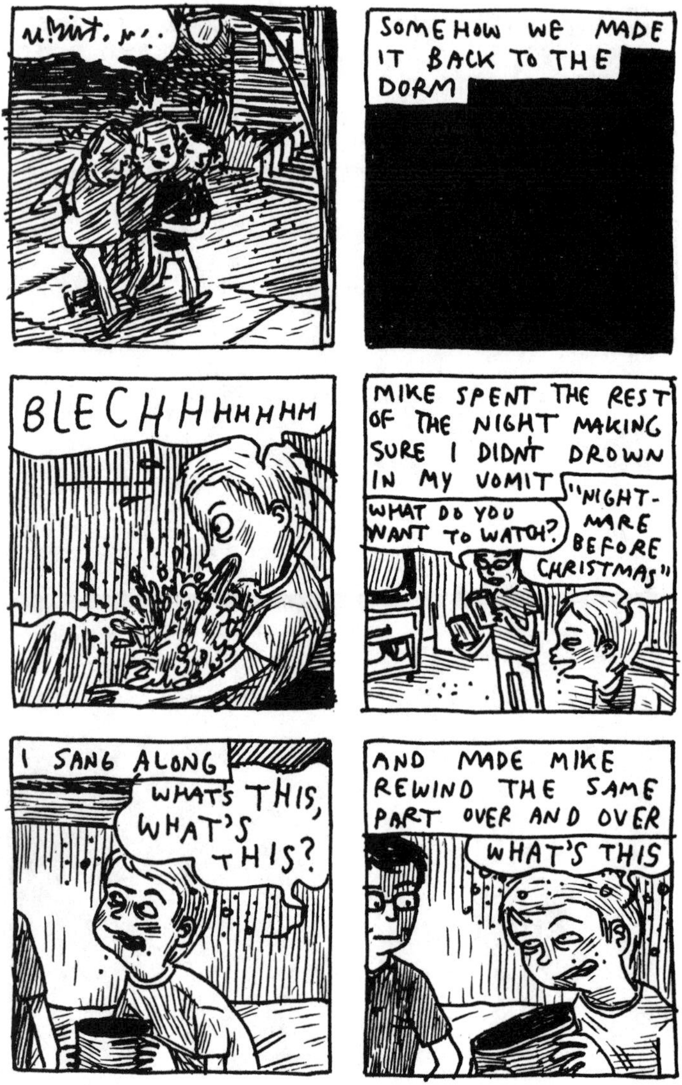
SOMEHOW WE MADE IT BACK TO THE DORM
BLECHHHHHHH
MIKE SPENT THE REST OF THE NIGHT MAKING SURE I DIDN'T DROWN IN MY VOMIT
WHAT DO YOU WANT TO WATCH?
"NIGHT-MARE BEFORE CHRISTMAS"
I SANG ALONG
WHAT'S THIS, WHAT'S THIS?
AND MADE MIKE REWIND THE SAME PART OVER AND OVER
WHAT'S THIS

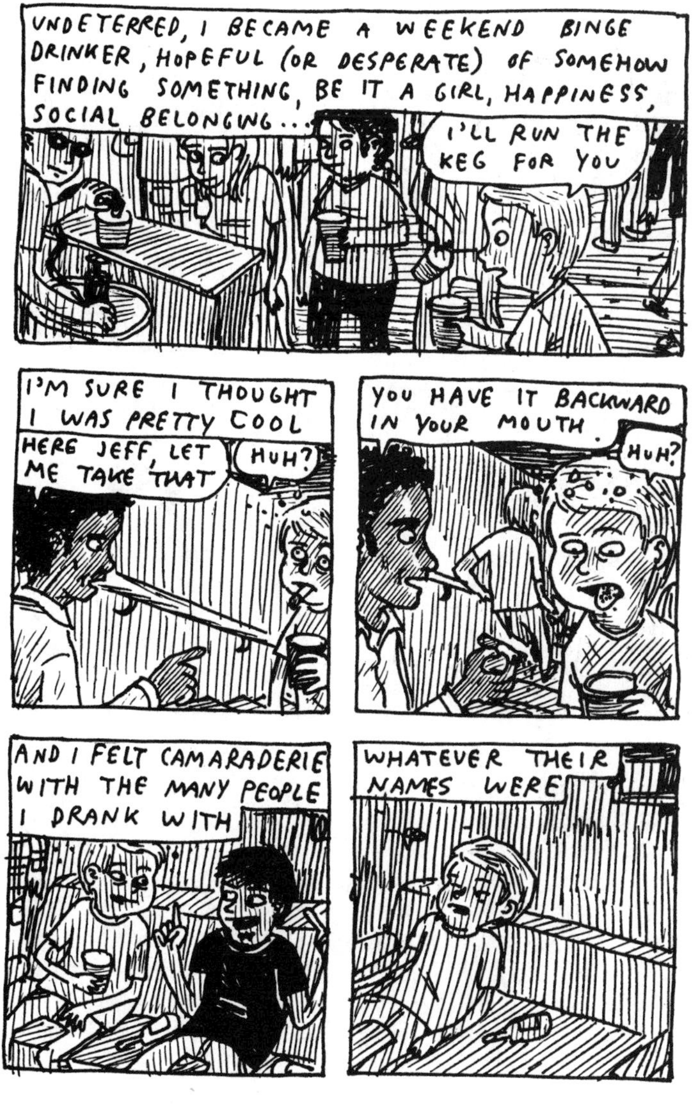
UNDETERRED, I BECAME A WEEKEND BINGE DRINKER, HOPEFUL (OR DESPERATE) OF SOMEHOW FINDING SOMETHING, BE IT A GIRL, HAPPINESS, SOCIAL BELONGING...
I'LL RUN THE KEG FOR YOU
I'M SURE I THOUGHT I WAS PRETTY COOL
HERE JEFF, LET ME TAKE THAT
HUH?
YOU HAVE IT BACKWARD IN YOUR MOUTH.
HUH?
AND I FELT CAMARADERIE WITH THE MANY PEOPLE I DRANK WITH
WHATEVER THEIR NAMES WERE

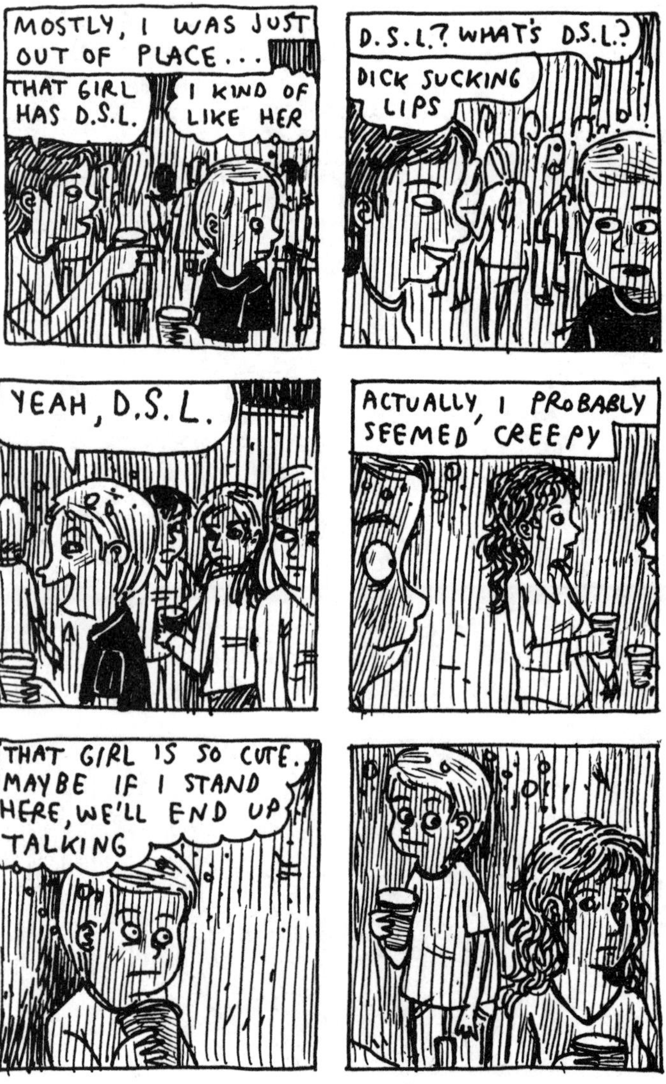
MOSTLY, I WAS JUST OUT OF PLACE...
THAT GIRL HAS D.S.L.
I KIND OF LIKE HER
D.S.L.? WHAT'S D.S.L.?
DICK SUCKING LIPS
YEAH, D.S.L.
ACTUALLY, I PROBABLY SEEMED CREEPY
THAT GIRL IS SO CUTE. MAYBE IF I STAND HERE, WE'LL END UP TALKING

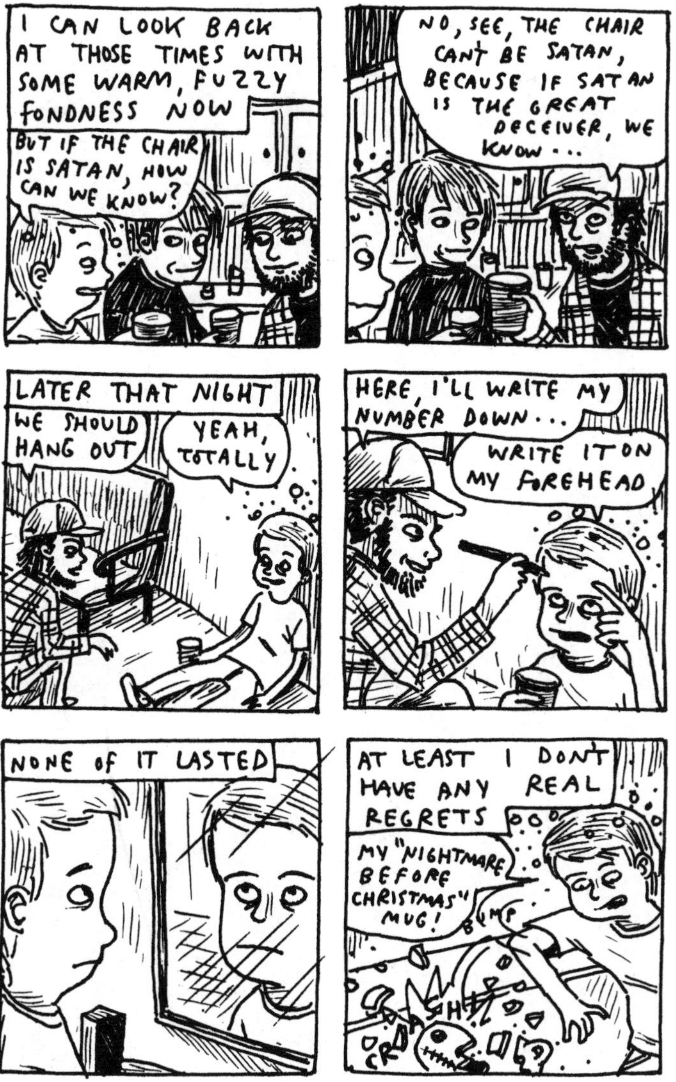
I CAN LOOK BACK AT THOSE TIMES WITH SOME WARM, FUZZY FONDNESS NOW
BUT IF THE CHAIR IS SATAN, HOW CAN WE KNOW?
NO, SEE, THE CHAIR CAN'T BE SATAN, BECAUSE IF SATAN IS THE GREAT DECEIVER, WE KNOW...
LATER THAT NIGHT
WE SHOULD HANG OUT
YEAH, TOTALLY
HERE, I'LL WRITE MY NUMBER DOWN...
WRITE IT ON MY FOREHEAD
NONE OF IT LASTED
AT LEAST I DON'T HAVE ANY REAL REGRETS
MY "NIGHTMARE BEFORE CHRISTMAS" MUG!

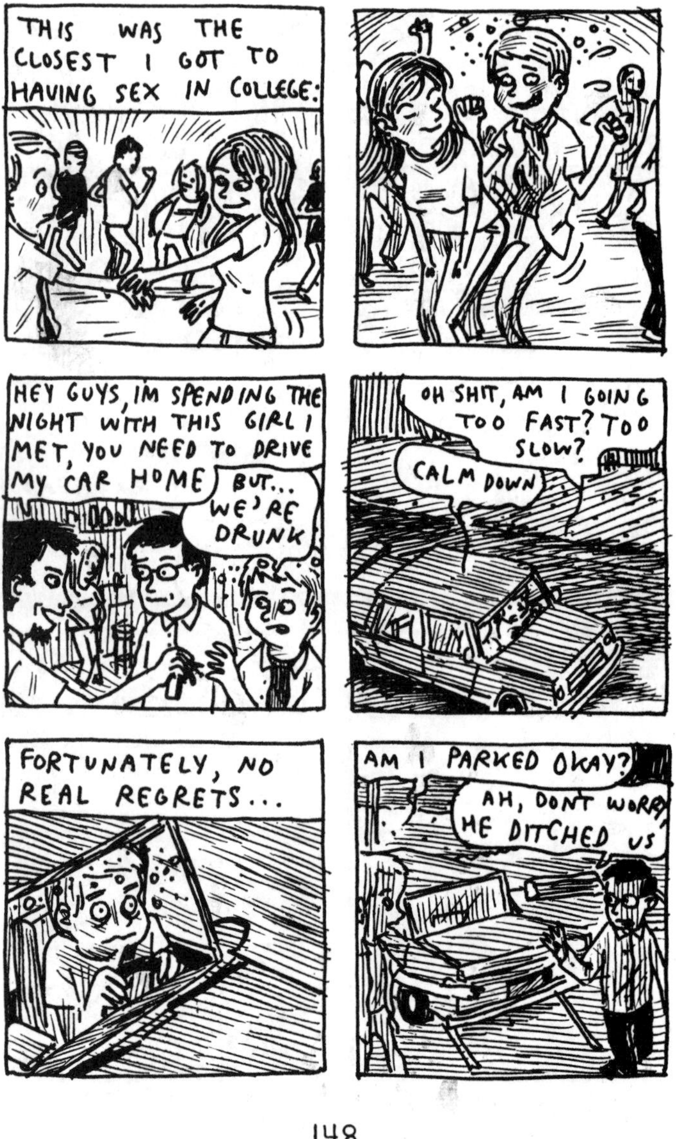
THIS WAS THE CLOSEST I GOT TO HAVING SEX IN COLLEGE:
HEY GUYS, IM SPENDING THE NIGHT WITH THIS GIRL I MET, YOU NEED TO DRIVE MY CAR HOME
BUT... WE'RE DRUNK
OH SHIT, AM I GOING TOO FAST? TOO SLOW?
CALM DOWN
FORTUNATELY, NO REAL REGRETS...
AM I PARKED OKAY?
AH, DONT WORRY, HE DITCHED US

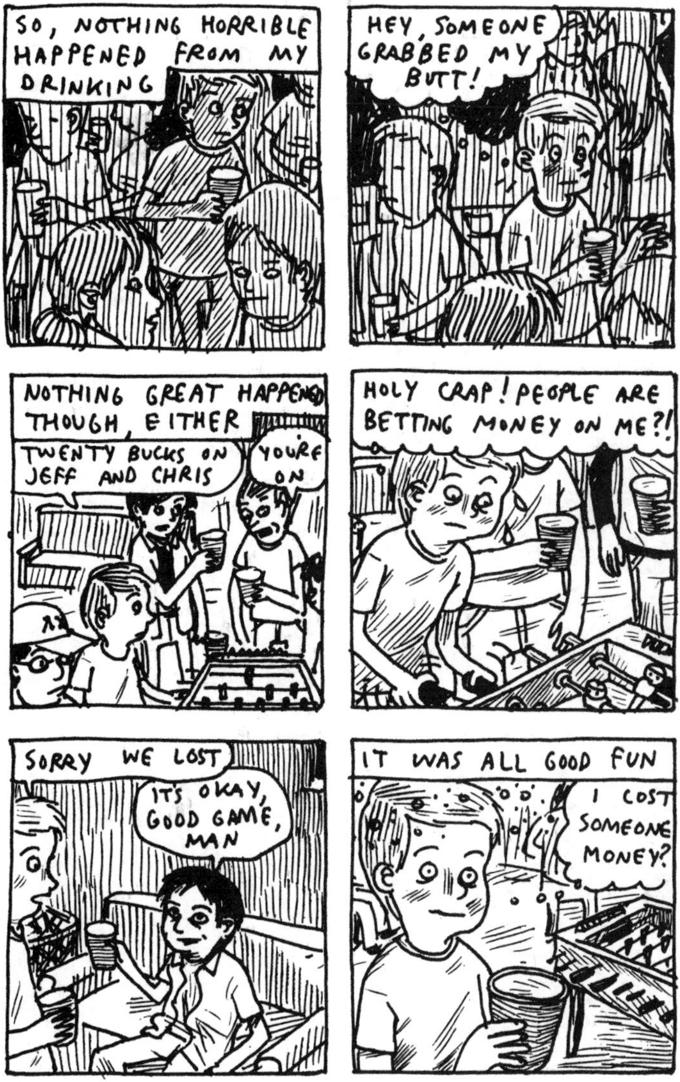
SO, NOTHING HORRIBLE HAPPENED FROM MY DRINKING
HEY, SOMEONE GRABBED MY BUTT!
NOTHING GREAT HAPPENED THOUGH, EITHER
TWENTY BUCKS ON JEFF AND CHRIS
YOU'RE ON
HOLY CRAP! PEOPLE ARE BETTING MONEY ON ME?!
SORRY WE LOST
IT'S OKAY, GOOD GAME, MAN
IT WAS ALL GOOD FUN
I COST SOMEONE MONEY?

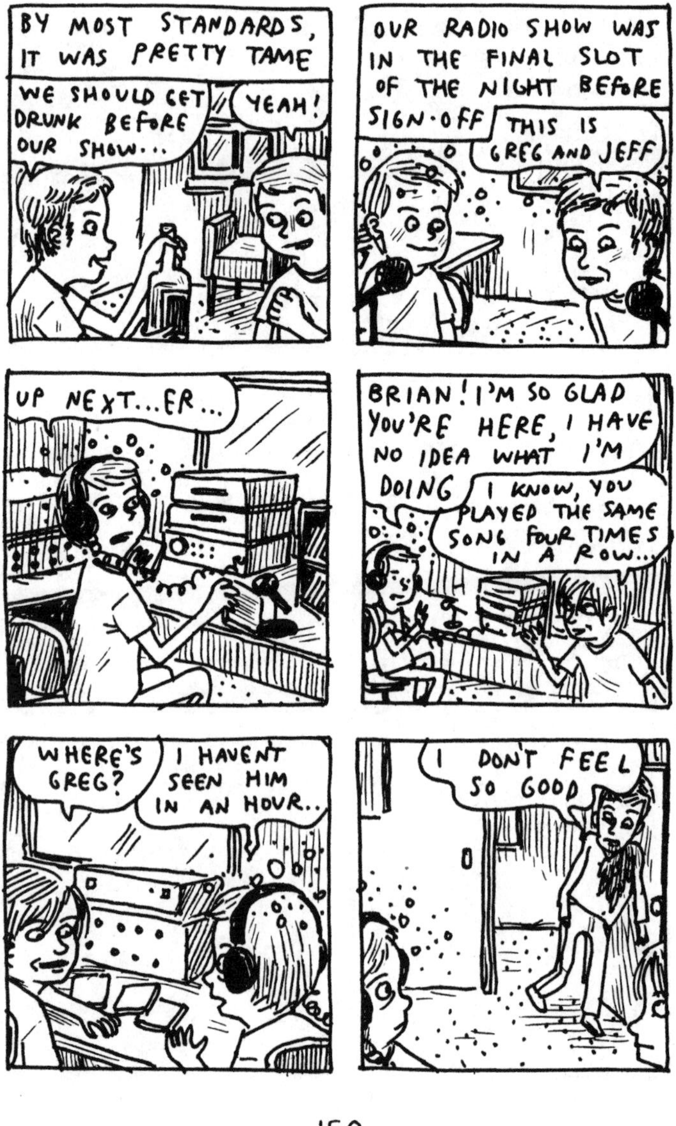
BY MOST STANDARDS, IT WAS PRETTY TAME
WE SHOULD GET DRUNK BEFORE OUR SHOW...
YEAH!
OUR RADIO SHOW WAS IN THE FINAL SLOT OF THE NIGHT BEFORE SIGN-OFF
THIS IS GREG AND JEFF
UP NEXT...ER...
BRIAN! I'M SO GLAD YOU'RE HERE, I HAVE NO IDEA WHAT I'M DOING
I KNOW, YOU PLAYED THE SAME SONG FOUR TIMES IN A ROW...
WHERE'S GREG?
I HAVENT SEEN HIM IN AN HOUR..
I DON'T FEEL SO GOOD

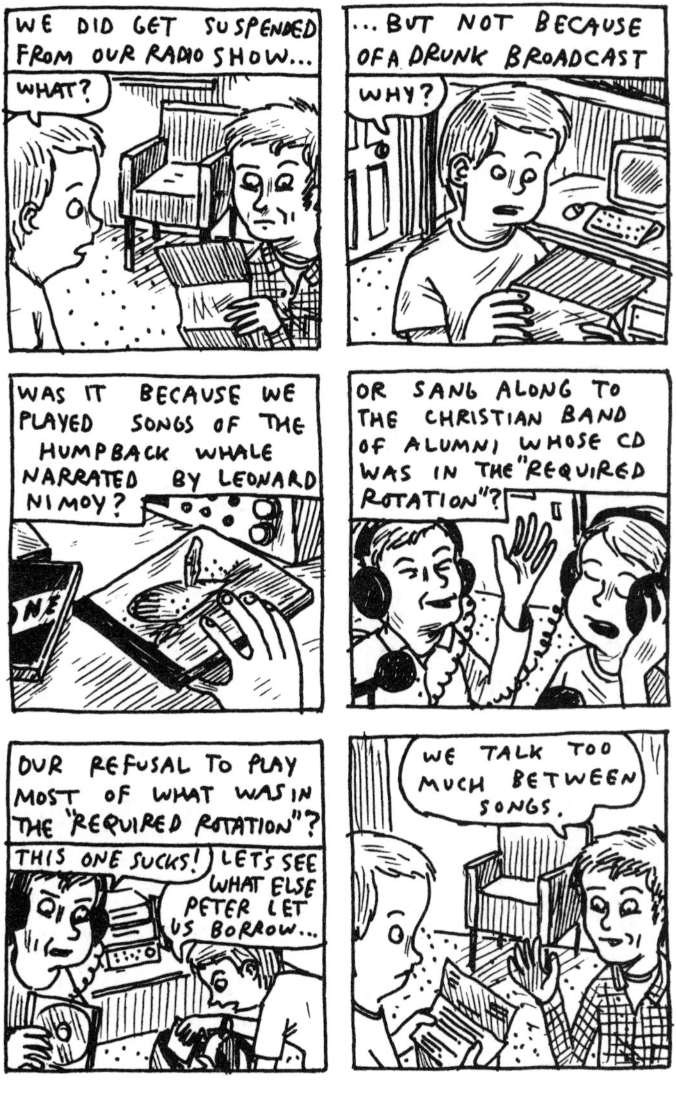
WE DID GET SUSPENDED FROM OUR RADIO SHOW...
WHAT?
...BUT NOT BECAUSE OF A DRUNK BROADCAST
WHY?
WAS IT BECAUSE WE PLAYED SONGS OF THE HUMPBACK WHALE NARRATED BY LEONARD NIMOY?
OR SANG ALONG TO THE CHRISTIAN BAND OF ALUMNI WHOSE CD WAS IN THE "REQUIRED ROTATION"?
OUR REFUSAL TO PLAY MOST OF WHAT WAS IN THE "REQUIRED ROTATION"?
THIS ONE SUCKS!
LET'S SEE WHAT ELSE PETER LET US BORROW...
WE TALK TOO MUCH BETWEEN SONGS.

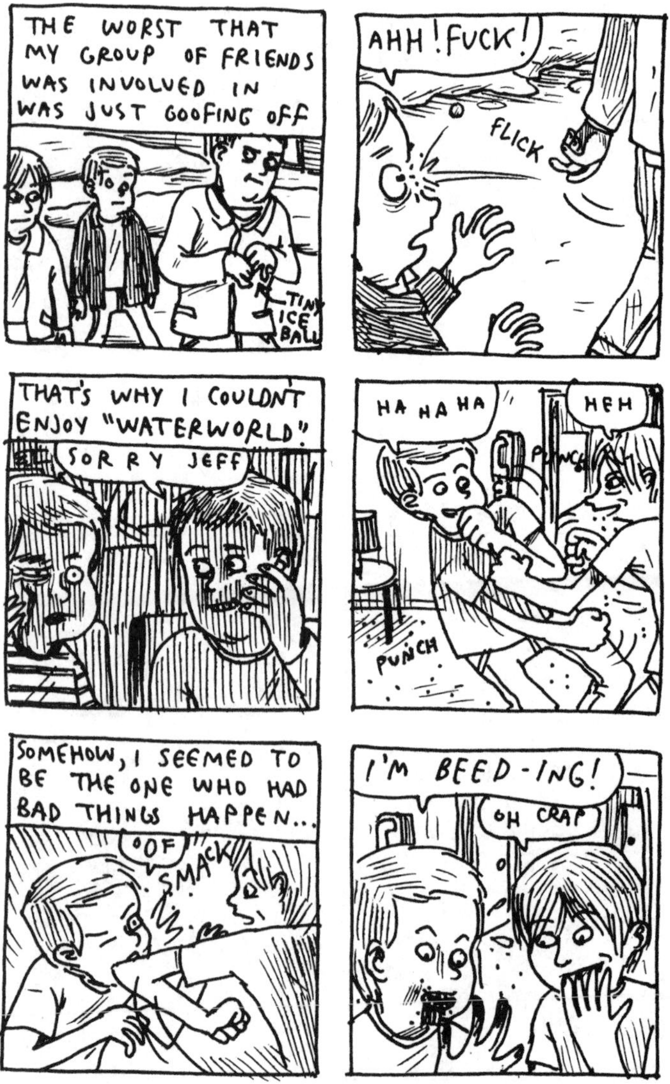
THE WORST THAT MY GROUP OF FRIENDS WAS INVOLVED IN WAS JUST GOOFING OFF
TINY ICE BALL
AHH! FUCK!
FLICK
THAT'S WHY I COULDN'T ENJOY "WATERWORLD"
SORRY JEFF
HA HA HA
HEH
PUNCH
PUNCH
SOMEHOW, I SEEMED TO BE THE ONE WHO HAD BAD THINGS HAPPEN...
OOF
SMACK
I'M BEED-ING!
OH CRAP

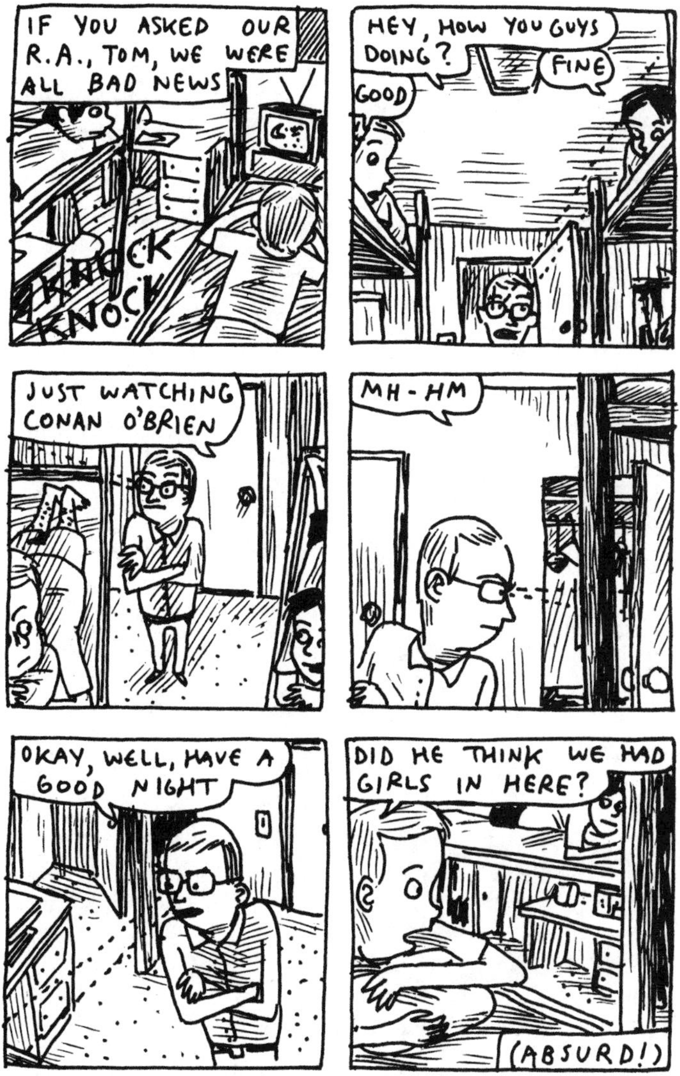
IF YOU ASKED OUR R.A., TOM, WE WERE ALL BAD NEWS
KNOCK KNOCK
HEY, HOW YOU GUYS DOING?
FINE
GOOD
JUST WATCHING CONAN O'BRIEN
MH-HM
OKAY, WELL, HAVE A GOOD NIGHT
DID HE THINK WE HAD GIRLS IN HERE?
(ABSURD!)

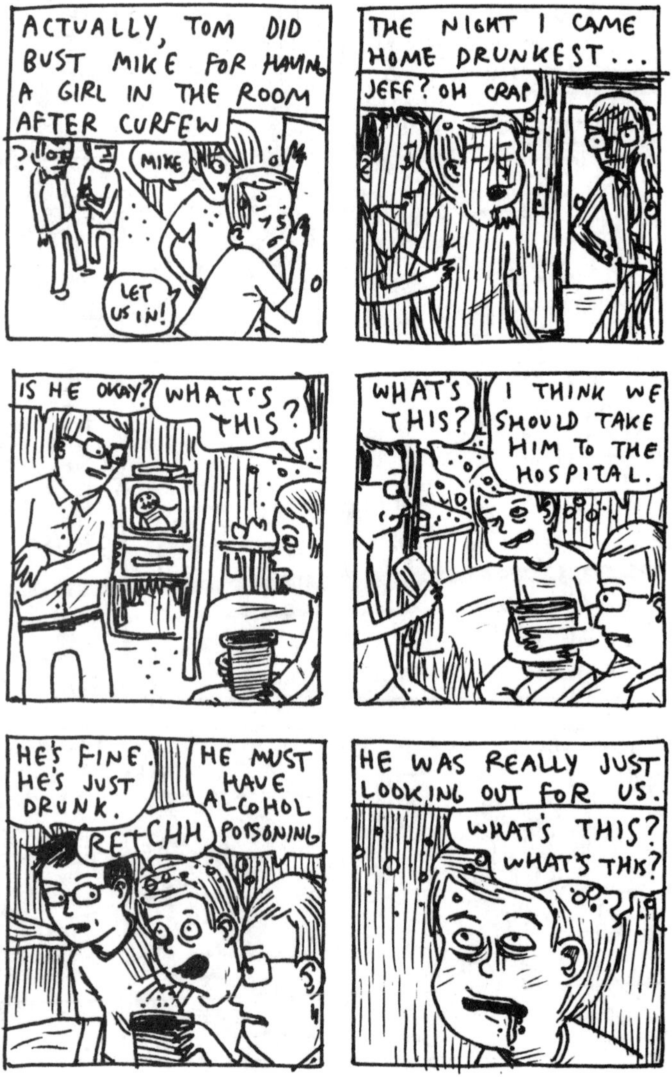
ACTUALLY, TOM DID BUST MIKE FOR HAVING A GIRL IN THE ROOM AFTER CURFEW
MIKE
LET US IN!
THE NIGHT I CAME HOME DRUNKEST...
JEFF? OH CRAP
IS HE OKAY?
WHAT'S THIS?
WHAT'S THIS?
I THINK WE SHOULD TAKE HIM TO THE HOSPITAL.
HE'S FINE. HE'S JUST DRUNK.
HE MUST HAVE ALCOHOL POISONING
RETCHH
HE WAS REALLY JUST LOOKING OUT FOR US.
WHAT'S THIS?
WHAT'S THIS?

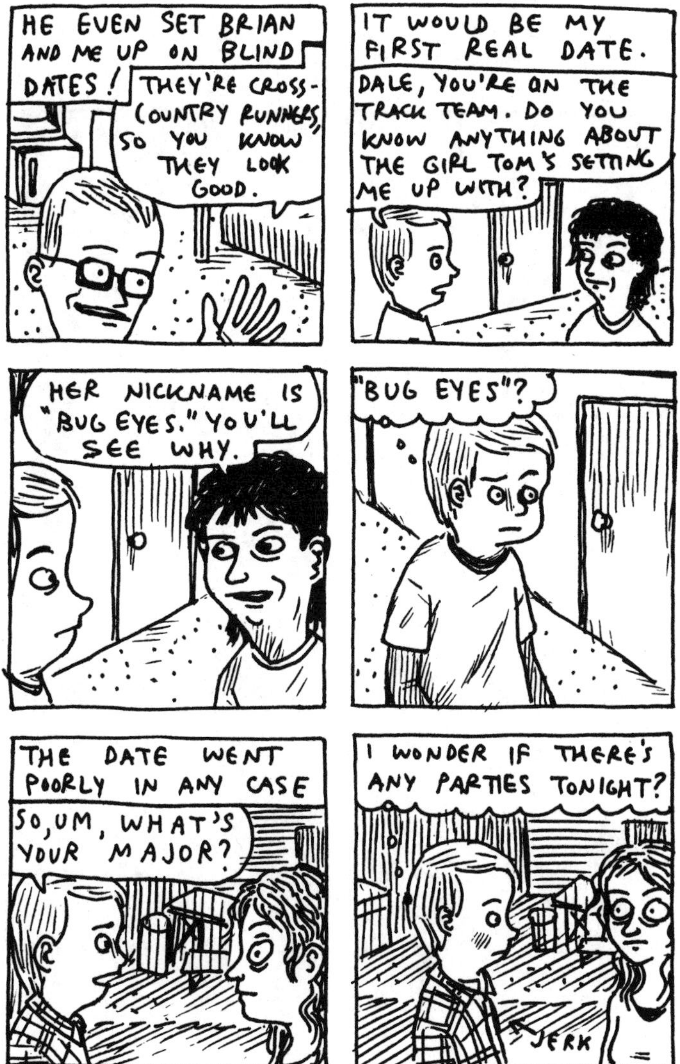
HE EVEN SET BRIAN AND ME UP ON BLIND DATES!
THEY'RE CROSS-COUNTRY RUNNERS, SO YOU KNOW THEY LOOK GOOD.
IT WOULD BE MY FIRST REAL DATE.
DALE, YOU'RE ON THE TRACK TEAM. DO YOU KNOW ANYTHING ABOUT THE GIRL TOM'S SETTING ME UP WITH?
HER NICKNAME IS "BUG EYES." YOU'LL SEE WHY.
"BUG EYES"?
THE DATE WENT POORLY IN ANY CASE
SO, UM, WHAT'S YOUR MAJOR?
I WONDER IF THERE'S ANY PARTIES TONIGHT?
JERK

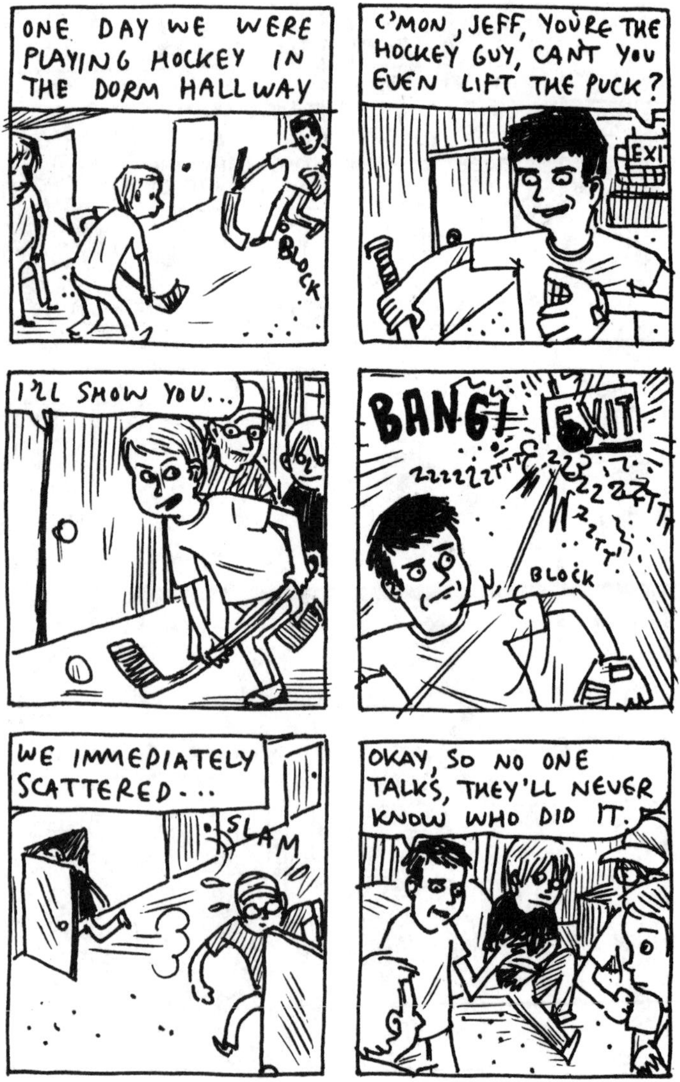
ONE DAY WE WERE PLAYING HOCKEY IN THE DORM HALLWAY
BLOCK
C'MON, JEFF, YOU'RE THE HOCKEY GUY, CAN'T YOU EVEN LIFT THE PUCK?
EXIT
I'LL SHOW YOU...
BANG!
EXIT
ZZZZZZTTT
BLOCK
WE IMMEDIATELY SCATTERED...
SLAM
OKAY, SO NO ONE TALKS, THEY'LL NEVER KNOW WHO DID IT.

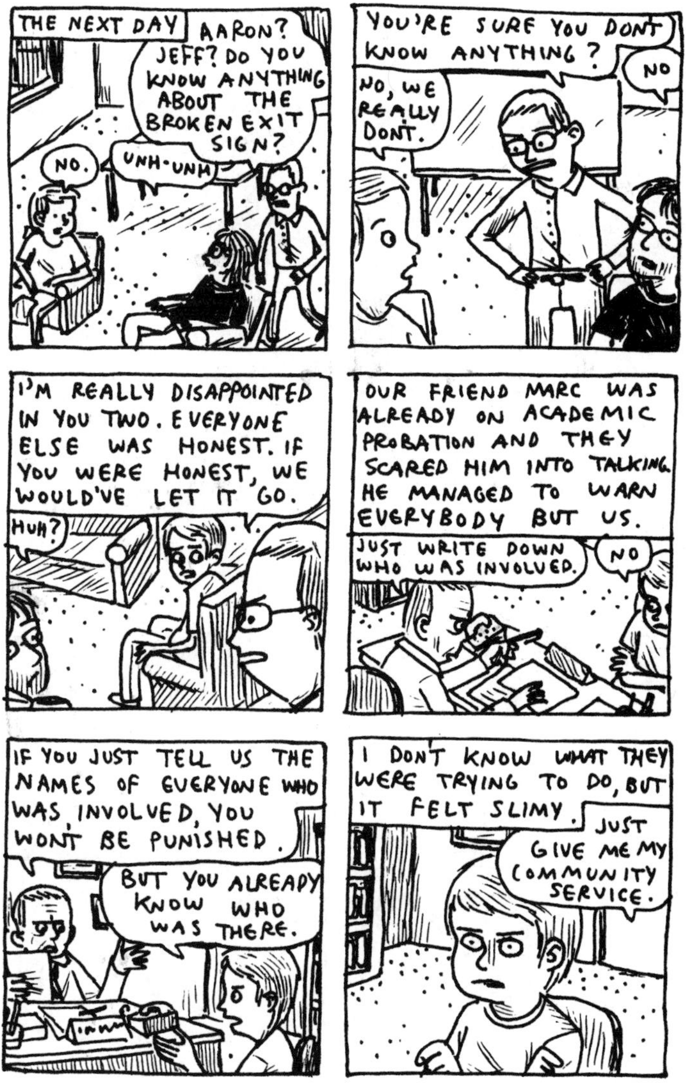
THE NEXT DAY
AARON? JEFF? DO YOU KNOW ANYTHING ABOUT THE BROKEN EXIT SIGN?
NO.
UNH-UNH
YOU'RE SURE YOU DON'T KNOW ANYTHING?
NO, WE REALLY DON'T.
NO
I'M REALLY DISAPPOINTED IN YOU TWO. EVERYONE ELSE WAS HONEST. IF YOU WERE HONEST, WE WOULD'VE LET IT GO.
HUH?
OUR FRIEND MARC WAS ALREADY ON ACADEMIC PROBATION AND THEY SCARED HIM INTO TALKING. HE MANAGED TO WARN EVERYBODY BUT US.
JUST WRITE DOWN WHO WAS INVOLVED.
NO
IF YOU JUST TELL US THE NAMES OF EVERYONE WHO WAS INVOLVED, YOU WON'T BE PUNISHED.
BUT YOU ALREADY KNOW WHO WAS THERE.
I DON'T KNOW WHAT THEY WERE TRYING TO DO, BUT IT FELT SLIMY.
JUST GIVE ME MY COMMUNITY SERVICE.

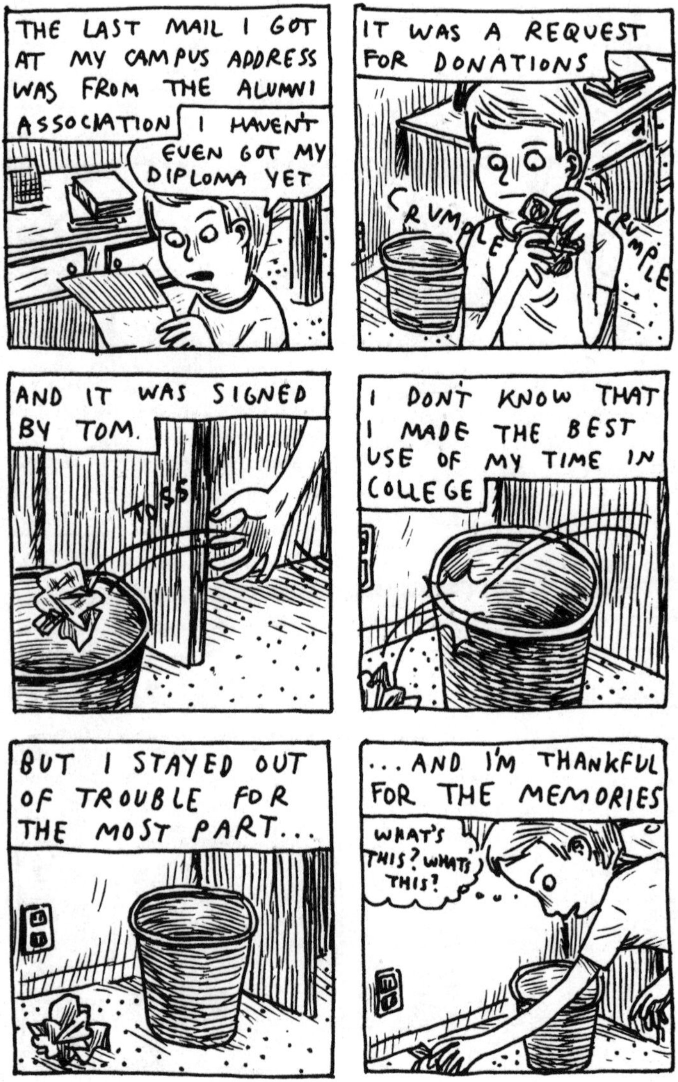
THE LAST MAIL I GOT AT MY CAMPUS ADDRESS WAS FROM THE ALUMNI ASSOCIATION
I HAVEN'T EVEN GOT MY DIPLOMA YET
IT WAS A REQUEST FOR DONATIONS
CRUMPLE
CRUMPLE
AND IT WAS SIGNED BY TOM.
TOSS
I DON'T KNOW THAT I MADE THE BEST USE OF MY TIME IN COLLEGE
BUT I STAYED OUT OF TROUBLE FOR THE MOST PART...
...AND I'M THANKFUL FOR THE MEMORIES
WHAT'S THIS? WHAT'S THIS?

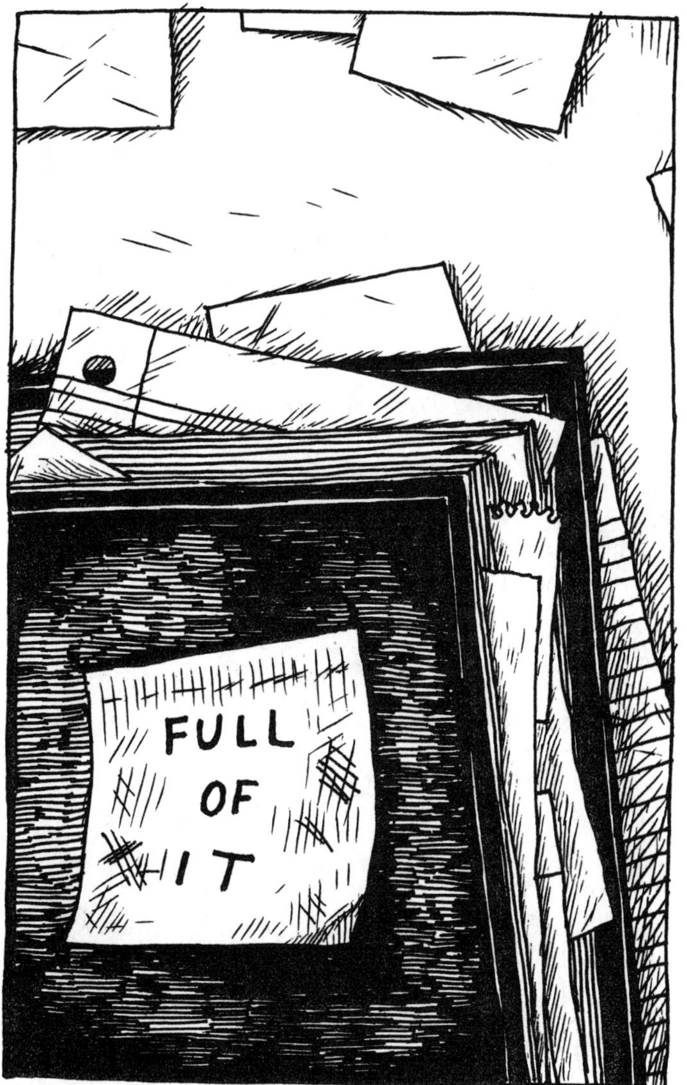
FULL
OF
IT

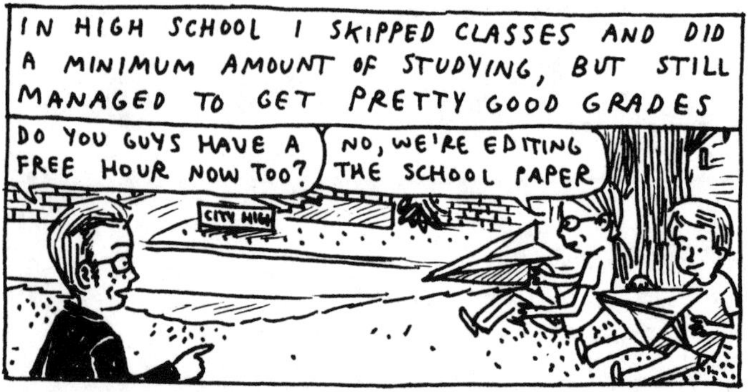
IN HIGH SCHOOL I SKIPPED CLASSES AND DID A MINIMUM AMOUNT OF STUDYING, BUT STILL MANAGED TO GET PRETTY GOOD GRADES
DO YOU GUYS HAVE A FREE HOUR NOW TOO?
NO, WE'RE EDITING THE SCHOOL PAPER
CITY HIGH

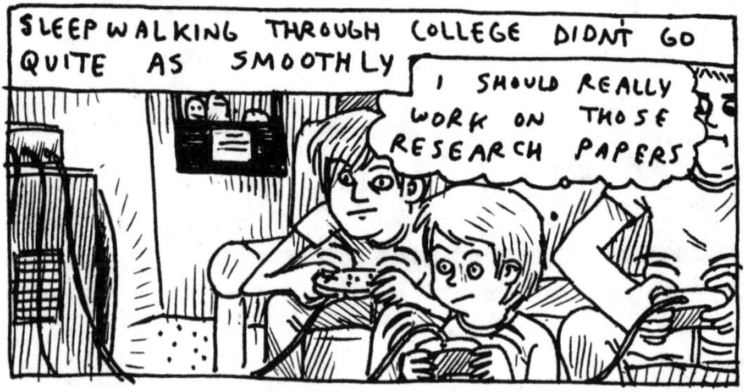
SLEEPWALKING THROUGH COLLEGE DIDN'T GO QUITE AS SMOOTHLY
I SHOULD REALLY WORK ON THOSE RESEARCH PAPERS

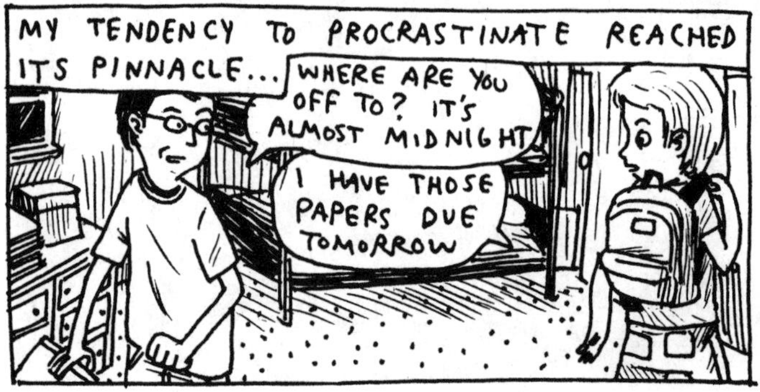
MY TENDENCY TO PROCRASTINATE REACHED ITS PINNACLE...
WHERE ARE YOU OFF TO? IT'S ALMOST MIDNIGHT
I HAVE THOSE PAPERS DUE TOMORROW

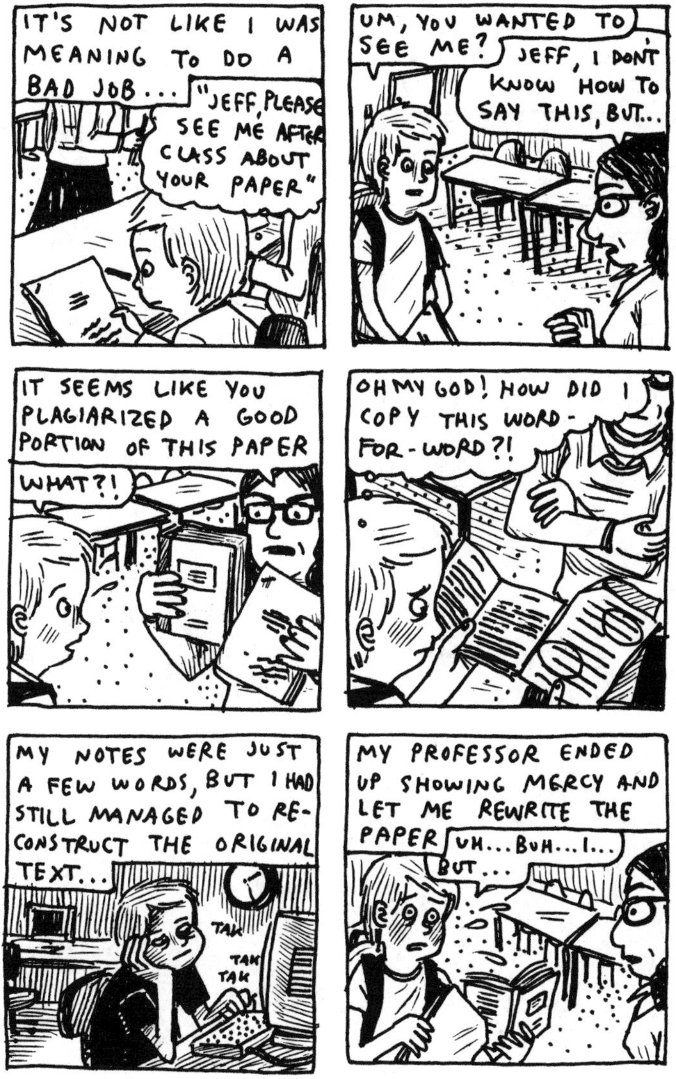
IT'S NOT LIKE I WAS MEANING TO DO A BAD JOB...
"JEFF, PLEASE SEE ME AFTER CLASS ABOUT YOUR PAPER"
UM, YOU WANTED TO SEE ME?
JEFF, I DON'T KNOW HOW TO SAY THIS, BUT...
IT SEEMS LIKE YOU PLAGIARIZED A GOOD PORTION OF THIS PAPER
WHAT?!
OH MY GOD! HOW DID I COPY THIS WORD-FOR-WORD?!
MY NOTES WERE JUST A FEW WORDS, BUT I HAD STILL MANAGED TO RE-CONSTRUCT THE ORIGINAL TEXT...
TAK
TAK
TAK
MY PROFESSOR ENDED UP SHOWING MERCY AND LET ME REWRITE THE PAPER
UH... BUH... I... BUT...

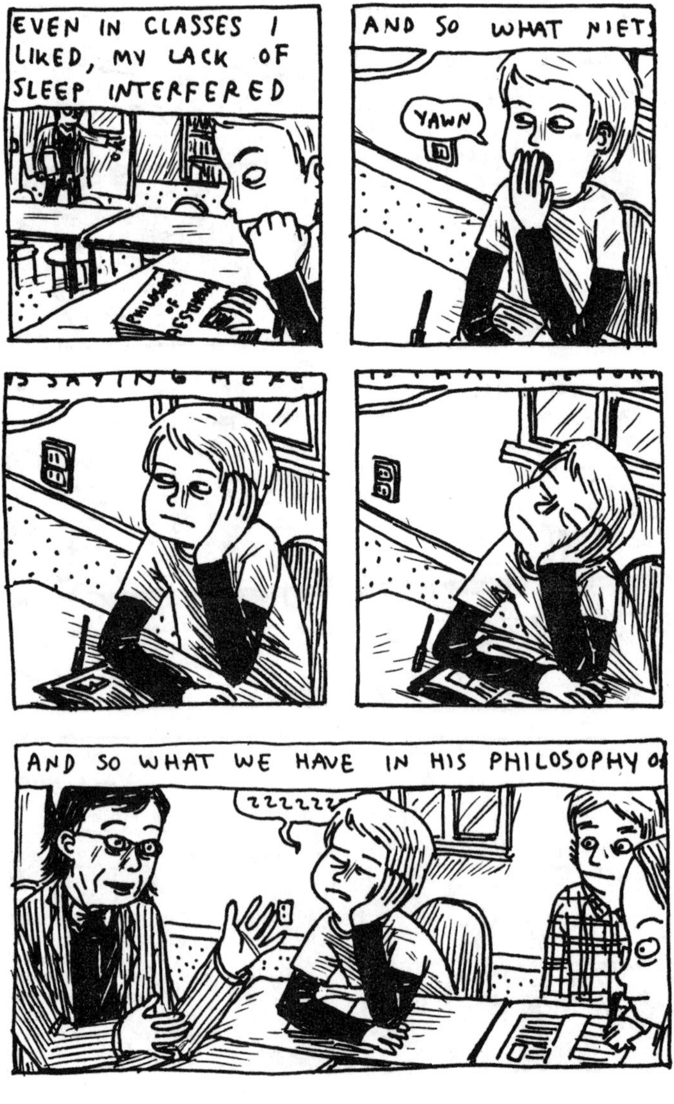
EVEN IN CLASSES I LIKED, MY LACK OF SLEEP INTERFERED
AND SO WHAT NIET
YAWN
AND SO WHAT WE HAVE IN HIS PHILOSOPHY O
ZZZZZZ

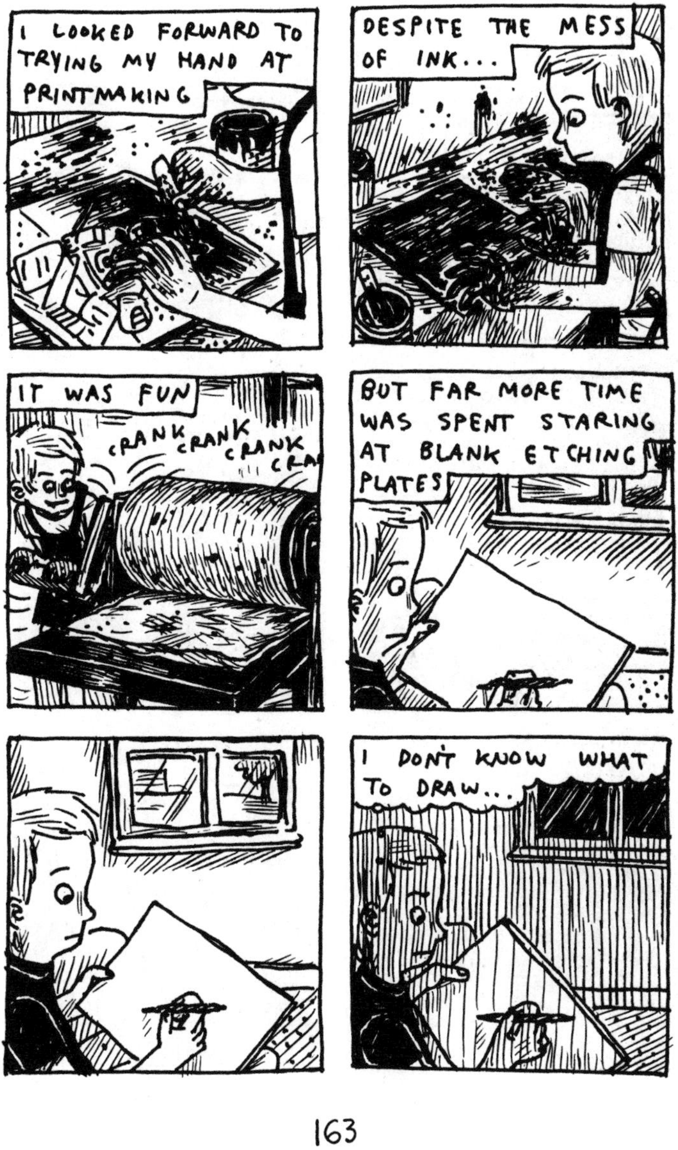
I LOOKED FORWARD TO TRYING MY HAND AT PRINTMAKING
DESPITE THE MESS OF INK...
IT WAS FUN
CRANK CRANK CRANK
BUT FAR MORE TIME WAS SPENT STARING AT BLANK ETCHING PLATES
I DON'T KNOW WHAT TO DRAW...

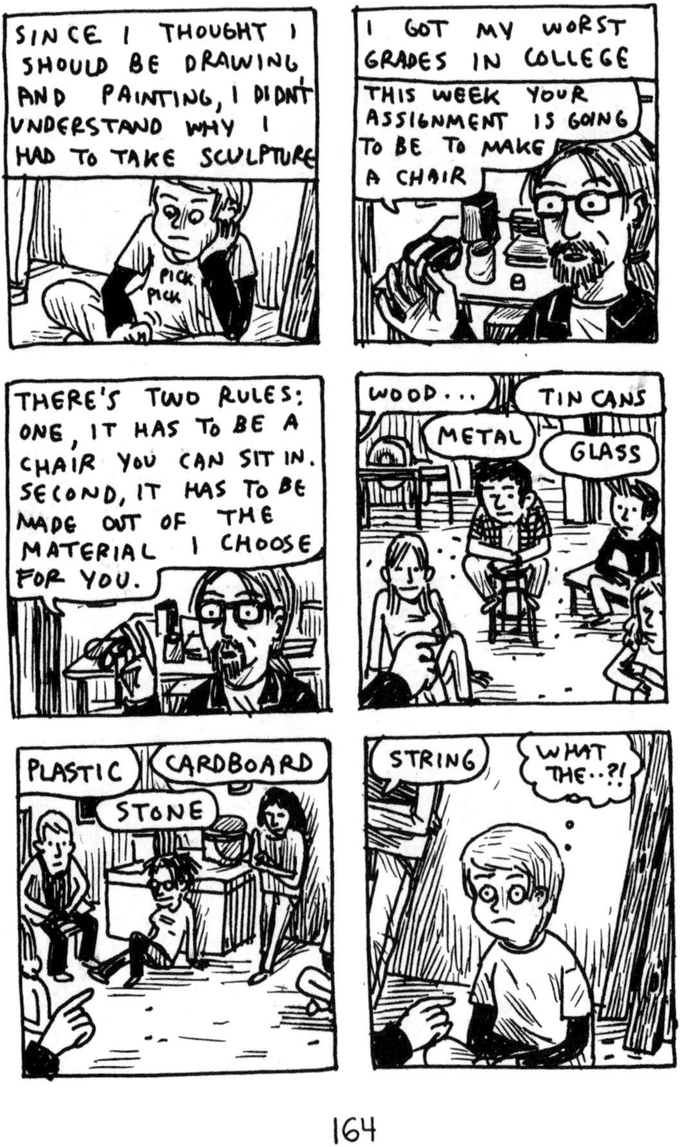
SINCE I THOUGHT I SHOULD BE DRAWING AND PAINTING, I DIDN'T UNDERSTAND WHY I HAD TO TAKE SCULPTURE
PICK PICK
I GOT MY WORST GRADES IN COLLEGE
THIS WEEK YOUR ASSIGNMENT IS GOING TO BE TO MAKE A CHAIR
THERE'S TWO RULES: ONE, IT HAS TO BE A CHAIR YOU CAN SIT IN. SECOND, IT HAS TO BE MADE OUT OF THE MATERIAL I CHOOSE FOR YOU.
WOOD...
TIN CANS
METAL
GLASS
PLASTIC
CARDBOARD
STONE
STRING
WHAT THE..?!

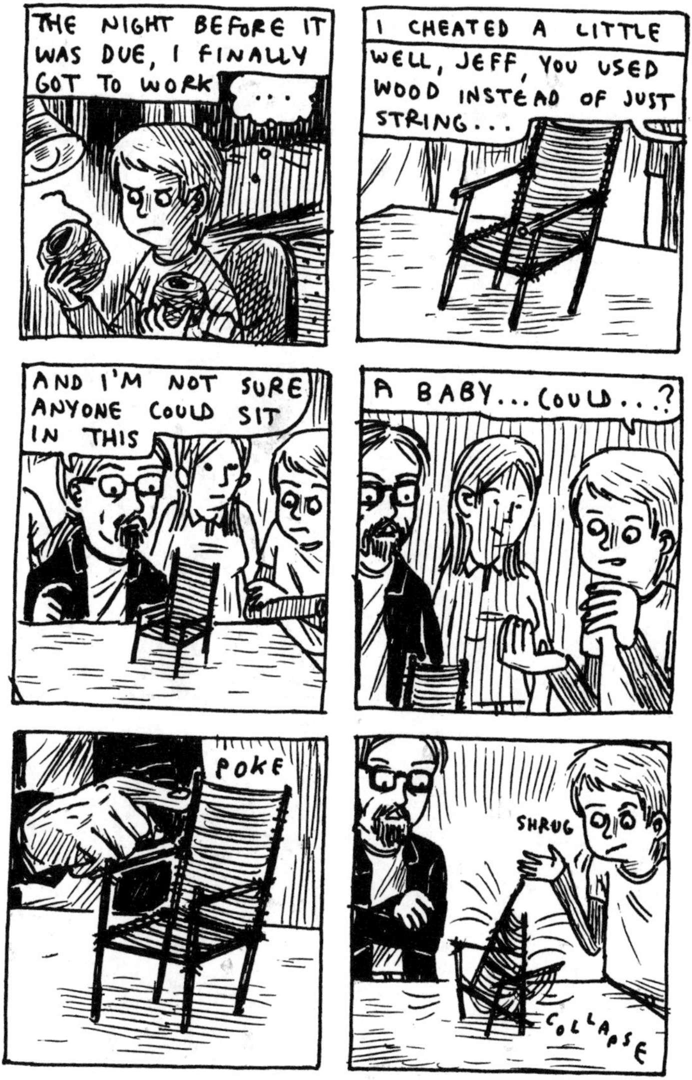
THE NIGHT BEFORE IT WAS DUE, I FINALLY GOT TO WORK
...
I CHEATED A LITTLE
WELL, JEFF, YOU USED WOOD INSTEAD OF JUST STRING...
AND I'M NOT SURE ANYONE COULD SIT IN THIS
A BABY... COULD...?
POKE
SHRUG
COLLAPSE

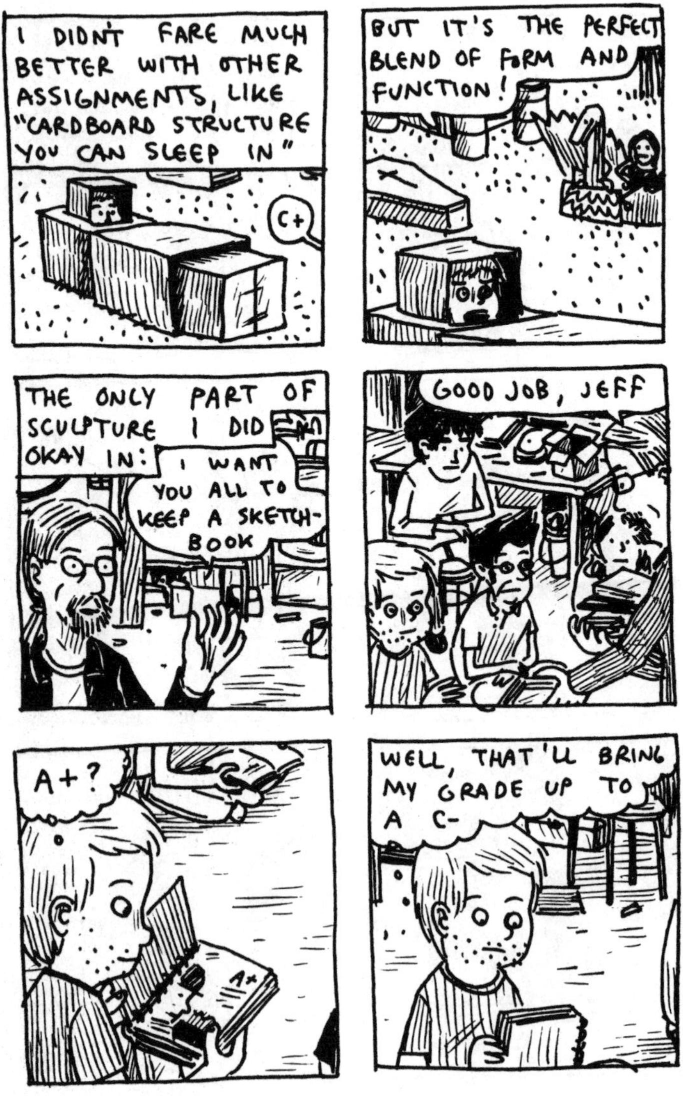
I DIDN'T FARE MUCH BETTER WITH OTHER ASSIGNMENTS, LIKE "CARDBOARD STRUCTURE YOU CAN SLEEP IN"
C+
BUT IT'S THE PERFECT BLEND OF FORM AND FUNCTION!
THE ONLY PART OF SCULPTURE I DID OKAY IN:
I WANT YOU ALL TO KEEP A SKETCH-BOOK
GOOD JOB, JEFF
A+?
A+
WELL, THAT'LL BRING MY GRADE UP TO A C-

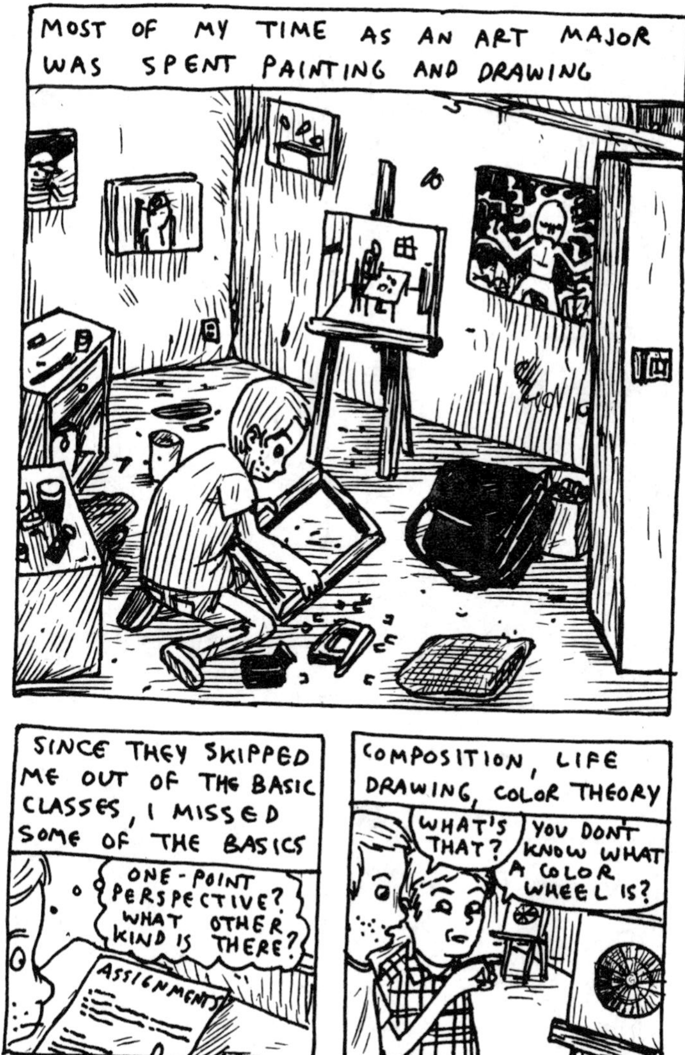
MOST OF MY TIME AS AN ART MAJOR WAS SPENT PAINTING AND DRAWING
SINCE THEY SKIPPED ME OUT OF THE BASIC CLASSES, I MISSED SOME OF THE BASICS
ONE-POINT PERSPECTIVE? WHAT OTHER KIND IS THERE?
ASSIGNMENT
COMPOSITION, LIFE DRAWING, COLOR THEORY
WHAT'S THAT?
YOU DON'T KNOW WHAT A COLOR WHEEL IS?

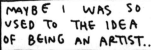
MAYBE I WAS SO USED TO THE IDEA OF BEING AN ARTIST...

I WASN'T REALLY WORKING TO BE ONE

LEFT MOSTLY TO MY OWN DEVICES, MY PAINTINGS WERE...

...UNREMARKABLE, AT BEST.

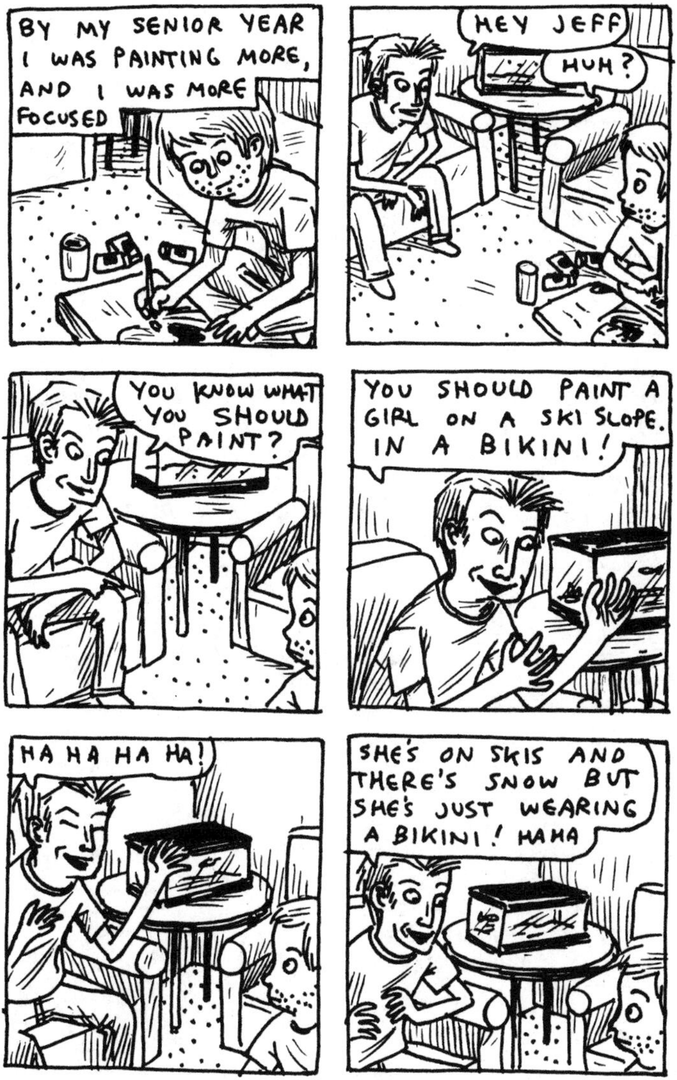
BY MY SENIOR YEAR I WAS PAINTING MORE, AND I WAS MORE FOCUSED
HEY JEFF
HUH?
YOU KNOW WHAT YOU SHOULD PAINT?
YOU SHOULD PAINT A GIRL ON A SKI SLOPE. IN A BIKINI!
HA HA HA HA!
SHE'S ON SKIS AND THERE'S SNOW BUT SHE'S JUST WEARING A BIKINI! HAHA

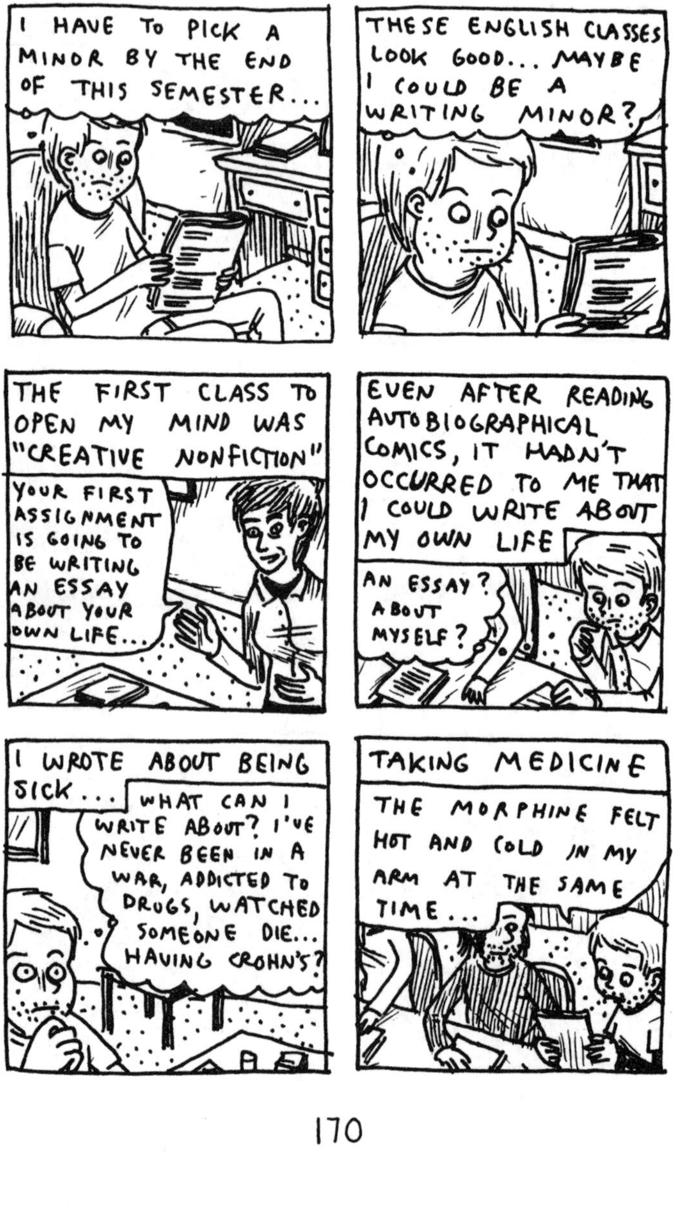
I HAVE TO PICK A MINOR BY THE END OF THIS SEMESTER...
THESE ENGLISH CLASSES LOOK GOOD... MAYBE I COULD BE A WRITING MINOR?
THE FIRST CLASS TO OPEN MY MIND WAS "CREATIVE NONFICTION"
YOUR FIRST ASSIGNMENT IS GOING TO BE WRITING AN ESSAY ABOUT YOUR OWN LIFE...
EVEN AFTER READING AUTOBIOGRAPHICAL COMICS, IT HADN'T OCCURRED TO ME THAT I COULD WRITE ABOUT MY OWN LIFE
AN ESSAY? ABOUT MYSELF?
I WROTE ABOUT BEING SICK...
WHAT CAN I WRITE ABOUT? I'VE NEVER BEEN IN A WAR, ADDICTED TO DRUGS, WATCHED SOMEONE DIE... HAVING CROHN'S?
TAKING MEDICINE
THE MORPHINE FELT HOT AND COLD IN MY ARM AT THE SAME TIME...

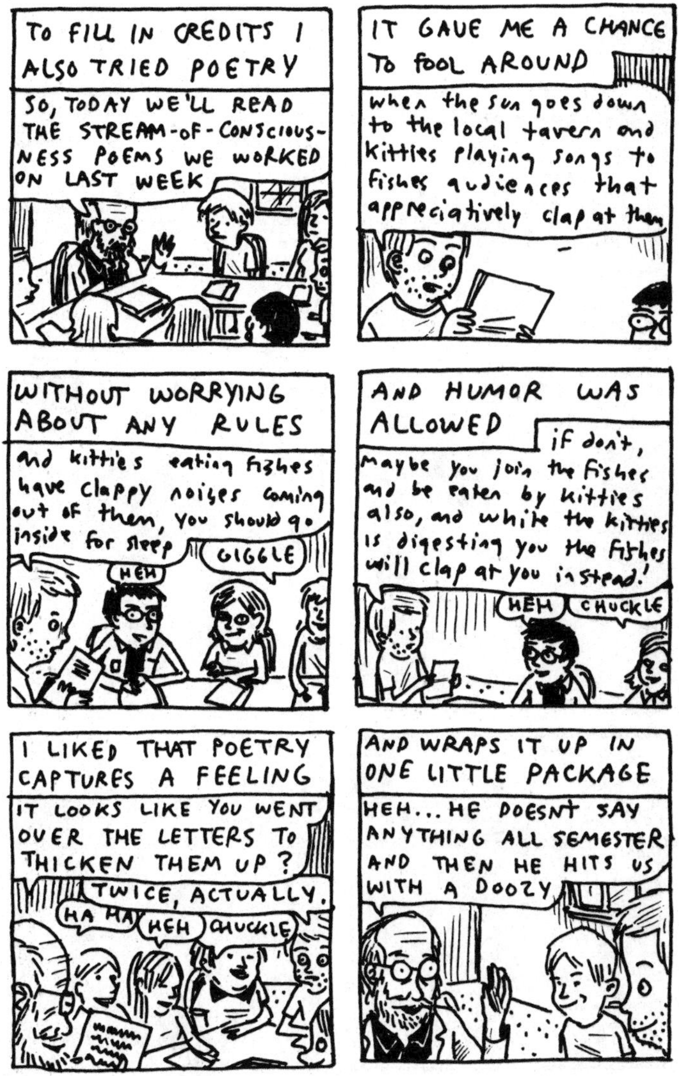
TO FILL IN CREDITS I ALSO TRIED POETRY
SO, TODAY WE'LL READ THE STREAM-OF-CONSCIOUSNESS POEMS WE WORKED ON LAST WEEK
IT GAVE ME A CHANCE TO FOOL AROUND
when the sun goes down to the local tavern and kitties playing songs to fishes audiences that appreciatively clap at them
WITHOUT WORRYING ABOUT ANY RULES
and kitties eating fishes have clappy noises coming out of them, you should go inside for sleep
HEH
GIGGLE
AND HUMOR WAS ALLOWED
if don't, maybe you join the fishes and be eaten by kitties also, and while the kitties is digesting you the fishes will clap at you instead!
HEH
CHUCKLE
I LIKED THAT POETRY CAPTURES A FEELING
IT LOOKS LIKE YOU WENT OVER THE LETTERS TO THICKEN THEM UP?
TWICE, ACTUALLY.
HA HA
HEH
CHUCKLE
AND WRAPS IT UP IN ONE LITTLE PACKAGE
HEH... HE DOESN'T SAY ANYTHING ALL SEMESTER AND THEN HE HITS US WITH A DOOZY

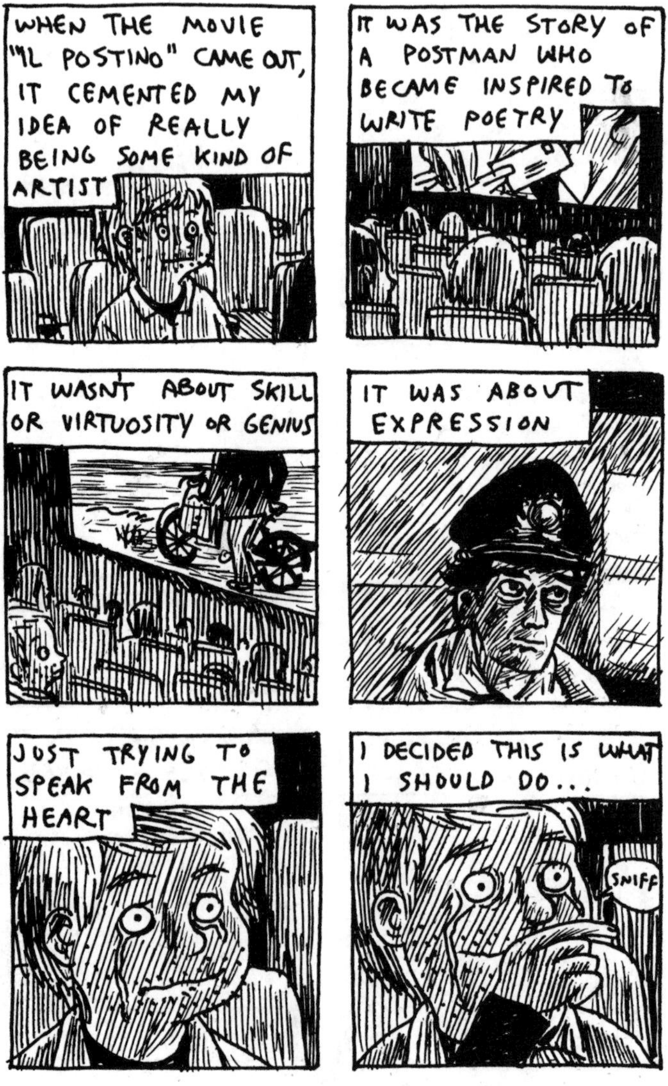
WHEN THE MOVIE "IL POSTINO" CAME OUT, IT CEMENTED MY IDEA OF REALLY BEING SOME KIND OF ARTIST
IT WAS THE STORY OF A POSTMAN WHO BECAME INSPIRED TO WRITE POETRY
IT WASN'T ABOUT SKILL OR VIRTUOSITY OR GENIUS
IT WAS ABOUT EXPRESSION
JUST TRYING TO SPEAK FROM THE HEART
I DECIDED THIS IS WHAT I SHOULD DO...
SNIFF

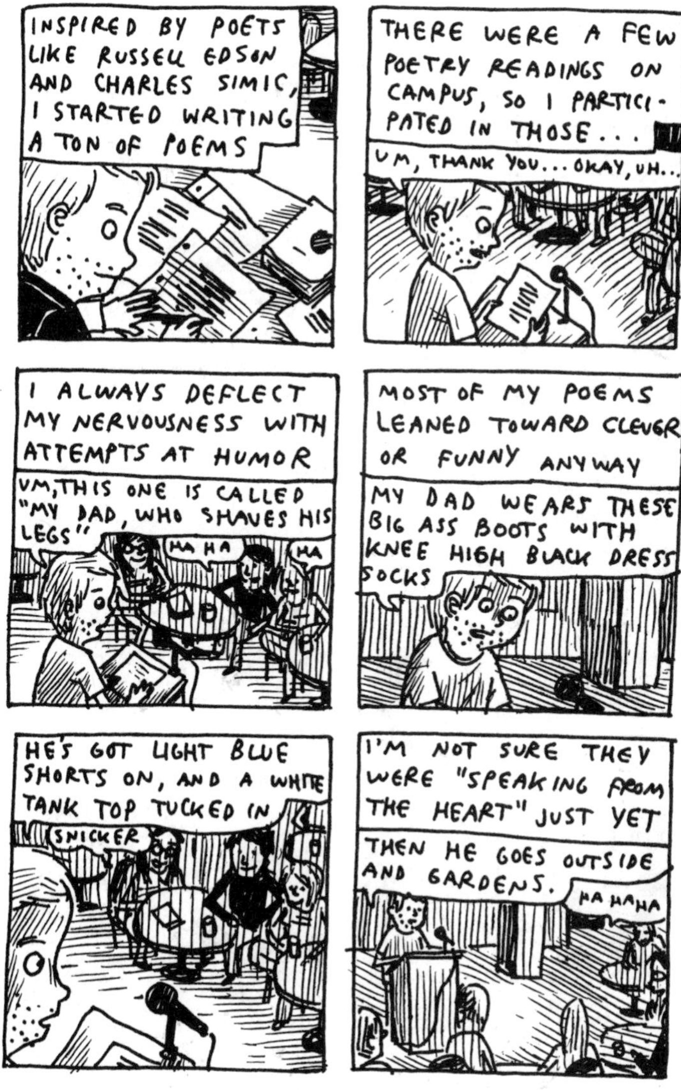
INSPIRED BY POETS LIKE RUSSELL EDSON AND CHARLES SIMIC, I STARTED WRITING A TON OF POEMS
THERE WERE A FEW POETRY READINGS ON CAMPUS, SO I PARTICIPATED IN THOSE...
UM, THANK YOU... OKAY, UH...
I ALWAYS DEFLECT MY NERVOUSNESS WITH ATTEMPTS AT HUMOR
UM, THIS ONE IS CALLED "MY DAD, WHO SHAVES HIS LEGS"
HA HA
HA
MOST OF MY POEMS LEANED TOWARD CLEVER OR FUNNY ANYWAY
MY DAD WEARS THESE BIG ASS BOOTS WITH KNEE HIGH BLACK DRESS SOCKS
HE'S GOT LIGHT BLUE SHORTS ON, AND A WHITE TANK TOP TUCKED IN
SNICKER
I'M NOT SURE THEY WERE "SPEAKING FROM THE HEART" JUST YET
THEN HE GOES OUTSIDE AND GARDENS.
HA HA HA

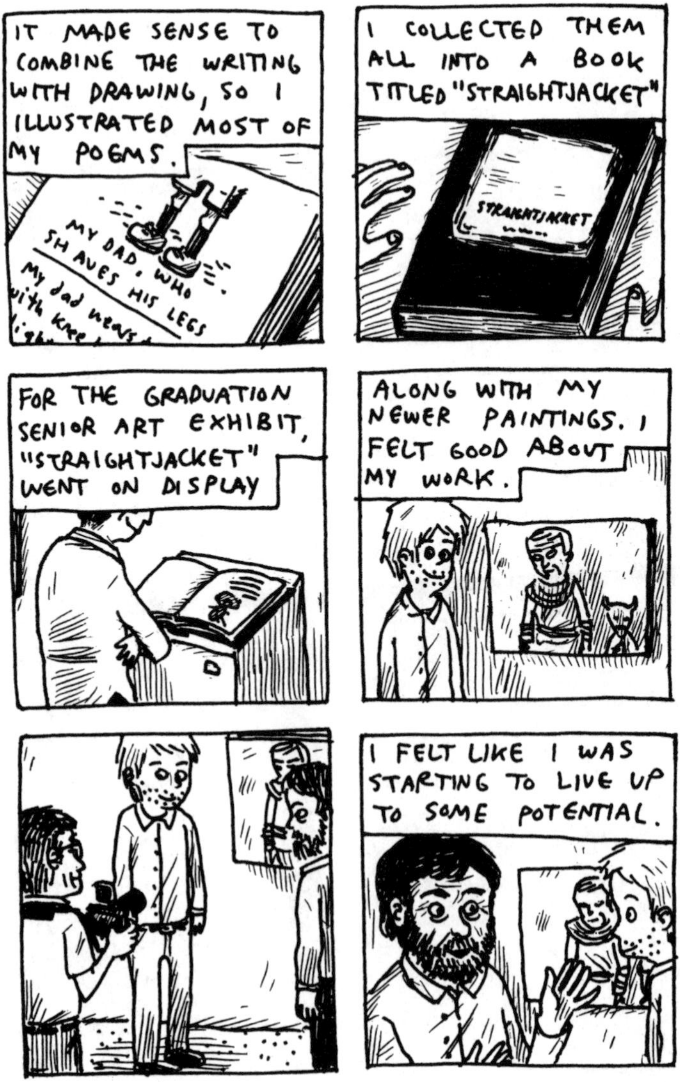
IT MADE SENSE TO COMBINE THE WRITING WITH DRAWING, SO I ILLUSTRATED MOST OF MY POEMS.
MY DAD, WHO SHAVES HIS LEGS
I COLLECTED THEM ALL INTO A BOOK TITLED "STRAIGHTJACKET"
STRAIGHTJACKET
FOR THE GRADUATION SENIOR ART EXHIBIT, "STRAIGHTJACKET" WENT ON DISPLAY
ALONG WITH MY NEWER PAINTINGS. I FELT GOOD ABOUT MY WORK.
I FELT LIKE I WAS STARTING TO LIVE UP TO SOME POTENTIAL.

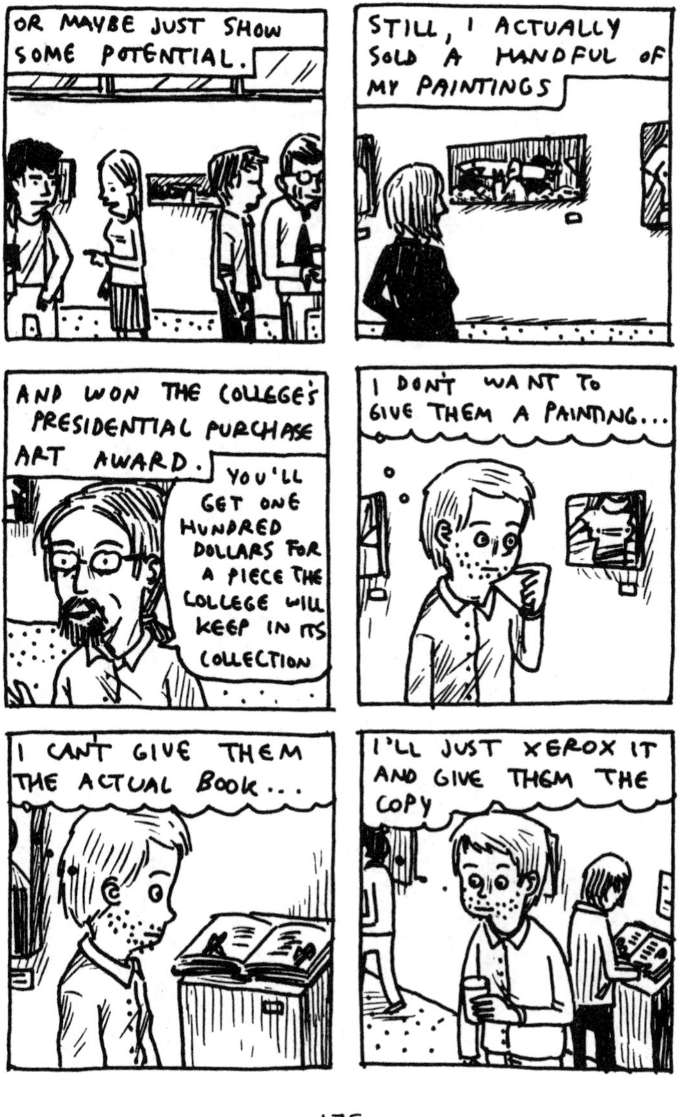
OR MAYBE JUST SHOW SOME POTENTIAL.
STILL, I ACTUALLY SOLD A HANDFUL OF MY PAINTINGS
AND WON THE COLLEGE'S PRESIDENTIAL PURCHASE ART AWARD.
YOU'LL GET ONE HUNDRED DOLLARS FOR A PIECE THE COLLEGE WILL KEEP IN ITS COLLECTION
I DON'T WANT TO GIVE THEM A PAINTING...
I CAN'T GIVE THEM THE ACTUAL BOOK...
I'LL JUST XEROX IT AND GIVE THEM THE COPY

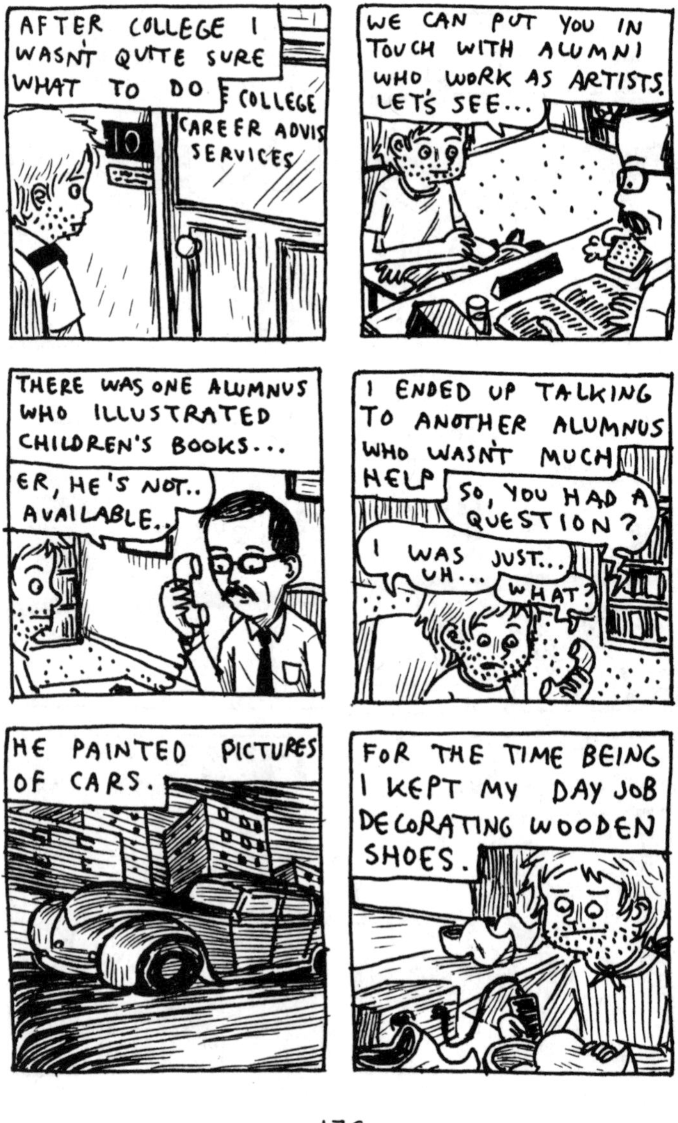
AFTER COLLEGE I WASN'T QUITE SURE WHAT TO DO
COLLEGE CAREER ADVIS SERVICES
WE CAN PUT YOU IN TOUCH WITH ALUMNI WHO WORK AS ARTISTS. LET'S SEE...
THERE WAS ONE ALUMNUS WHO ILLUSTRATED CHILDREN'S BOOKS...
ER, HE'S NOT.. AVAILABLE..
I ENDED UP TALKING TO ANOTHER ALUMNUS WHO WASN'T MUCH HELP
SO, YOU HAD A QUESTION?
I WAS JUST... UH...
WHAT?
HE PAINTED PICTURES OF CARS.
FOR THE TIME BEING I KEPT MY DAY JOB DECORATING WOODEN SHOES.

I DECIDED I REALLY WANTED TO MAKE ILLUSTRATED BOOKS.

I'LL BET SOMEONE COULD PUBLISH THIS

I BEGAN TO REDRAW "STRAIGHTJACKET"

I LOOKED UP HOW TO PITCH A BOOK PROPOSAL

HOW TO GET PUBLISHED

GUIDE TO WRITE

WRITER MARKET 1997

I THINK I KNEW POETRY WASN'T A BOOMING MARKET...

MY BOOK-SHELVES

HM

POETRY

...BUT I FIGURED MY BOOK BEING DIFFERENT WAS AN ADVANTAGE...

THERE'S NEVER BEEN A POETRY BOOK LIKE THIS!

EVER!

SOMETHING TO MAKE IT STAND OUT.

STRAIGHTJACKET

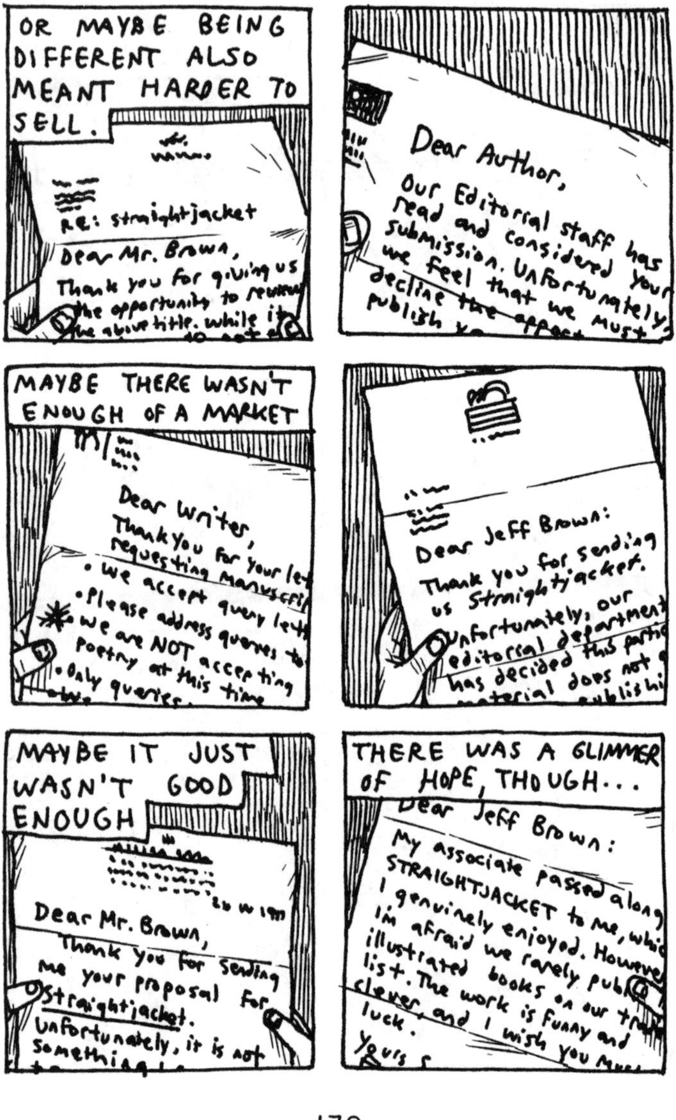
OR MAYBE BEING DIFFERENT ALSO MEANT HARDER TO SELL.
RE: straightjacket
Dear Mr. Brown,
Thank you for giving us
the opportunity to
Dear Author,
Our Editorial staff has read and considered your submission. Unfortunately, we feel that we must decline the
MAYBE THERE WASN'T ENOUGH OF A MARKET
Dear Writer,
Thank you for your
requesting
• We accept query
• Please address queries to
We are NOT accepting poetry at this time
• Only queries
Dear Jeff Brown:
Thank you for sending us Straightjacket.
Unfortunately, our editorial department has decided this
material does not
MAYBE IT JUST WASN'T GOOD ENOUGH
Dear Mr. Brown,
Thank you for sending me your proposal for Straightjacket.
Unfortunately, it is not something
THERE WAS A GLIMMER OF HOPE, THOUGH...
Dear Jeff Brown:
My associate passed along STRAIGHTJACKET to me, which I genuinely enjoyed. However, I'm afraid we rarely publish illustrated books on our
list. The work is funny and clever, and I wish you
luck.
Yours

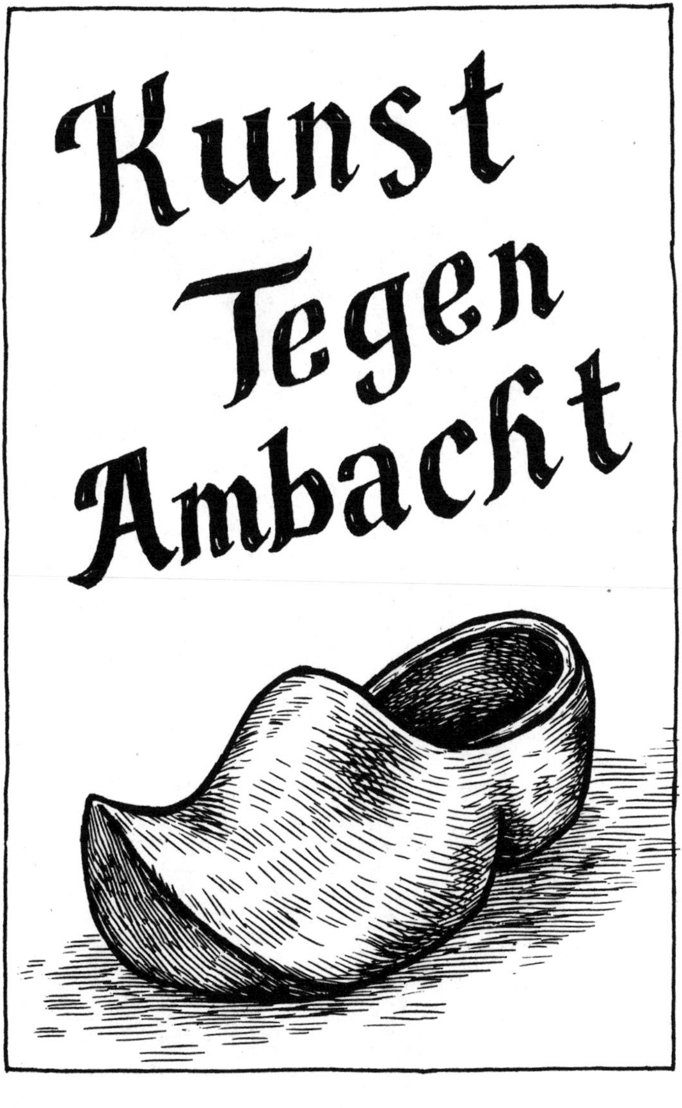
Kunst
Tegen
Ambacht

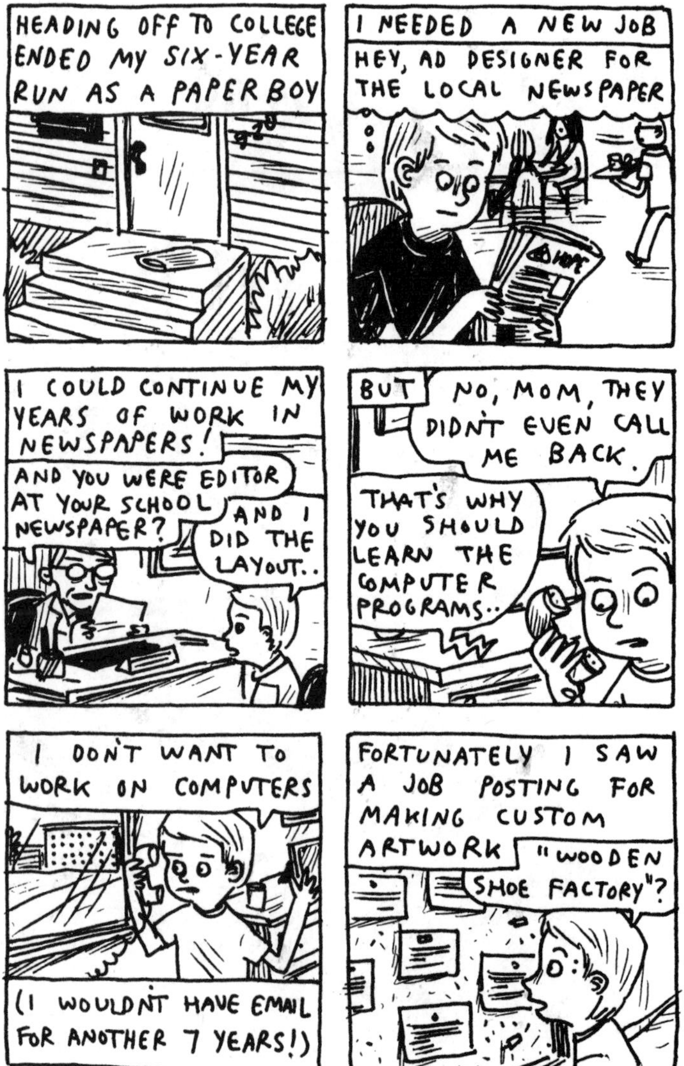
HEADING OFF TO COLLEGE ENDED MY SIX-YEAR RUN AS A PAPERBOY
I NEEDED A NEW JOB
HEY, AD DESIGNER FOR THE LOCAL NEWSPAPER
I COULD CONTINUE MY YEARS OF WORK IN NEWSPAPERS!
AND YOU WERE EDITOR AT YOUR SCHOOL NEWSPAPER?
AND I DID THE LAYOUT..
BUT
NO, MOM, THEY DIDN'T EVEN CALL ME BACK.
THAT'S WHY YOU SHOULD LEARN THE COMPUTER PROGRAMS..
I DON'T WANT TO WORK ON COMPUTERS
(I WOULDN'T HAVE EMAIL FOR ANOTHER 7 YEARS!)
FORTUNATELY I SAW A JOB POSTING FOR MAKING CUSTOM ARTWORK
"WOODEN SHOE FACTORY"?

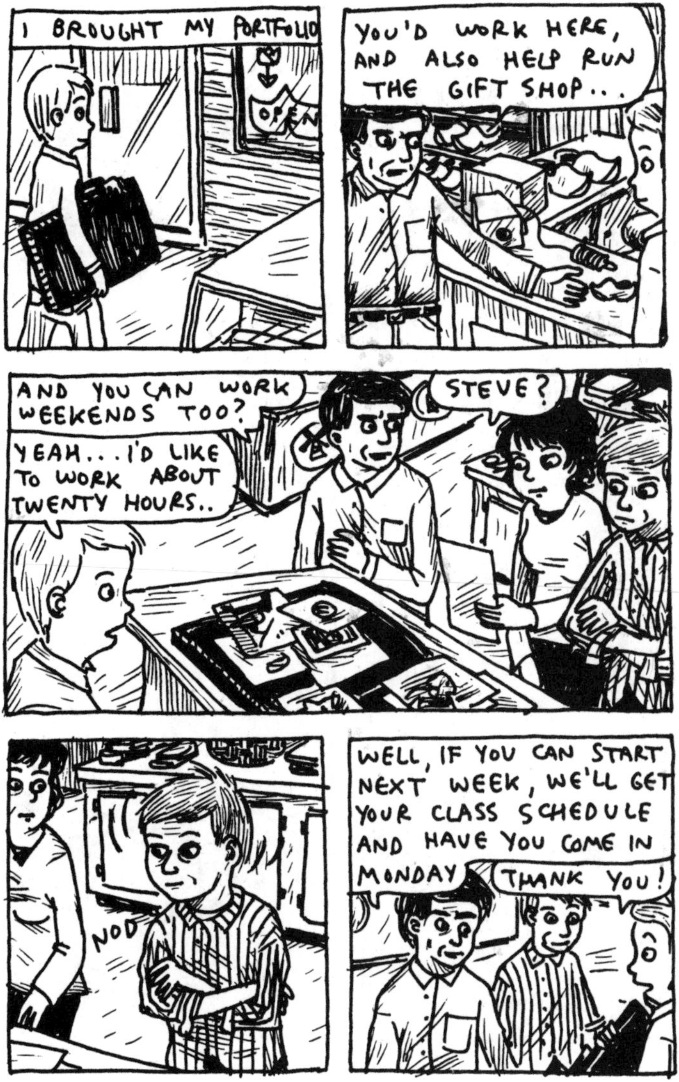
I BROUGHT MY PORTFOLIO
OPEN
YOU'D WORK HERE, AND ALSO HELP RUN THE GIFT SHOP...
AND YOU CAN WORK WEEKENDS TOO?
STEVE?
YEAH... I'D LIKE TO WORK ABOUT TWENTY HOURS..
NOD
WELL, IF YOU CAN START NEXT WEEK, WE'LL GET YOUR CLASS SCHEDULE AND HAVE YOU COME IN MONDAY
THANK YOU!

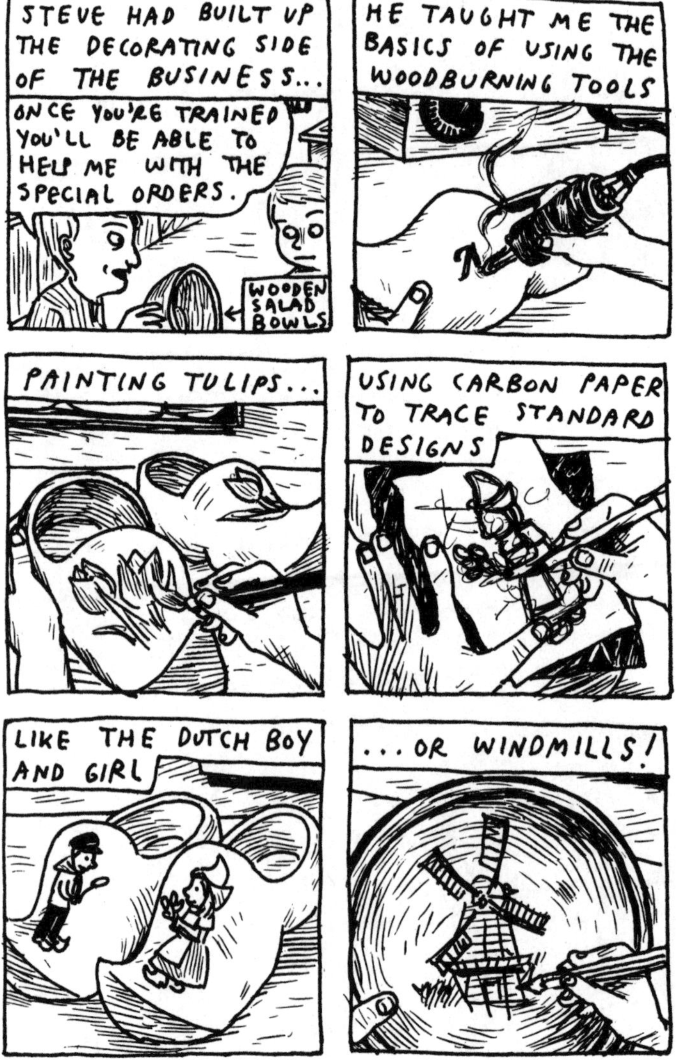
STEVE HAD BUILT UP THE DECORATING SIDE OF THE BUSINESS...
ONCE YOU'RE TRAINED YOU'LL BE ABLE TO HELP ME WITH THE SPECIAL ORDERS.
WOODEN SALAD BOWLS
HE TAUGHT ME THE BASICS OF USING THE WOODBURNING TOOLS
PAINTING TULIPS...
USING CARBON PAPER TO TRACE STANDARD DESIGNS
LIKE THE DUTCH BOY AND GIRL
...OR WINDMILLS!

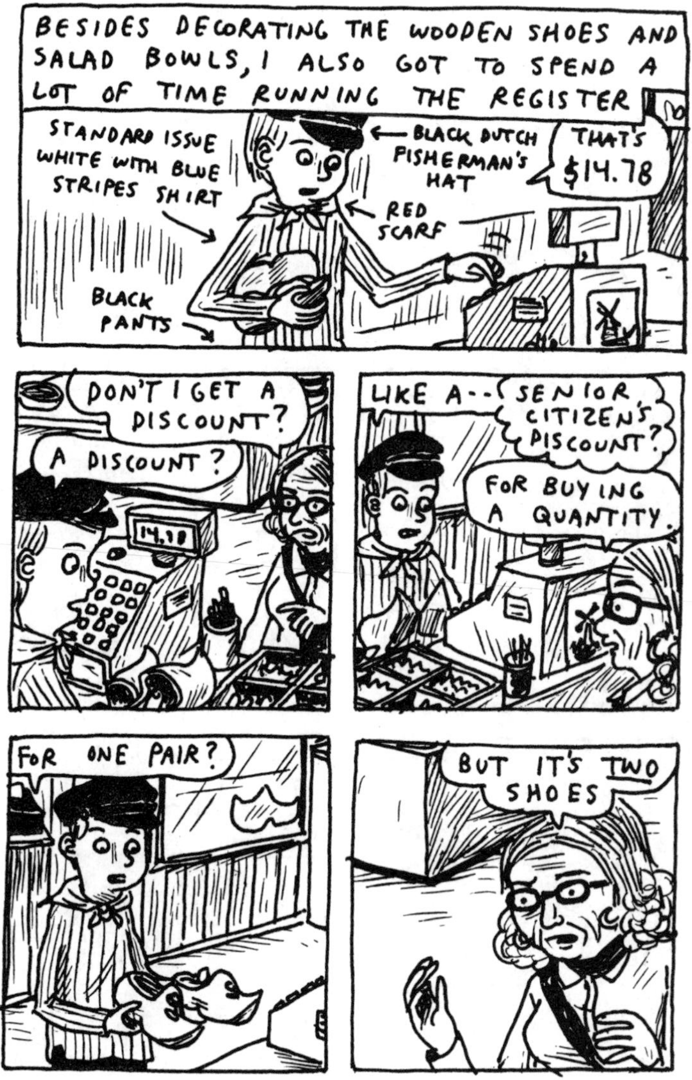
BESIDES DECORATING THE WOODEN SHOES AND SALAD BOWLS, I ALSO GOT TO SPEND A LOT OF TIME RUNNING THE REGISTER
STANDARD ISSUE WHITE WITH BLUE STRIPES SHIRT
BLACK DUTCH FISHERMAN'S HAT
RED SCARF
BLACK PANTS
THAT'S $14.78
DON'T I GET A DISCOUNT?
A DISCOUNT?
14.78
LIKE A--
SENIOR CITIZEN'S DISCOUNT?
FOR BUYING A QUANTITY.
FOR ONE PAIR?
BUT IT'S TWO SHOES

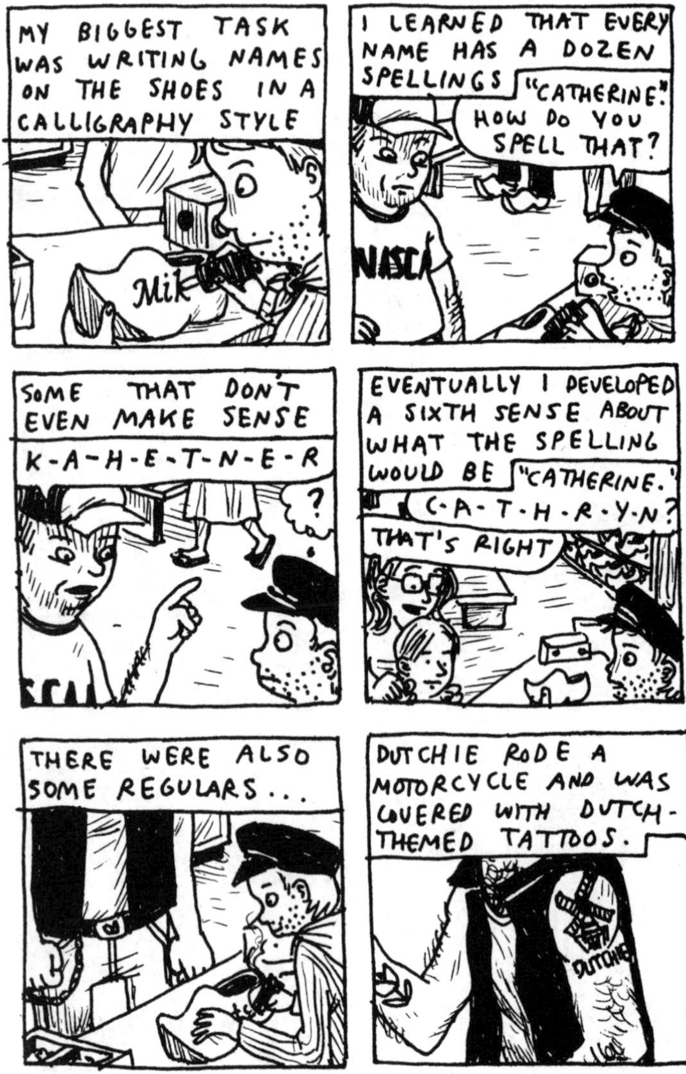
MY BIGGEST TASK WAS WRITING NAMES ON THE SHOES IN A CALLIGRAPHY STYLE
Mik
I LEARNED THAT EVERY NAME HAS A DOZEN SPELLINGS
"CATHERINE." HOW DO YOU SPELL THAT?
NASCA
SOME THAT DON'T EVEN MAKE SENSE
K-A-H-E-T-N-E-R
?
EVENTUALLY I DEVELOPED A SIXTH SENSE ABOUT WHAT THE SPELLING WOULD BE
"CATHERINE."
C-A-T-H-R-Y-N?
THAT'S RIGHT
THERE WERE ALSO SOME REGULARS...
DUTCHIE RODE A MOTORCYCLE AND WAS COVERED WITH DUTCH-THEMED TATTOOS.
DUTCHIE

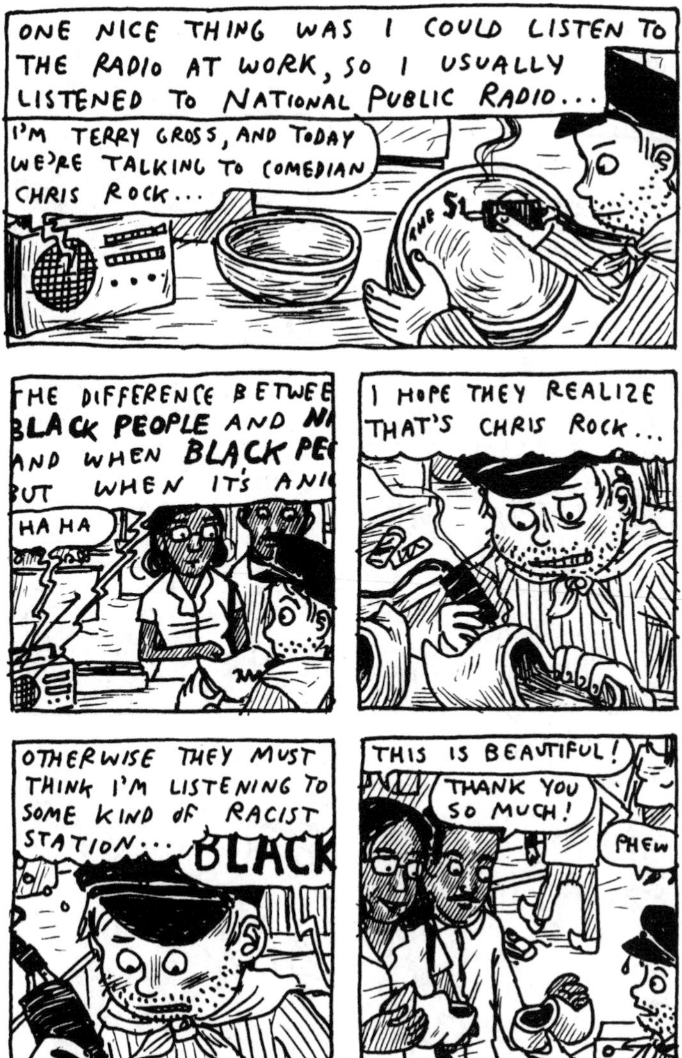
ONE NICE THING WAS I COULD LISTEN TO THE RADIO AT WORK, SO I USUALLY LISTENED TO NATIONAL PUBLIC RADIO...
I'M TERRY GROSS, AND TODAY WE'RE TALKING TO COMEDIAN CHRIS ROCK...
THE DIFFERENCE BETWEE
BLACK PEOPLE AND N
AND WHEN BLACK PE
BUT WHEN IT'S AN
HA HA
I HOPE THEY REALIZE THAT'S CHRIS ROCK...
OTHERWISE THEY MUST THINK I'M LISTENING TO SOME KIND OF RACIST STATION...
BLACK
THIS IS BEAUTIFUL!
THANK YOU SO MUCH!
PHEW

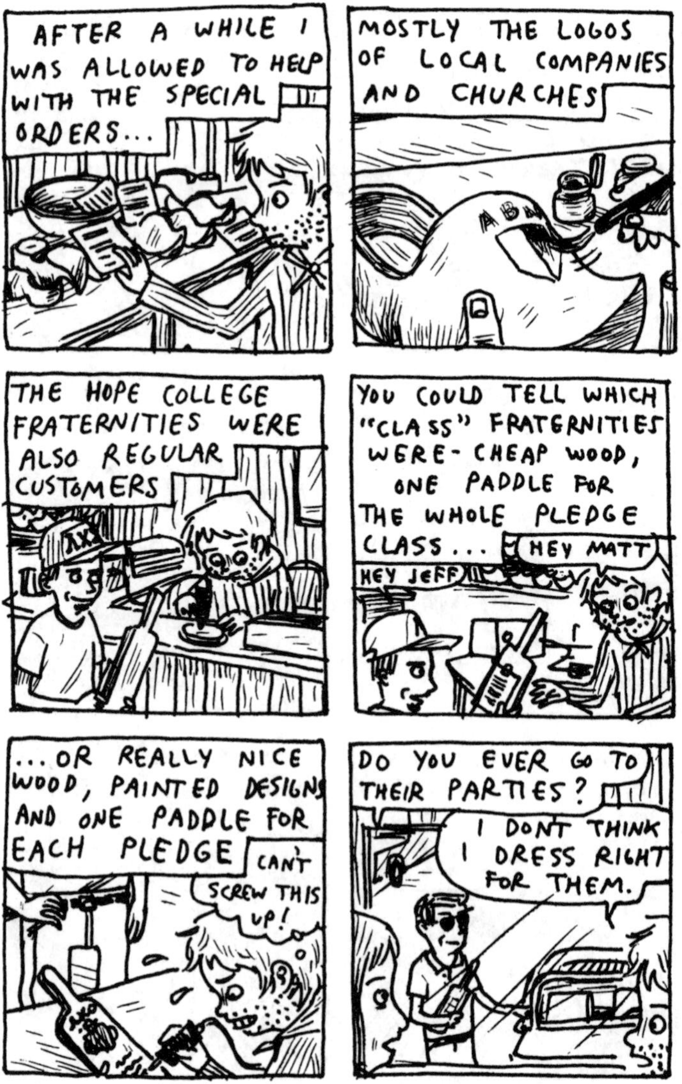
AFTER A WHILE I WAS ALLOWED TO HELP WITH THE SPECIAL ORDERS...
MOSTLY THE LOGOS OF LOCAL COMPANIES AND CHURCHES
THE HOPE COLLEGE FRATERNITIES WERE ALSO REGULAR CUSTOMERS
YOU COULD TELL WHICH "CLASS" FRATERNITIES WERE - CHEAP WOOD, ONE PADDLE FOR THE WHOLE PLEDGE CLASS...
HEY MATT
HEY JEFF
...OR REALLY NICE WOOD, PAINTED DESIGNS AND ONE PADDLE FOR EACH PLEDGE
CAN'T SCREW THIS UP!
DO YOU EVER GO TO THEIR PARTIES?
I DON'T THINK I DRESS RIGHT FOR THEM.

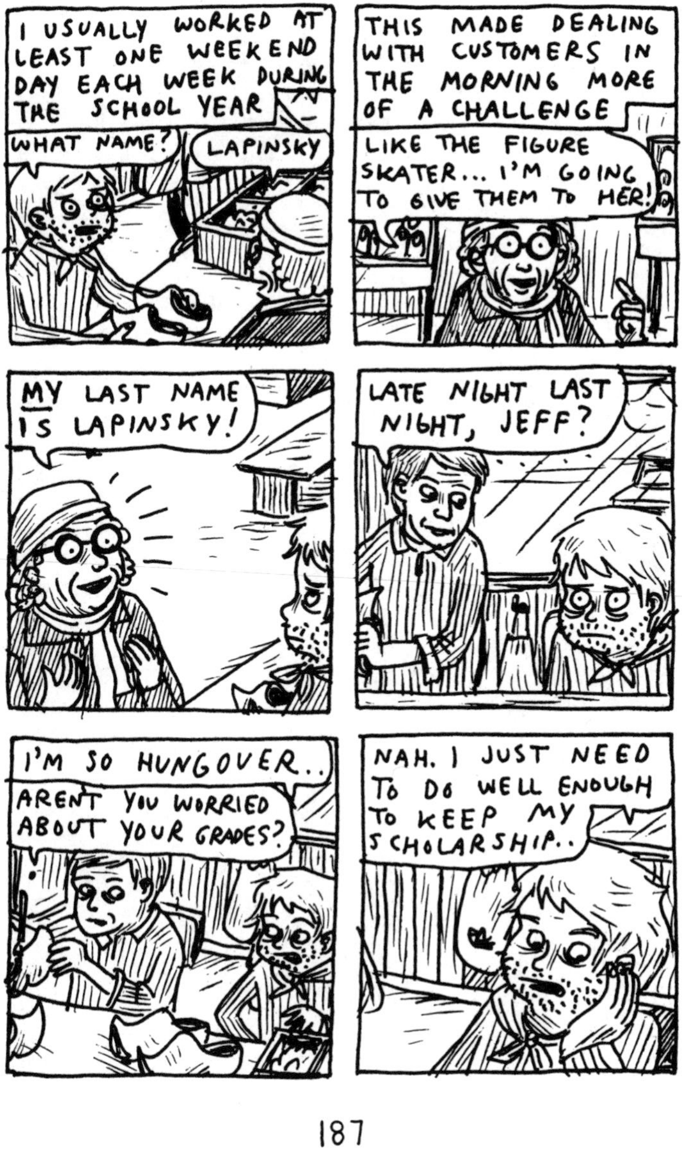
I USUALLY WORKED AT LEAST ONE WEEKEND DAY EACH WEEK DURING THE SCHOOL YEAR
WHAT NAME?
LAPINSKY
THIS MADE DEALING WITH CUSTOMERS IN THE MORNING MORE OF A CHALLENGE
LIKE THE FIGURE SKATER... I'M GOING TO GIVE THEM TO HER!
MY LAST NAME IS LAPINSKY!
LATE NIGHT LAST NIGHT, JEFF?
I'M SO HUNGOVER..
ARENT YOU WORRIED ABOUT YOUR GRADES?
NAH. I JUST NEED TO DO WELL ENOUGH TO KEEP MY SCHOLARSHIP..

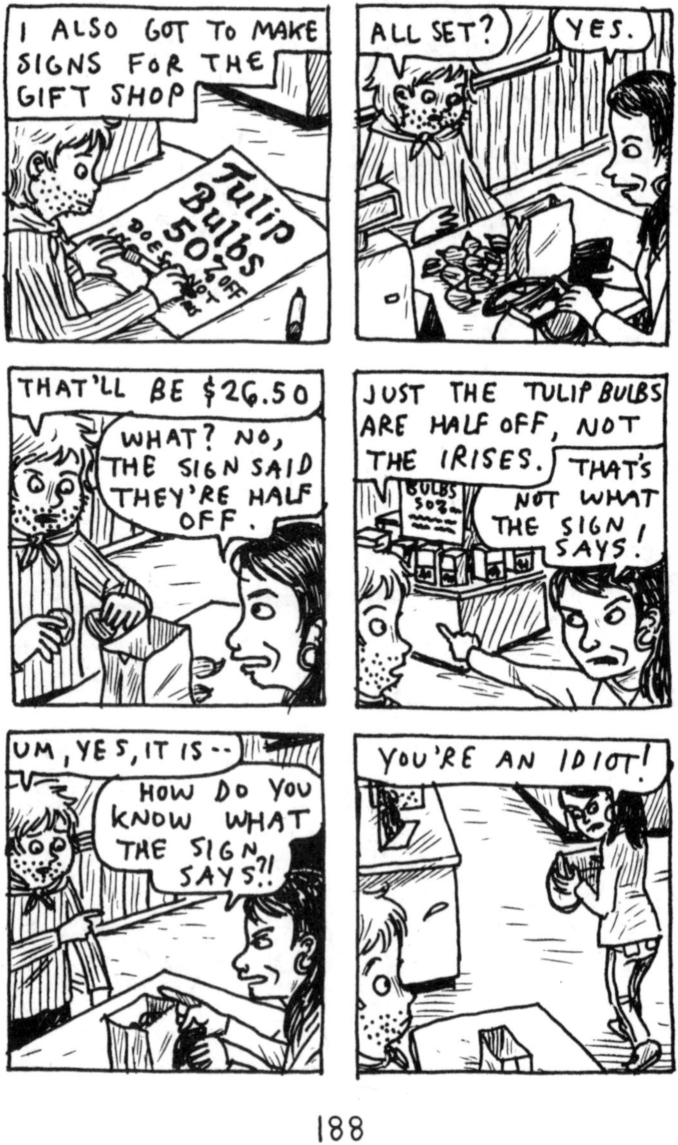
I ALSO GOT TO MAKE SIGNS FOR THE GIFT SHOP
Tulip Bulbs 50% OFF
ALL SET?
YES.
THAT'LL BE $26.50
WHAT? NO, THE SIGN SAID THEY'RE HALF OFF.
JUST THE TULIP BULBS ARE HALF OFF, NOT THE IRISES.
THAT'S NOT WHAT THE SIGN SAYS!
UM, YES, IT IS--
HOW DO YOU KNOW WHAT THE SIGN SAYS?!
YOU'RE AN IDIOT!

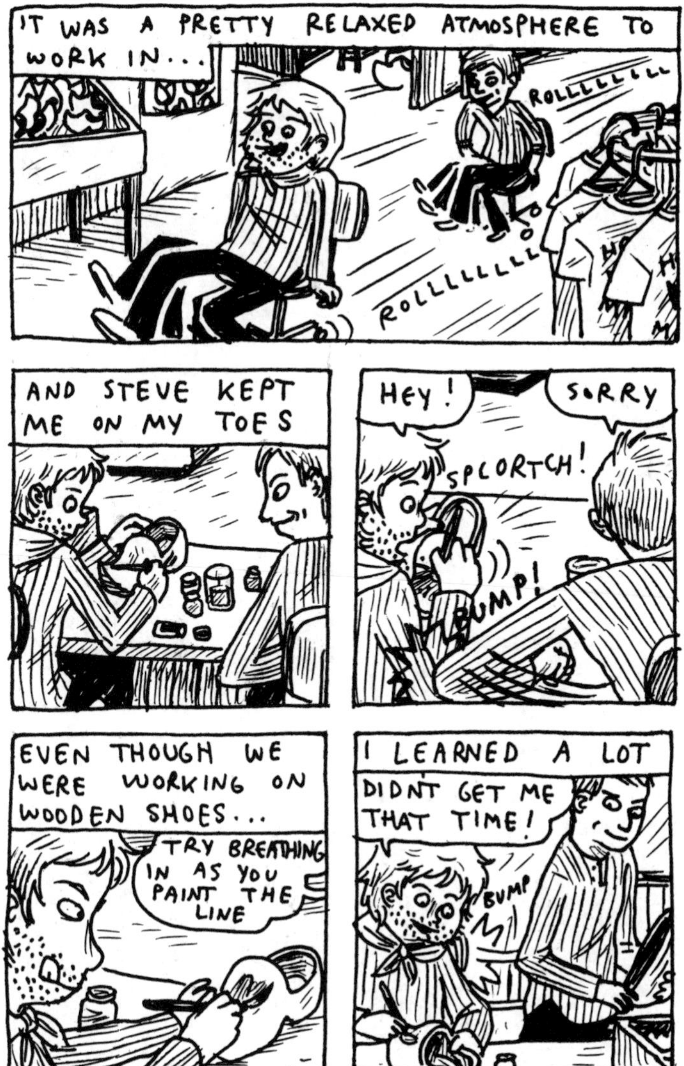

IT WAS A PRETTY RELAXED ATMOSPHERE TO WORK IN...
ROLLLLLLLL
ROLLLLLLLLL
AND STEVE KEPT ME ON MY TOES
HEY!
SORRY
SPLORTCH!
BUMP!
EVEN THOUGH WE WERE WORKING ON WOODEN SHOES...
TRY BREATHING IN AS YOU PAINT THE LINE
I LEARNED A LOT
DIDN'T GET ME THAT TIME!
BUMP

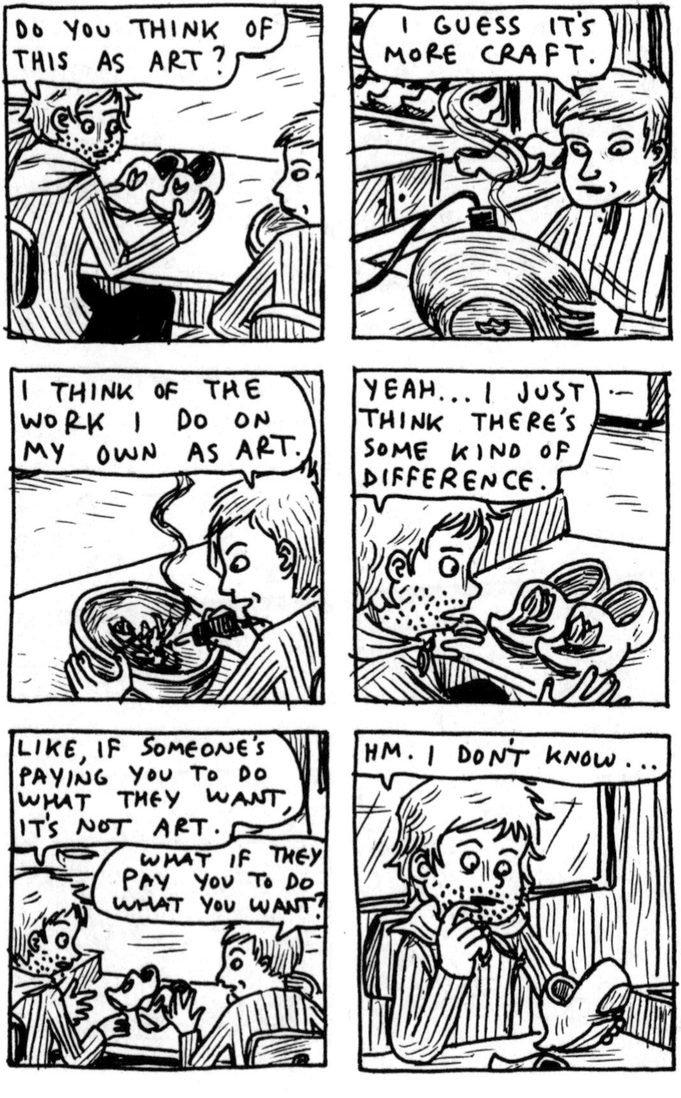
DO YOU THINK OF THIS AS ART?
I GUESS IT'S MORE CRAFT.
I THINK OF THE WORK I DO ON MY OWN AS ART.
YEAH... I JUST THINK THERE'S SOME KIND OF DIFFERENCE.
LIKE, IF SOMEONE'S PAYING YOU TO DO WHAT THEY WANT, IT'S NOT ART.
WHAT IF THEY PAY YOU TO DO WHAT YOU WANT?
HM. I DON'T KNOW...

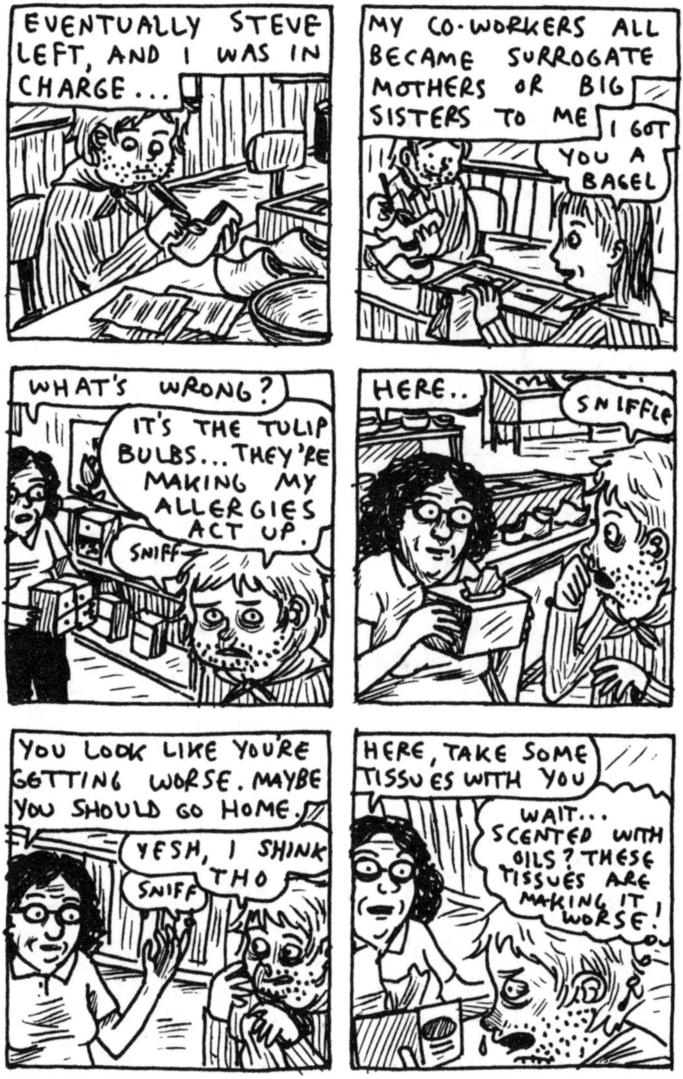
EVENTUALLY STEVE LEFT, AND I WAS IN CHARGE...
MY CO-WORKERS ALL BECAME SURROGATE MOTHERS OR BIG SISTERS TO ME
I GOT YOU A BAGEL
WHAT'S WRONG?
IT'S THE TULIP BULBS... THEY'RE MAKING MY ALLERGIES ACT UP.
SNIFF
HERE..
SNIFFLE
YOU LOOK LIKE YOU'RE GETTING WORSE. MAYBE YOU SHOULD GO HOME.
YESH, I SHINK THO
SNIFF
HERE, TAKE SOME TISSUES WITH YOU
WAIT... SCENTED WITH OILS? THESE TISSUES ARE MAKING IT WORSE!

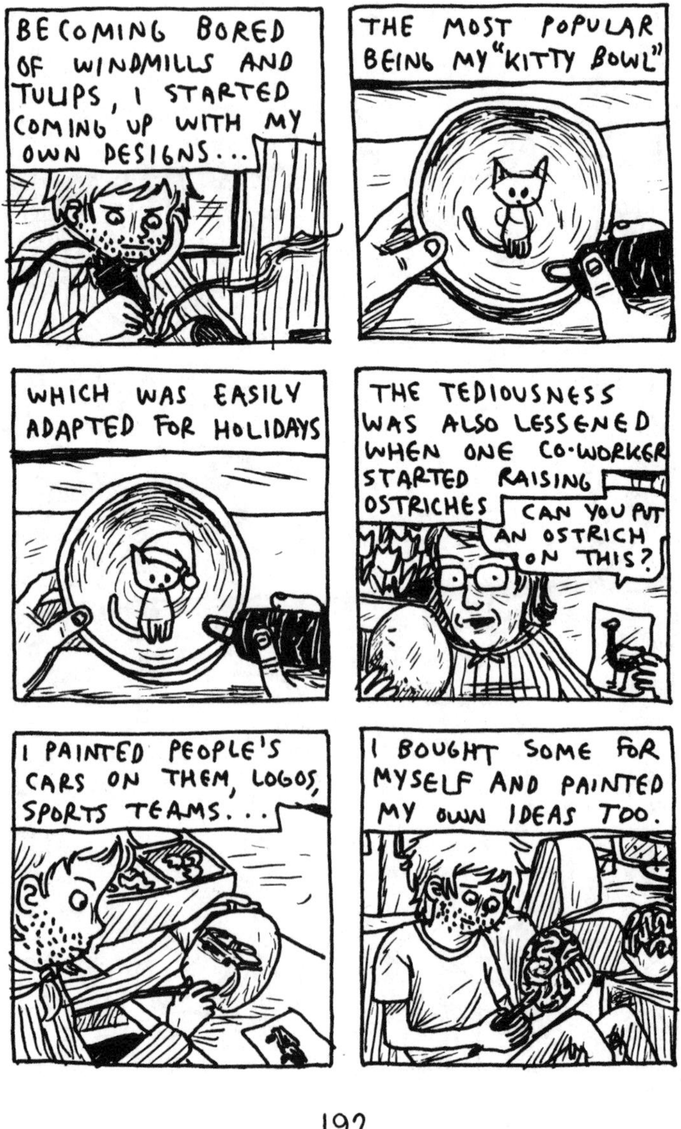
BECOMING BORED OF WINDMILLS AND TULIPS, I STARTED COMING UP WITH MY OWN DESIGNS...
THE MOST POPULAR BEING MY "KITTY BOWL"
WHICH WAS EASILY ADAPTED FOR HOLIDAYS
THE TEDIOUSNESS WAS ALSO LESSENED WHEN ONE CO-WORKER STARTED RAISING OSTRICHES
CAN YOU PUT AN OSTRICH ON THIS?
I PAINTED PEOPLE'S CARS ON THEM, LOGOS, SPORTS TEAMS...
I BOUGHT SOME FOR MYSELF AND PAINTED MY OWN IDEAS TOO.

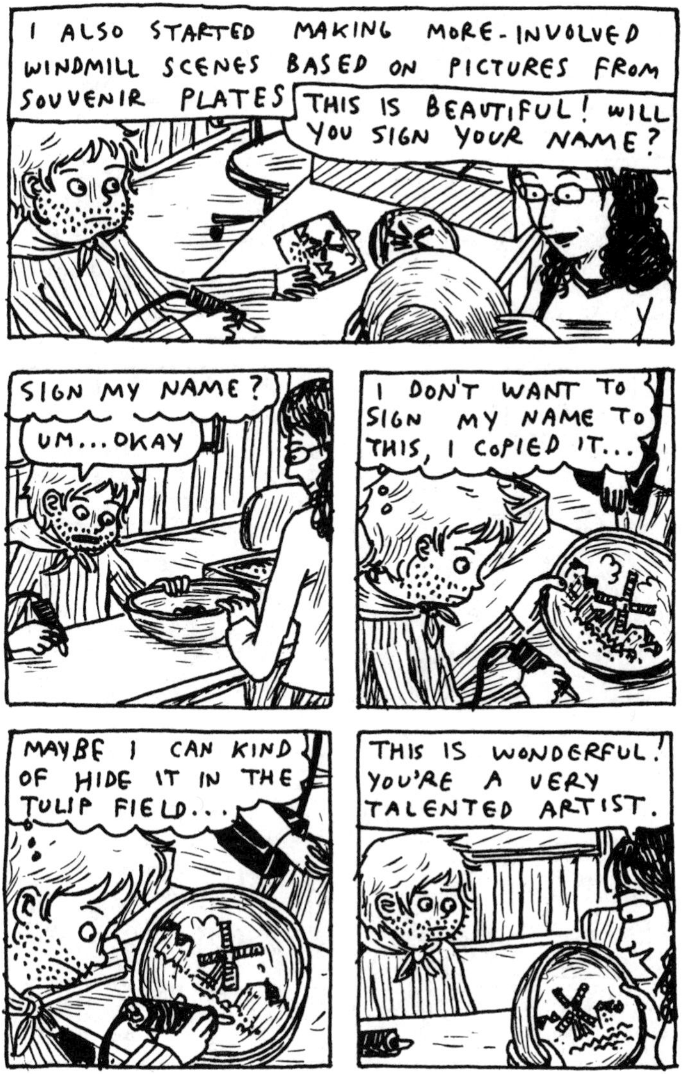
I ALSO STARTED MAKING MORE-INVOLVED WINDMILL SCENES BASED ON PICTURES FROM SOUVENIR PLATES
THIS IS BEAUTIFUL! WILL YOU SIGN YOUR NAME?
SIGN MY NAME?
UM...OKAY
I DON'T WANT TO SIGN MY NAME TO THIS, I COPIED IT...
MAYBE I CAN KIND OF HIDE IT IN THE TULIP FIELD...
THIS IS WONDERFUL! YOU'RE A VERY TALENTED ARTIST.

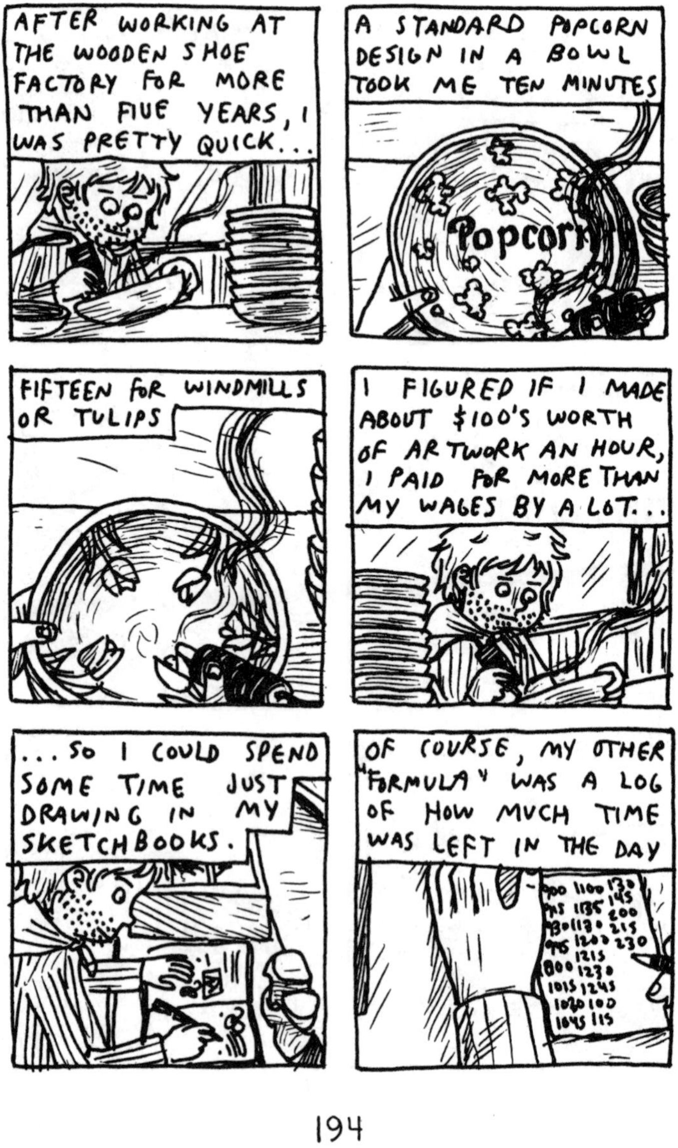
AFTER WORKING AT THE WOODEN SHOE FACTORY FOR MORE THAN FIVE YEARS, I WAS PRETTY QUICK...
A STANDARD POPCORN DESIGN IN A BOWL TOOK ME TEN MINUTES
Popcorn
FIFTEEN FOR WINDMILLS OR TULIPS
I FIGURED IF I MADE ABOUT $100'S WORTH OF ARTWORK AN HOUR, I PAID FOR MORE THAN MY WAGES BY A LOT...
...SO I COULD SPEND SOME TIME JUST DRAWING IN MY SKETCHBOOKS.
OF COURSE, MY OTHER "FORMULA" WAS A LOG OF HOW MUCH TIME WAS LEFT IN THE DAY

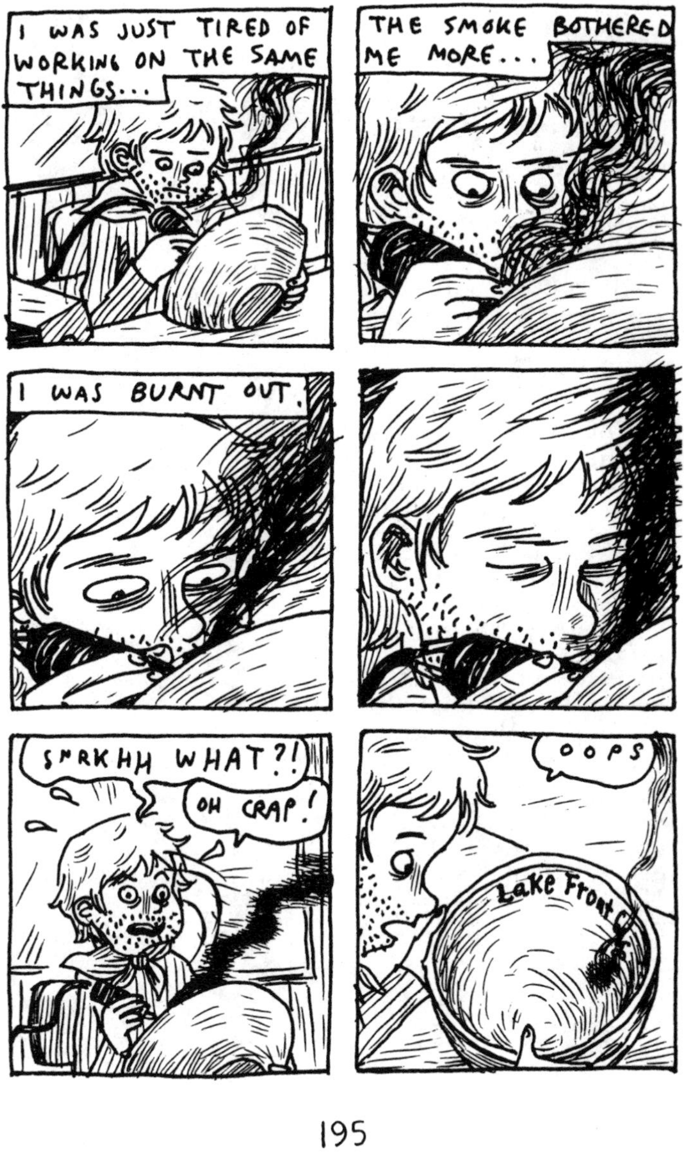
I WAS JUST TIRED OF WORKING ON THE SAME THINGS...
THE SMOKE BOTHERED ME MORE...
I WAS BURNT OUT.
SNRKHH WHAT?!
OH CRAP!
OOPS
Lake Front

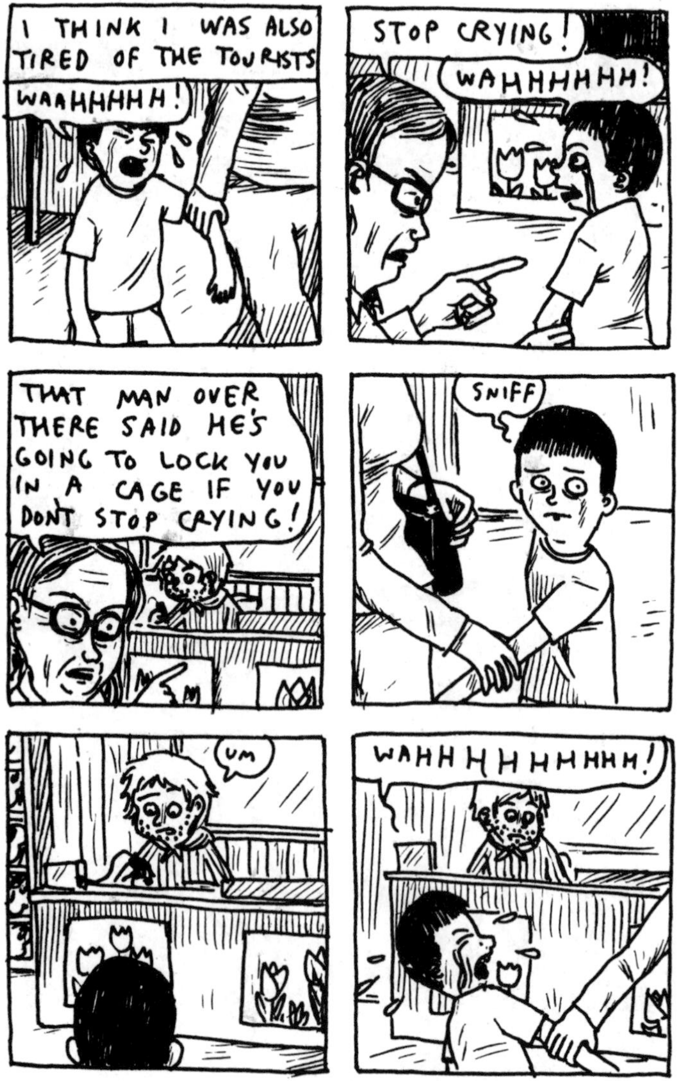
I THINK I WAS ALSO TIRED OF THE TOURISTS
WAAHHHHH!
STOP CRYING!
WAHHHHHH!
THAT MAN OVER THERE SAID HE'S GOING TO LOCK YOU IN A CAGE IF YOU DONT STOP CRYING!
SNIFF
UM
WAHHHHHHHHHH!

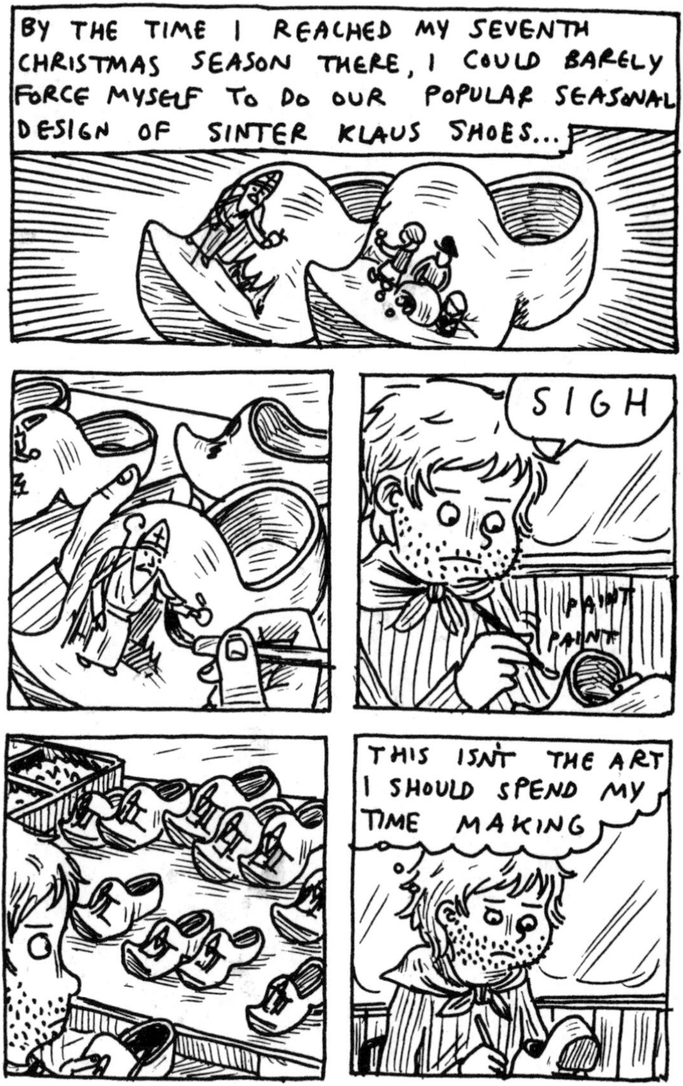
BY THE TIME I REACHED MY SEVENTH CHRISTMAS SEASON THERE, I COULD BARELY FORCE MYSELF TO DO OUR POPULAR SEASONAL DESIGN OF SINTER KLAUS SHOES...
SIGH
PAINT
PAINT
THIS ISN'T THE ART I SHOULD SPEND MY TIME MAKING

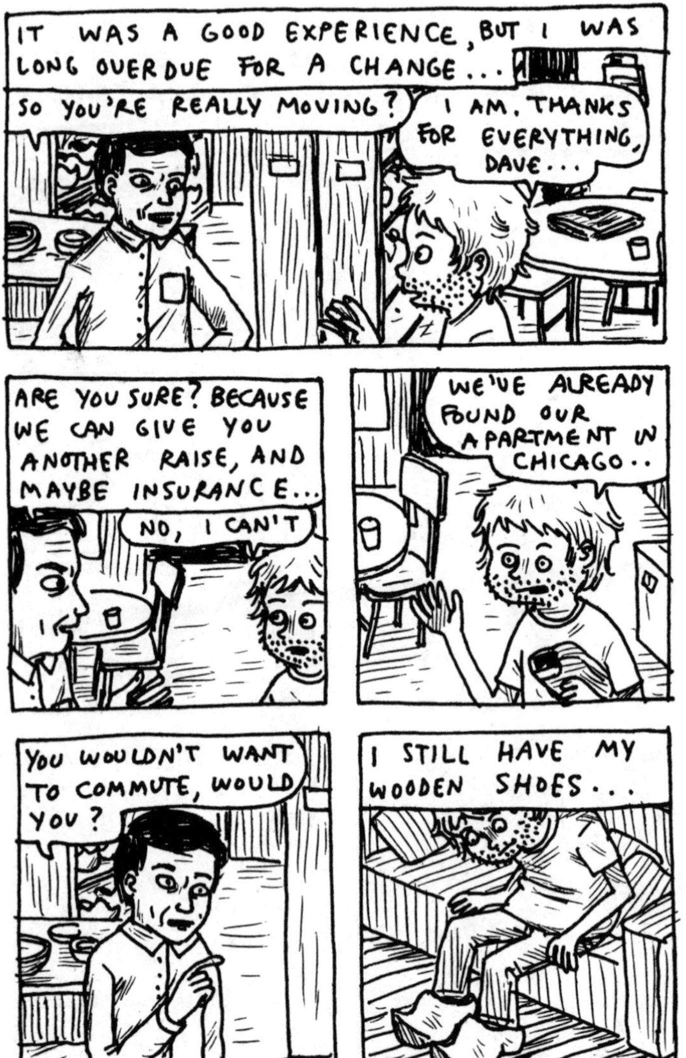
IT WAS A GOOD EXPERIENCE, BUT I WAS LONG OVERDUE FOR A CHANGE...
SO YOU'RE REALLY MOVING?
I AM. THANKS FOR EVERYTHING, DAVE...
ARE YOU SURE? BECAUSE WE CAN GIVE YOU ANOTHER RAISE, AND MAYBE INSURANCE...
NO, I CAN'T
WE'VE ALREADY FOUND OUR APARTMENT IN CHICAGO..
YOU WOULDN'T WANT TO COMMUTE, WOULD YOU?
I STILL HAVE MY WOODEN SHOES...

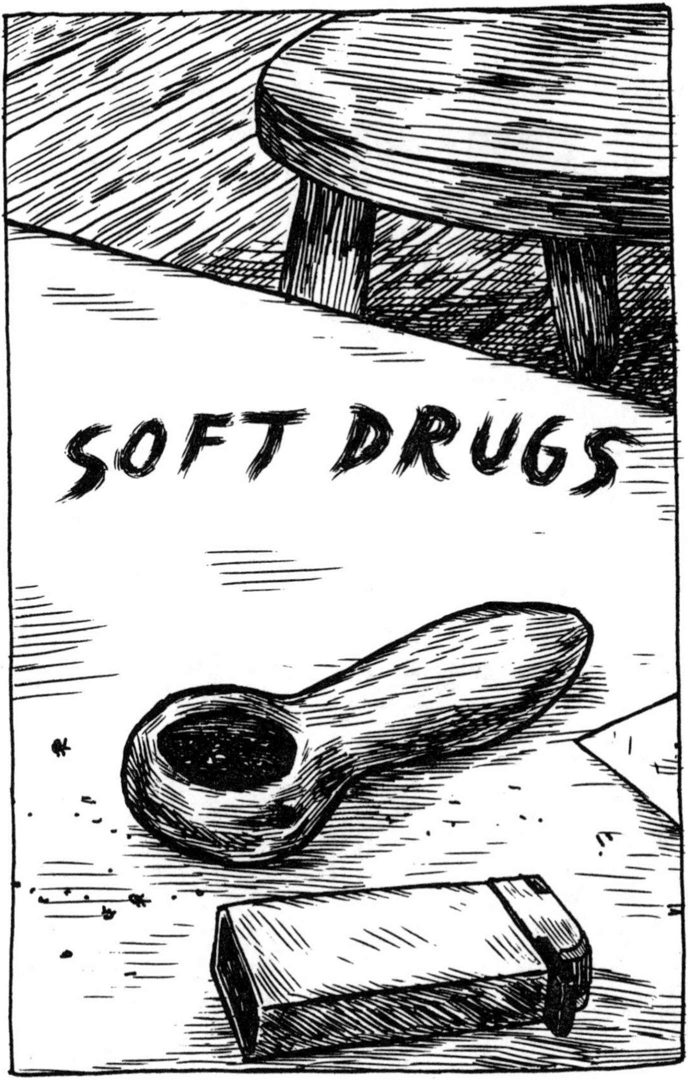
SOFT DRUGS

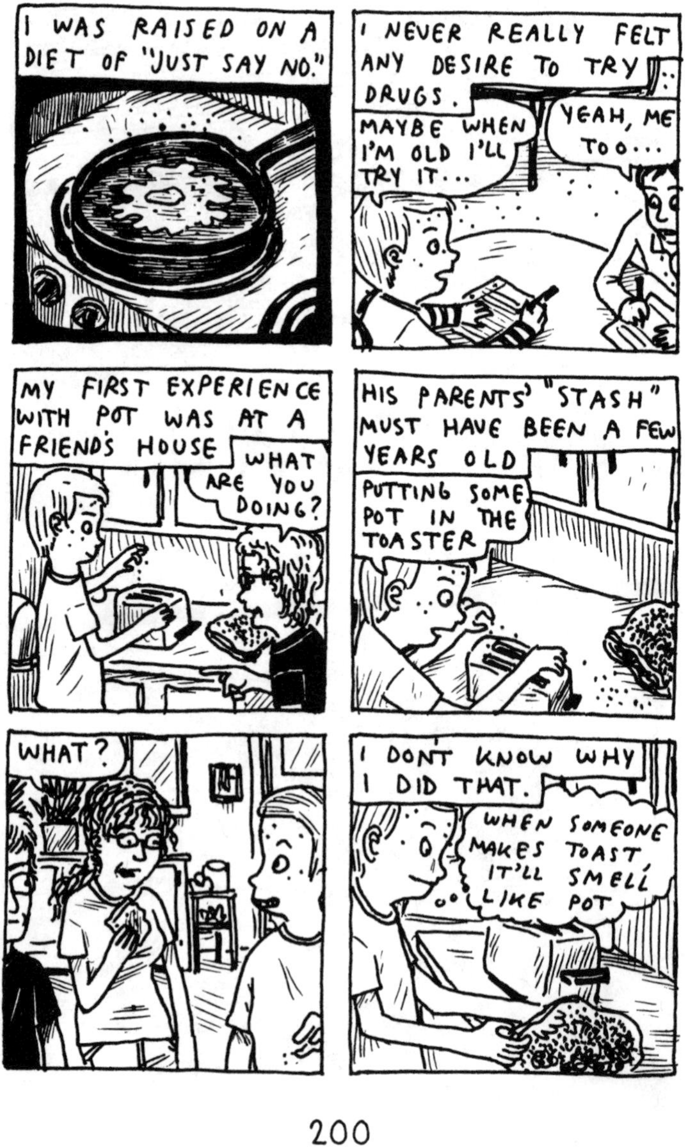
I WAS RAISED ON A DIET OF "JUST SAY NO."
I NEVER REALLY FELT ANY DESIRE TO TRY DRUGS.
MAYBE WHEN I'M OLD I'LL TRY IT...
YEAH, ME TOO...
MY FIRST EXPERIENCE WITH POT WAS AT A FRIEND'S HOUSE
WHAT ARE YOU DOING?
HIS PARENTS' "STASH" MUST HAVE BEEN A FEW YEARS OLD
PUTTING SOME POT IN THE TOASTER
WHAT?
I DON'T KNOW WHY I DID THAT.
WHEN SOMEONE MAKES TOAST, IT'LL SMELL LIKE POT

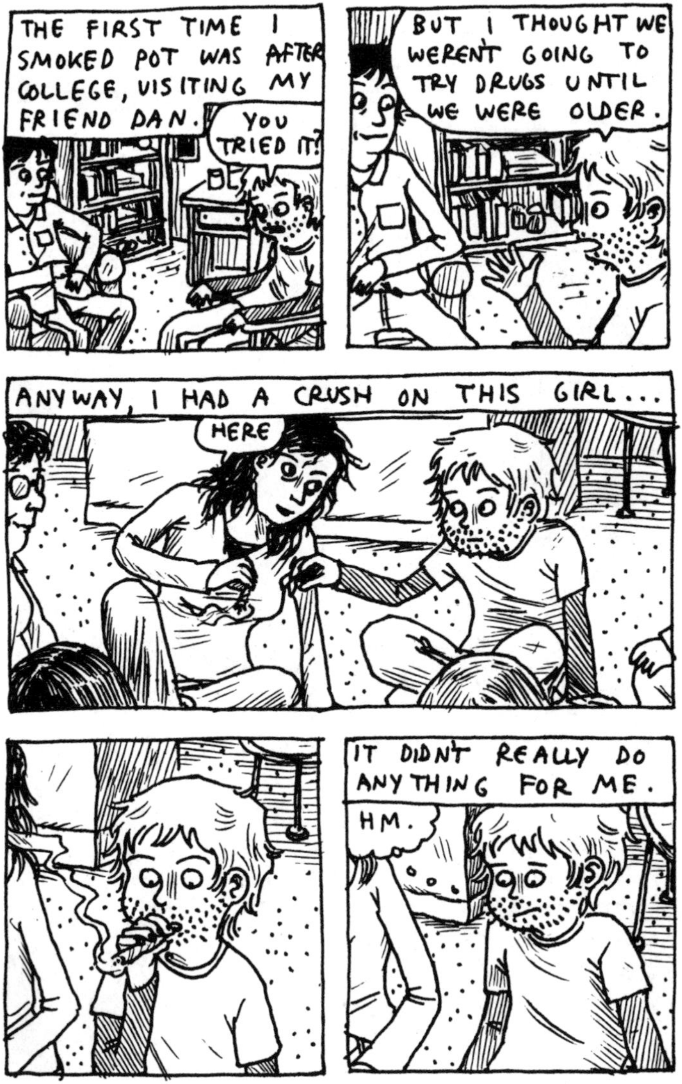
THE FIRST TIME I SMOKED POT WAS AFTER COLLEGE, VISITING MY FRIEND DAN.
YOU TRIED IT?
BUT I THOUGHT WE WEREN'T GOING TO TRY DRUGS UNTIL WE WERE OLDER.
ANYWAY, I HAD A CRUSH ON THIS GIRL...
HERE
IT DIDN'T REALLY DO ANYTHING FOR ME.
HM.

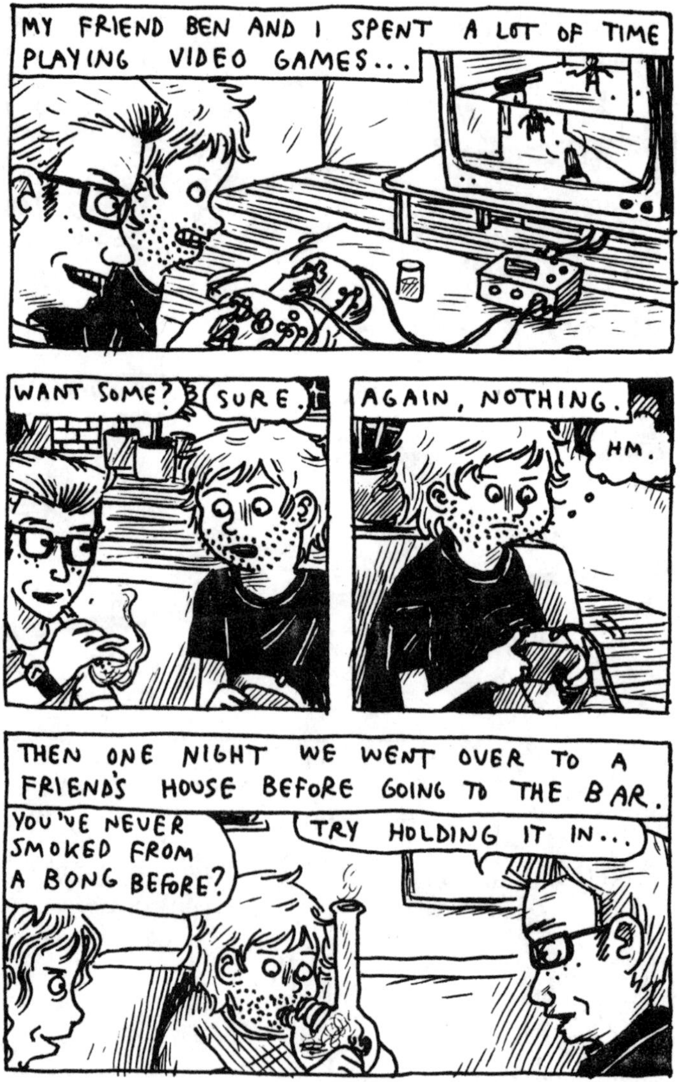
MY FRIEND BEN AND I SPENT A LOT OF TIME PLAYING VIDEO GAMES...
WANT SOME?
SURE.
AGAIN, NOTHING.
HM.
THEN ONE NIGHT WE WENT OVER TO A FRIEND'S HOUSE BEFORE GOING TO THE BAR.
YOU'VE NEVER SMOKED FROM A BONG BEFORE?
TRY HOLDING IT IN...

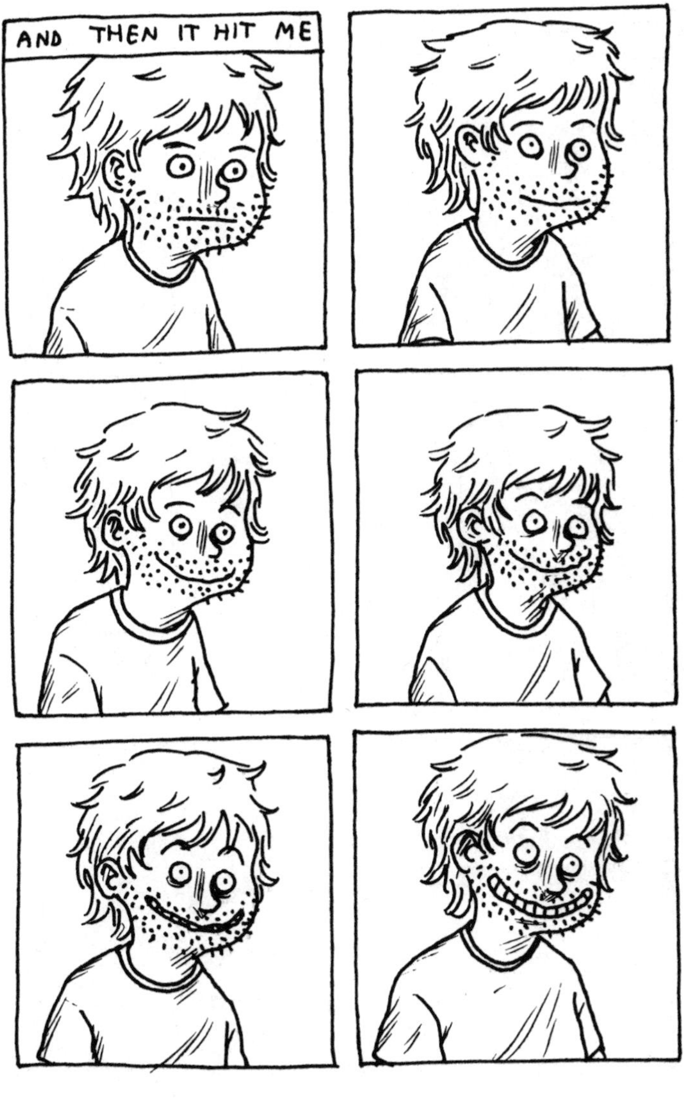
AND THEN IT HIT ME

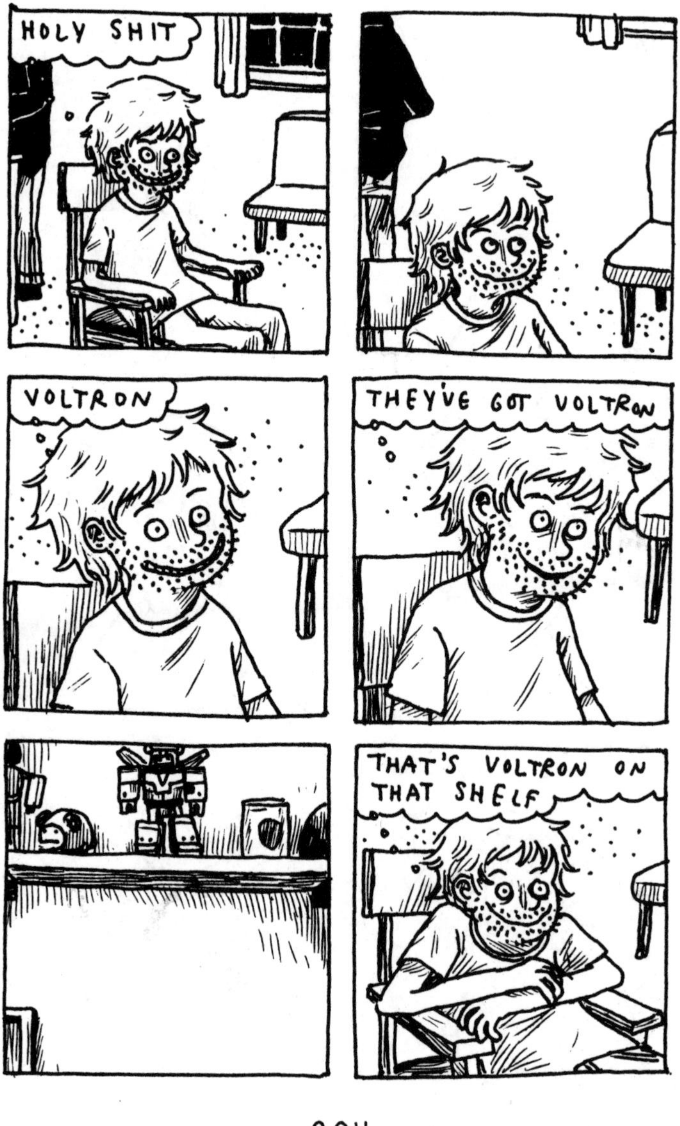
HOLY SHIT
VOLTRON
THEY'VE GOT VOLTRON
THAT'S VOLTRON ON THAT SHELF

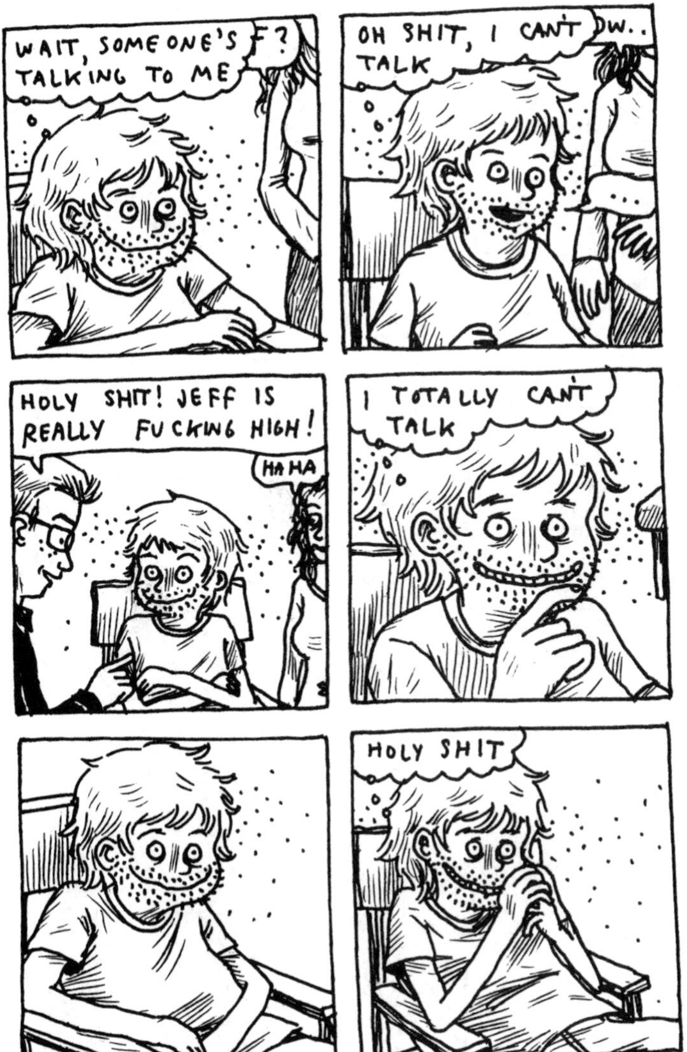
WAIT, SOMEONE'S TALKING TO ME
F?
OH SHIT, I CAN'T TALK
W..
HOLY SHIT! JEFF IS REALLY FUCKING HIGH!
HA HA
I TOTALLY CAN'T TALK
HOLY SHIT

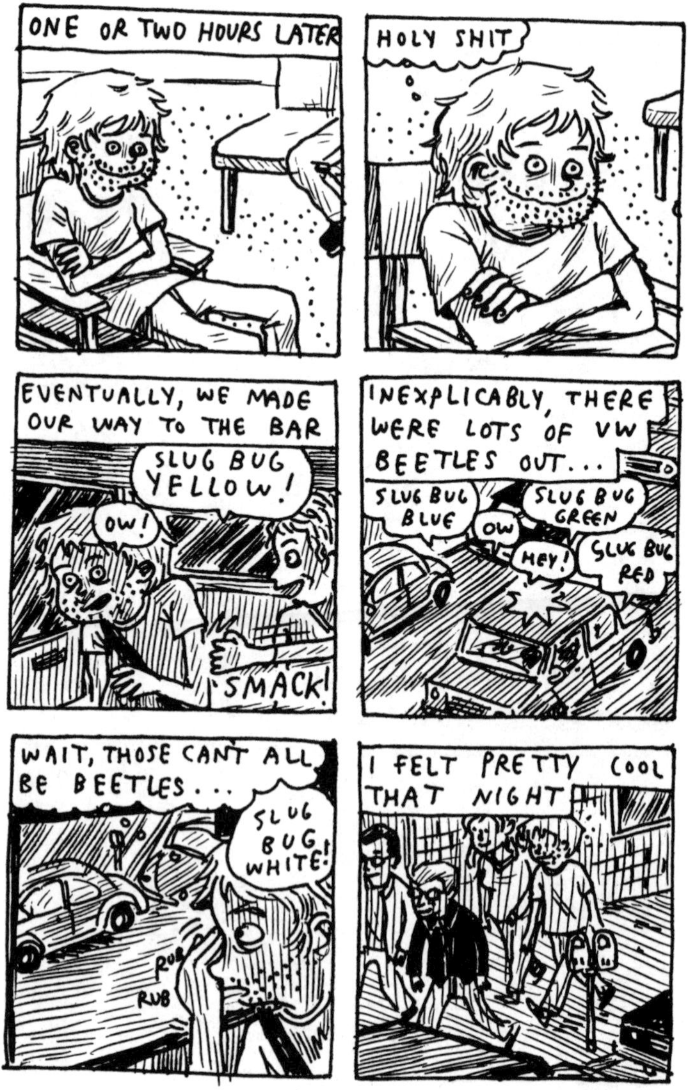
ONE OR TWO HOURS LATER
HOLY SHIT
EVENTUALLY, WE MADE OUR WAY TO THE BAR
SLUG BUG YELLOW!
OW!
SMACK!
INEXPLICABLY, THERE WERE LOTS OF VW BEETLES OUT...
SLUG BUG BLUE
OW
SLUG BUG GREEN
HEY!
SLUG BUG RED
WAIT, THOSE CAN'T ALL BE BEETLES...
SLUG BUG WHITE!
RUB
RUB
I FELT PRETTY COOL THAT NIGHT

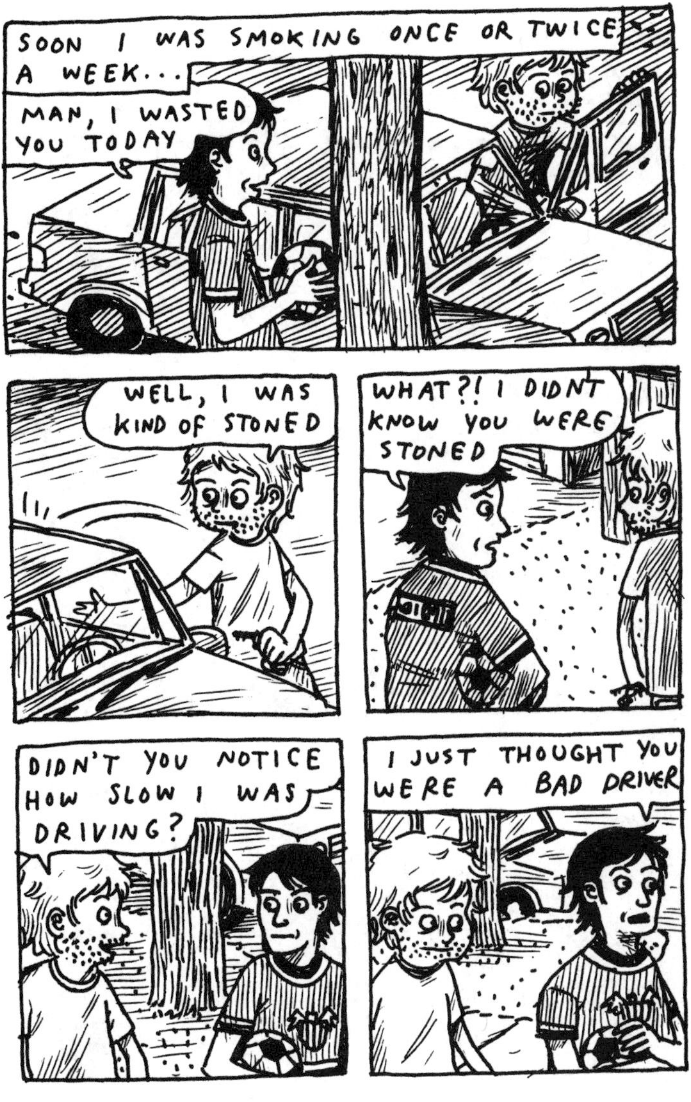
SOON I WAS SMOKING ONCE OR TWICE A WEEK...
MAN, I WASTED YOU TODAY
WELL, I WAS KIND OF STONED
WHAT?! I DIDNT KNOW YOU WERE STONED
DIDN'T YOU NOTICE HOW SLOW I WAS DRIVING?
I JUST THOUGHT YOU WERE A BAD DRIVER

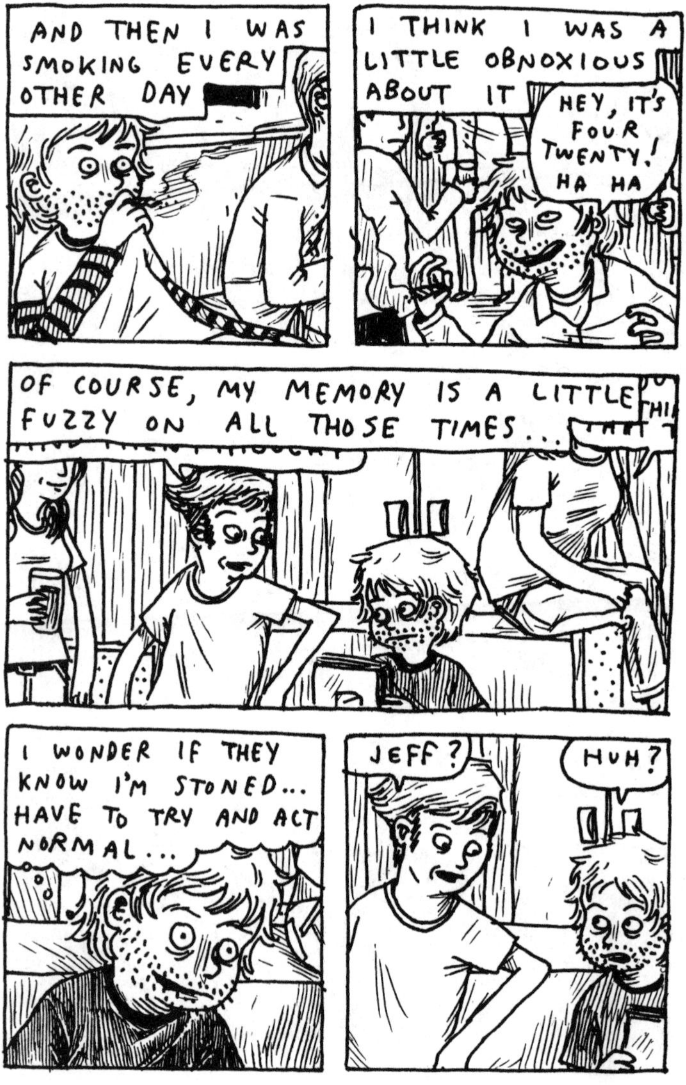
AND THEN I WAS SMOKING EVERY OTHER DAY
I THINK I WAS A LITTLE OBNOXIOUS ABOUT IT
HEY, IT'S FOUR TWENTY! HA HA
OF COURSE, MY MEMORY IS A LITTLE FUZZY ON ALL THOSE TIMES...
I WONDER IF THEY KNOW I'M STONED... HAVE TO TRY AND ACT NORMAL...
JEFF?
HUH?

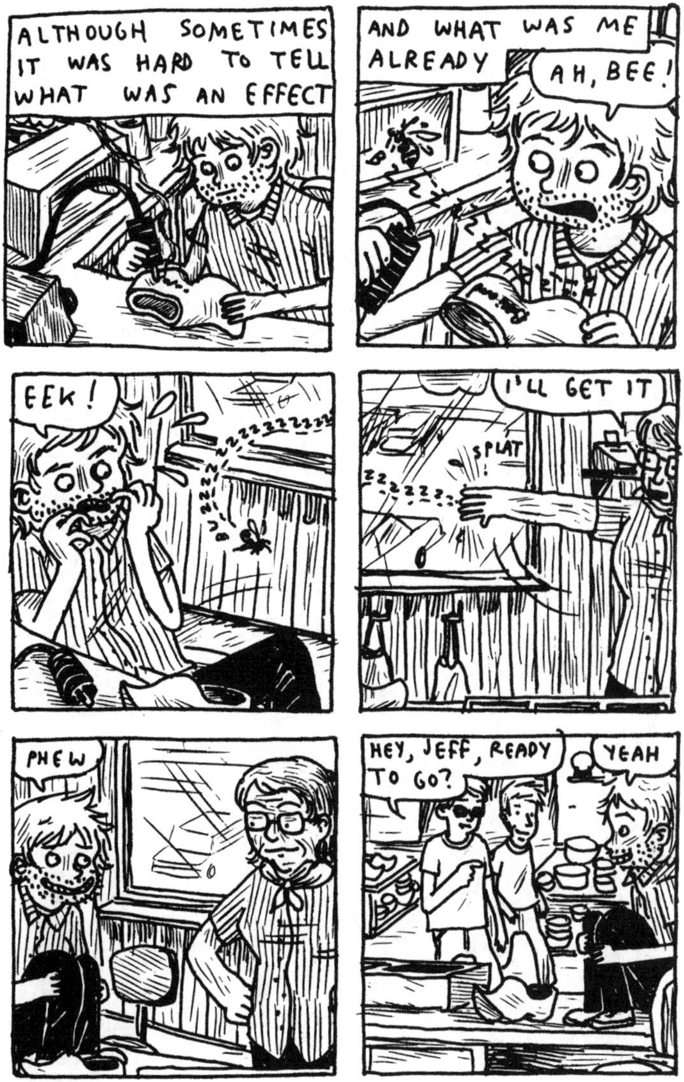
ALTHOUGH SOMETIMES IT WAS HARD TO TELL WHAT WAS AN EFFECT
AND WHAT WAS ME ALREADY
AH, BEE!
EEK!
I'LL GET IT
SPLAT
PHEW
HEY, JEFF, READY TO GO?
YEAH

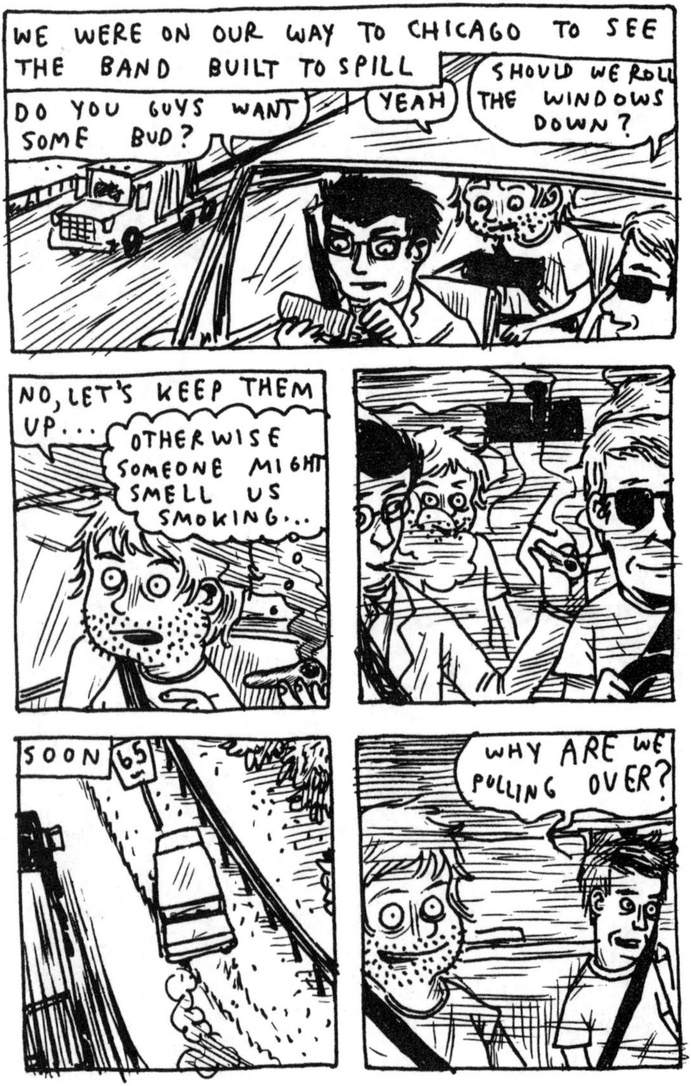
WE WERE ON OUR WAY TO CHICAGO TO SEE THE BAND BUILT TO SPILL
DO YOU GUYS WANT SOME BUD?
YEAH
SHOULD WE ROLL THE WINDOWS DOWN?
NO, LET'S KEEP THEM UP...
OTHERWISE SOMEONE MIGHT SMELL US SMOKING...
SOON
65
WHY ARE WE PULLING OVER?

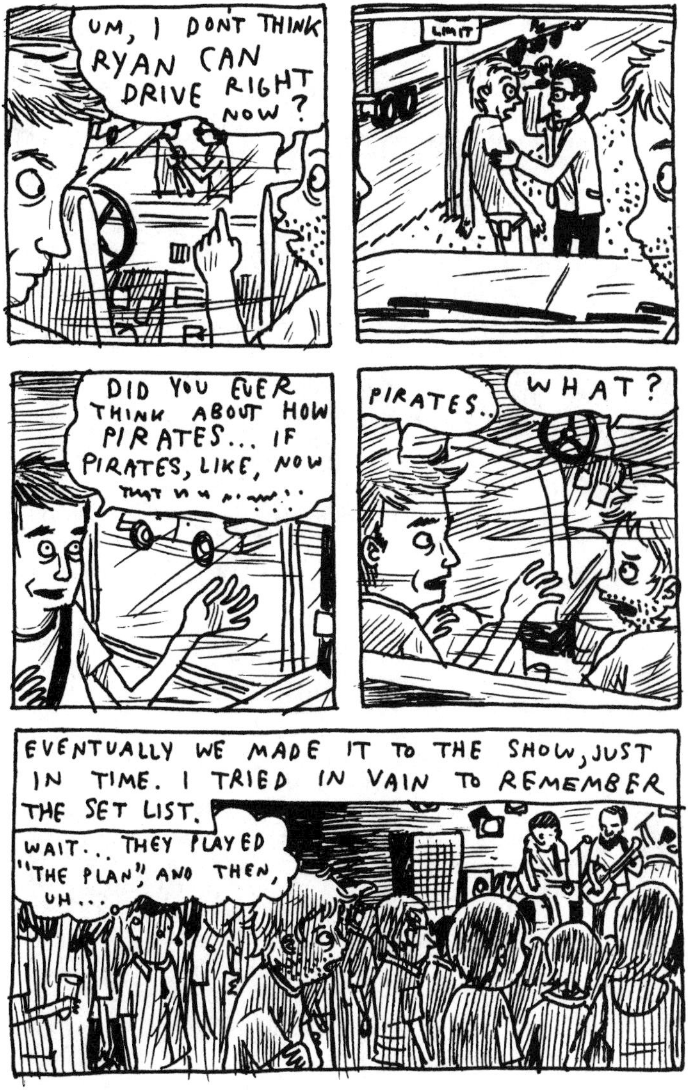
UM, I DON'T THINK RYAN CAN DRIVE RIGHT NOW?
LIMIT
DID YOU EVER THINK ABOUT HOW PIRATES... IF PIRATES, LIKE, NOW
PIRATES..
WHAT?
EVENTUALLY WE MADE IT TO THE SHOW, JUST IN TIME. I TRIED IN VAIN TO REMEMBER THE SET LIST.
WAIT... THEY PLAYED "THE PLAN," AND THEN, UH...

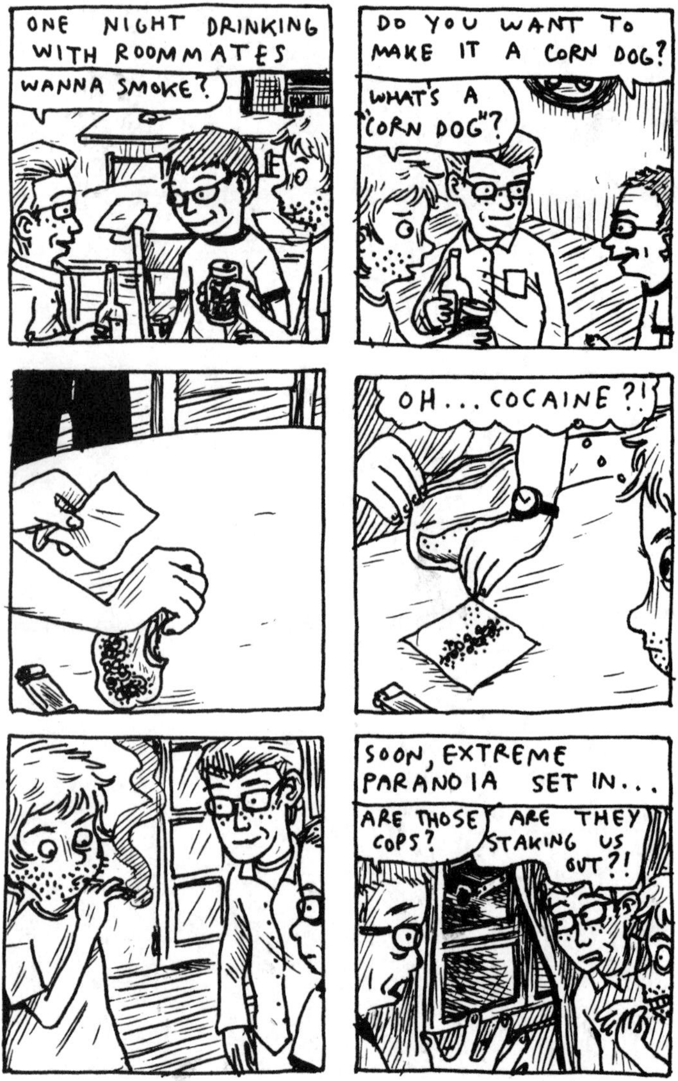
ONE NIGHT DRINKING WITH ROOMMATES
WANNA SMOKE?
DO YOU WANT TO MAKE IT A CORN DOG?
WHAT'S A "CORN DOG"?
OH... COCAINE?!
SOON, EXTREME PARANOIA SET IN...
ARE THOSE COPS?
ARE THEY STAKING US OUT?!

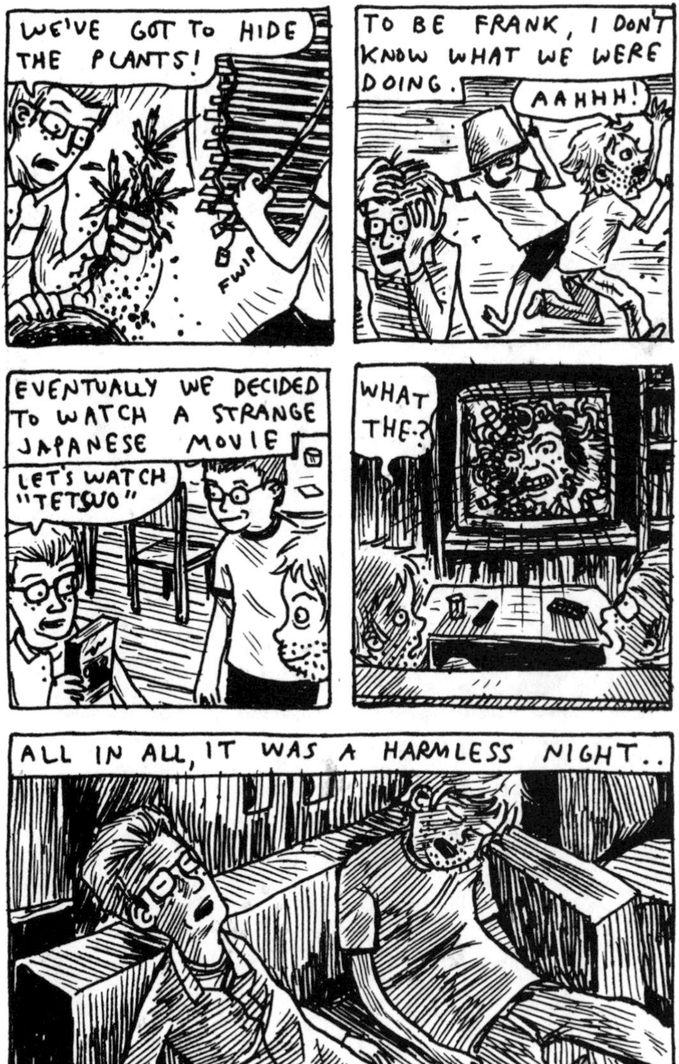
WE'VE GOT TO HIDE THE PLANTS!
FWIP
TO BE FRANK, I DON'T KNOW WHAT WE WERE DOING.
AAHHH!
EVENTUALLY WE DECIDED TO WATCH A STRANGE JAPANESE MOVIE
LET'S WATCH "TETSUO"
WHAT THE-?
ALL IN ALL, IT WAS A HARMLESS NIGHT..

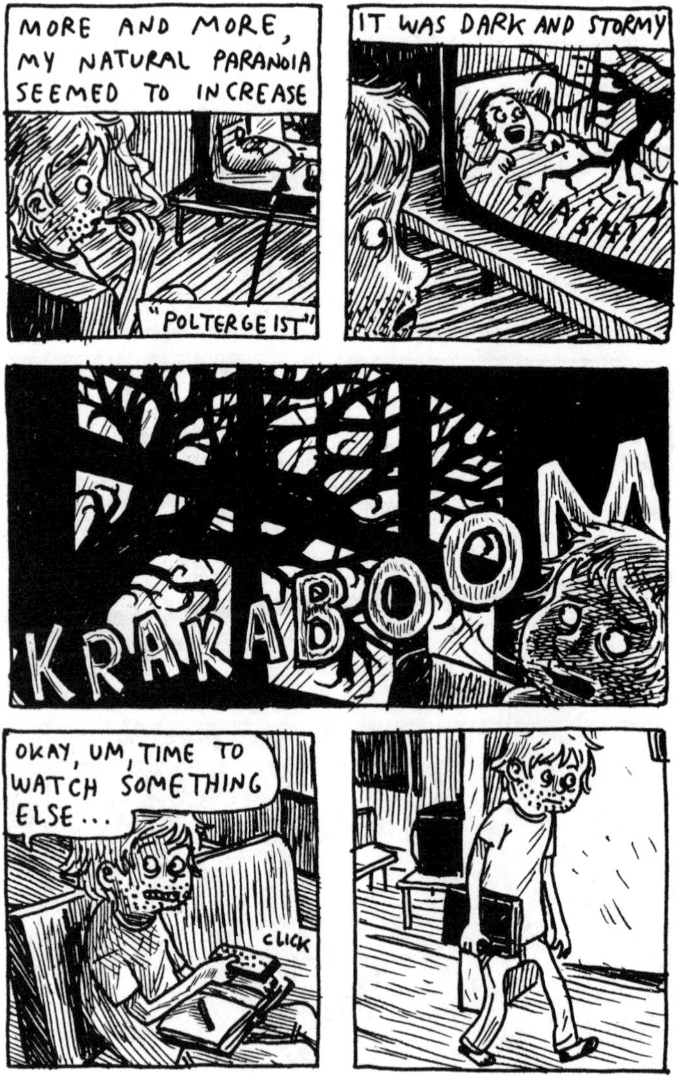
MORE AND MORE, MY NATURAL PARANOIA SEEMED TO INCREASE
"POLTERGEIST"
IT WAS DARK AND STORMY
CRASH!
KRAKABOOM
OKAY, UM, TIME TO WATCH SOMETHING ELSE...
CLICK

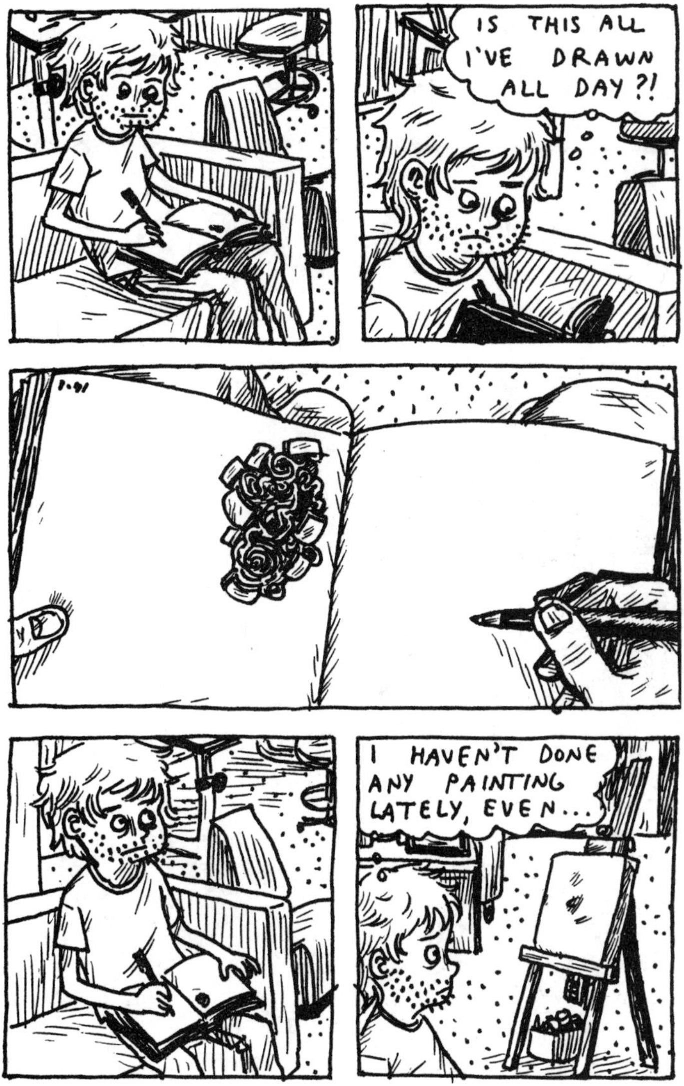
IS THIS ALL I'VE DRAWN ALL DAY ?!
I HAVEN'T DONE ANY PAINTING LATELY, EVEN...

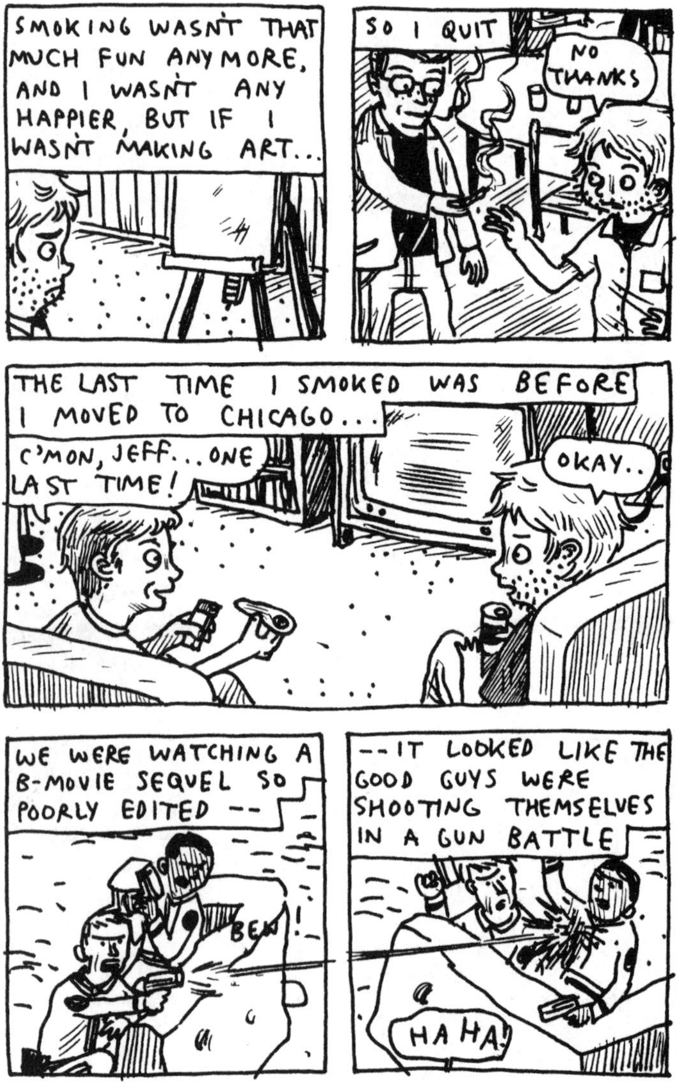
SMOKING WASN'T THAT MUCH FUN ANYMORE, AND I WASN'T ANY HAPPIER, BUT IF I WASN'T MAKING ART...
SO I QUIT
NO THANKS
THE LAST TIME I SMOKED WAS BEFORE I MOVED TO CHICAGO...
C'MON, JEFF...ONE LAST TIME!
OKAY..
WE WERE WATCHING A B-MOVIE SEQUEL SO POORLY EDITED --
BEW!
--IT LOOKED LIKE THE GOOD GUYS WERE SHOOTING THEMSELVES IN A GUN BATTLE
HA HA!

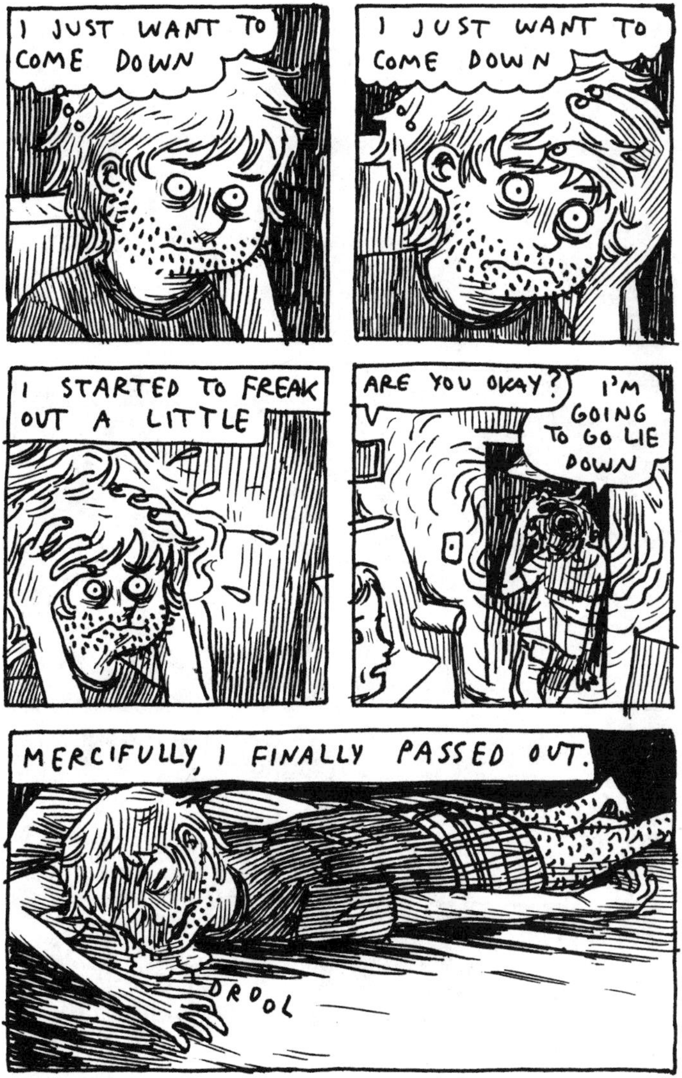
I JUST WANT TO COME DOWN
I JUST WANT TO COME DOWN
I STARTED TO FREAK OUT A LITTLE
ARE YOU OKAY?
I'M GOING TO GO LIE DOWN
MERCIFULLY, I FINALLY PASSED OUT.
DROOL

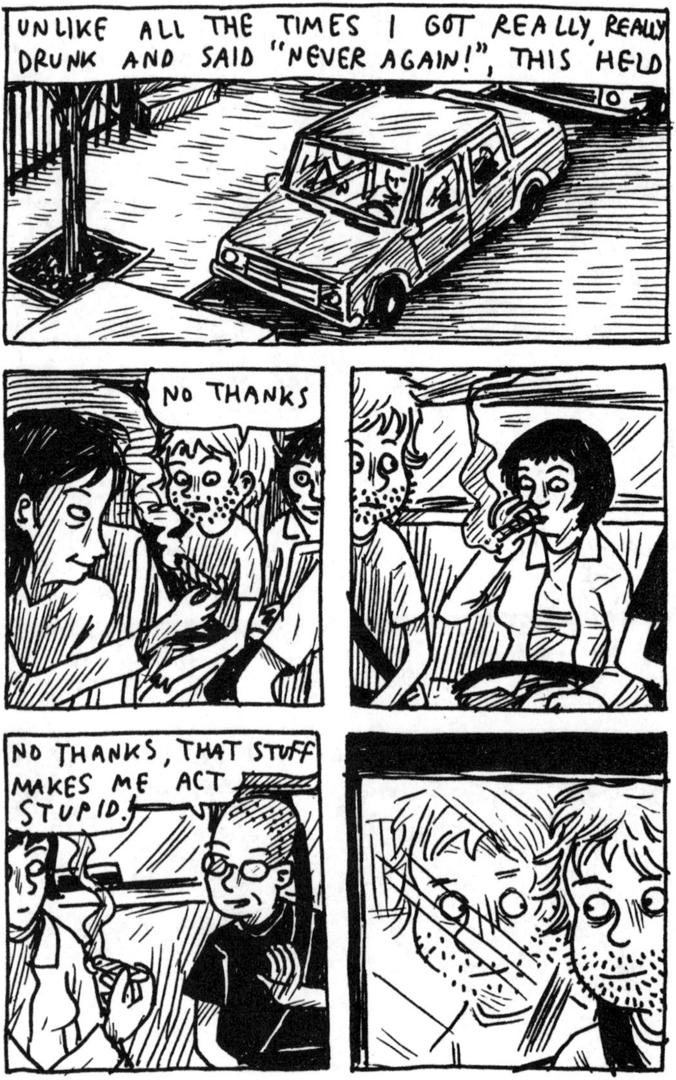
UNLIKE ALL THE TIMES I GOT REALLY, REALLY DRUNK AND SAID "NEVER AGAIN!", THIS HELD
NO THANKS
NO THANKS, THAT STUFF MAKES ME ACT STUPID.

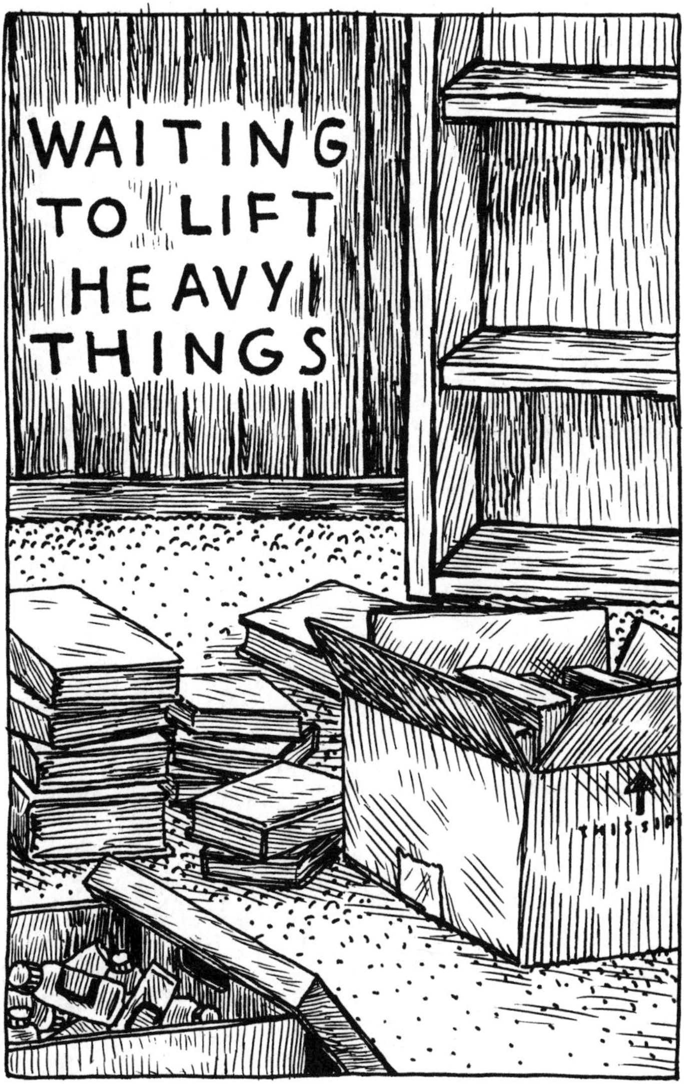
WAITING
TO LIFT
HEAVY
THINGS

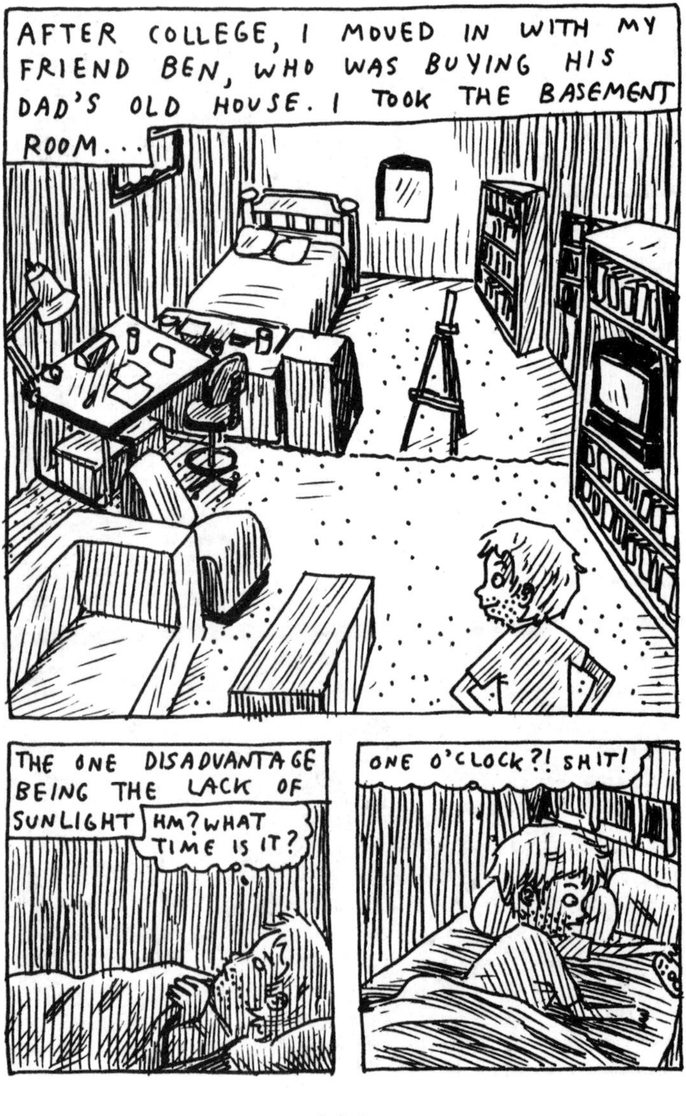
AFTER COLLEGE, I MOVED IN WITH MY FRIEND BEN, WHO WAS BUYING HIS DAD'S OLD HOUSE. I TOOK THE BASEMENT ROOM...
THE ONE DISADVANTAGE BEING THE LACK OF SUNLIGHT
HM? WHAT TIME IS IT?
ONE O'CLOCK?! SHIT!

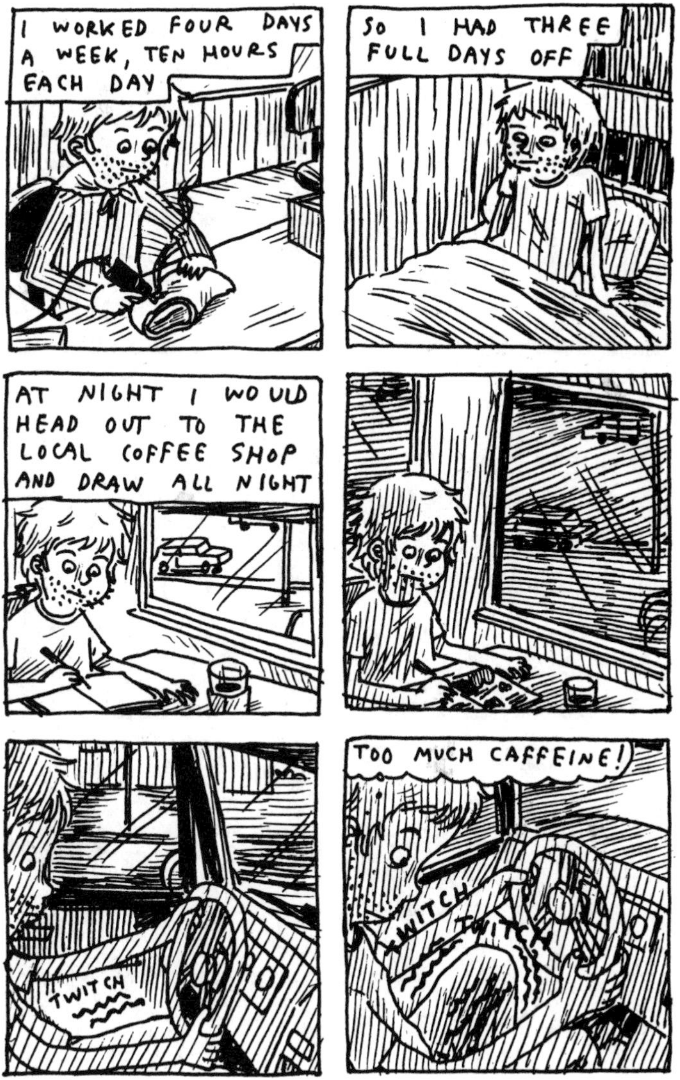
I WORKED FOUR DAYS A WEEK, TEN HOURS EACH DAY
SO I HAD THREE FULL DAYS OFF
AT NIGHT I WOULD HEAD OUT TO THE LOCAL COFFEE SHOP AND DRAW ALL NIGHT
TWITCH
TOO MUCH CAFFEINE!
TWITCH
TWITCH

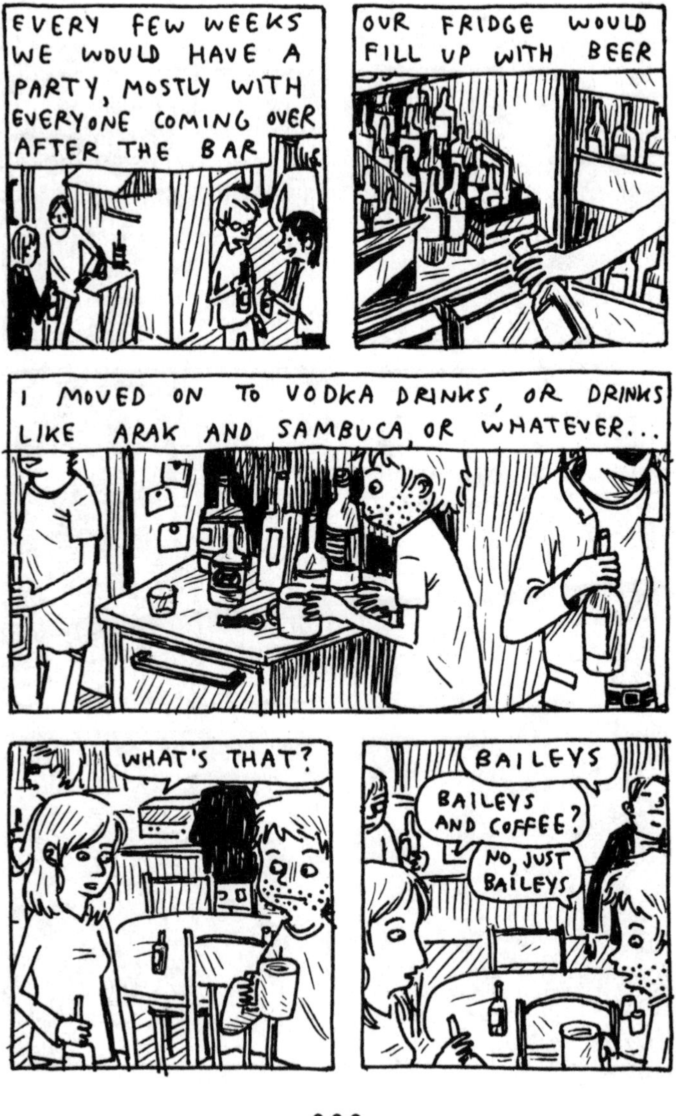
EVERY FEW WEEKS WE WOULD HAVE A PARTY, MOSTLY WITH EVERYONE COMING OVER AFTER THE BAR
OUR FRIDGE WOULD FILL UP WITH BEER
I MOVED ON TO VODKA DRINKS, OR DRINKS LIKE ARAK AND SAMBUCA, OR WHATEVER...
WHAT'S THAT?
BAILEYS
BAILEYS AND COFFEE?
NO, JUST BAILEYS

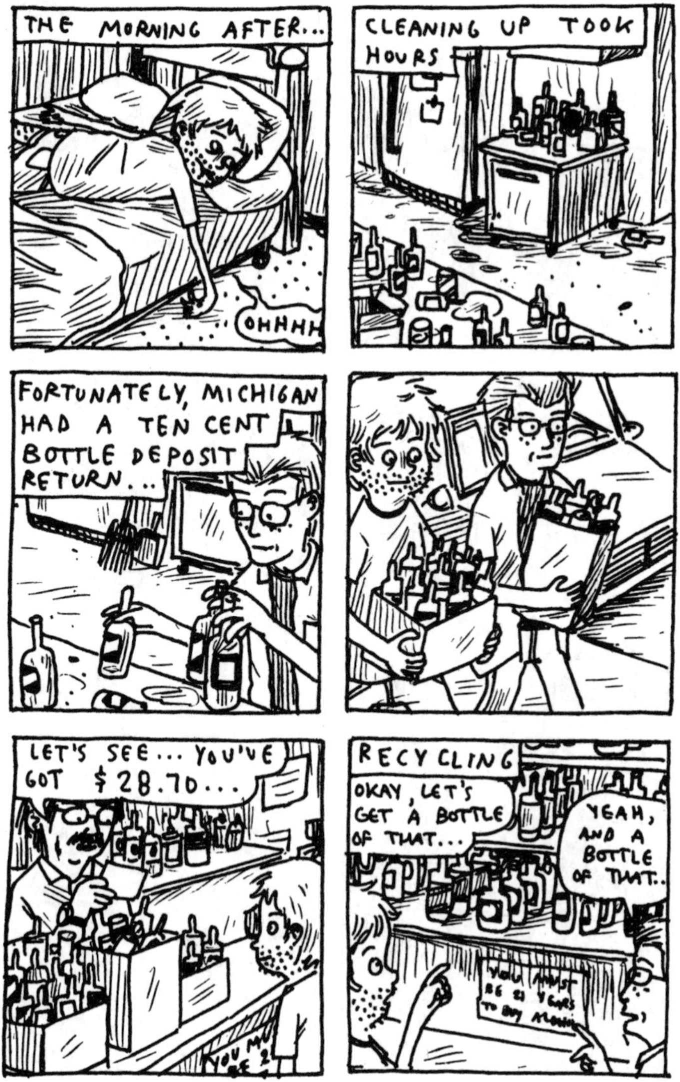
THE MORNING AFTER...
OHHHH
CLEANING UP TOOK HOURS
FORTUNATELY, MICHIGAN HAD A TEN CENT BOTTLE DEPOSIT RETURN...
LET'S SEE... YOU'VE GOT $28.70...
RECYCLING
OKAY, LET'S GET A BOTTLE OF THAT...
YEAH, AND A BOTTLE OF THAT...

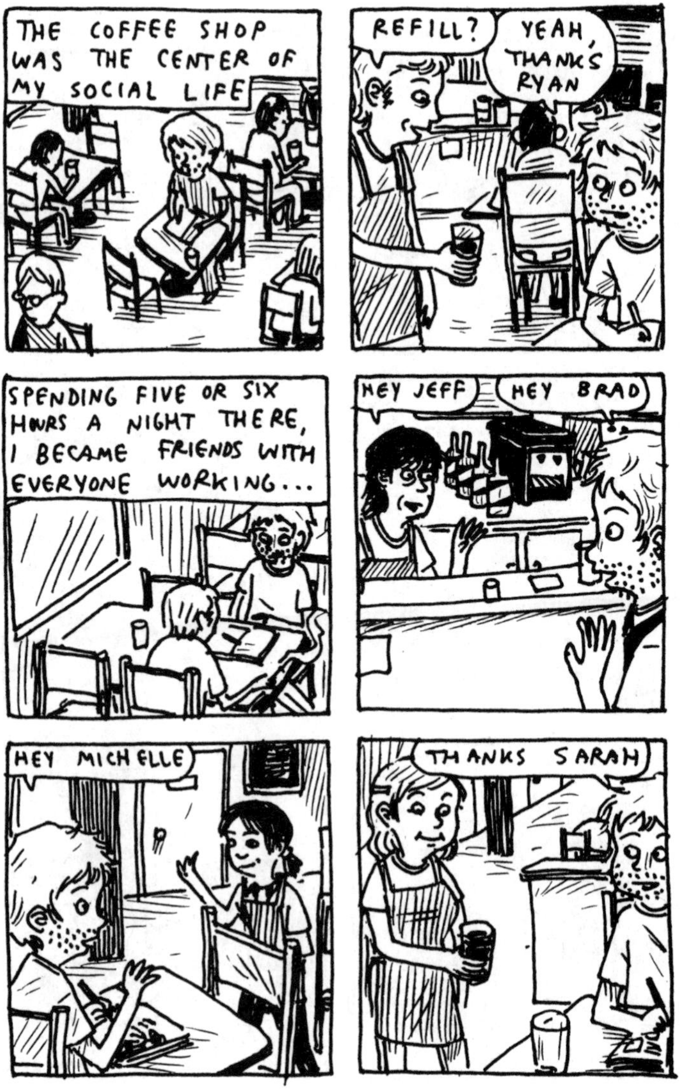
THE COFFEE SHOP WAS THE CENTER OF MY SOCIAL LIFE
REFILL?
YEAH, THANKS RYAN
SPENDING FIVE OR SIX HOURS A NIGHT THERE, I BECAME FRIENDS WITH EVERYONE WORKING...
HEY JEFF
HEY BRAD
HEY MICHELLE
THANKS SARAH

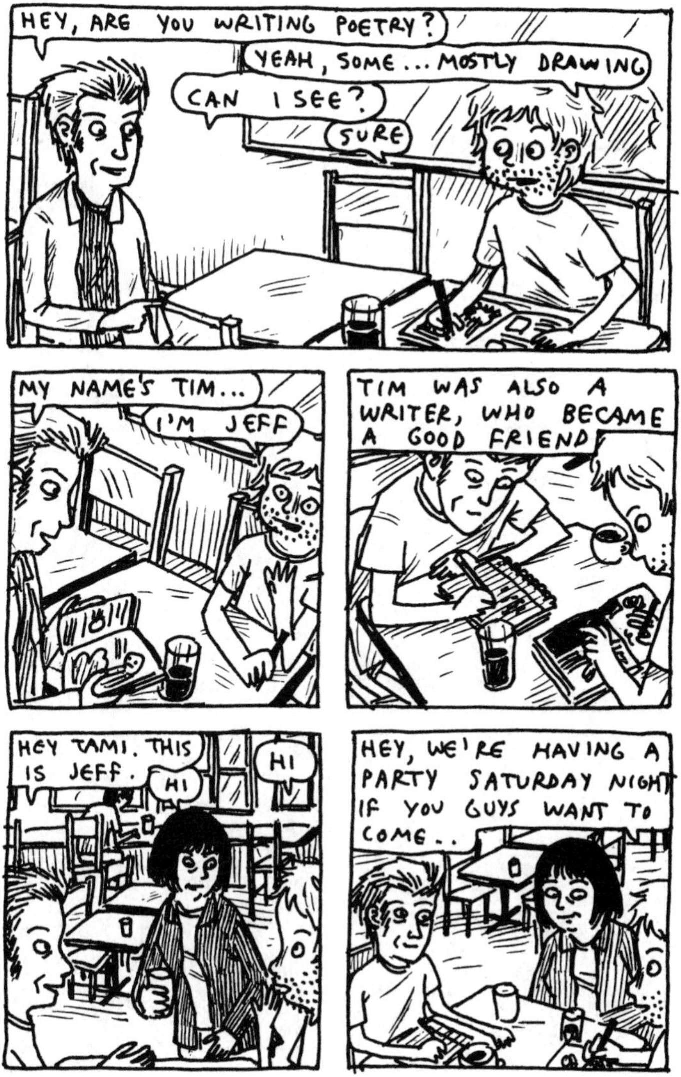
HEY, ARE YOU WRITING POETRY?
YEAH, SOME... MOSTLY DRAWING
CAN I SEE?
SURE
MY NAME'S TIM...
I'M JEFF
TIM WAS ALSO A WRITER, WHO BECAME A GOOD FRIEND
HEY TAMI. THIS IS JEFF.
HI
HI
HEY, WE'RE HAVING A PARTY SATURDAY NIGHT IF YOU GUYS WANT TO COME..

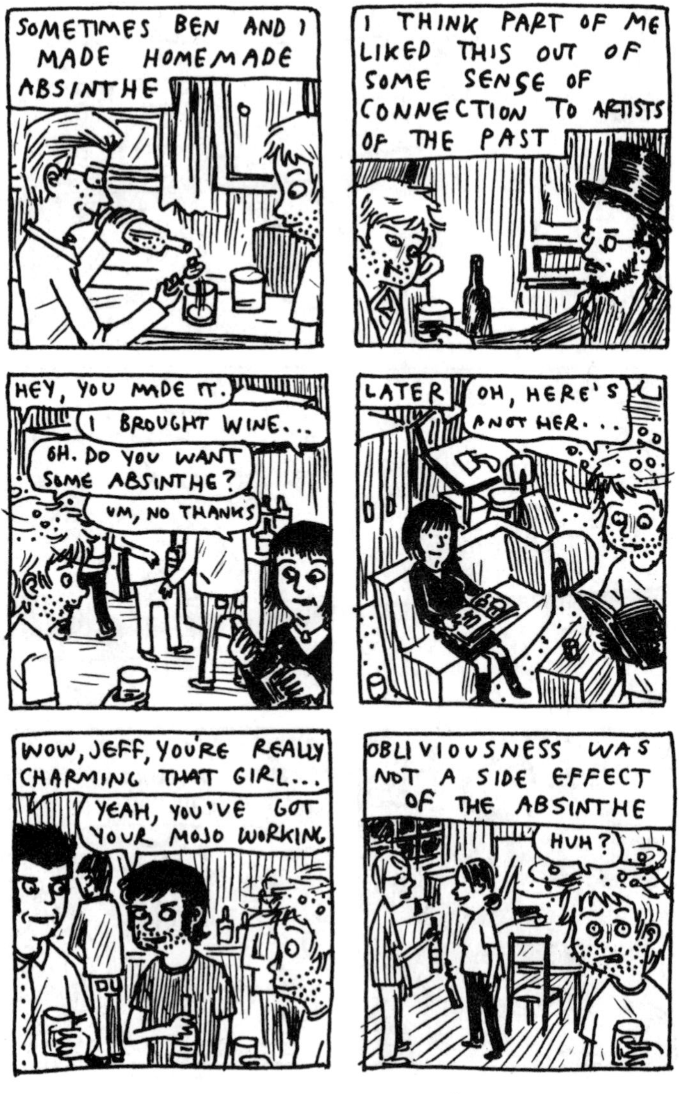
SOMETIMES BEN AND I MADE HOMEMADE ABSINTHE
I THINK PART OF ME LIKED THIS OUT OF SOME SENSE OF CONNECTION TO ARTISTS OF THE PAST
HEY, YOU MADE IT.
I BROUGHT WINE...
OH. DO YOU WANT SOME ABSINTHE?
UM, NO THANKS
LATER
OH, HERE'S ANOTHER...
WOW, JEFF, YOU'RE REALLY CHARMING THAT GIRL...
YEAH, YOU'VE GOT YOUR MOJO WORKING
OBLIVIOUSNESS WAS NOT A SIDE EFFECT OF THE ABSINTHE
HUH?

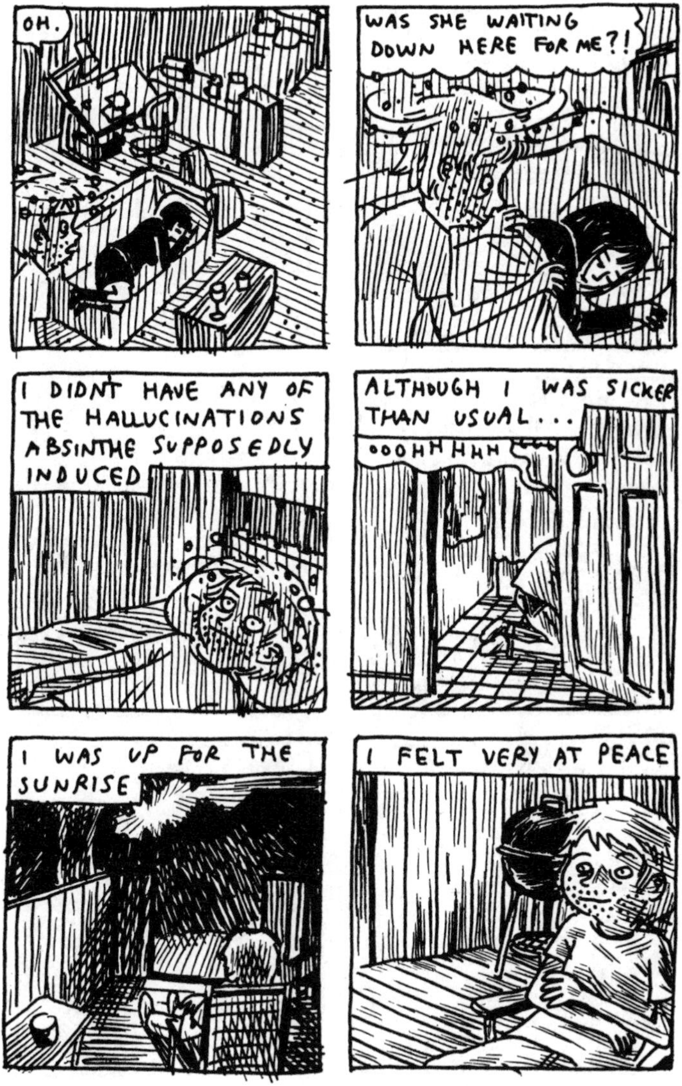
OH.
WAS SHE WAITING DOWN HERE FOR ME?!
I DIDN'T HAVE ANY OF THE HALLUCINATIONS ABSINTHE SUPPOSEDLY INDUCED
ALTHOUGH I WAS SICKER THAN USUAL...
OOOHHHHHH
I WAS UP FOR THE SUNRISE
I FELT VERY AT PEACE

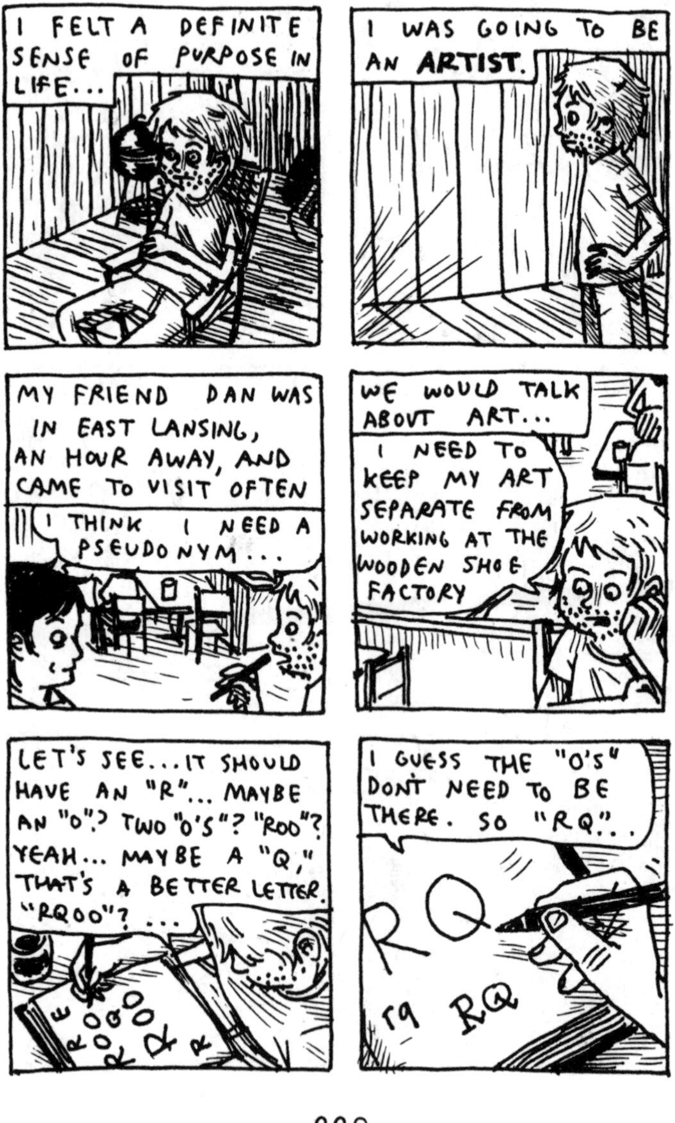
I FELT A DEFINITE SENSE OF PURPOSE IN LIFE...
I WAS GOING TO BE AN **ARTIST**.
MY FRIEND DAN WAS IN EAST LANSING, AN HOUR AWAY, AND CAME TO VISIT OFTEN
I THINK I NEED A PSEUDONYM...
WE WOULD TALK ABOUT ART...
I NEED TO KEEP MY ART SEPARATE FROM WORKING AT THE WOODEN SHOE FACTORY
LET'S SEE... IT SHOULD HAVE AN "R"... MAYBE AN "O"? TWO "O'S"? "ROO"? YEAH... MAYBE A "Q," THAT'S A BETTER LETTER. "RQOO"? ...
I GUESS THE "O'S" DON'T NEED TO BE THERE. SO "RQ"...
RQ
rq RQ

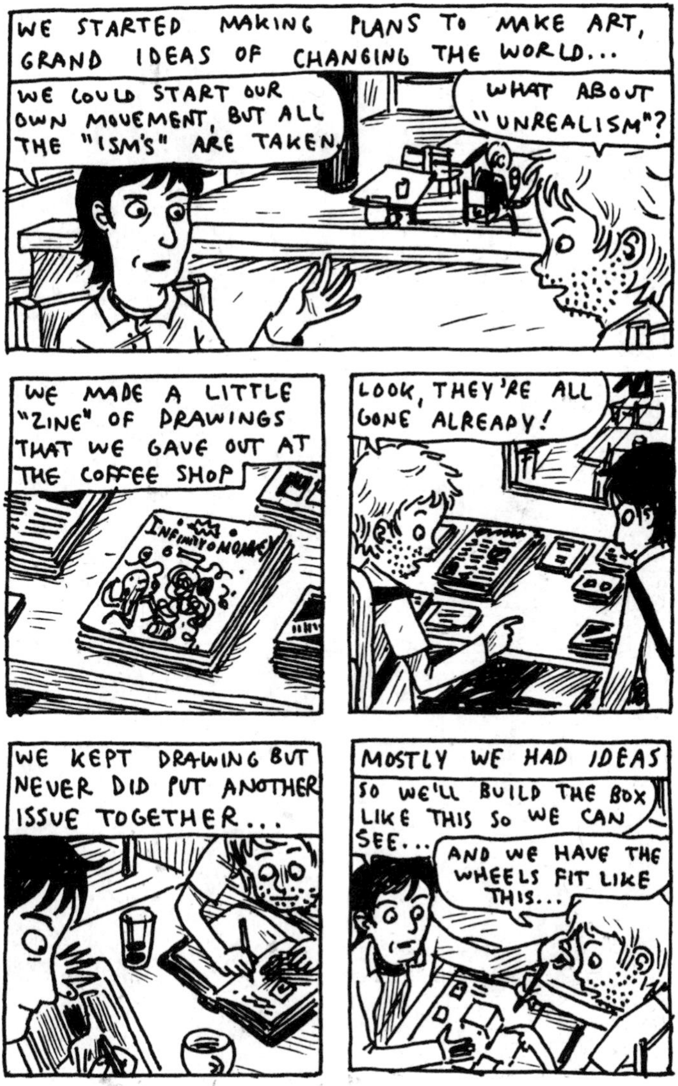
WE STARTED MAKING PLANS TO MAKE ART, GRAND IDEAS OF CHANGING THE WORLD...
WE COULD START OUR OWN MOVEMENT, BUT ALL THE "ISM'S" ARE TAKEN.
WHAT ABOUT "UNREALISM"?
WE MADE A LITTLE "ZINE" OF DRAWINGS THAT WE GAVE OUT AT THE COFFEE SHOP
LOOK, THEY'RE ALL GONE ALREADY!
WE KEPT DRAWING BUT NEVER DID PUT ANOTHER ISSUE TOGETHER...
MOSTLY WE HAD IDEAS
SO WE'LL BUILD THE BOX LIKE THIS SO WE CAN SEE...
AND WE HAVE THE WHEELS FIT LIKE THIS...

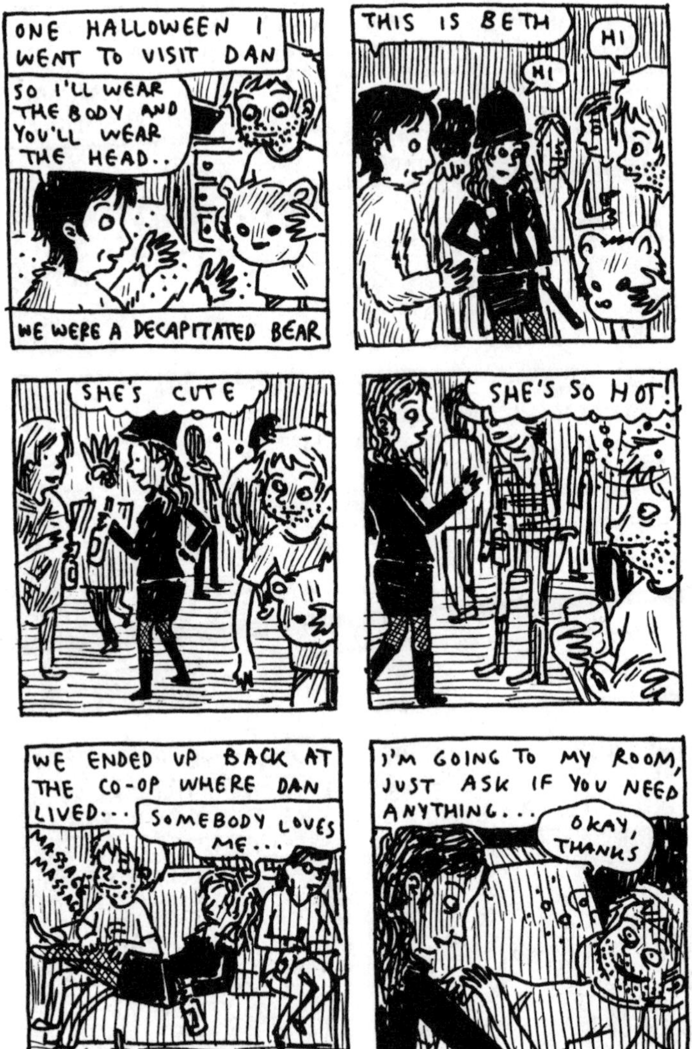
ONE HALLOWEEN I WENT TO VISIT DAN
SO I'LL WEAR THE BODY AND YOU'LL WEAR THE HEAD..
WE WERE A DECAPITATED BEAR
THIS IS BETH
HI
HI
SHE'S CUTE
SHE'S SO HOT!
WE ENDED UP BACK AT THE CO-OP WHERE DAN LIVED...
SOMEBODY LOVES ME...
I'M GOING TO MY ROOM, JUST ASK IF YOU NEED ANYTHING...
OKAY, THANKS

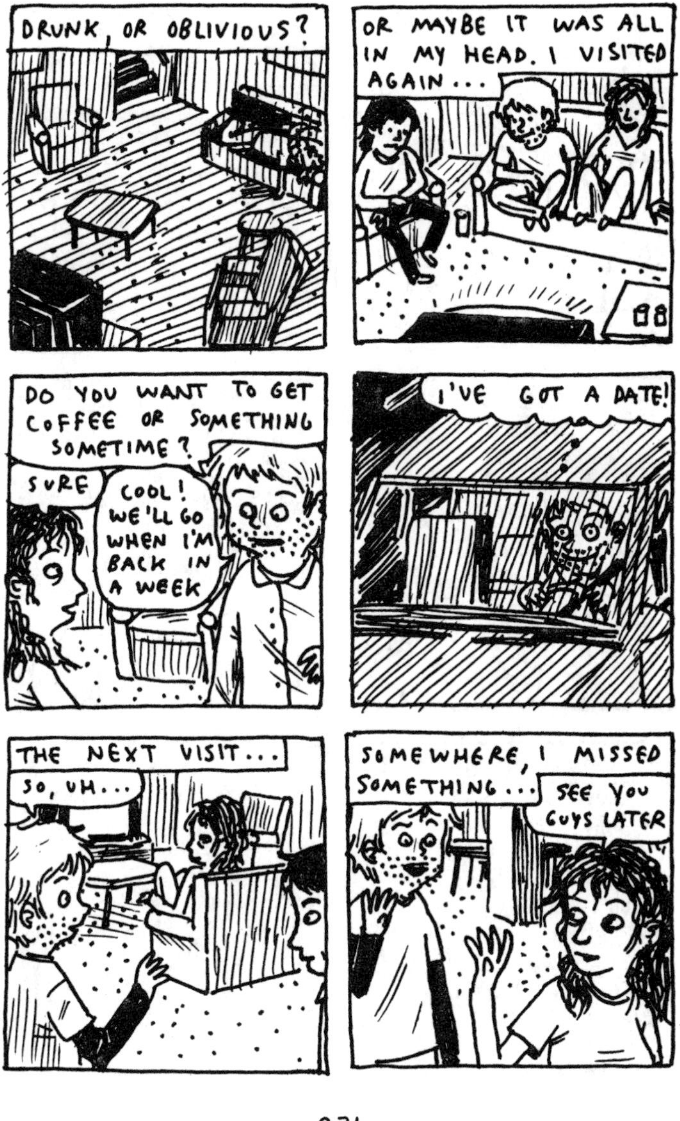
DRUNK, OR OBLIVIOUS?
OR MAYBE IT WAS ALL IN MY HEAD. I VISITED AGAIN...
DO YOU WANT TO GET COFFEE OR SOMETHING SOMETIME?
SURE
COOL! WE'LL GO WHEN I'M BACK IN A WEEK
I'VE GOT A DATE!
THE NEXT VISIT...
SO, UH...
SOMEWHERE, I MISSED SOMETHING...
SEE YOU GUYS LATER

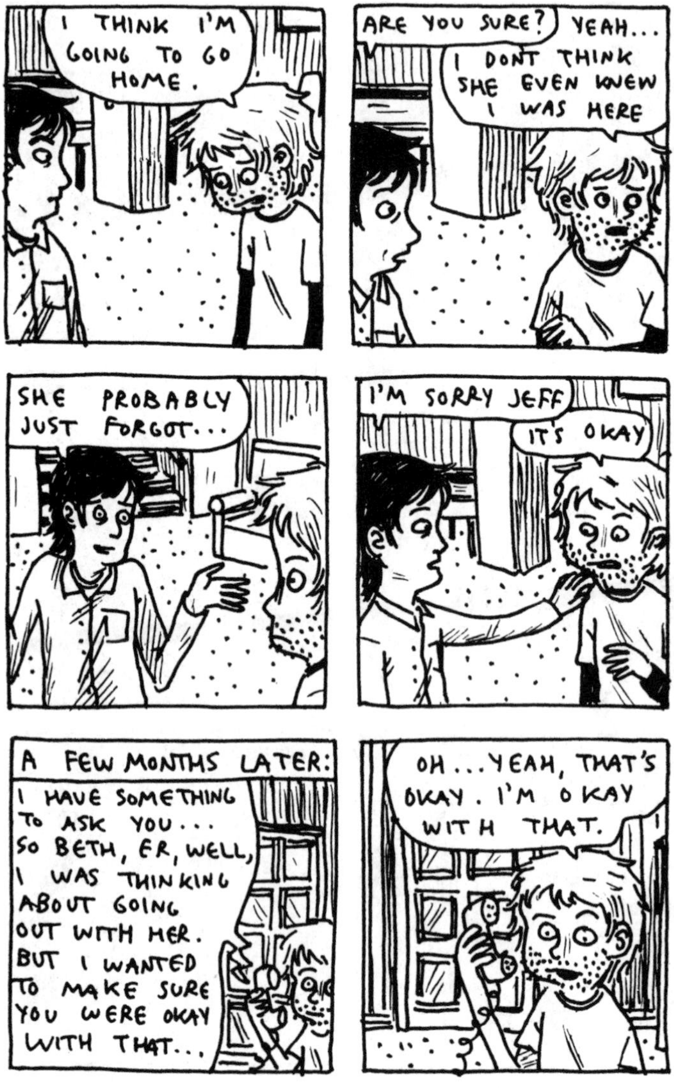
I THINK I'M GOING TO GO HOME.
ARE YOU SURE?
YEAH... I DONT THINK SHE EVEN KNEW I WAS HERE
SHE PROBABLY JUST FORGOT...
I'M SORRY JEFF
IT'S OKAY
A FEW MONTHS LATER:
I HAVE SOMETHING TO ASK YOU... SO BETH, ER, WELL, I WAS THINKING ABOUT GOING OUT WITH HER. BUT I WANTED TO MAKE SURE YOU WERE OKAY WITH THAT...
OH... YEAH, THAT'S OKAY. I'M OKAY WITH THAT.

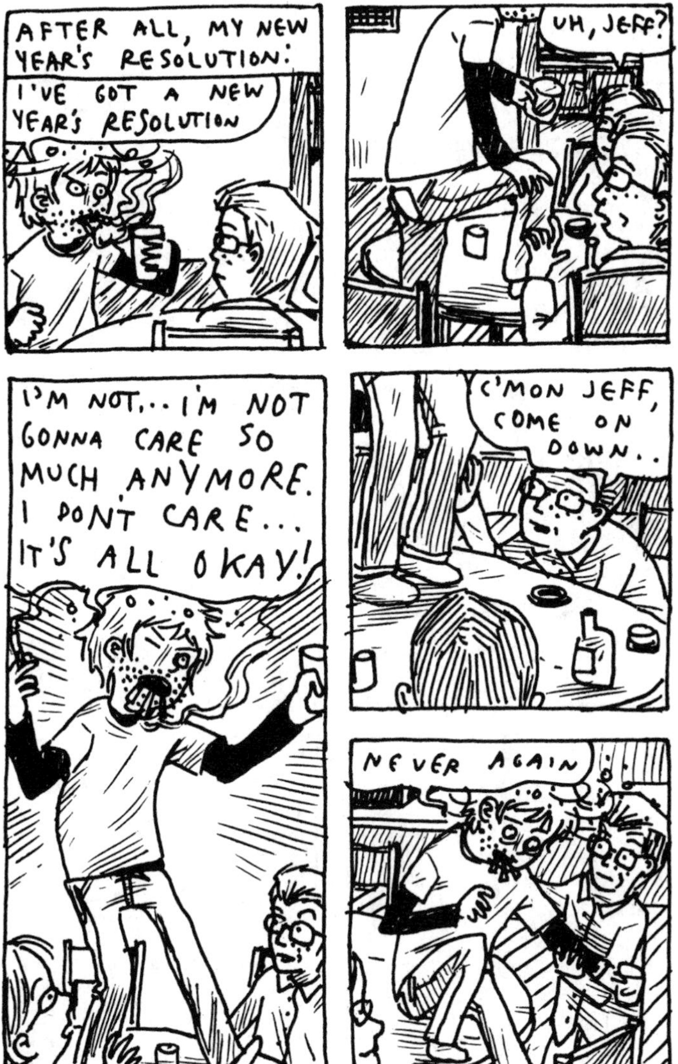
AFTER ALL, MY NEW YEAR'S RESOLUTION:
I'VE GOT A NEW YEAR'S RESOLUTION
UH, JEFF?
I'M NOT... I'M NOT GONNA CARE SO MUCH ANYMORE. I DON'T CARE... IT'S ALL OKAY!
C'MON JEFF, COME ON DOWN..
NEVER AGAIN

NATURALLY, IT WOULD BE YEARS BEFORE THAT SENTIMENT FINALLY SANK IN

WHY DOESN'T SHE NOTICE ME?

BUT I WAS TRYING TO FOCUS ON MY ART

MY ROOM WAS FILLING UP WITH STACKS OF PAINTINGS

SOMETIMES I'D BRING THEM TO SHOW FRIENDS AT THE COFFEE HOUSE

OH MY GOD! THIS IS THE MOST HORRIBLE THING I'VE EVER SEEN.

AND I WAS FILLING UP SKETCHBOOKS BY THE DOZEN

SOMETIMES WITH VERY EMBARRASSING RANTS ABOUT GIRLS...

"I WILL ALWAYS HOLD A SPECIAL PLACE IN MY HEART FOR YOU," SHE TOLD ME. YES, A VERY SMALL PLACE, TUCKED AWAY IN A CORNER IN UN MAR...

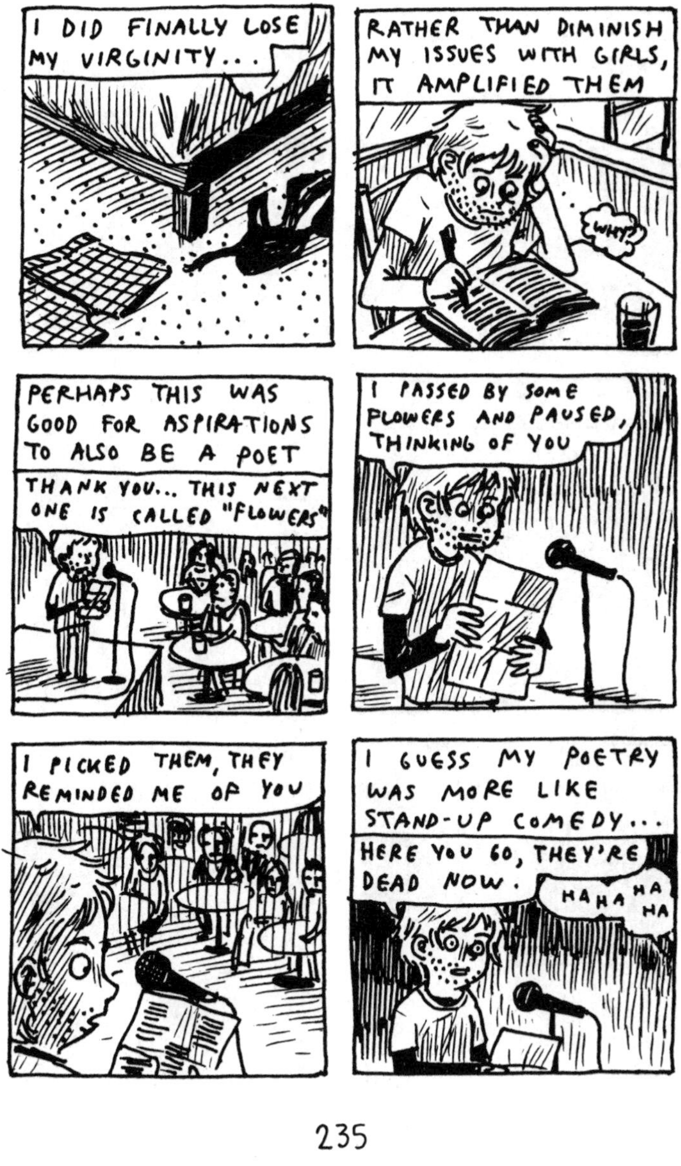
I DID FINALLY LOSE MY VIRGINITY...
RATHER THAN DIMINISH MY ISSUES WITH GIRLS, IT AMPLIFIED THEM
WHY?
PERHAPS THIS WAS GOOD FOR ASPIRATIONS TO ALSO BE A POET
THANK YOU... THIS NEXT ONE IS CALLED "FLOWERS"
I PASSED BY SOME FLOWERS AND PAUSED, THINKING OF YOU
I PICKED THEM, THEY REMINDED ME OF YOU
I GUESS MY POETRY WAS MORE LIKE STAND-UP COMEDY...
HERE YOU GO, THEY'RE DEAD NOW.
HAHAHA HA

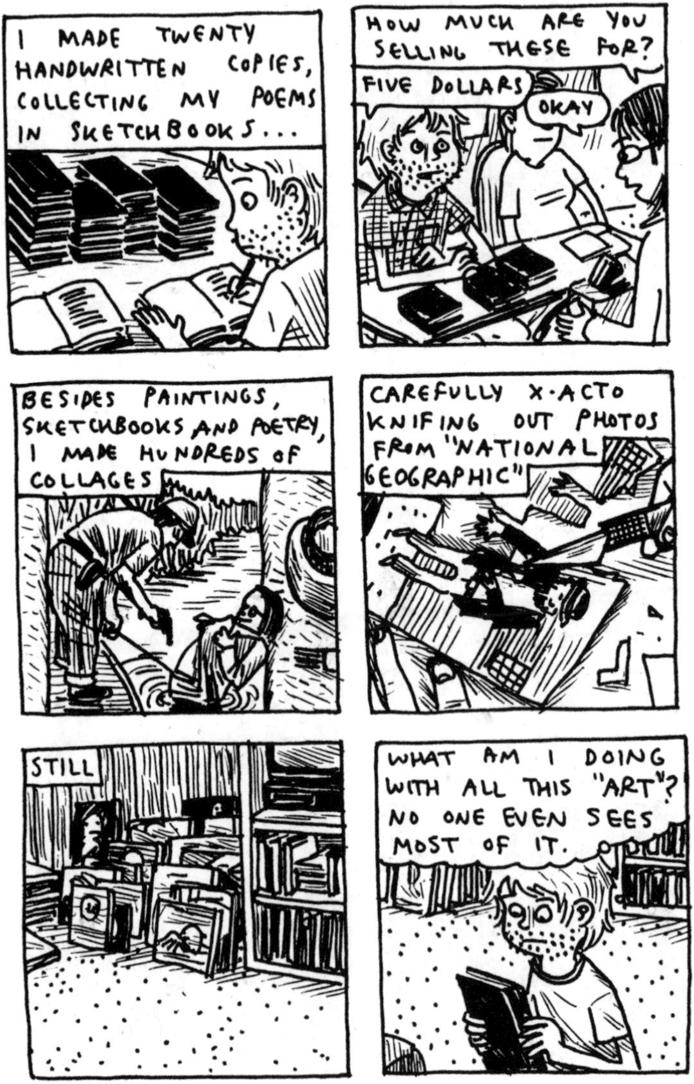
I MADE TWENTY HANDWRITTEN COPIES, COLLECTING MY POEMS IN SKETCHBOOKS...
HOW MUCH ARE YOU SELLING THESE FOR?
FIVE DOLLARS
OKAY
BESIDES PAINTINGS, SKETCHBOOKS AND POETRY, I MADE HUNDREDS OF COLLAGES
CAREFULLY X-ACTO KNIFING OUT PHOTOS FROM "NATIONAL GEOGRAPHIC"
STILL
WHAT AM I DOING WITH ALL THIS "ART"? NO ONE EVEN SEES MOST OF IT.

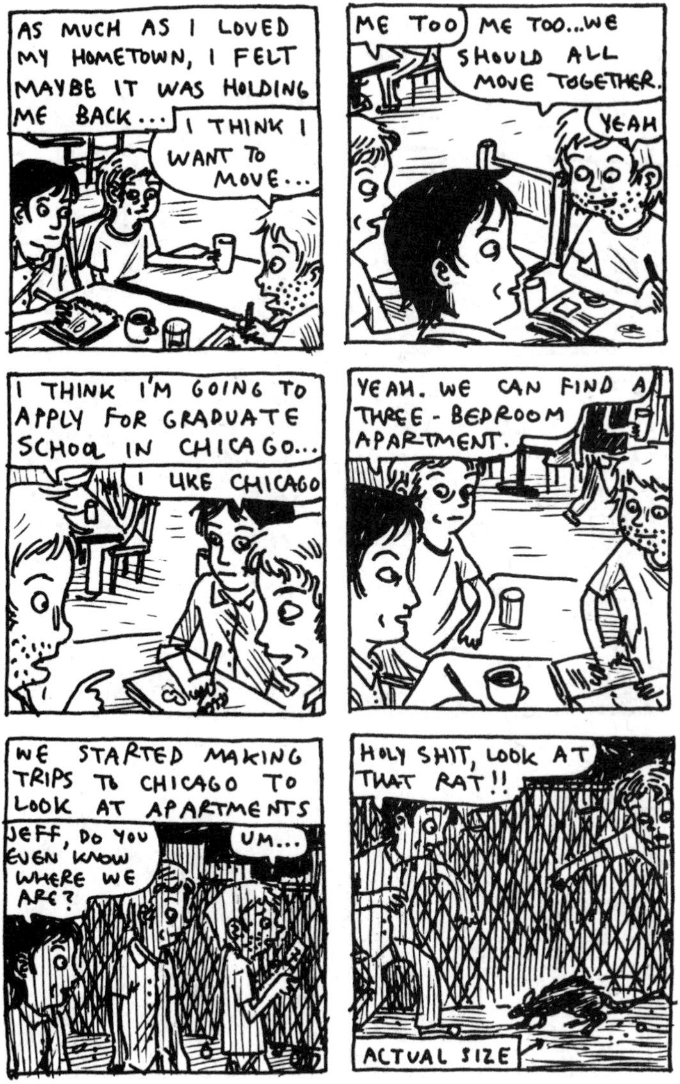
AS MUCH AS I LOVED MY HOMETOWN, I FELT MAYBE IT WAS HOLDING ME BACK...
I THINK I WANT TO MOVE...
ME TOO
ME TOO...WE SHOULD ALL MOVE TOGETHER.
YEAH
I THINK I'M GOING TO APPLY FOR GRADUATE SCHOOL IN CHICAGO...
I LIKE CHICAGO
YEAH. WE CAN FIND A THREE-BEDROOM APARTMENT.
WE STARTED MAKING TRIPS TO CHICAGO TO LOOK AT APARTMENTS
JEFF, DO YOU EVEN KNOW WHERE WE ARE?
UM...
HOLY SHIT, LOOK AT THAT RAT!!
ACTUAL SIZE

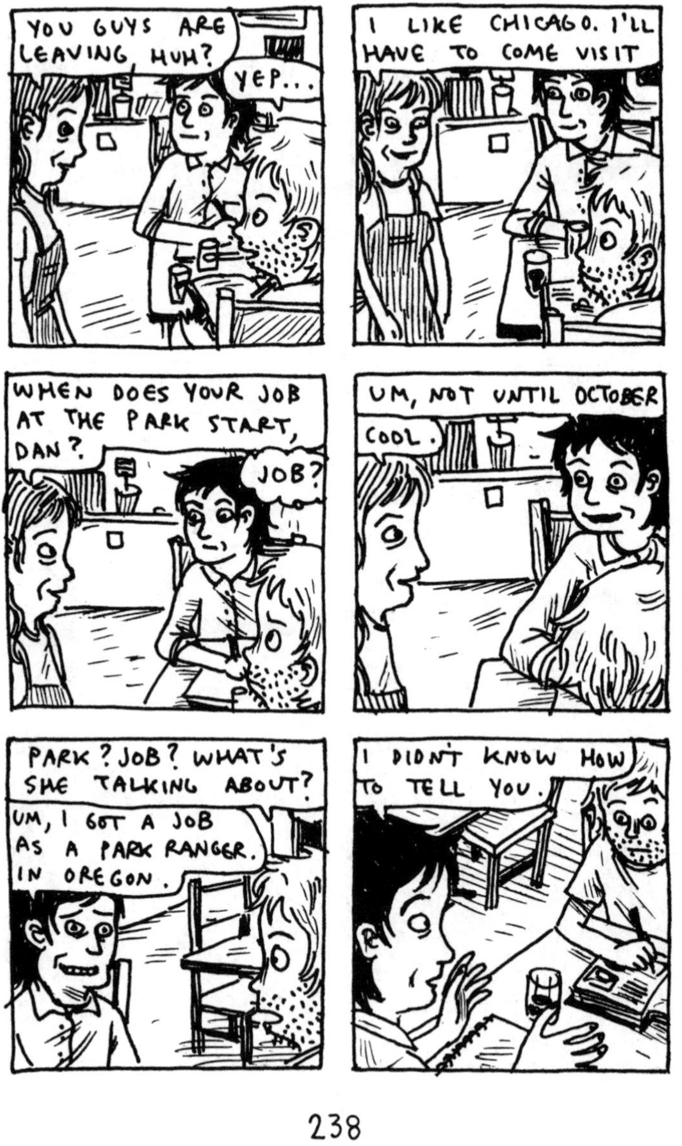
YOU GUYS ARE LEAVING, HUH?
YEP...
I LIKE CHICAGO. I'LL HAVE TO COME VISIT
WHEN DOES YOUR JOB AT THE PARK START, DAN?
JOB?
UM, NOT UNTIL OCTOBER
COOL.
PARK? JOB? WHAT'S SHE TALKING ABOUT?
UM, I GOT A JOB AS A PARK RANGER. IN OREGON.
I DIDN'T KNOW HOW TO TELL YOU.

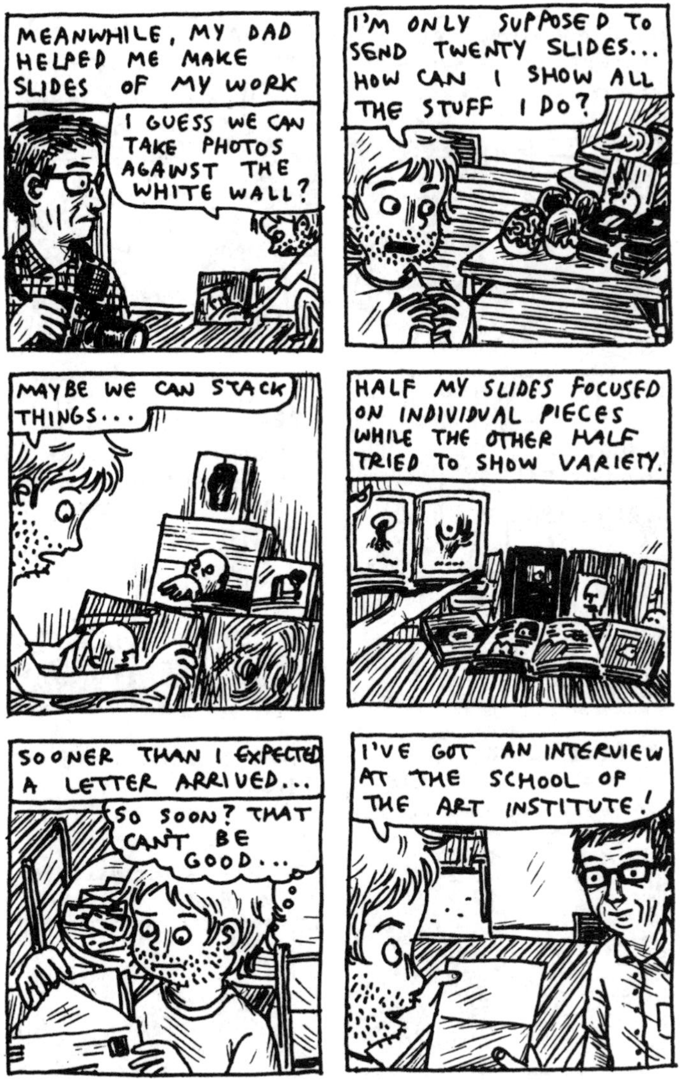
MEANWHILE, MY DAD HELPED ME MAKE SLIDES OF MY WORK
I GUESS WE CAN TAKE PHOTOS AGAINST THE WHITE WALL?
I'M ONLY SUPPOSED TO SEND TWENTY SLIDES... HOW CAN I SHOW ALL THE STUFF I DO?
MAYBE WE CAN STACK THINGS...
HALF MY SLIDES FOCUSED ON INDIVIDUAL PIECES WHILE THE OTHER HALF TRIED TO SHOW VARIETY.
SOONER THAN I EXPECTED A LETTER ARRIVED...
SO SOON? THAT CAN'T BE GOOD...
I'VE GOT AN INTERVIEW AT THE SCHOOL OF THE ART INSTITUTE!

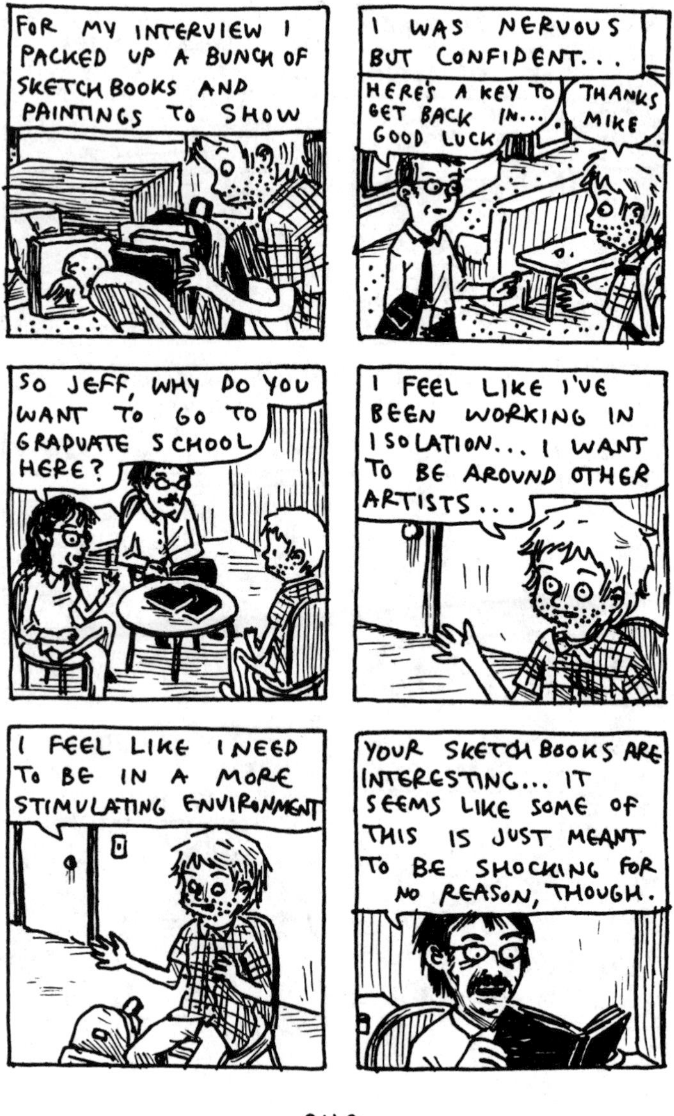
FOR MY INTERVIEW I PACKED UP A BUNCH OF SKETCHBOOKS AND PAINTINGS TO SHOW
I WAS NERVOUS BUT CONFIDENT...
HERE'S A KEY TO GET BACK IN... GOOD LUCK
THANKS MIKE
SO JEFF, WHY DO YOU WANT TO GO TO GRADUATE SCHOOL HERE?
I FEEL LIKE I'VE BEEN WORKING IN ISOLATION... I WANT TO BE AROUND OTHER ARTISTS...
I FEEL LIKE I NEED TO BE IN A MORE STIMULATING ENVIRONMENT
YOUR SKETCHBOOKS ARE INTERESTING... IT SEEMS LIKE SOME OF THIS IS JUST MEANT TO BE SHOCKING FOR NO REASON, THOUGH.

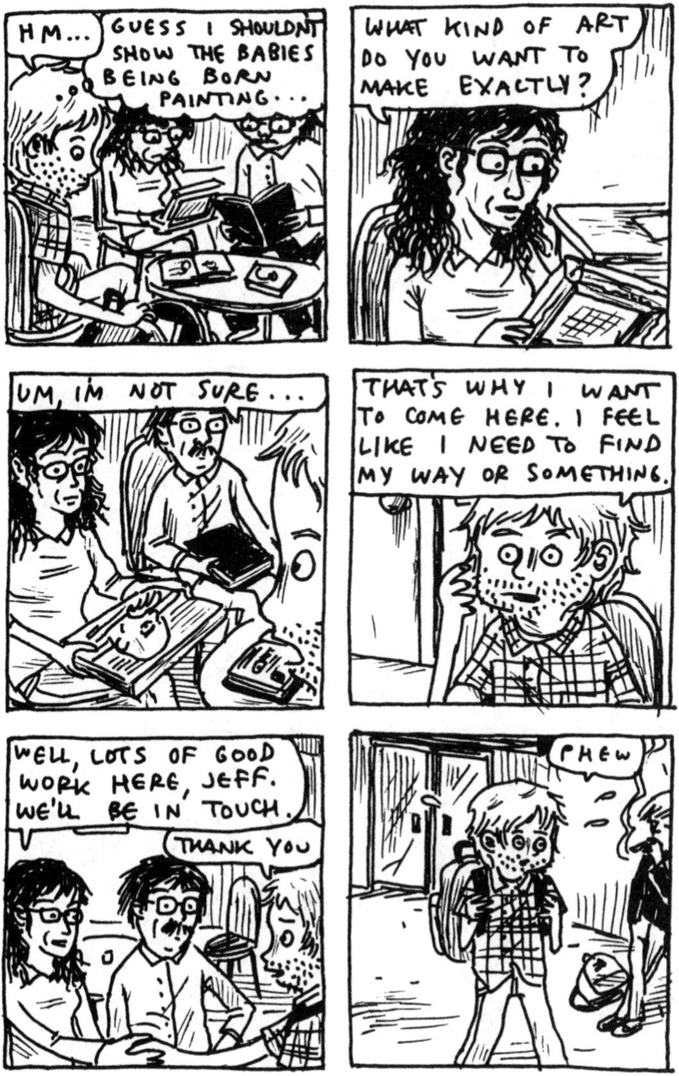
HM...
GUESS I SHOULDN'T SHOW THE BABIES BEING BORN PAINTING...
WHAT KIND OF ART DO YOU WANT TO MAKE EXACTLY?
UM, I'M NOT SURE...
THAT'S WHY I WANT TO COME HERE. I FEEL LIKE I NEED TO FIND MY WAY OR SOMETHING.
WELL, LOTS OF GOOD WORK HERE, JEFF. WE'LL BE IN TOUCH.
THANK YOU
PHEW

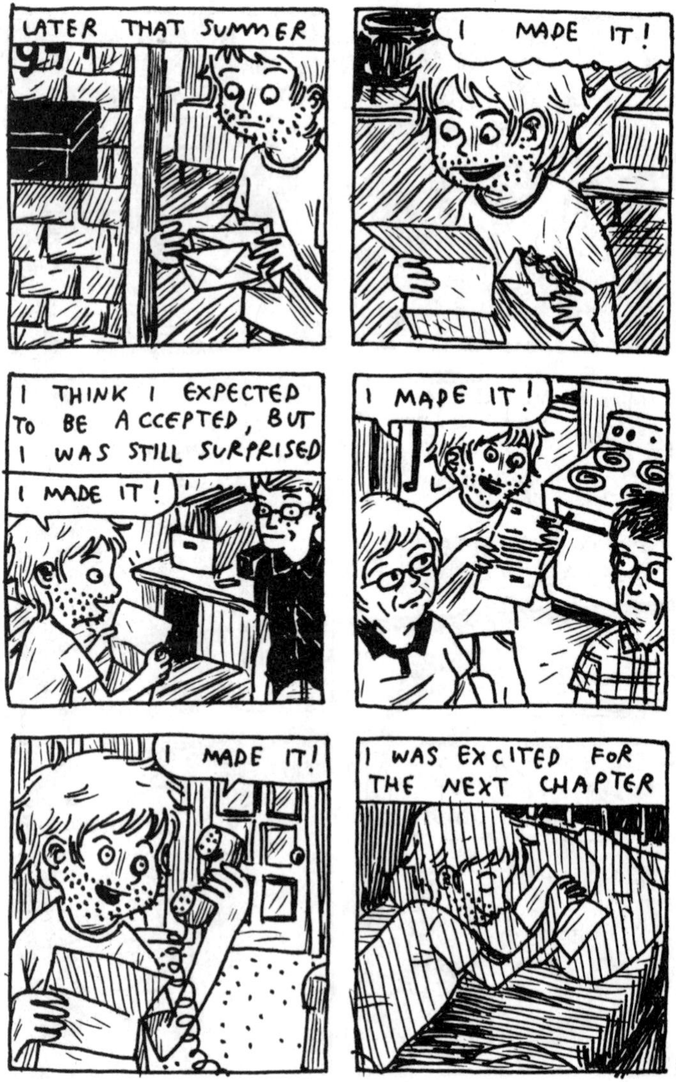
LATER THAT SUMMER
I MADE IT!
I THINK I EXPECTED TO BE ACCEPTED, BUT I WAS STILL SURPRISED
I MADE IT!
I MADE IT!
I MADE IT!
I WAS EXCITED FOR THE NEXT CHAPTER

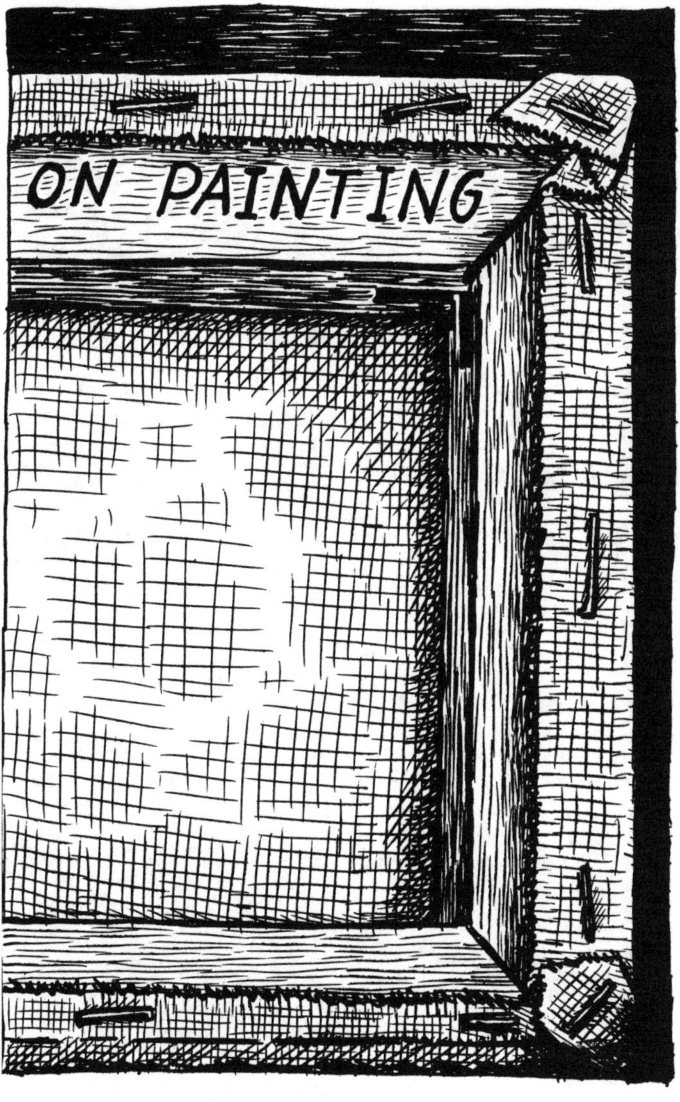
ON PAINTING

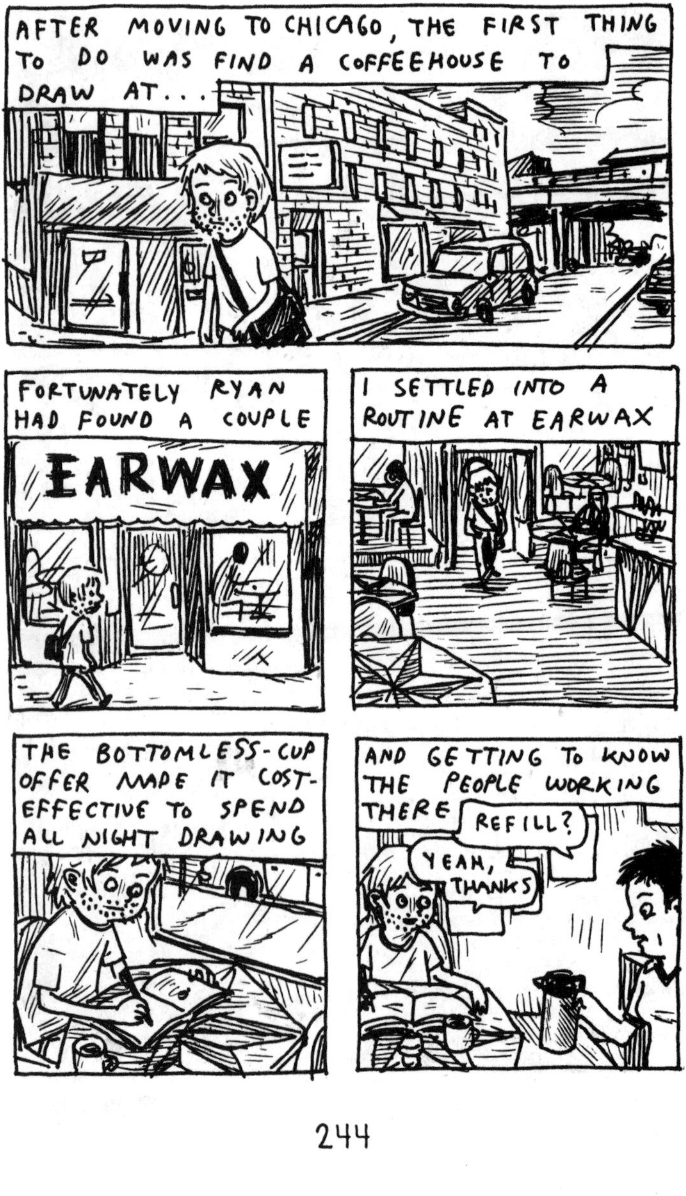
AFTER MOVING TO CHICAGO, THE FIRST THING TO DO WAS FIND A COFFEEHOUSE TO DRAW AT...
FORTUNATELY RYAN HAD FOUND A COUPLE
EARWAX
I SETTLED INTO A ROUTINE AT EARWAX
THE BOTTOMLESS-CUP OFFER MADE IT COST-EFFECTIVE TO SPEND ALL NIGHT DRAWING
AND GETTING TO KNOW THE PEOPLE WORKING THERE
REFILL?
YEAH, THANKS

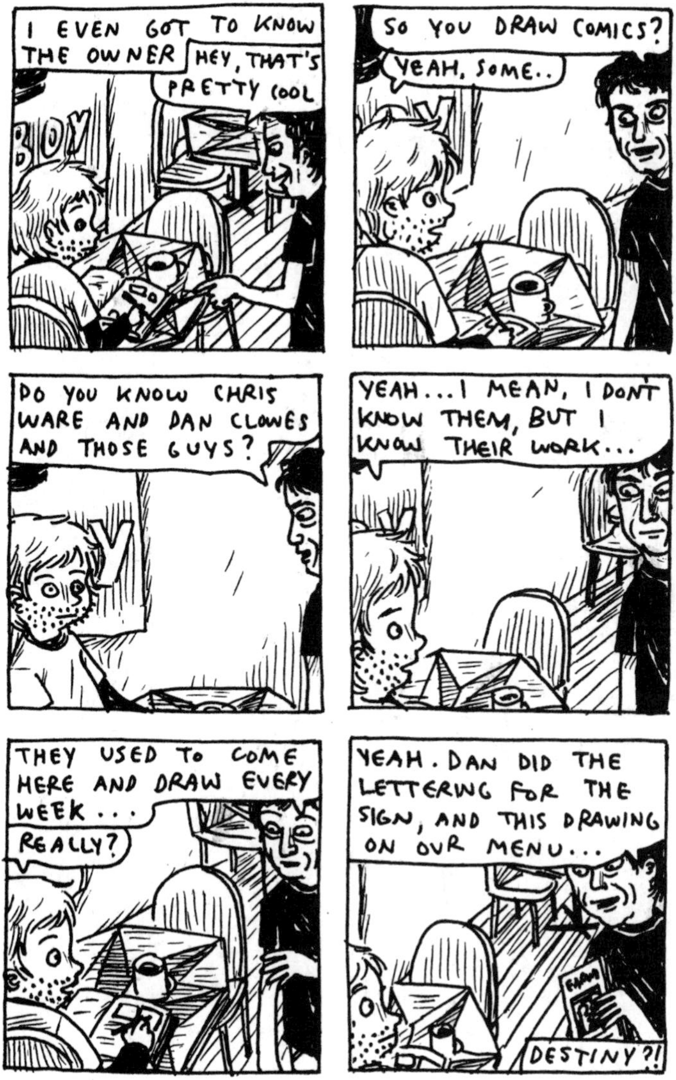
I EVEN GOT TO KNOW THE OWNER
HEY, THAT'S PRETTY COOL
SO YOU DRAW COMICS?
YEAH, SOME..
DO YOU KNOW CHRIS WARE AND DAN CLOWES AND THOSE GUYS?
YEAH...I MEAN, I DONT KNOW THEM, BUT I KNOW THEIR WORK...
THEY USED TO COME HERE AND DRAW EVERY WEEK...
REALLY?
YEAH. DAN DID THE LETTERING FOR THE SIGN, AND THIS DRAWING ON OUR MENU...
DESTINY?!

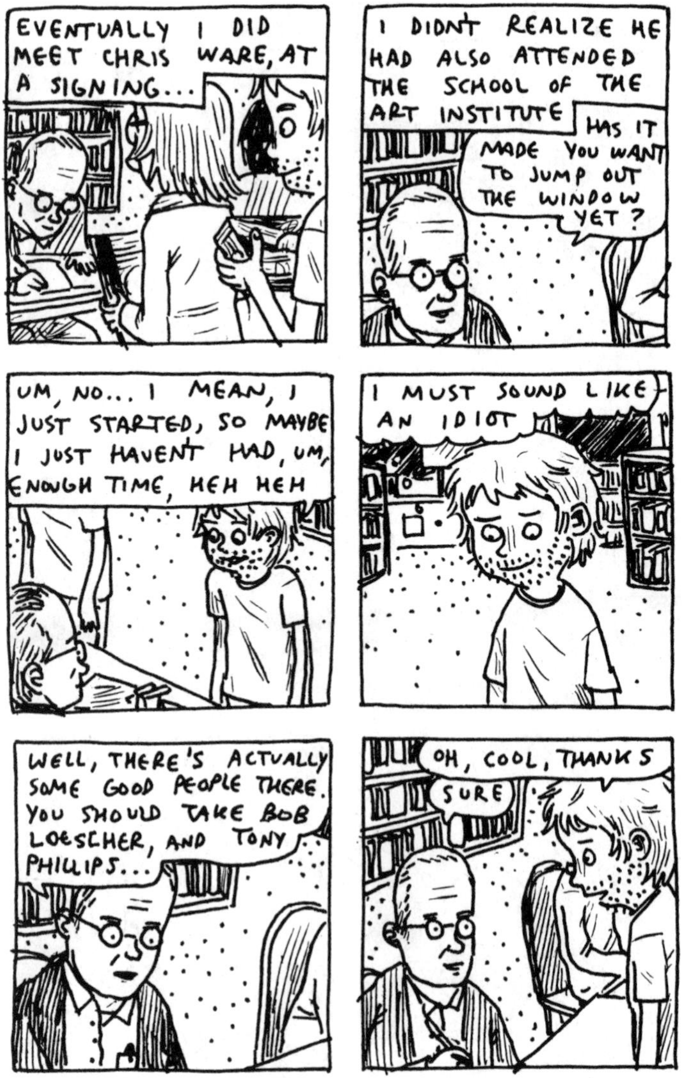
EVENTUALLY I DID MEET CHRIS WARE, AT A SIGNING...
I DIDN'T REALIZE HE HAD ALSO ATTENDED THE SCHOOL OF THE ART INSTITUTE
HAS IT MADE YOU WANT TO JUMP OUT THE WINDOW YET?
UM, NO... I MEAN, I JUST STARTED, SO MAYBE I JUST HAVEN'T HAD, UM, ENOUGH TIME, HEH HEH
I MUST SOUND LIKE AN IDIOT
WELL, THERE'S ACTUALLY SOME GOOD PEOPLE THERE. YOU SHOULD TAKE BOB LOESCHER, AND TONY PHILLIPS...
OH, COOL, THANKS
SURE

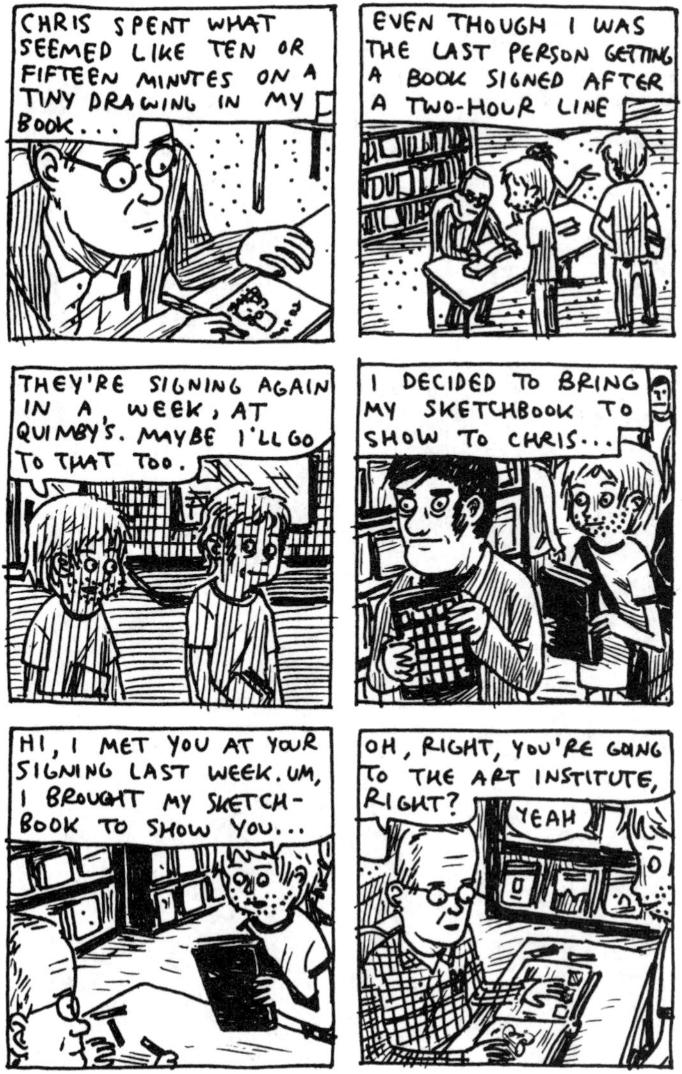
CHRIS SPENT WHAT SEEMED LIKE TEN OR FIFTEEN MINUTES ON A TINY DRAWING IN MY BOOK...
EVEN THOUGH I WAS THE LAST PERSON GETTING A BOOK SIGNED AFTER A TWO-HOUR LINE
THEY'RE SIGNING AGAIN IN A WEEK, AT QUIMBY'S. MAYBE I'LL GO TO THAT TOO.
I DECIDED TO BRING MY SKETCHBOOK TO SHOW TO CHRIS...
HI, I MET YOU AT YOUR SIGNING LAST WEEK. UM, I BROUGHT MY SKETCH-BOOK TO SHOW YOU...
OH, RIGHT, YOU'RE GOING TO THE ART INSTITUTE, RIGHT?
YEAH

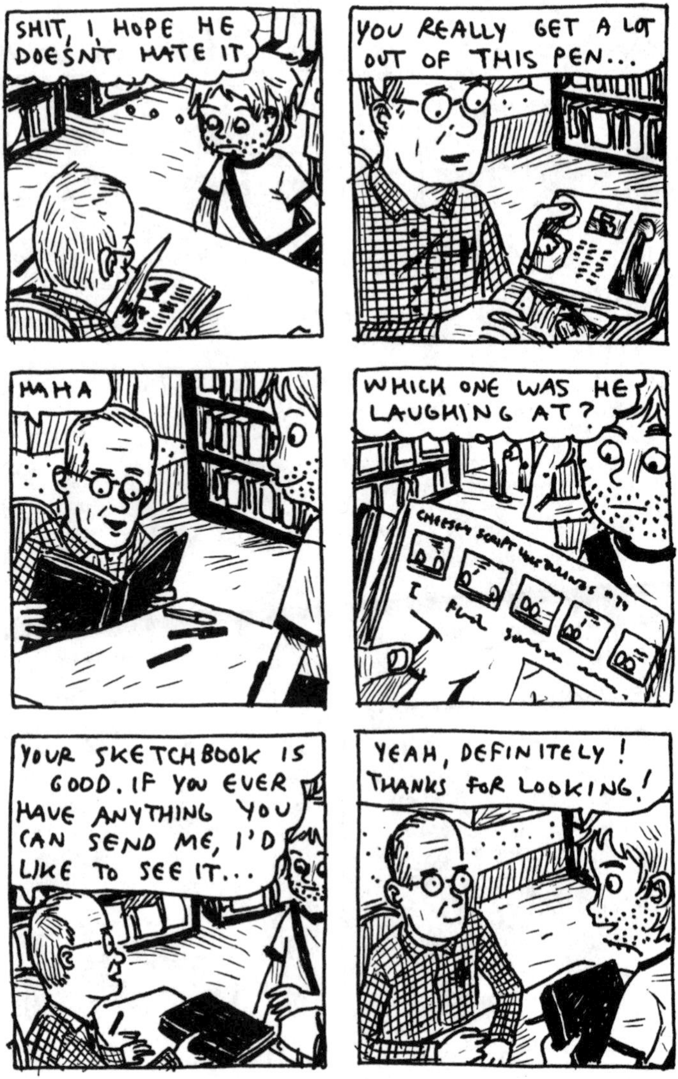
SHIT, I HOPE HE DOESN'T HATE IT
YOU REALLY GET A LOT OUT OF THIS PEN...
HAHA
WHICH ONE WAS HE LAUGHING AT?
YOUR SKETCHBOOK IS GOOD. IF YOU EVER HAVE ANYTHING YOU CAN SEND ME, I'D LIKE TO SEE IT...
YEAH, DEFINITELY! THANKS FOR LOOKING!

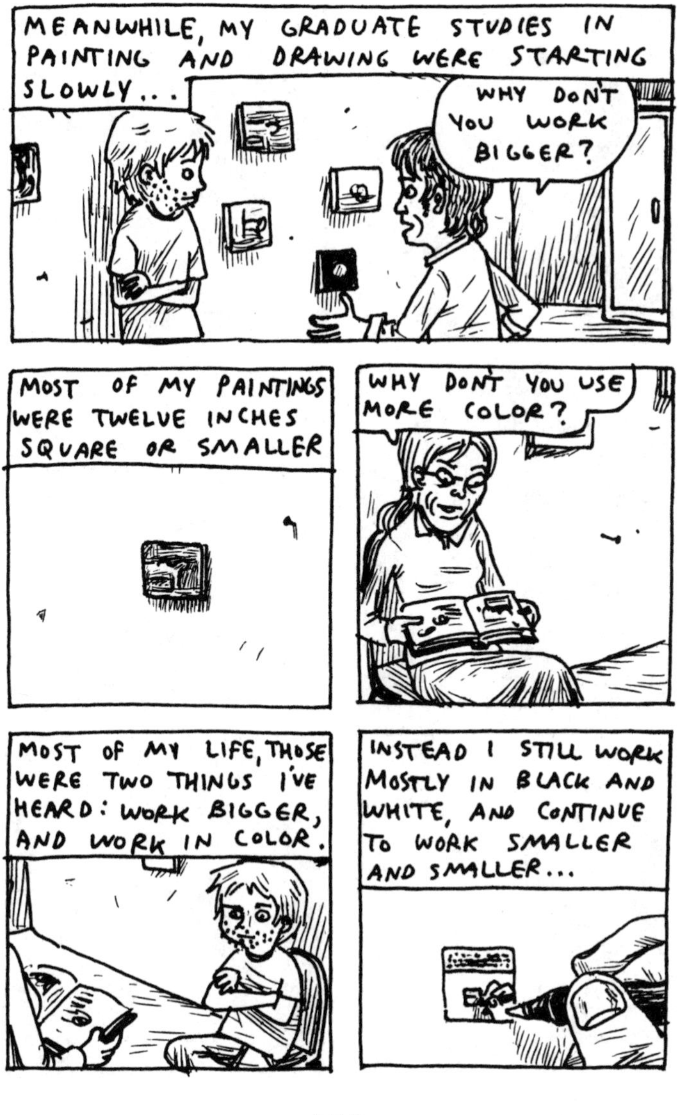
MEANWHILE, MY GRADUATE STUDIES IN PAINTING AND DRAWING WERE STARTING SLOWLY...
WHY DON'T YOU WORK BIGGER?
MOST OF MY PAINTINGS WERE TWELVE INCHES SQUARE OR SMALLER
WHY DON'T YOU USE MORE COLOR?
MOST OF MY LIFE, THOSE WERE TWO THINGS I'VE HEARD: WORK BIGGER, AND WORK IN COLOR.
INSTEAD I STILL WORK MOSTLY IN BLACK AND WHITE, AND CONTINUE TO WORK SMALLER AND SMALLER...

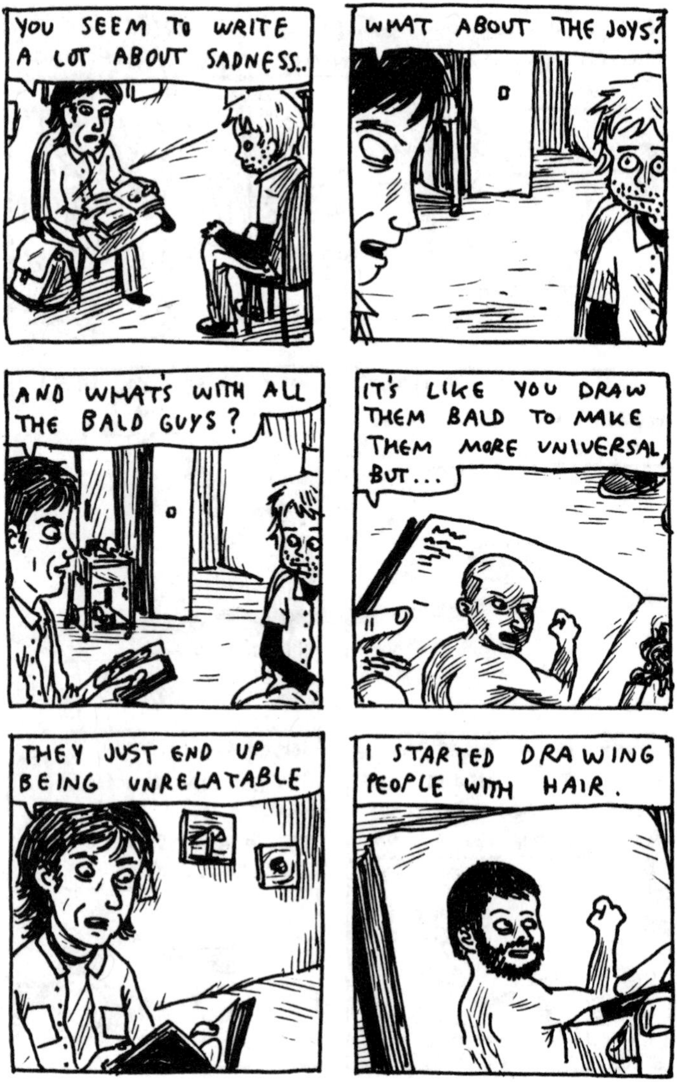
YOU SEEM TO WRITE A LOT ABOUT SADNESS..
WHAT ABOUT THE JOYS?
AND WHAT'S WITH ALL THE BALD GUYS?
IT'S LIKE YOU DRAW THEM BALD TO MAKE THEM MORE UNIVERSAL, BUT...
THEY JUST END UP BEING UNRELATABLE
I STARTED DRAWING PEOPLE WITH HAIR.

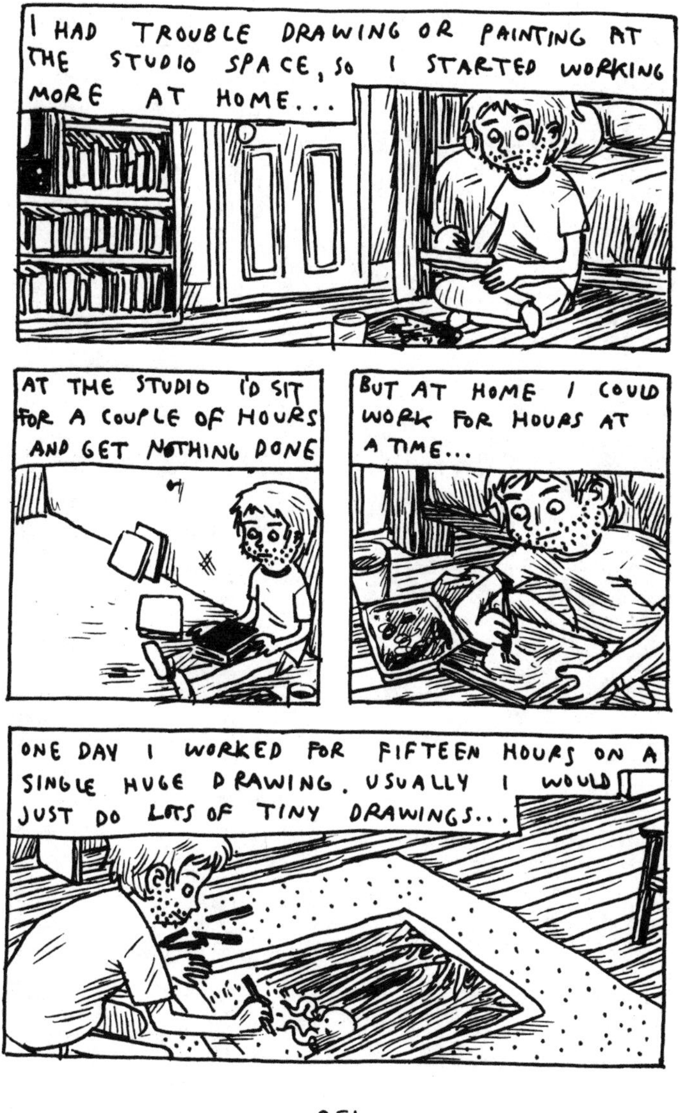
I HAD TROUBLE DRAWING OR PAINTING AT THE STUDIO SPACE, SO I STARTED WORKING MORE AT HOME...
AT THE STUDIO I'D SIT FOR A COUPLE OF HOURS AND GET NOTHING DONE
BUT AT HOME I COULD WORK FOR HOURS AT A TIME...
ONE DAY I WORKED FOR FIFTEEN HOURS ON A SINGLE HUGE DRAWING. USUALLY I WOULD JUST DO LOTS OF TINY DRAWINGS...

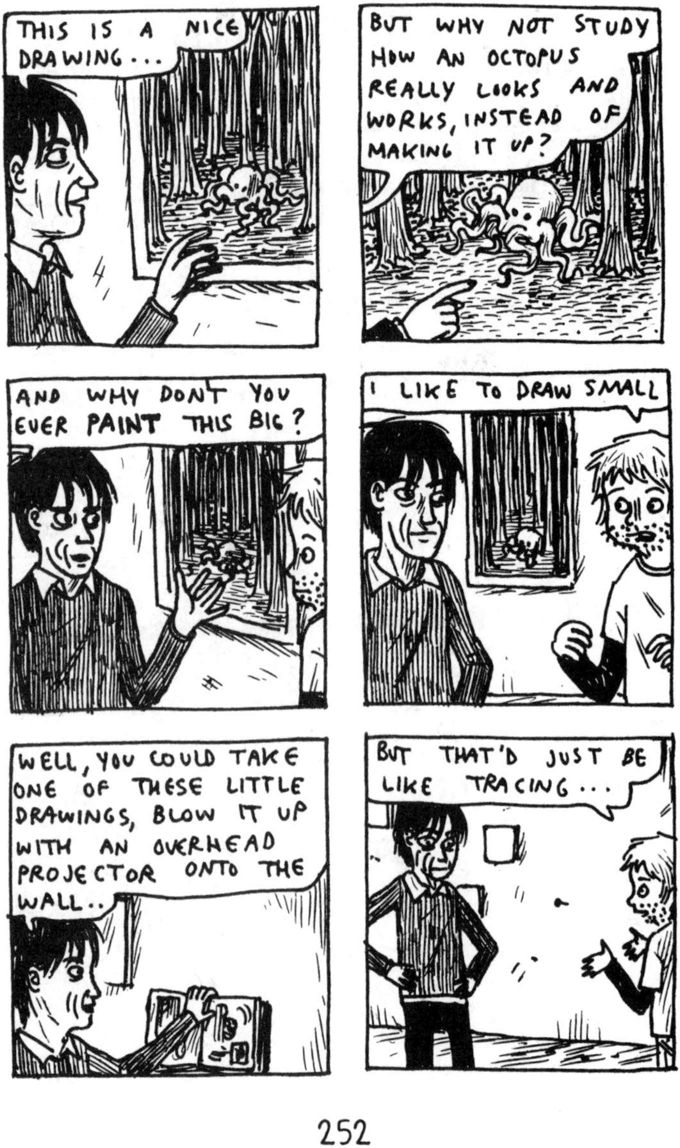
THIS IS A NICE DRAWING...
BUT WHY NOT STUDY HOW AN OCTOPUS REALLY LOOKS AND WORKS, INSTEAD OF MAKING IT UP?
AND WHY DON'T YOU EVER PAINT THIS BIG?
I LIKE TO DRAW SMALL
WELL, YOU COULD TAKE ONE OF THESE LITTLE DRAWINGS, BLOW IT UP WITH AN OVERHEAD PROJECTOR ONTO THE WALL..
BUT THAT'D JUST BE LIKE TRACING...

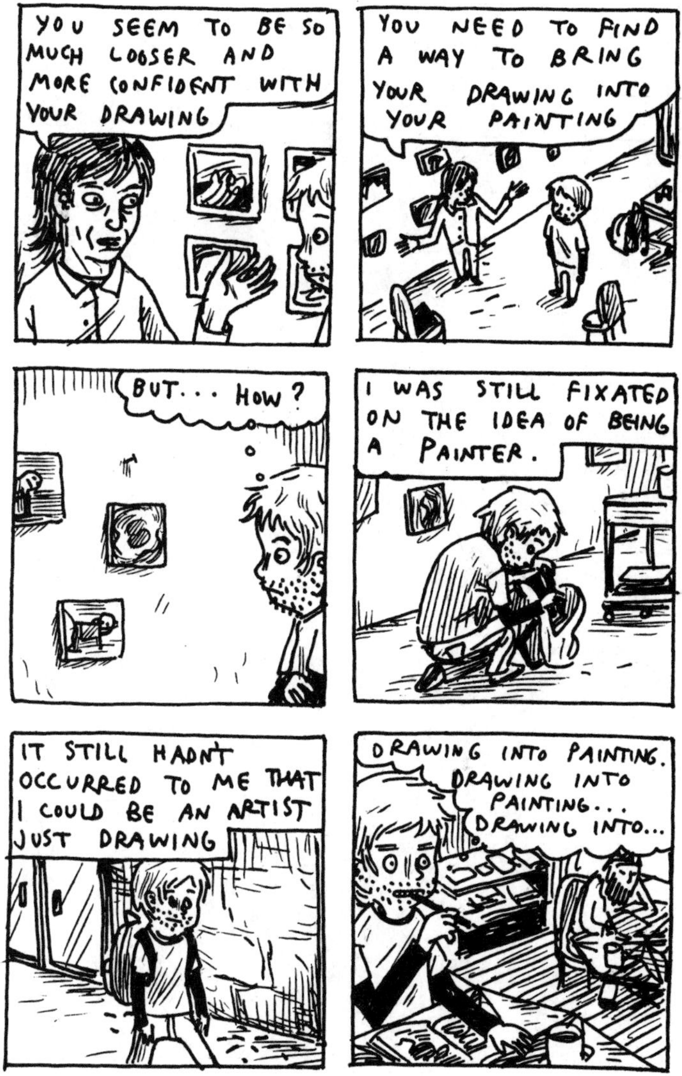
YOU SEEM TO BE SO MUCH LOOSER AND MORE CONFIDENT WITH YOUR DRAWING
YOU NEED TO FIND A WAY TO BRING YOUR DRAWING INTO YOUR PAINTING
BUT... HOW?
I WAS STILL FIXATED ON THE IDEA OF BEING A PAINTER.
IT STILL HADN'T OCCURRED TO ME THAT I COULD BE AN ARTIST JUST DRAWING
DRAWING INTO PAINTING. DRAWING INTO PAINTING... DRAWING INTO...

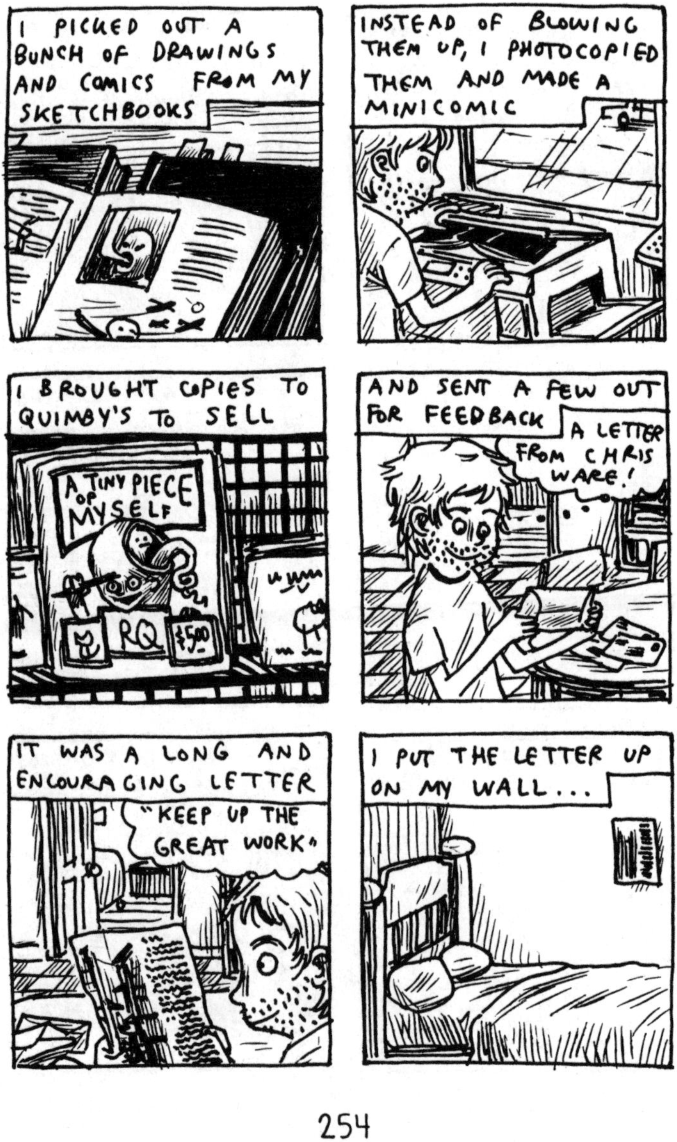
I PICKED OUT A BUNCH OF DRAWINGS AND COMICS FROM MY SKETCHBOOKS
INSTEAD OF BLOWING THEM UP, I PHOTOCOPIED THEM AND MADE A MINICOMIC
I BROUGHT COPIES TO QUIMBY'S TO SELL
A TINY PIECE OF MYSELF
RQ
$5.00
AND SENT A FEW OUT FOR FEEDBACK
A LETTER FROM CHRIS WARE!
IT WAS A LONG AND ENCOURAGING LETTER
"KEEP UP THE GREAT WORK"
I PUT THE LETTER UP ON MY WALL...

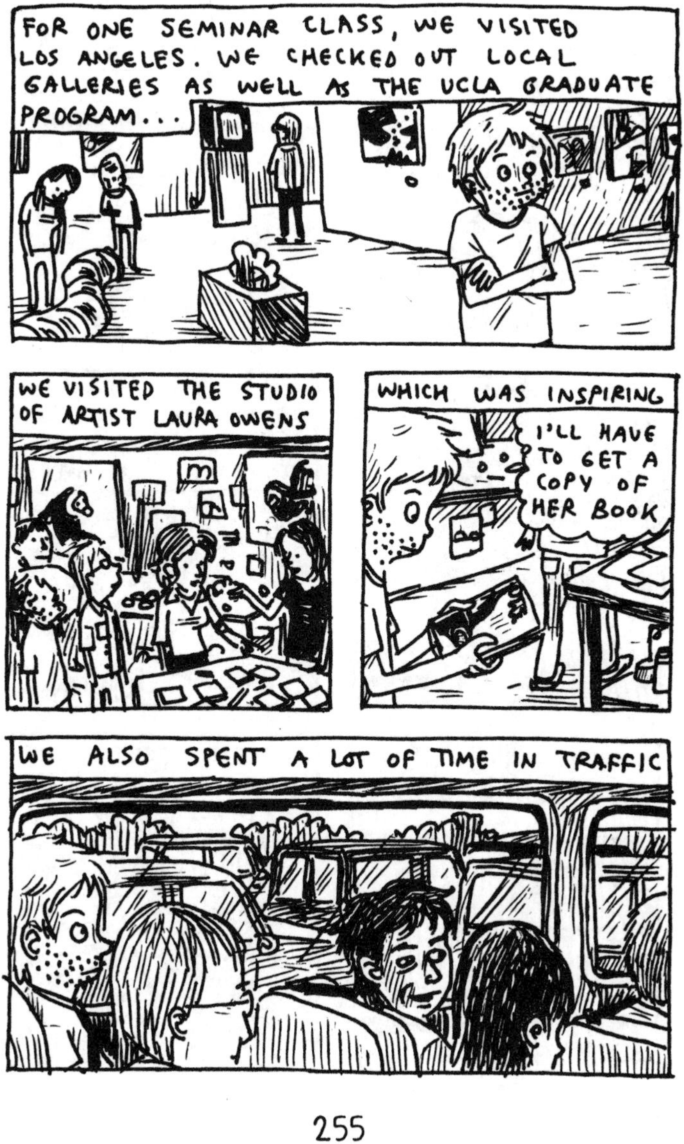
FOR ONE SEMINAR CLASS, WE VISITED LOS ANGELES. WE CHECKED OUT LOCAL GALLERIES AS WELL AS THE UCLA GRADUATE PROGRAM...
WE VISITED THE STUDIO OF ARTIST LAURA OWENS
WHICH WAS INSPIRING
I'LL HAVE TO GET A COPY OF HER BOOK
WE ALSO SPENT A LOT OF TIME IN TRAFFIC

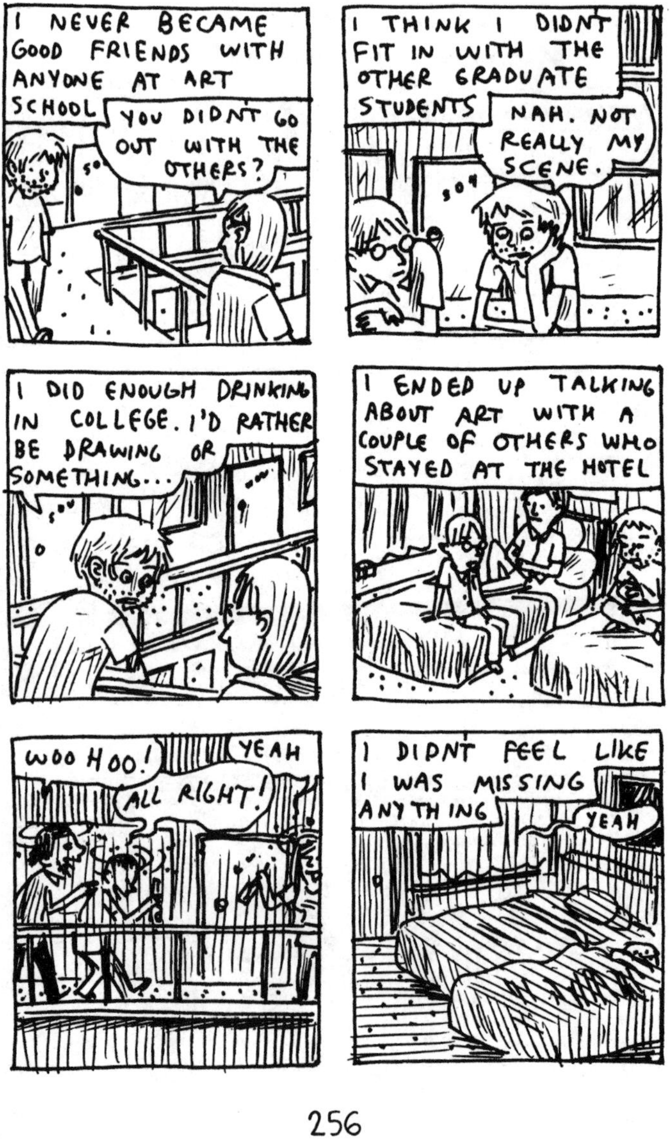
I NEVER BECAME GOOD FRIENDS WITH ANYONE AT ART SCHOOL
YOU DIDN'T GO OUT WITH THE OTHERS?
I THINK I DIDN'T FIT IN WITH THE OTHER GRADUATE STUDENTS
NAH. NOT REALLY MY SCENE.
I DID ENOUGH DRINKING IN COLLEGE. I'D RATHER BE DRAWING OR SOMETHING...
I ENDED UP TALKING ABOUT ART WITH A COUPLE OF OTHERS WHO STAYED AT THE HOTEL
WOO HOO!
YEAH
ALL RIGHT!
I DIDN'T FEEL LIKE I WAS MISSING ANYTHING
YEAH

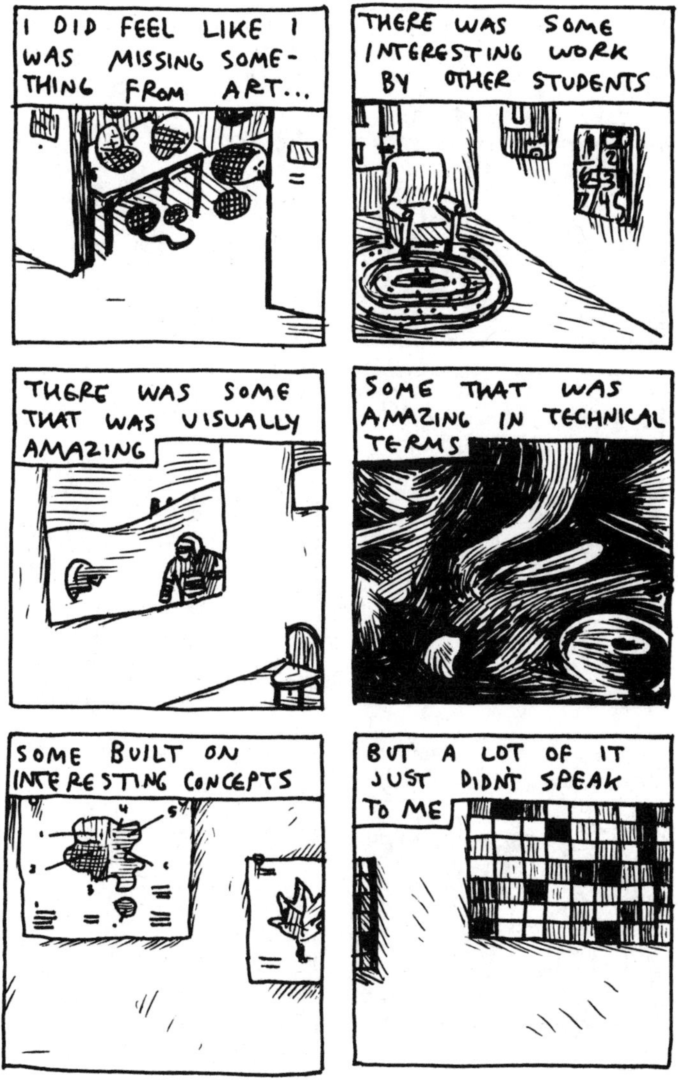
I DID FEEL LIKE I WAS MISSING SOME-THING FROM ART...
THERE WAS SOME INTERESTING WORK BY OTHER STUDENTS
THERE WAS SOME THAT WAS VISUALLY AMAZING
SOME THAT WAS AMAZING IN TECHNICAL TERMS
SOME BUILT ON INTERESTING CONCEPTS
BUT A LOT OF IT JUST DIDN'T SPEAK TO ME

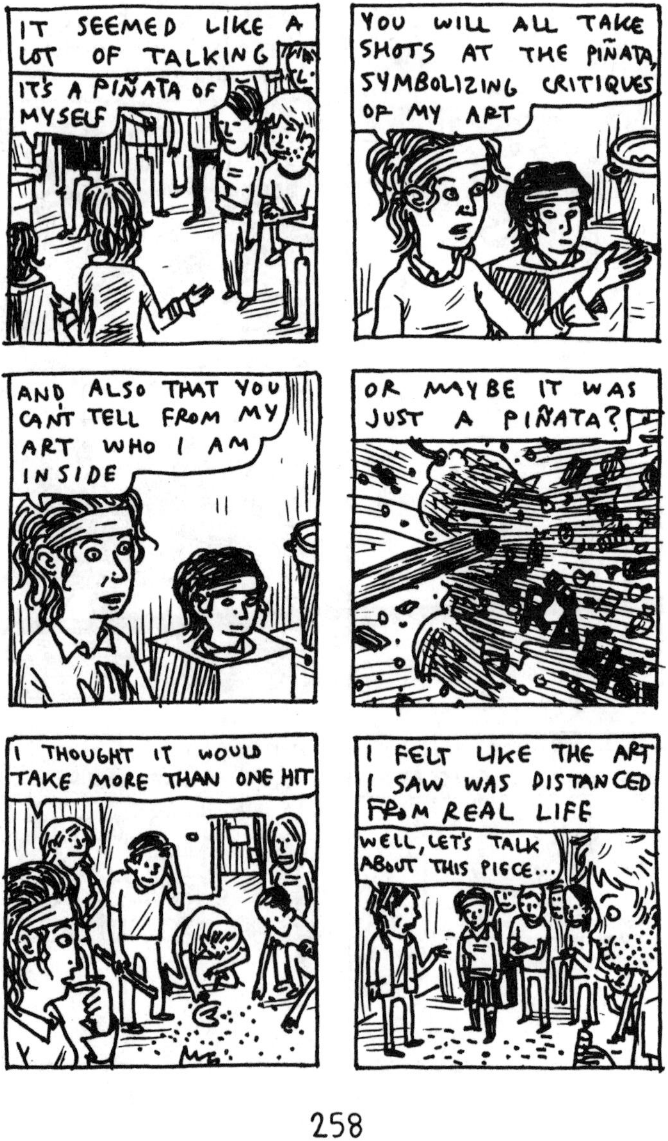
IT SEEMED LIKE A LOT OF TALKING
IT'S A PIÑATA OF MYSELF
YOU WILL ALL TAKE SHOTS AT THE PIÑATA, SYMBOLIZING CRITIQUES OF MY ART
AND ALSO THAT YOU CAN'T TELL FROM MY ART WHO I AM INSIDE
OR MAYBE IT WAS JUST A PIÑATA?
I THOUGHT IT WOULD TAKE MORE THAN ONE HIT
I FELT LIKE THE ART I SAW WAS DISTANCED FROM REAL LIFE
WELL, LET'S TALK ABOUT THIS PIECE...

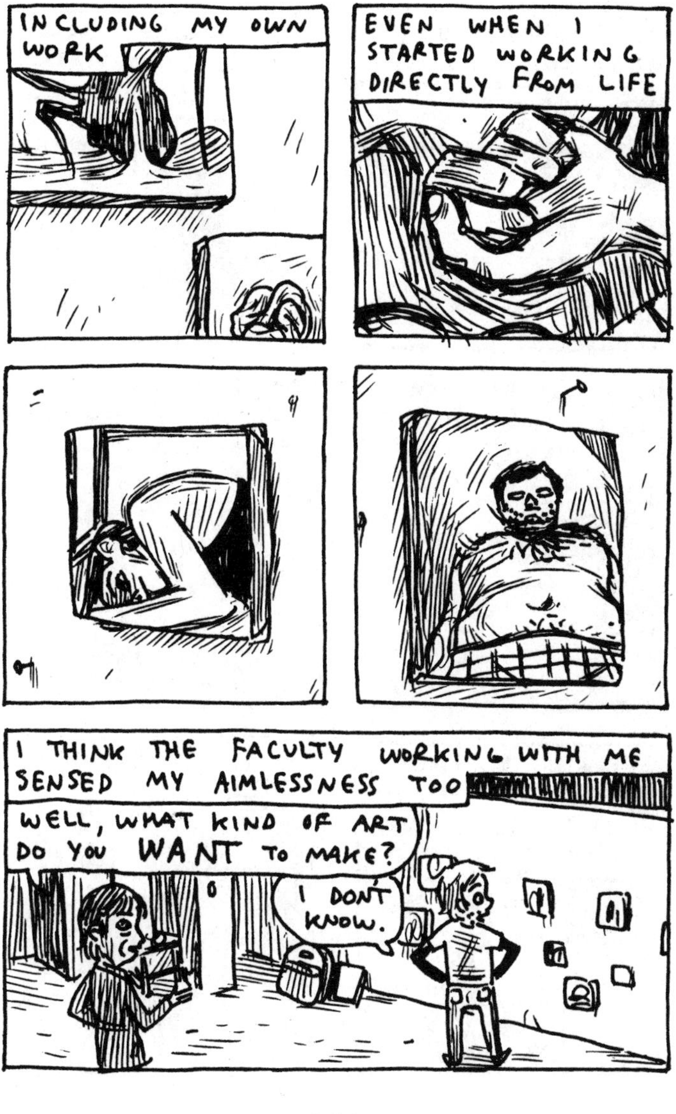
INCLUDING MY OWN WORK
EVEN WHEN I STARTED WORKING DIRECTLY FROM LIFE
I THINK THE FACULTY WORKING WITH ME SENSED MY AIMLESSNESS TOO
WELL, WHAT KIND OF ART DO YOU WANT TO MAKE?
I DON'T KNOW.

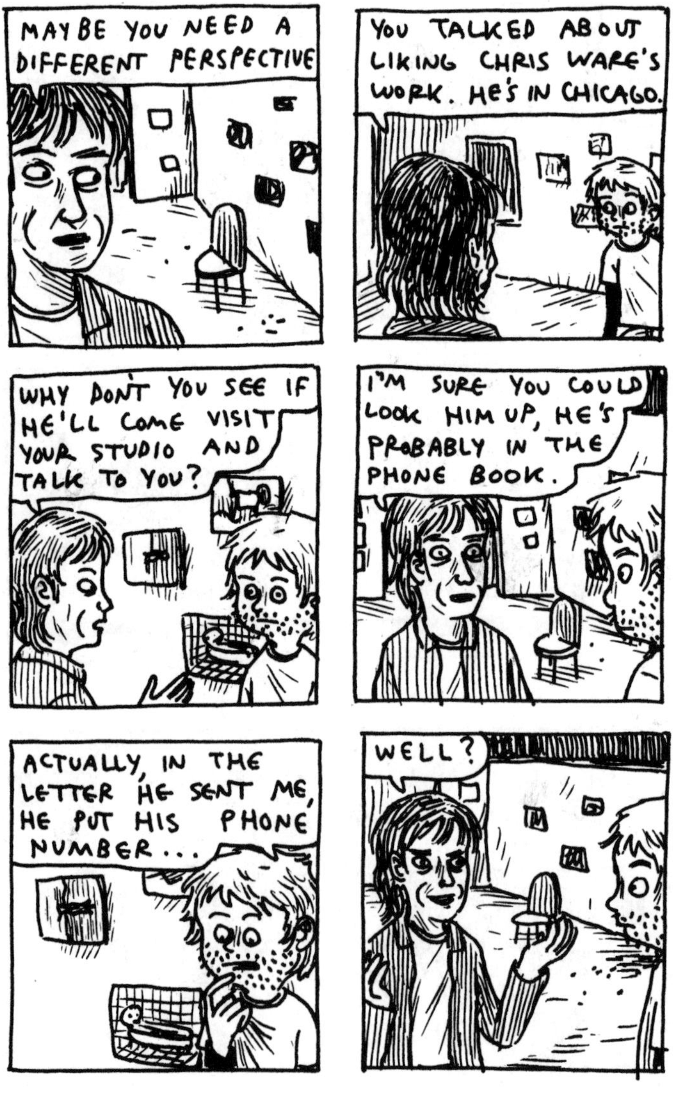
MAYBE YOU NEED A DIFFERENT PERSPECTIVE
YOU TALKED ABOUT LIKING CHRIS WARE'S WORK. HE'S IN CHICAGO.
WHY DON'T YOU SEE IF HE'LL COME VISIT YOUR STUDIO AND TALK TO YOU?
I'M SURE YOU COULD LOOK HIM UP, HE'S PROBABLY IN THE PHONE BOOK.
ACTUALLY, IN THE LETTER HE SENT ME, HE PUT HIS PHONE NUMBER...
WELL?

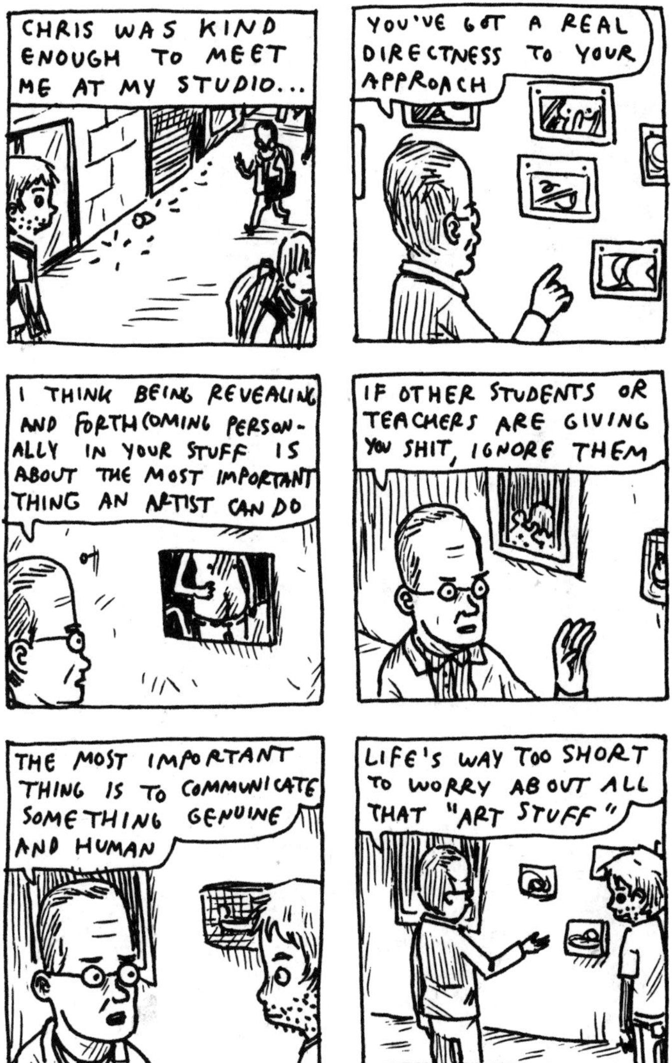
CHRIS WAS KIND ENOUGH TO MEET ME AT MY STUDIO...
YOU'VE GOT A REAL DIRECTNESS TO YOUR APPROACH
I THINK BEING REVEALING AND FORTHCOMING PERSONALLY IN YOUR STUFF IS ABOUT THE MOST IMPORTANT THING AN ARTIST CAN DO
IF OTHER STUDENTS OR TEACHERS ARE GIVING YOU SHIT, IGNORE THEM
THE MOST IMPORTANT THING IS TO COMMUNICATE SOMETHING GENUINE AND HUMAN
LIFE'S WAY TOO SHORT TO WORRY ABOUT ALL THAT "ART STUFF"

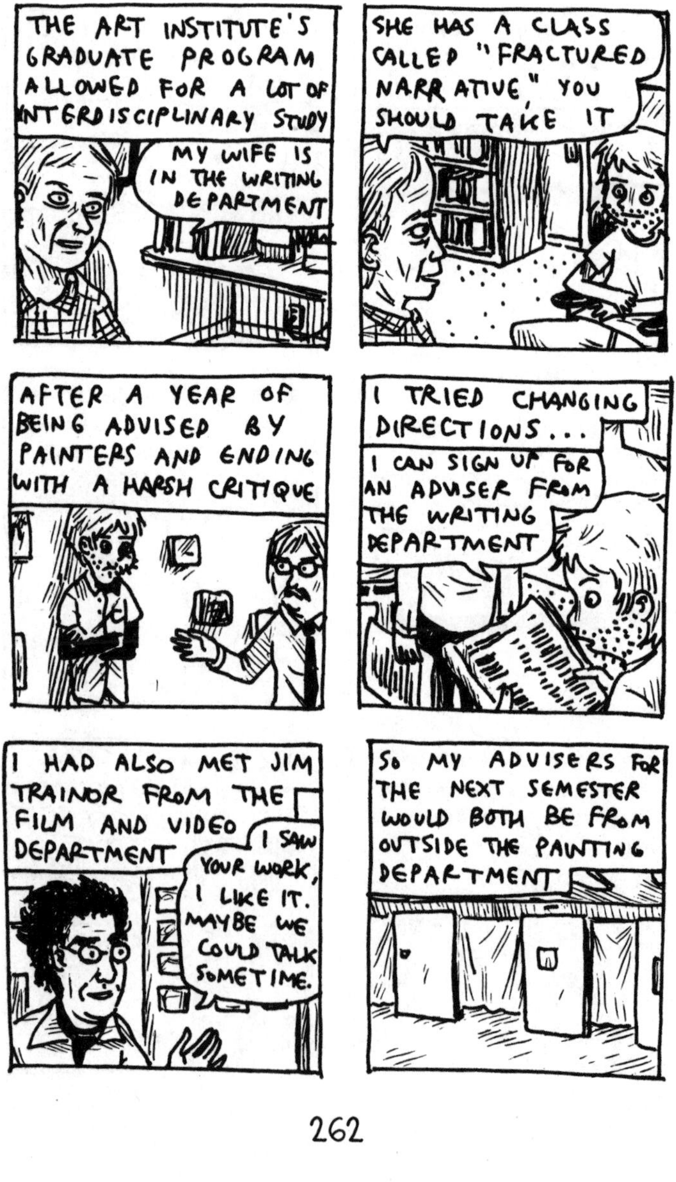
THE ART INSTITUTE'S GRADUATE PROGRAM ALLOWED FOR A LOT OF INTERDISCIPLINARY STUDY
MY WIFE IS IN THE WRITING DEPARTMENT
SHE HAS A CLASS CALLED "FRACTURED NARRATIVE," YOU SHOULD TAKE IT
AFTER A YEAR OF BEING ADVISED BY PAINTERS AND ENDING WITH A HARSH CRITIQUE
I TRIED CHANGING DIRECTIONS...
I CAN SIGN UP FOR AN ADVISER FROM THE WRITING DEPARTMENT
I HAD ALSO MET JIM TRAINOR FROM THE FILM AND VIDEO DEPARTMENT
I SAW YOUR WORK, I LIKE IT. MAYBE WE COULD TALK SOMETIME.
SO MY ADVISERS FOR THE NEXT SEMESTER WOULD BOTH BE FROM OUTSIDE THE PAINTING DEPARTMENT

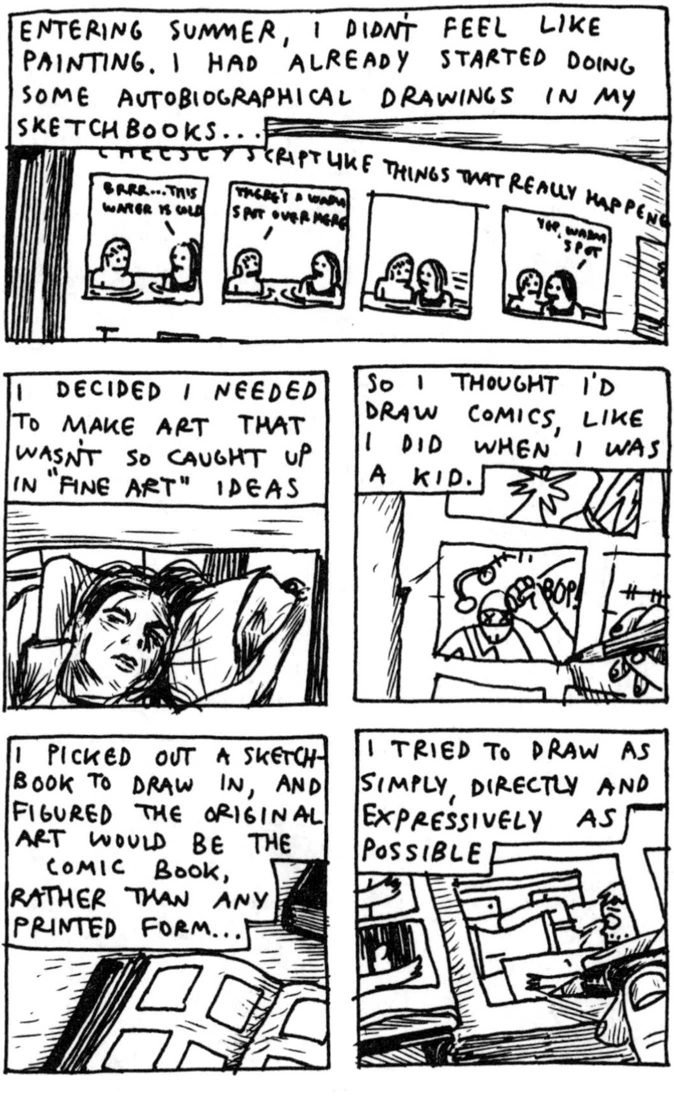
ENTERING SUMMER, I DIDN'T FEEL LIKE PAINTING. I HAD ALREADY STARTED DOING SOME AUTOBIOGRAPHICAL DRAWINGS IN MY SKETCHBOOKS...
SCRIPT LIKE THINGS THAT REALLY
BRRR...THIS WATER IS COLD
THERE'S A WARM SPOT OVER HERE
YEP, WARM SPOT
I DECIDED I NEEDED TO MAKE ART THAT WASN'T SO CAUGHT UP IN "FINE ART" IDEAS
SO I THOUGHT I'D DRAW COMICS, LIKE I DID WHEN I WAS A KID.
BOP!
I PICKED OUT A SKETCHBOOK TO DRAW IN, AND FIGURED THE ORIGINAL ART WOULD BE THE COMIC BOOK, RATHER THAN ANY PRINTED FORM...
I TRIED TO DRAW AS SIMPLY, DIRECTLY AND EXPRESSIVELY AS POSSIBLE

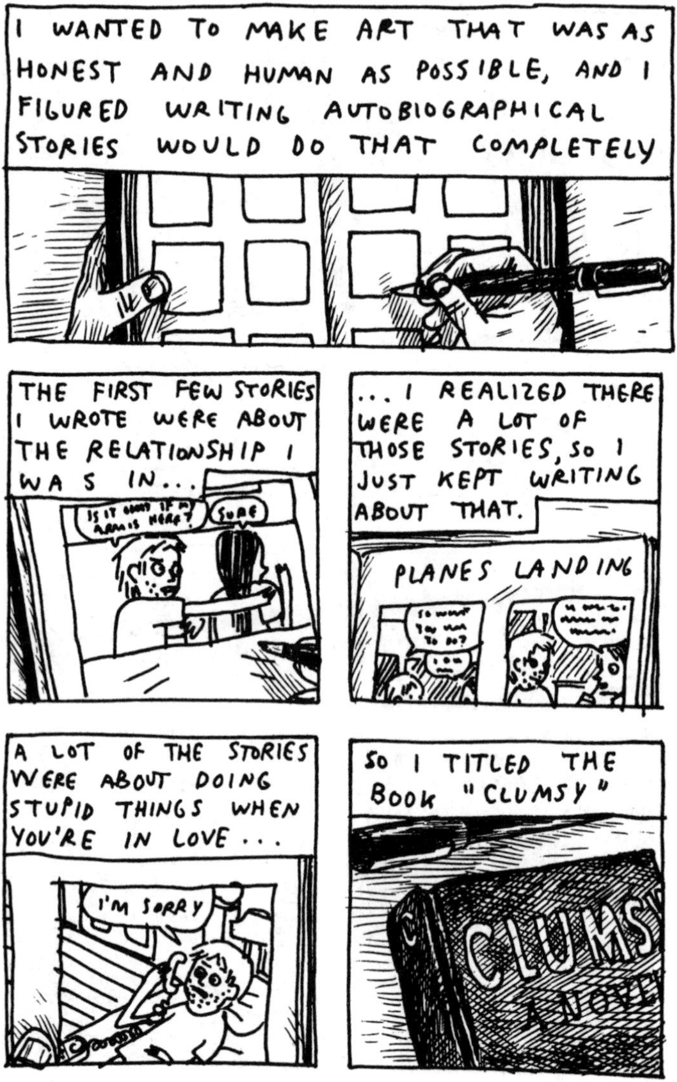
I WANTED TO MAKE ART THAT WAS AS HONEST AND HUMAN AS POSSIBLE, AND I FIGURED WRITING AUTOBIOGRAPHICAL STORIES WOULD DO THAT COMPLETELY
THE FIRST FEW STORIES I WROTE WERE ABOUT THE RELATIONSHIP I WAS IN...
SURE
...I REALIZED THERE WERE A LOT OF THOSE STORIES, SO I JUST KEPT WRITING ABOUT THAT.
PLANES LANDING
A LOT OF THE STORIES WERE ABOUT DOING STUPID THINGS WHEN YOU'RE IN LOVE...
I'M SORRY
SO I TITLED THE BOOK "CLUMSY"
CLUMSY
A NOVEL

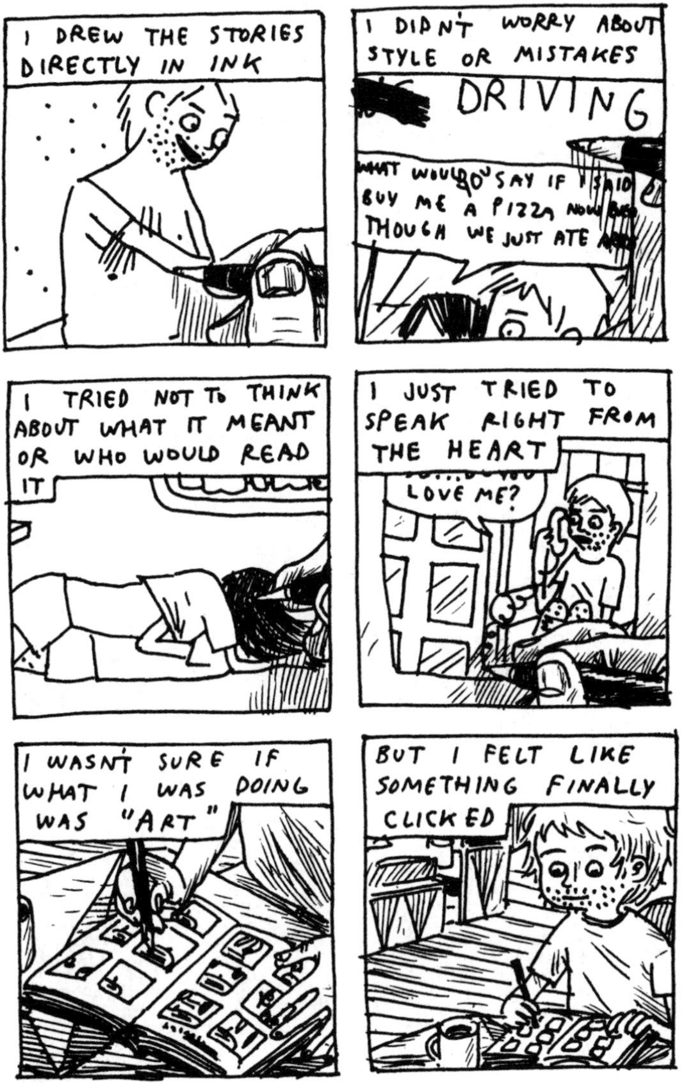
I DREW THE STORIES DIRECTLY IN INK
I DIDN'T WORRY ABOUT STYLE OR MISTAKES
DRIVING
WHAT WOULD YOU SAY IF I SAID BUY ME A PIZZA NOW THOUGH WE JUST ATE
I TRIED NOT TO THINK ABOUT WHAT IT MEANT OR WHO WOULD READ IT
I JUST TRIED TO SPEAK RIGHT FROM THE HEART
LOVE ME?
I WASN'T SURE IF WHAT I WAS DOING WAS "ART"
BUT I FELT LIKE SOMETHING FINALLY CLICKED

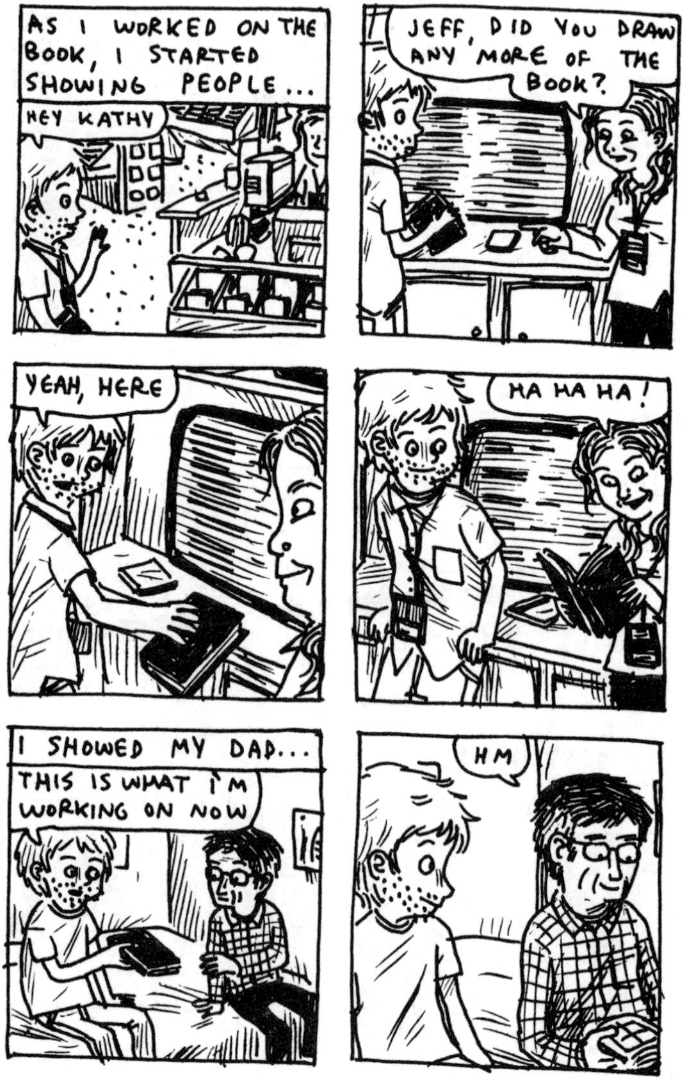
AS I WORKED ON THE BOOK, I STARTED SHOWING PEOPLE...
HEY KATHY
JEFF, DID YOU DRAW ANY MORE OF THE BOOK?
YEAH, HERE
HA HA HA!
I SHOWED MY DAD...
THIS IS WHAT I'M WORKING ON NOW
HM

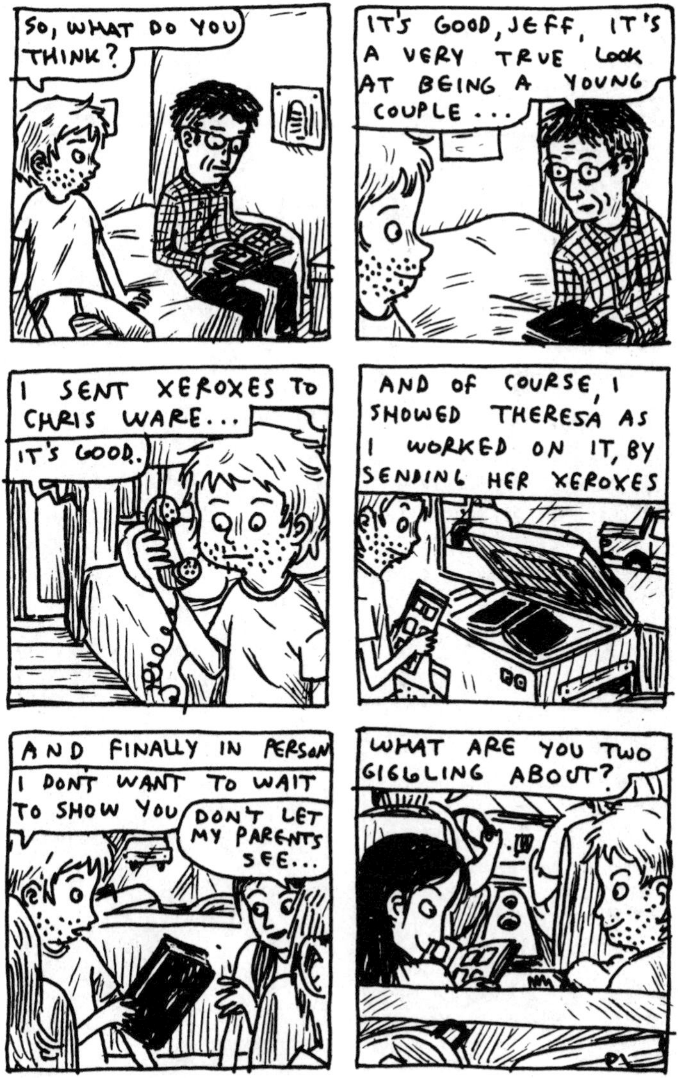
SO, WHAT DO YOU THINK?
IT'S GOOD, JEFF, IT'S A VERY TRUE LOOK AT BEING A YOUNG COUPLE...
I SENT XEROXES TO CHRIS WARE...
IT'S GOOD.
AND OF COURSE, I SHOWED THERESA AS I WORKED ON IT, BY SENDING HER XEROXES
AND FINALLY IN PERSON
I DON'T WANT TO WAIT TO SHOW YOU
DON'T LET MY PARENTS SEE...
WHAT ARE YOU TWO GIGGLING ABOUT?

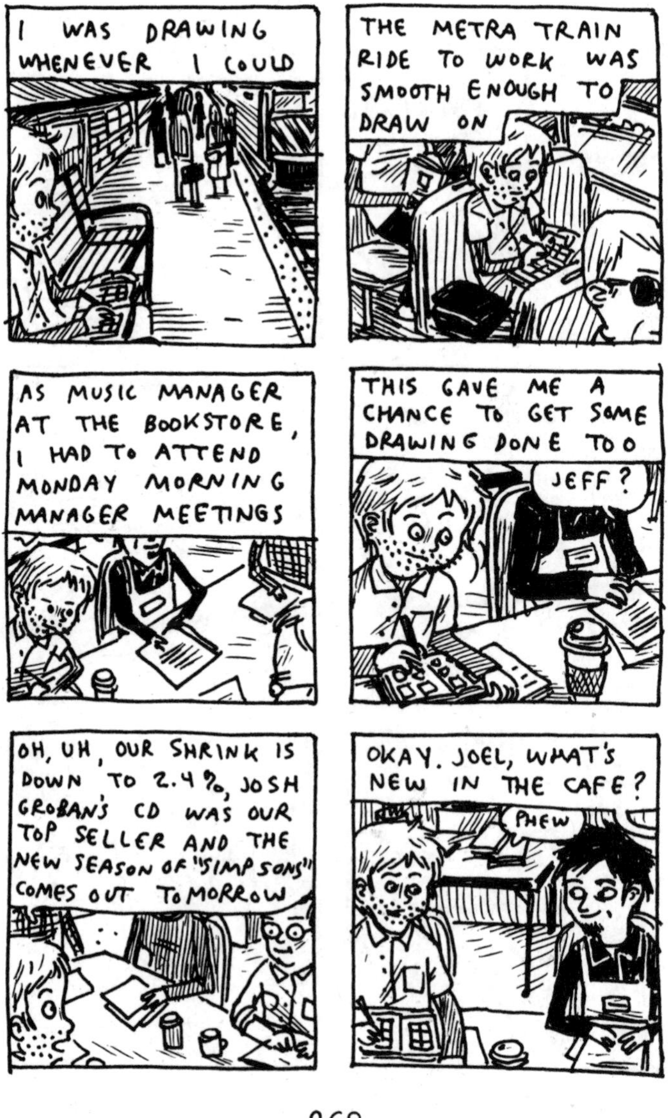
I WAS DRAWING WHENEVER I COULD
THE METRA TRAIN RIDE TO WORK WAS SMOOTH ENOUGH TO DRAW ON
AS MUSIC MANAGER AT THE BOOKSTORE, I HAD TO ATTEND MONDAY MORNING MANAGER MEETINGS
THIS GAVE ME A CHANCE TO GET SOME DRAWING DONE TOO
JEFF?
OH, UH, OUR SHRINK IS DOWN TO 2.4%, JOSH GROBAN'S CD WAS OUR TOP SELLER AND THE NEW SEASON OF "SIMPSONS" COMES OUT TOMORROW
OKAY. JOEL, WHAT'S NEW IN THE CAFE?
PHEW

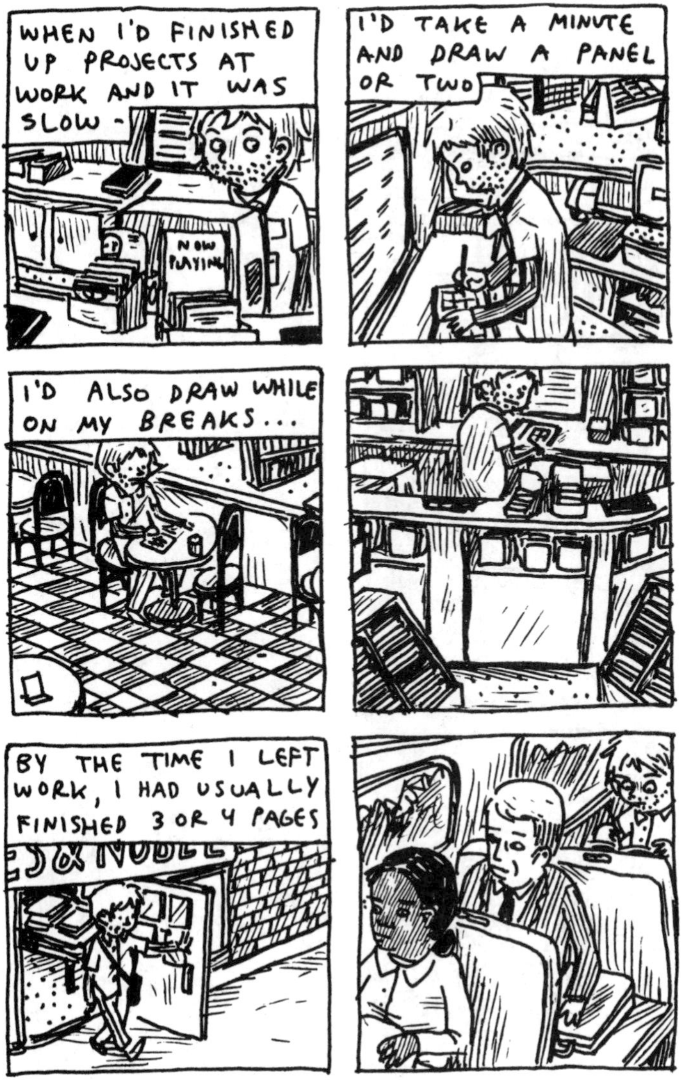
WHEN I'D FINISHED UP PROJECTS AT WORK AND IT WAS SLOW -
NOW PLAYING
I'D TAKE A MINUTE AND DRAW A PANEL OR TWO
I'D ALSO DRAW WHILE ON MY BREAKS...
BY THE TIME I LEFT WORK, I HAD USUALLY FINISHED 3 OR 4 PAGES

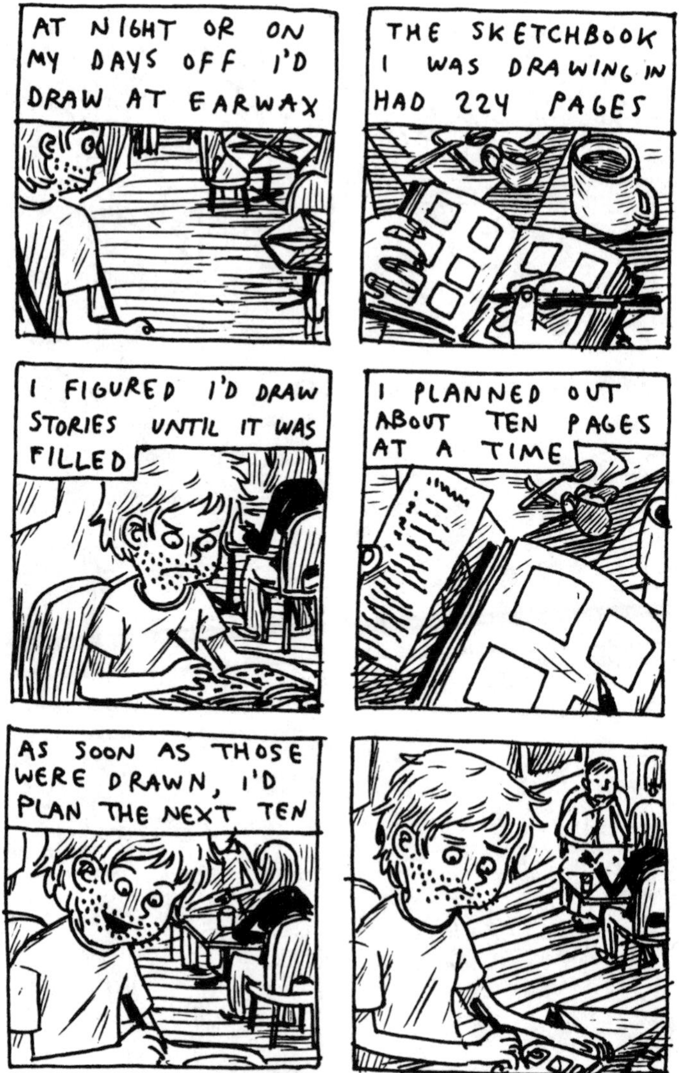
AT NIGHT OR ON MY DAYS OFF I'D DRAW AT EARWAX
THE SKETCHBOOK I WAS DRAWING IN HAD 224 PAGES
I FIGURED I'D DRAW STORIES UNTIL IT WAS FILLED
I PLANNED OUT ABOUT TEN PAGES AT A TIME
AS SOON AS THOSE WERE DRAWN, I'D PLAN THE NEXT TEN

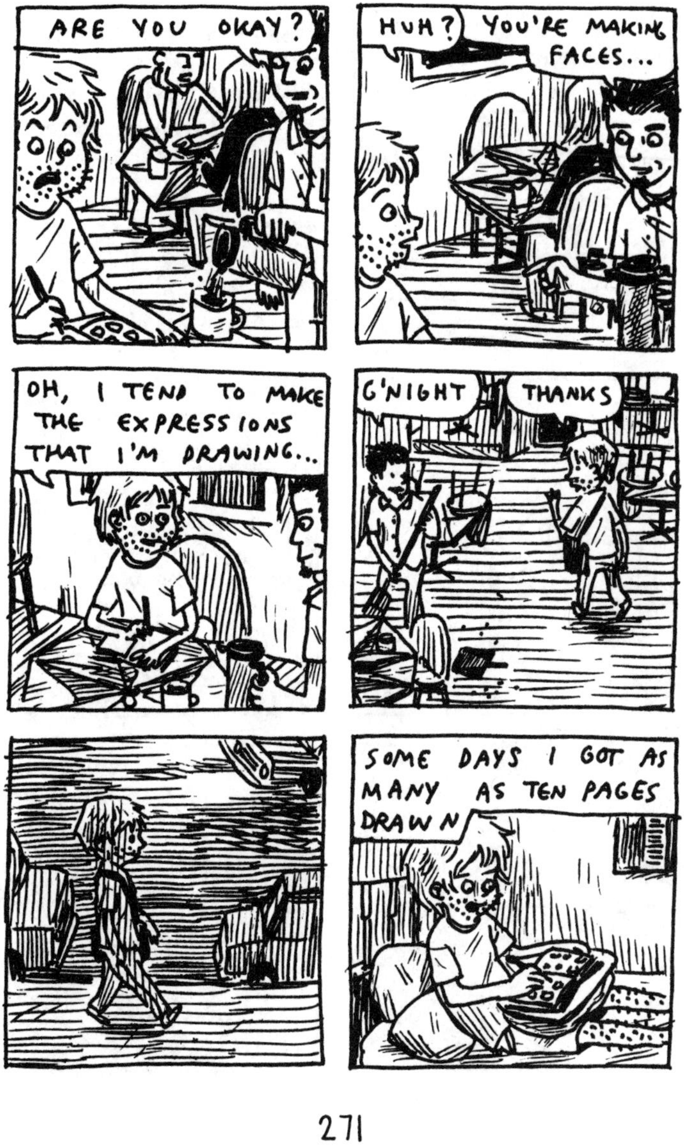
ARE YOU OKAY?
HUH?
YOU'RE MAKING FACES...
OH, I TEND TO MAKE THE EXPRESSIONS THAT I'M DRAWING...
G'NIGHT
THANKS
SOME DAYS I GOT AS MANY AS TEN PAGES DRAWN

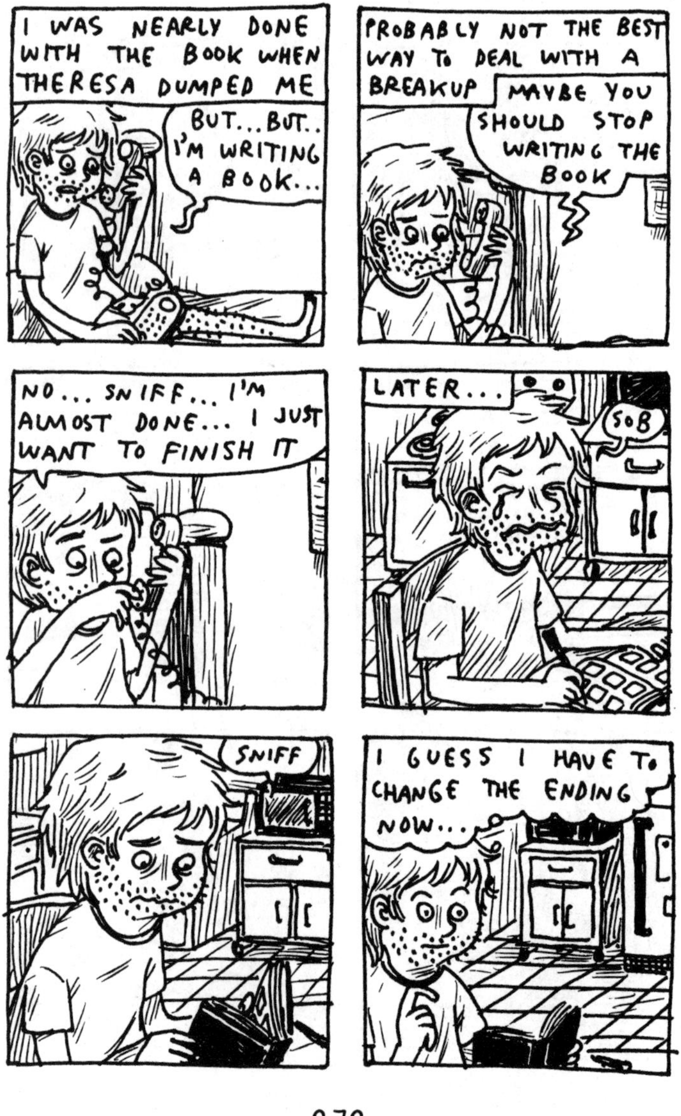
I WAS NEARLY DONE WITH THE BOOK WHEN THERESA DUMPED ME
BUT... BUT.. I'M WRITING A BOOK...
PROBABLY NOT THE BEST WAY TO DEAL WITH A BREAKUP
MAYBE YOU SHOULD STOP WRITING THE BOOK
NO... SNIFF... I'M ALMOST DONE... I JUST WANT TO FINISH IT
LATER...
SOB
SNIFF
I GUESS I HAVE TO CHANGE THE ENDING NOW...

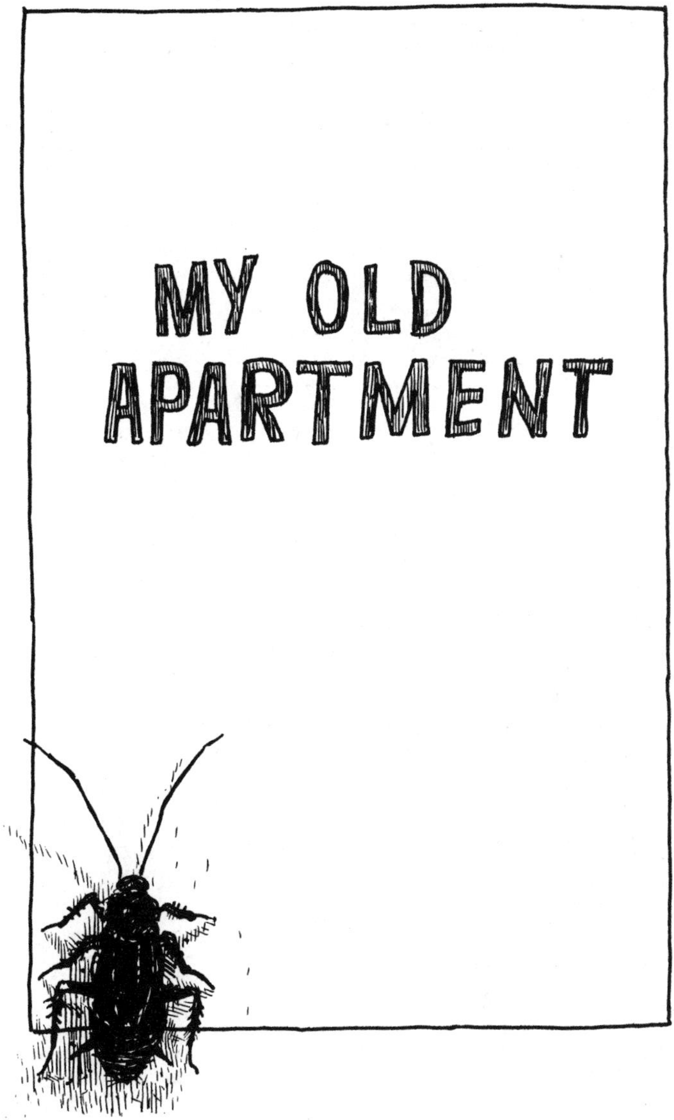
MY OLD
APARTMENT

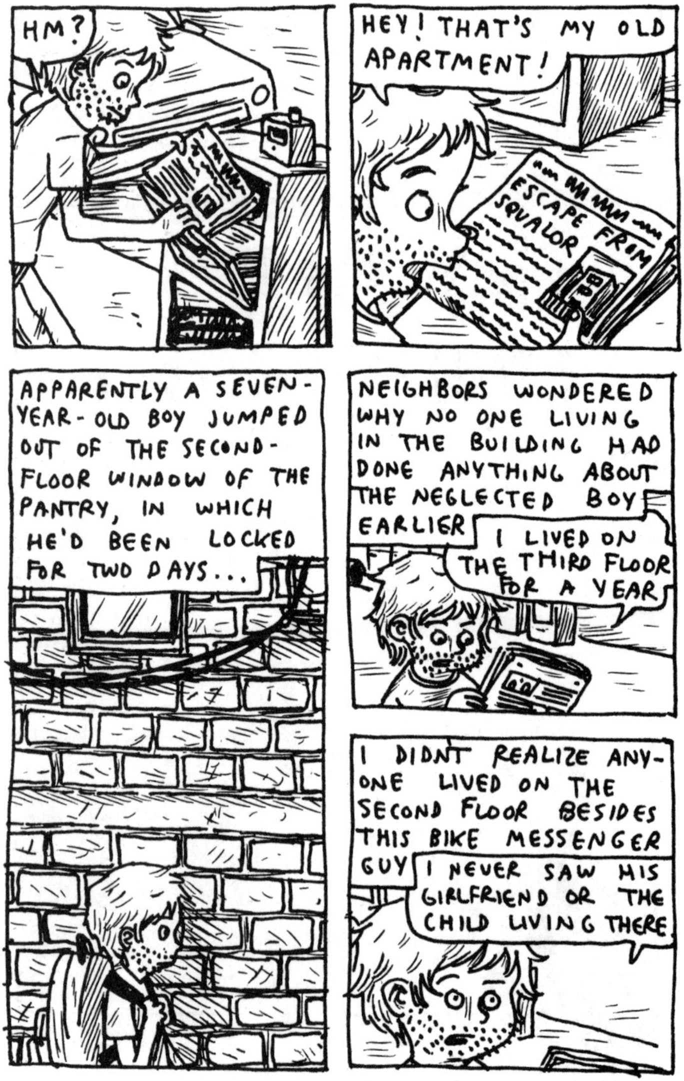
HM?
HEY! THAT'S MY OLD APARTMENT!
ESCAPE FROM SQUALOR
APPARENTLY A SEVEN-YEAR-OLD BOY JUMPED OUT OF THE SECOND-FLOOR WINDOW OF THE PANTRY, IN WHICH HE'D BEEN LOCKED FOR TWO DAYS...
NEIGHBORS WONDERED WHY NO ONE LIVING IN THE BUILDING HAD DONE ANYTHING ABOUT THE NEGLECTED BOY EARLIER
I LIVED ON THE THIRD FLOOR FOR A YEAR
I DIDN'T REALIZE ANYONE LIVED ON THE SECOND FLOOR BESIDES THIS BIKE MESSENGER GUY
I NEVER SAW HIS GIRLFRIEND OR THE CHILD LIVING THERE

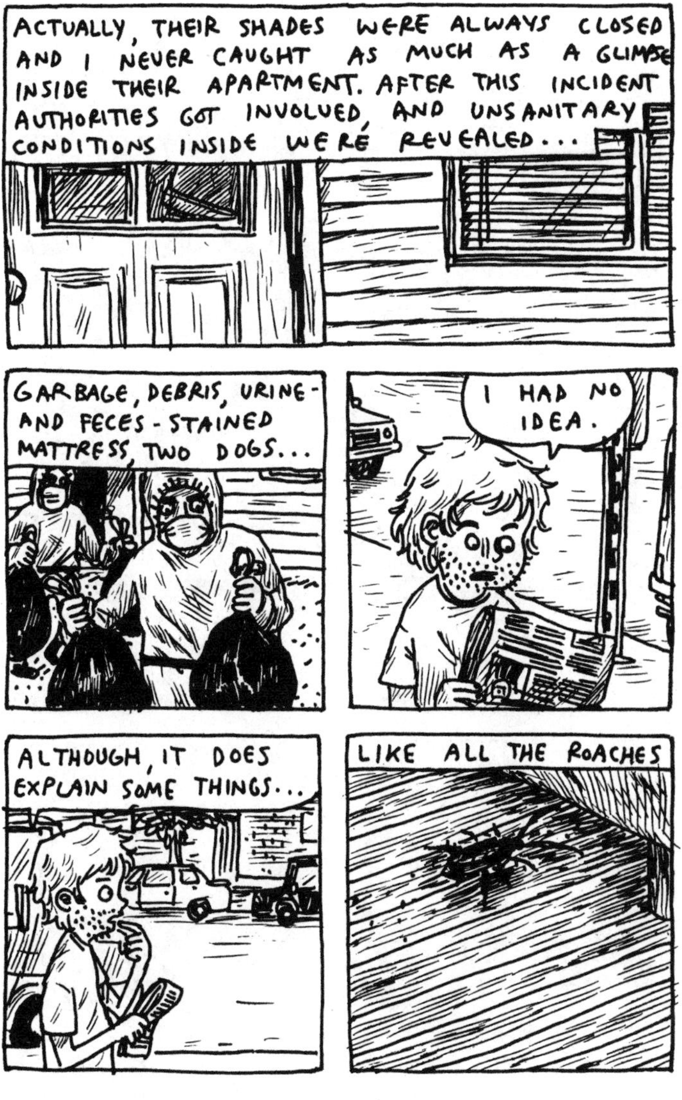
ACTUALLY, THEIR SHADES WERE ALWAYS CLOSED AND I NEVER CAUGHT AS MUCH AS A GLIMPSE INSIDE THEIR APARTMENT. AFTER THIS INCIDENT AUTHORITIES GOT INVOLVED, AND UNSANITARY CONDITIONS INSIDE WERE REVEALED...
GARBAGE, DEBRIS, URINE-AND FECES-STAINED MATTRESS, TWO DOGS...
I HAD NO IDEA.
ALTHOUGH, IT DOES EXPLAIN SOME THINGS...
LIKE ALL THE ROACHES

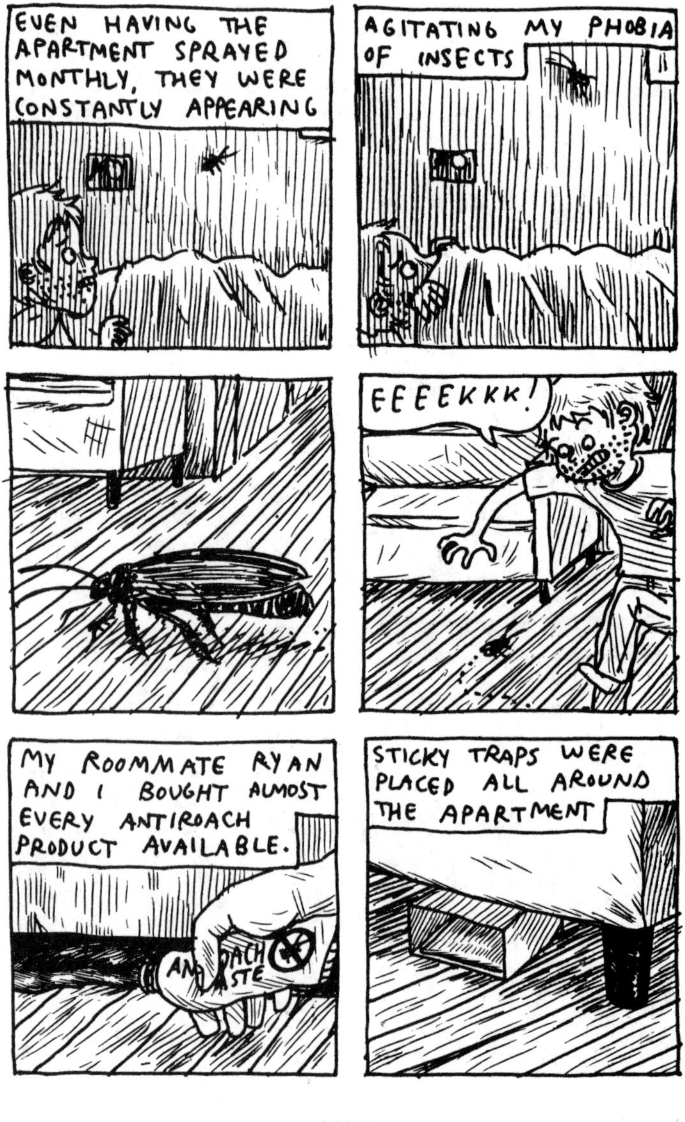
EVEN HAVING THE APARTMENT SPRAYED MONTHLY, THEY WERE CONSTANTLY APPEARING
AGITATING MY PHOBIA OF INSECTS
EEEEKKK!
MY ROOMMATE RYAN AND I BOUGHT ALMOST EVERY ANTIROACH PRODUCT AVAILABLE.
STICKY TRAPS WERE PLACED ALL AROUND THE APARTMENT

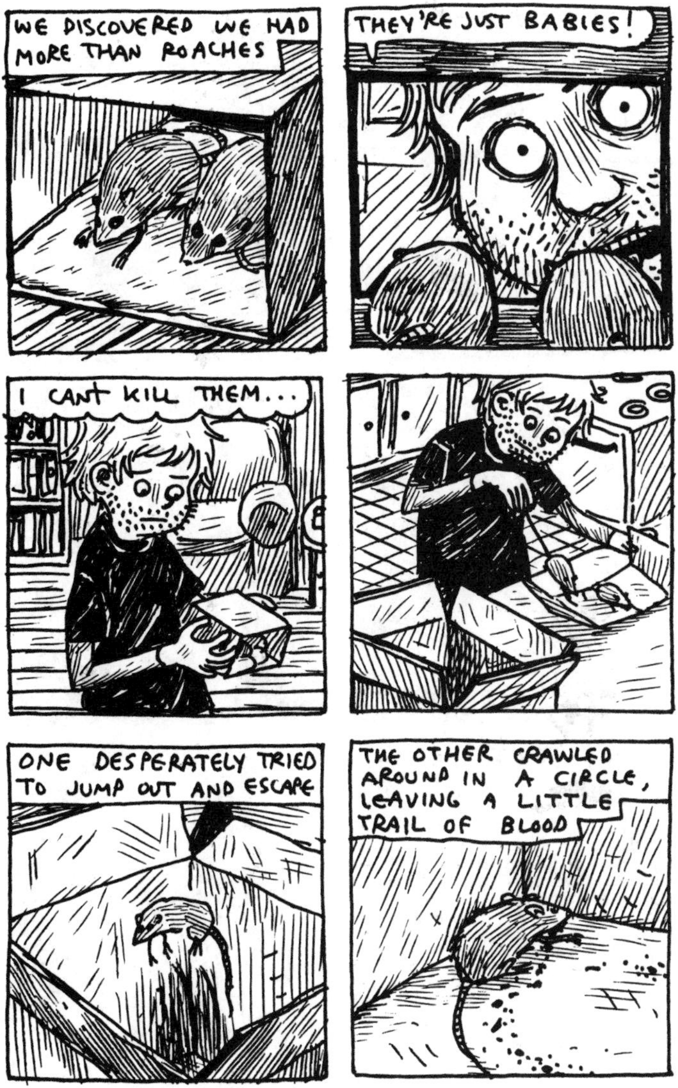
WE DISCOVERED WE HAD MORE THAN ROACHES
THEY'RE JUST BABIES!
I CANT KILL THEM...
ONE DESPERATELY TRIED TO JUMP OUT AND ESCAPE
THE OTHER CRAWLED AROUND IN A CIRCLE, LEAVING A LITTLE TRAIL OF BLOOD

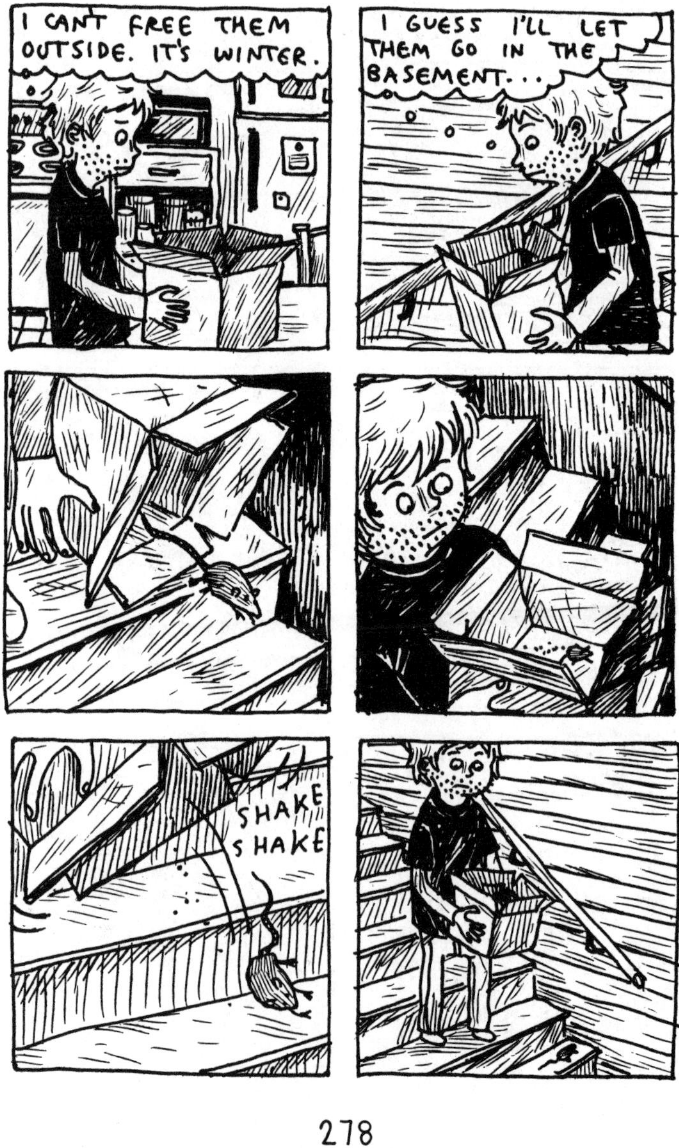
I CAN'T FREE THEM OUTSIDE. IT'S WINTER.
I GUESS I'LL LET THEM GO IN THE BASEMENT...
SHAKE SHAKE

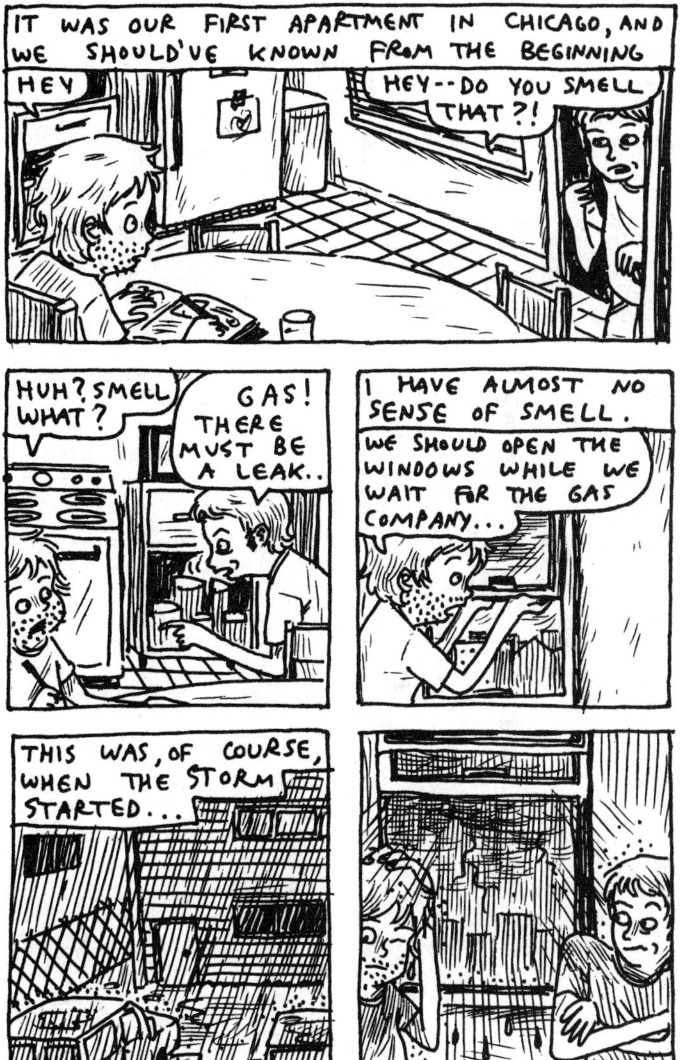
IT WAS OUR FIRST APARTMENT IN CHICAGO, AND WE SHOULD'VE KNOWN FROM THE BEGINNING
HEY
HEY--DO YOU SMELL THAT?!
HUH? SMELL WHAT?
GAS! THERE MUST BE A LEAK..
I HAVE ALMOST NO SENSE OF SMELL.
WE SHOULD OPEN THE WINDOWS WHILE WE WAIT FOR THE GAS COMPANY...
THIS WAS, OF COURSE, WHEN THE STORM STARTED...

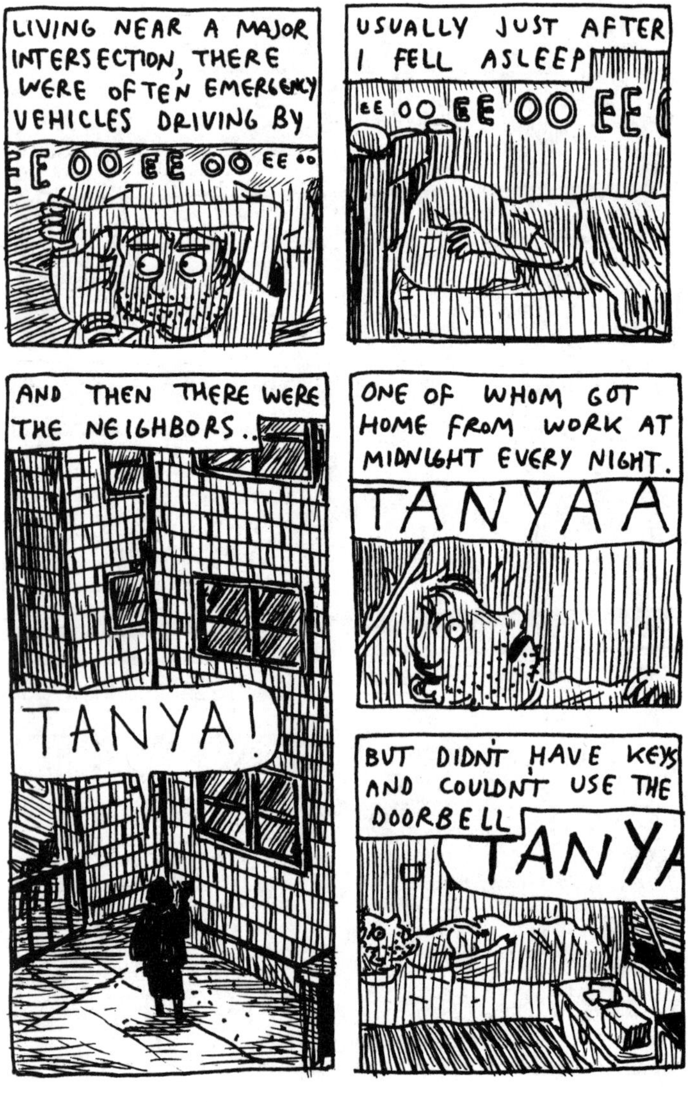
LIVING NEAR A MAJOR INTERSECTION, THERE WERE OFTEN EMERGENCY VEHICLES DRIVING BY
EE OO EE OO EE OO
USUALLY JUST AFTER I FELL ASLEEP
EE OO EE OO EE
AND THEN THERE WERE THE NEIGHBORS..
TANYA!
ONE OF WHOM GOT HOME FROM WORK AT MIDNIGHT EVERY NIGHT.
TANYAA
BUT DIDN'T HAVE KEYS AND COULDN'T USE THE DOORBELL
TANYA

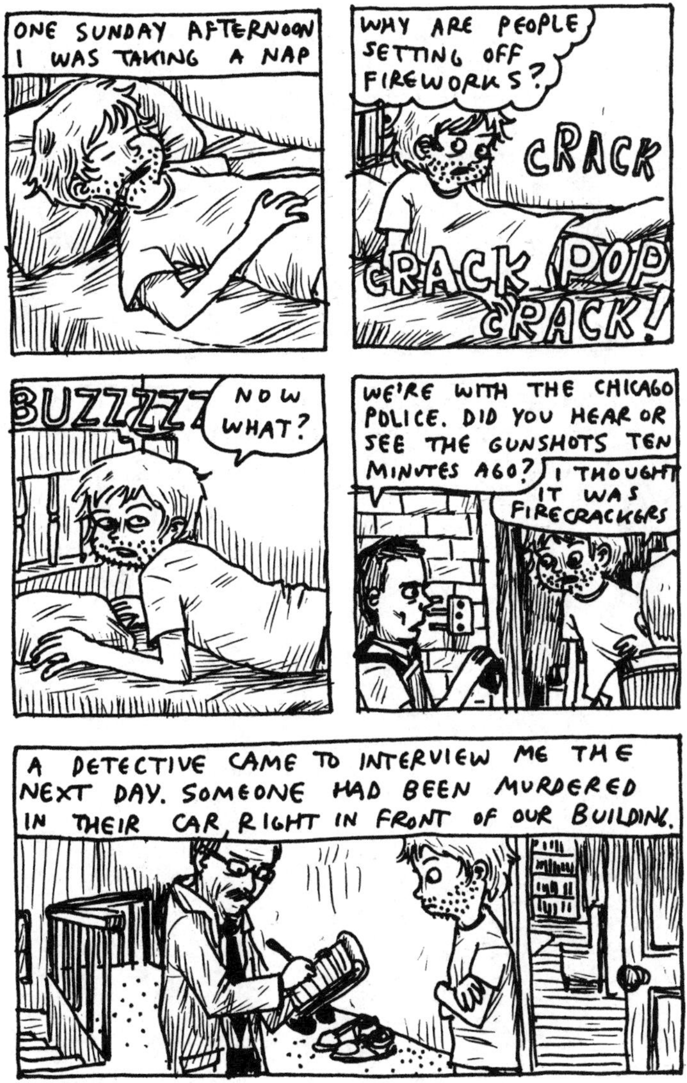
ONE SUNDAY AFTERNOON I WAS TAKING A NAP
WHY ARE PEOPLE SETTING OFF FIREWORKS?
CRACK
CRACK POP
CRACK!
BUZZZZZ
NOW WHAT?
WE'RE WITH THE CHICAGO POLICE. DID YOU HEAR OR SEE THE GUNSHOTS TEN MINUTES AGO?
I THOUGHT IT WAS FIRECRACKERS
A DETECTIVE CAME TO INTERVIEW ME THE NEXT DAY. SOMEONE HAD BEEN MURDERED IN THEIR CAR RIGHT IN FRONT OF OUR BUILDING.

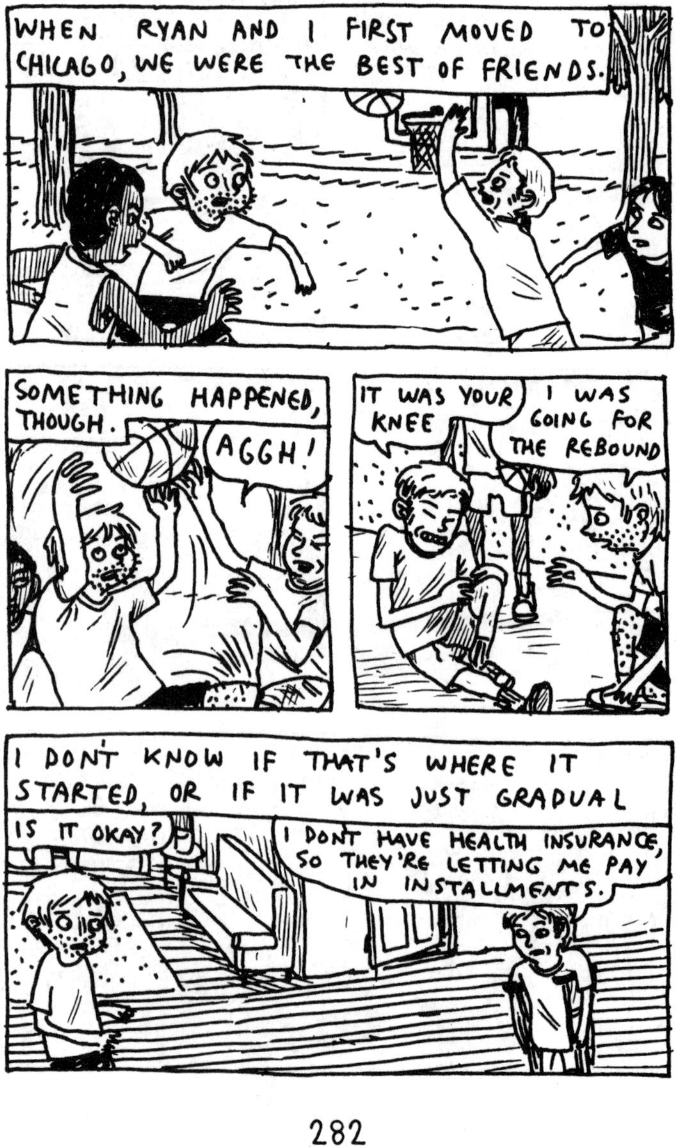
WHEN RYAN AND I FIRST MOVED TO CHICAGO, WE WERE THE BEST OF FRIENDS.
SOMETHING HAPPENED, THOUGH.
AGGH!
IT WAS YOUR KNEE
I WAS GOING FOR THE REBOUND
I DON'T KNOW IF THAT'S WHERE IT STARTED, OR IF IT WAS JUST GRADUAL
IS IT OKAY?
I DONT HAVE HEALTH INSURANCE, SO THEY'RE LETTING ME PAY IN INSTALLMENTS.

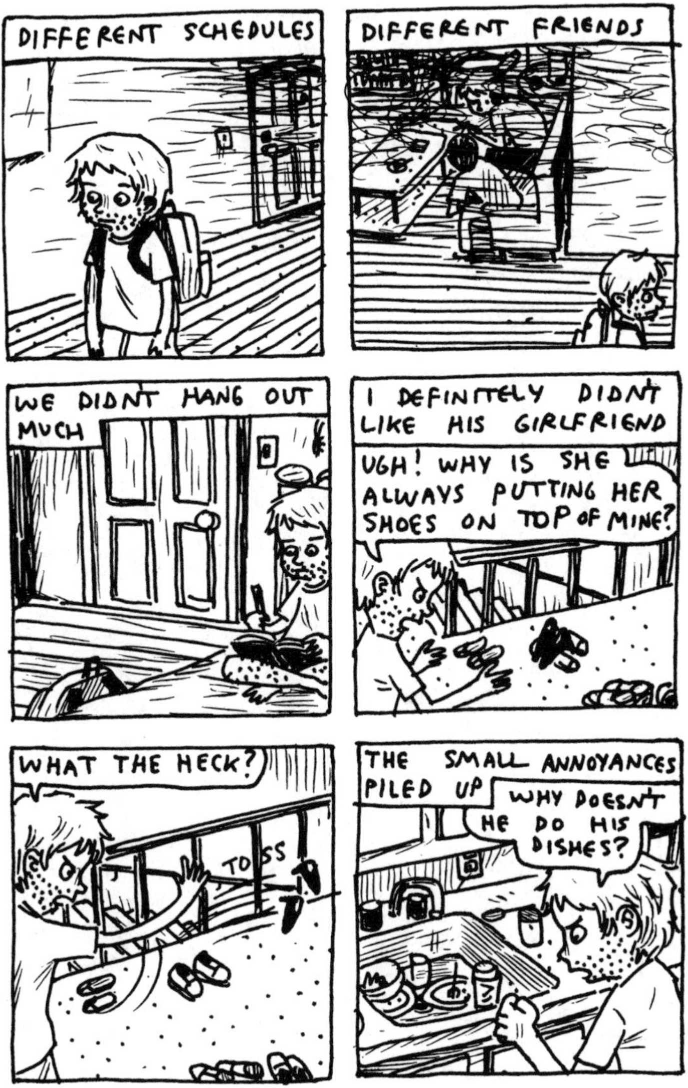
DIFFERENT SCHEDULES
DIFFERENT FRIENDS
WE DIDN'T HANG OUT MUCH
I DEFINITELY DIDN'T LIKE HIS GIRLFRIEND
UGH! WHY IS SHE ALWAYS PUTTING HER SHOES ON TOP OF MINE?
WHAT THE HECK?
TOSS
THE SMALL ANNOYANCES PILED UP
WHY DOESN'T HE DO HIS DISHES?

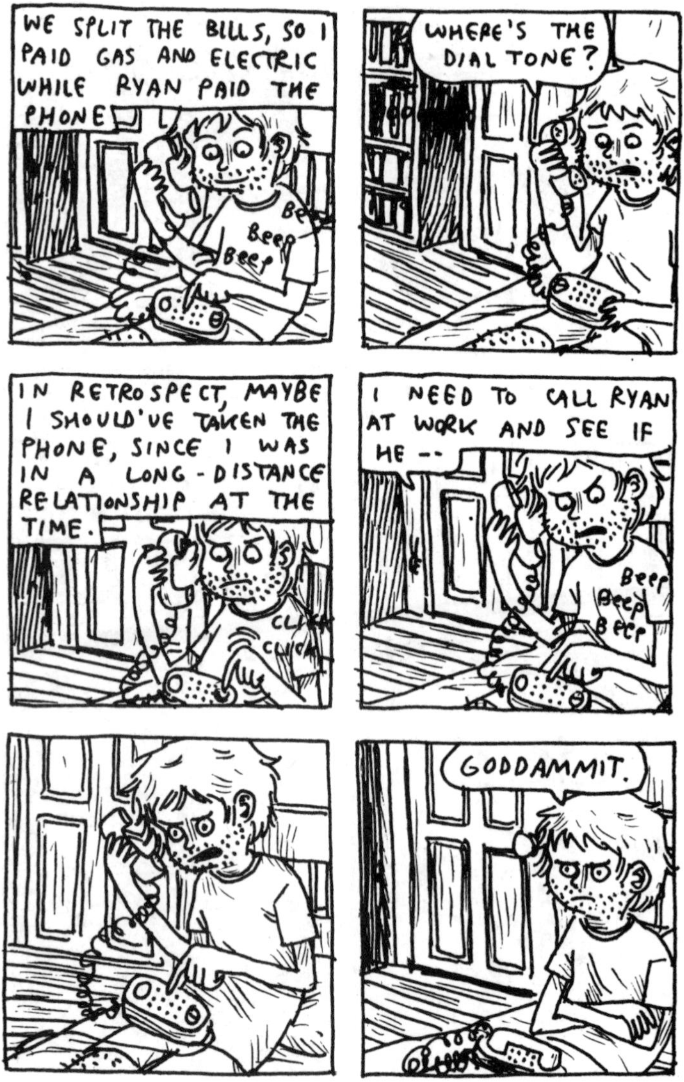
WE SPLIT THE BILLS, SO I PAID GAS AND ELECTRIC WHILE RYAN PAID THE PHONE.
Beep
Beep
WHERE'S THE DIAL TONE?
IN RETROSPECT, MAYBE I SHOULD'VE TAKEN THE PHONE, SINCE I WAS IN A LONG-DISTANCE RELATIONSHIP AT THE TIME.
I NEED TO CALL RYAN AT WORK AND SEE IF HE --
Beep
Beep
Beep
GODDAMMIT.

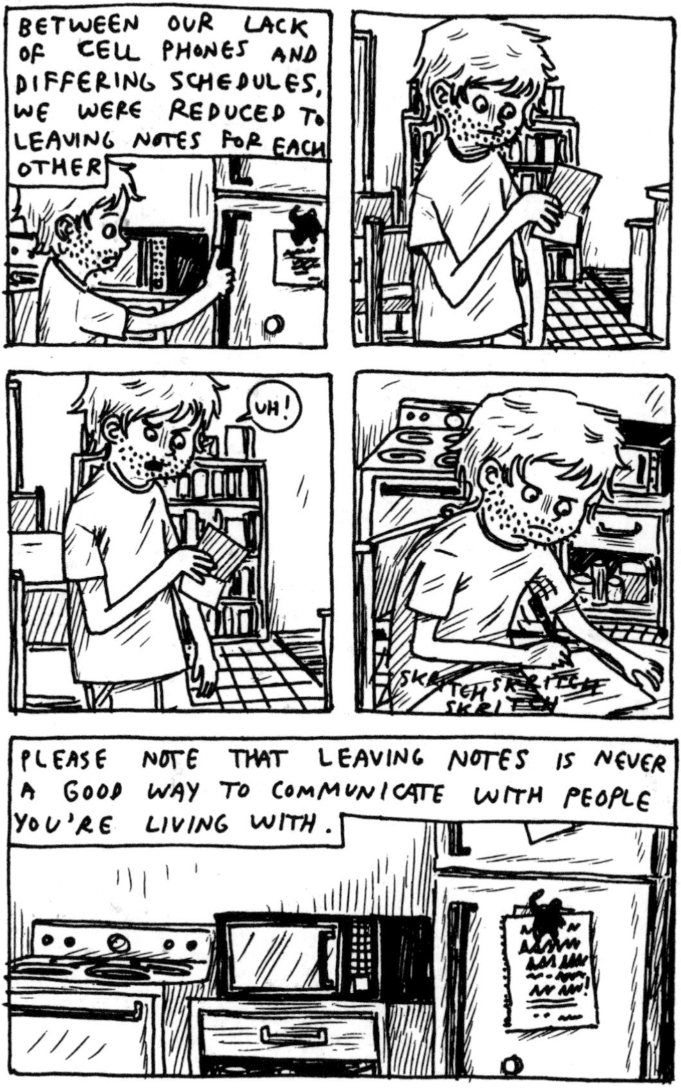
BETWEEN OUR LACK OF CELL PHONES AND DIFFERING SCHEDULES, WE WERE REDUCED TO LEAVING NOTES FOR EACH OTHER
UH!
SKRITCH SKRITCH SKRITCH
PLEASE NOTE THAT LEAVING NOTES IS NEVER A GOOD WAY TO COMMUNICATE WITH PEOPLE YOU'RE LIVING WITH.

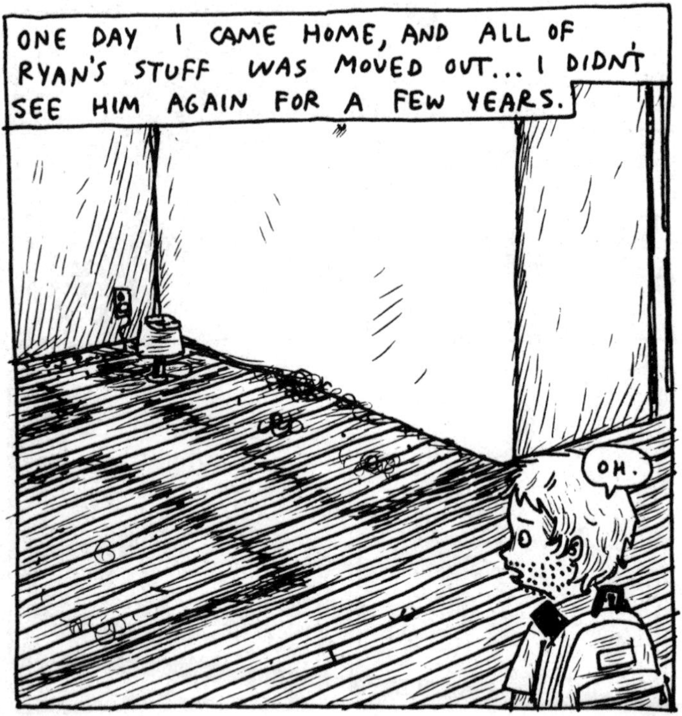
ONE DAY I CAME HOME, AND ALL OF RYAN'S STUFF WAS MOVED OUT... I DIDN'T SEE HIM AGAIN FOR A FEW YEARS.
OH.

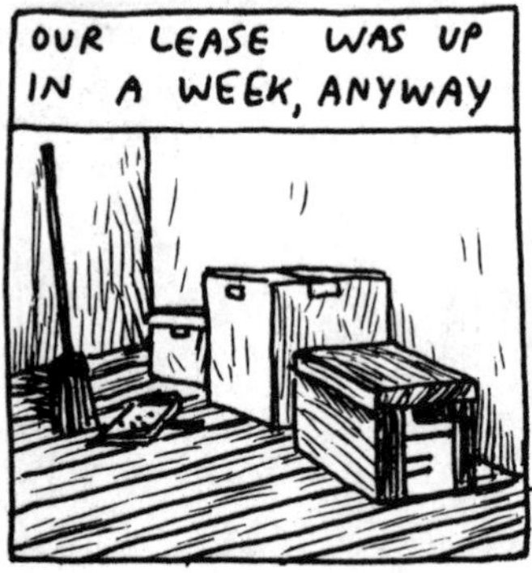
OUR LEASE WAS UP IN A WEEK, ANYWAY

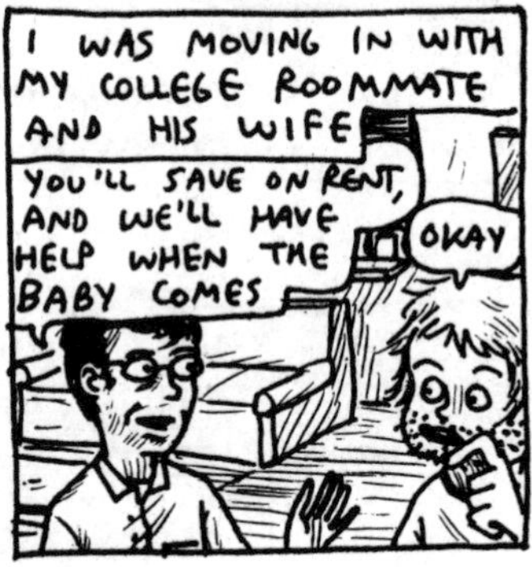
I WAS MOVING IN WITH MY COLLEGE ROOMMATE AND HIS WIFE
YOU'LL SAVE ON RENT, AND WE'LL HAVE HELP WHEN THE BABY COMES
OKAY

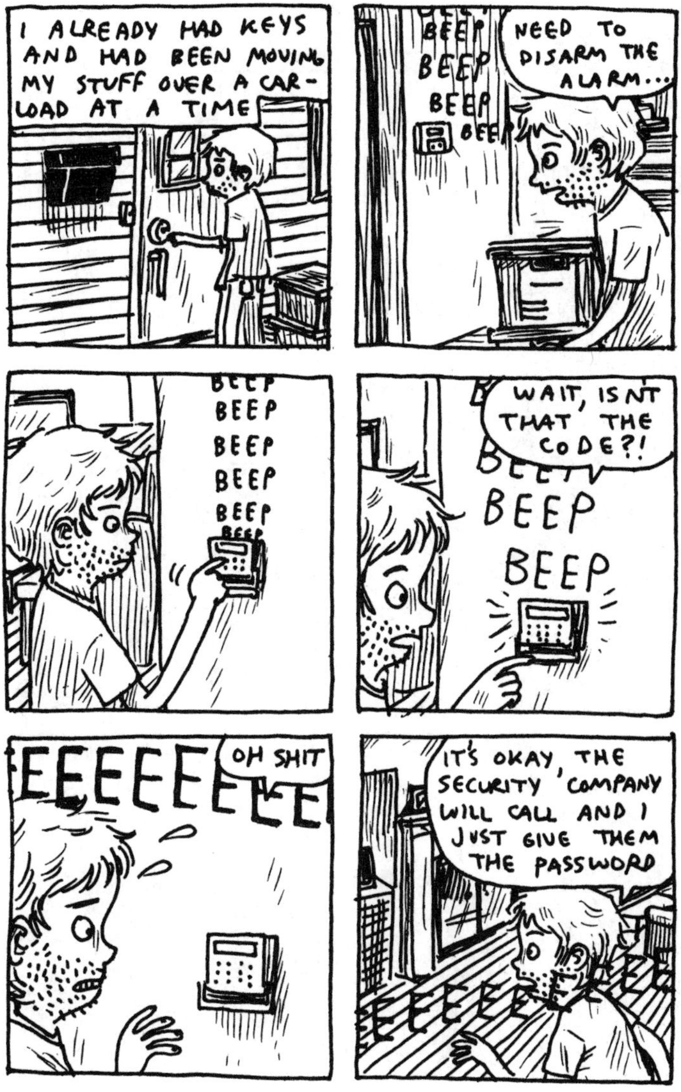

I ALREADY HAD KEYS AND HAD BEEN MOVING MY STUFF OVER A CAR-LOAD AT A TIME
BEEP BEEP BEEP BEEP
NEED TO DISARM THE ALARM...
BEEP BEEP BEEP BEEP
WAIT, ISN'T THAT THE CODE?!
BEEP BEEP
EEEEEEEE
OH SHIT
IT'S OKAY, THE SECURITY COMPANY WILL CALL AND I JUST GIVE THEM THE PASSWORD
EEEEEEEE

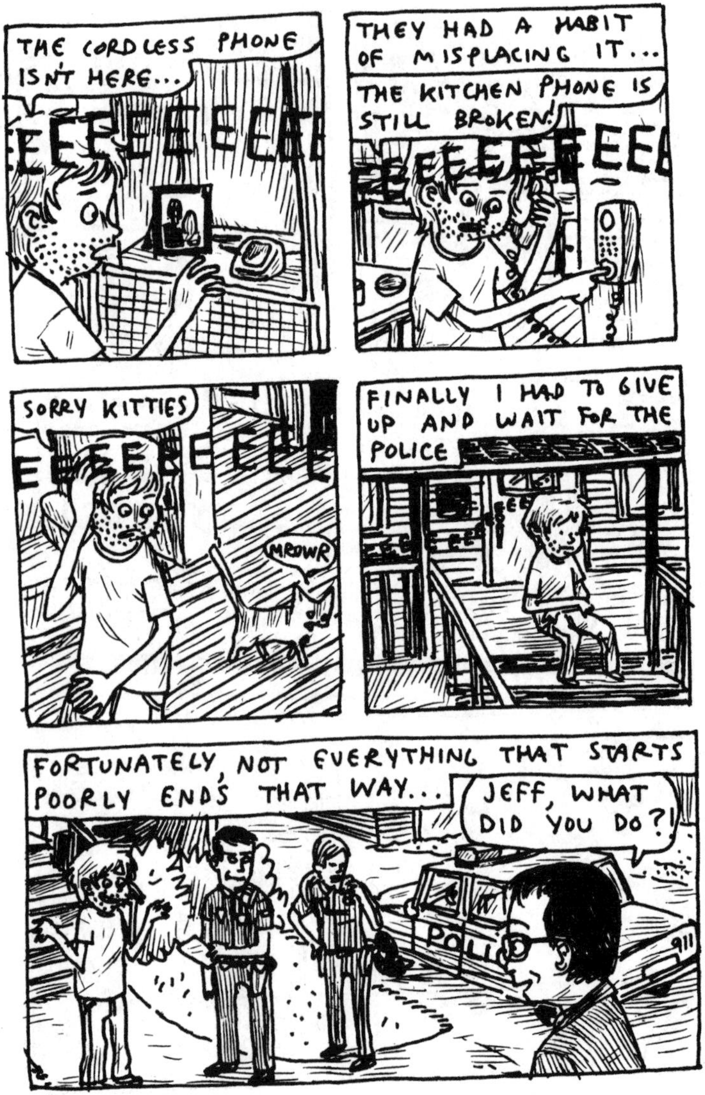
THE CORDLESS PHONE ISN'T HERE...
THEY HAD A HABIT OF MISPLACING IT...
THE KITCHEN PHONE IS STILL BROKEN!
SORRY KITTIES
MROWR
FINALLY I HAD TO GIVE UP AND WAIT FOR THE POLICE
FORTUNATELY, NOT EVERYTHING THAT STARTS POORLY ENDS THAT WAY...
JEFF, WHAT DID YOU DO?!
POLI
911

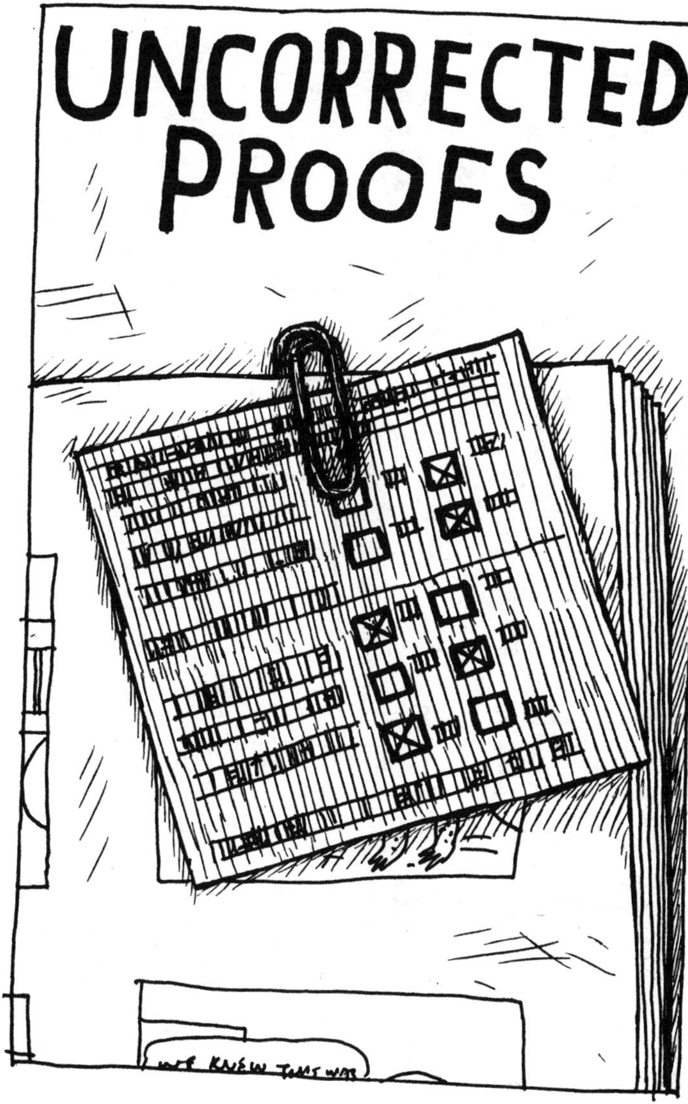
UNCORRECTED PROOFS

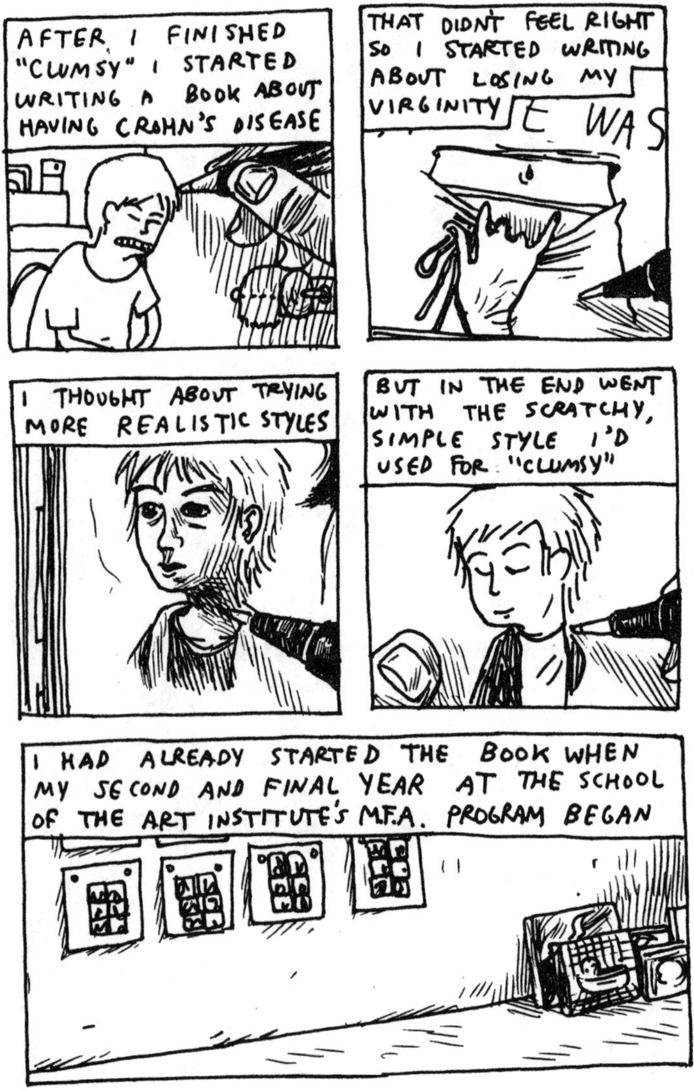
AFTER I FINISHED "CLUMSY" I STARTED WRITING A BOOK ABOUT HAVING CROHN'S DISEASE
THAT DIDN'T FEEL RIGHT SO I STARTED WRITING ABOUT LOSING MY VIRGINITY
E WAS
I THOUGHT ABOUT TRYING MORE REALISTIC STYLES
BUT IN THE END WENT WITH THE SCRATCHY, SIMPLE STYLE I'D USED FOR "CLUMSY"
I HAD ALREADY STARTED THE BOOK WHEN MY SECOND AND FINAL YEAR AT THE SCHOOL OF THE ART INSTITUTE'S M.F.A. PROGRAM BEGAN

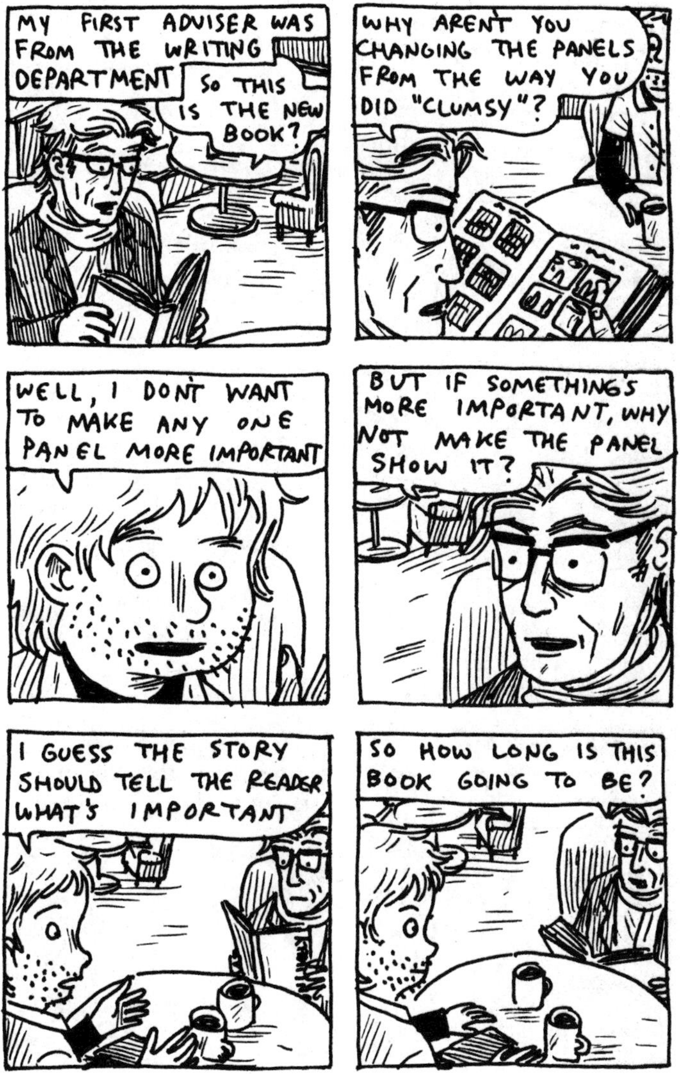
MY FIRST ADVISER WAS FROM THE WRITING DEPARTMENT
SO THIS IS THE NEW BOOK?
WHY AREN'T YOU CHANGING THE PANELS FROM THE WAY YOU DID "CLUMSY"?
WELL, I DON'T WANT TO MAKE ANY ONE PANEL MORE IMPORTANT
BUT IF SOMETHING'S MORE IMPORTANT, WHY NOT MAKE THE PANEL SHOW IT?
I GUESS THE STORY SHOULD TELL THE READER WHAT'S IMPORTANT
SO HOW LONG IS THIS BOOK GOING TO BE?

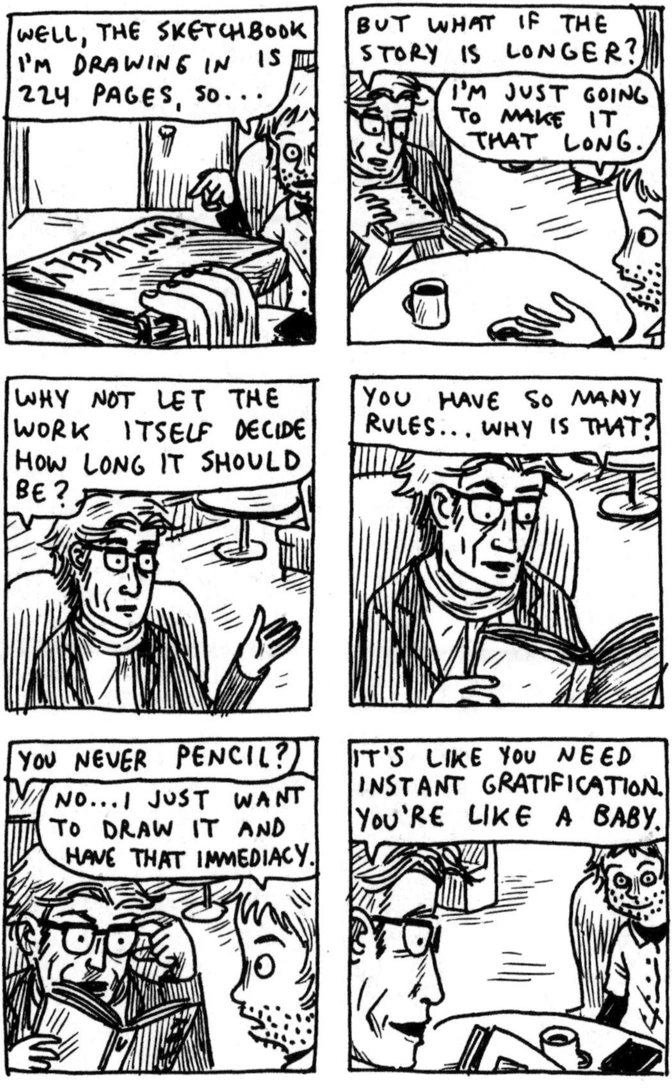
WELL, THE SKETCHBOOK I'M DRAWING IN IS 224 PAGES, SO...
UNLIKELY
BUT WHAT IF THE STORY IS LONGER?
I'M JUST GOING TO MAKE IT THAT LONG.
WHY NOT LET THE WORK ITSELF DECIDE HOW LONG IT SHOULD BE?
YOU HAVE SO MANY RULES... WHY IS THAT?
YOU NEVER PENCIL?
NO...I JUST WANT TO DRAW IT AND HAVE THAT IMMEDIACY.
IT'S LIKE YOU NEED INSTANT GRATIFICATION. YOU'RE LIKE A BABY.

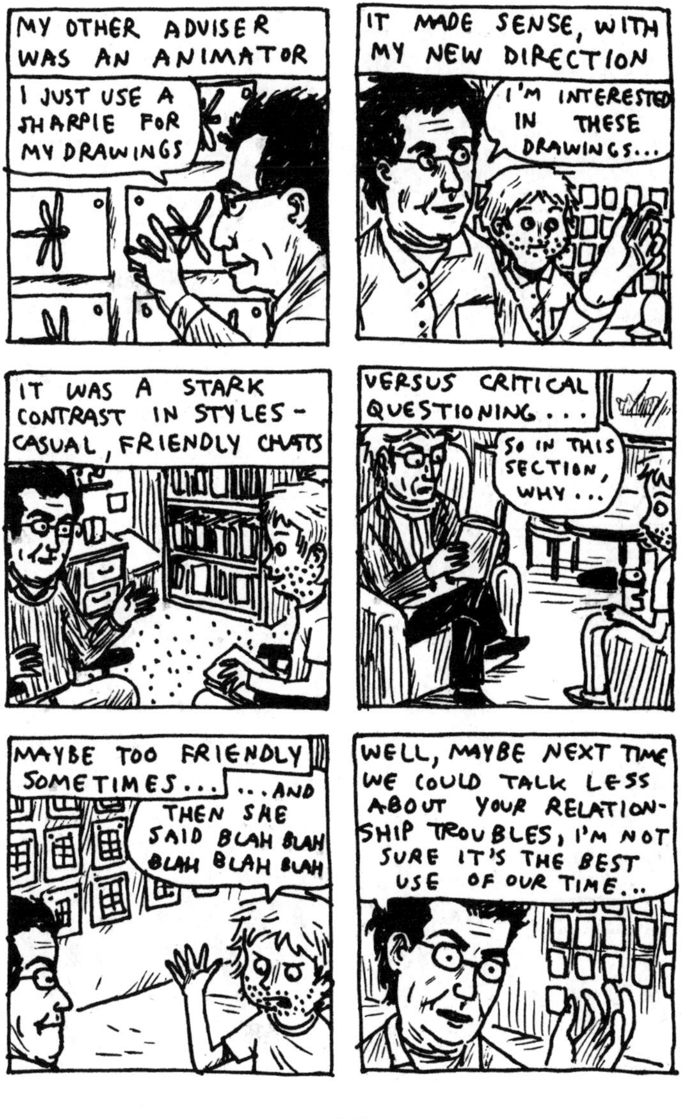
MY OTHER ADVISER WAS AN ANIMATOR
I JUST USE A SHARPIE FOR MY DRAWINGS
IT MADE SENSE, WITH MY NEW DIRECTION
I'M INTERESTED IN THESE DRAWINGS...
IT WAS A STARK CONTRAST IN STYLES - CASUAL, FRIENDLY CHATS
VERSUS CRITICAL QUESTIONING...
SO IN THIS SECTION, WHY...
MAYBE TOO FRIENDLY SOMETIMES...
...AND THEN SHE SAID BLAH BLAH BLAH BLAH BLAH
WELL, MAYBE NEXT TIME WE COULD TALK LESS ABOUT YOUR RELATIONSHIP TROUBLES, I'M NOT SURE IT'S THE BEST USE OF OUR TIME...

I ALSO STARTED TAKING WRITING CLASSES

EACH WEEK YOU'LL PASS OUT YOUR WORK FOR CRITIQUING...

I SHOWED MY COMICS, AND I ALSO WROTE NEW PROSE FOR FEEDBACK...

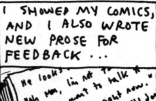

I WAS HANDWRITING ALL OF MY PAPERS

CRAP! I SCREWED THIS PAGE UP... NOW I HAVE TO START OVER...

SO I WAS WORKING MOSTLY JUST IN A BUNCH OF DIFFERENT BOOKS

BOOK FOR WRITING

GENERAL SKETCHBOOK

COMICS

BOTH MY PARENTS LOVED BOOKS AND I INHERITED THAT LOVE

YOU CAN PICK OUT A BOOK TO GET, JEFF

THIS ONE

I MADE PHOTOCOPIES OF "CLUMSY" AND NOW I HAD 100 COPIES OF MY FIRST BOOK

CLUMSY
A NOVEL
BY JEFF

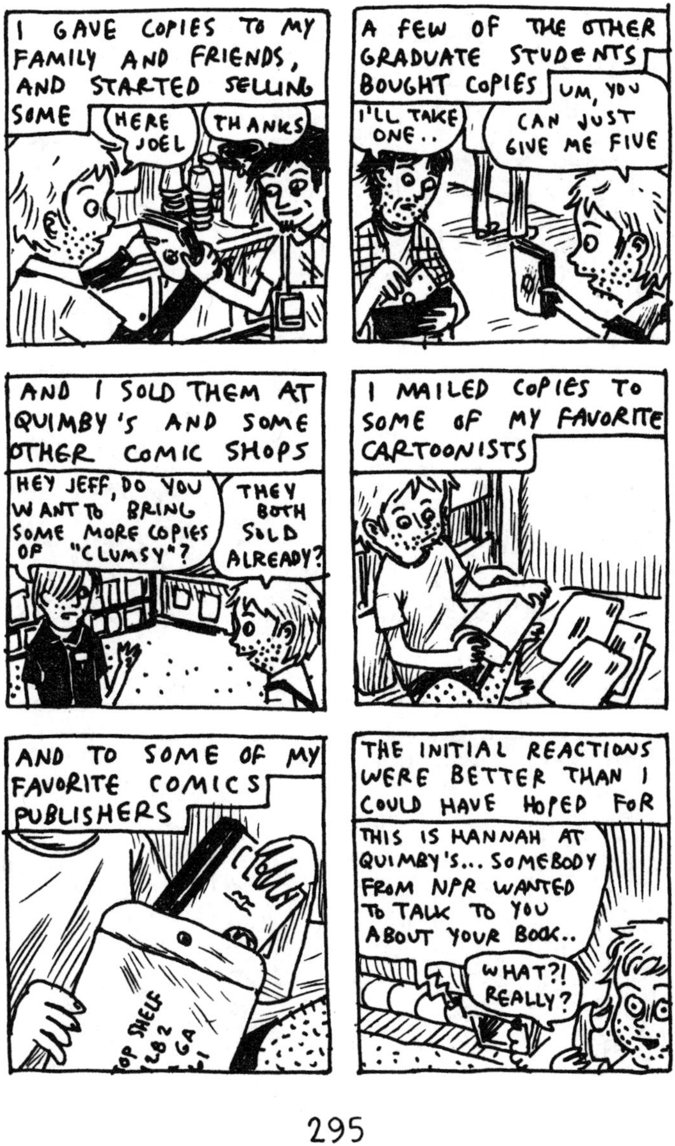
I GAVE COPIES TO MY FAMILY AND FRIENDS, AND STARTED SELLING SOME
HERE JOEL
THANKS
A FEW OF THE OTHER GRADUATE STUDENTS BOUGHT COPIES
I'LL TAKE ONE..
UM, YOU CAN JUST GIVE ME FIVE
AND I SOLD THEM AT QUIMBY'S AND SOME OTHER COMIC SHOPS
HEY JEFF, DO YOU WANT TO BRING SOME MORE COPIES OF "CLUMSY"?
THEY BOTH SOLD ALREADY?
I MAILED COPIES TO SOME OF MY FAVORITE CARTOONISTS
AND TO SOME OF MY FAVORITE COMICS PUBLISHERS
TOP SHELF
THE INITIAL REACTIONS WERE BETTER THAN I COULD HAVE HOPED FOR
THIS IS HANNAH AT QUIMBY'S... SOMEBODY FROM NPR WANTED TO TALK TO YOU ABOUT YOUR BOOK..
WHAT?! REALLY?

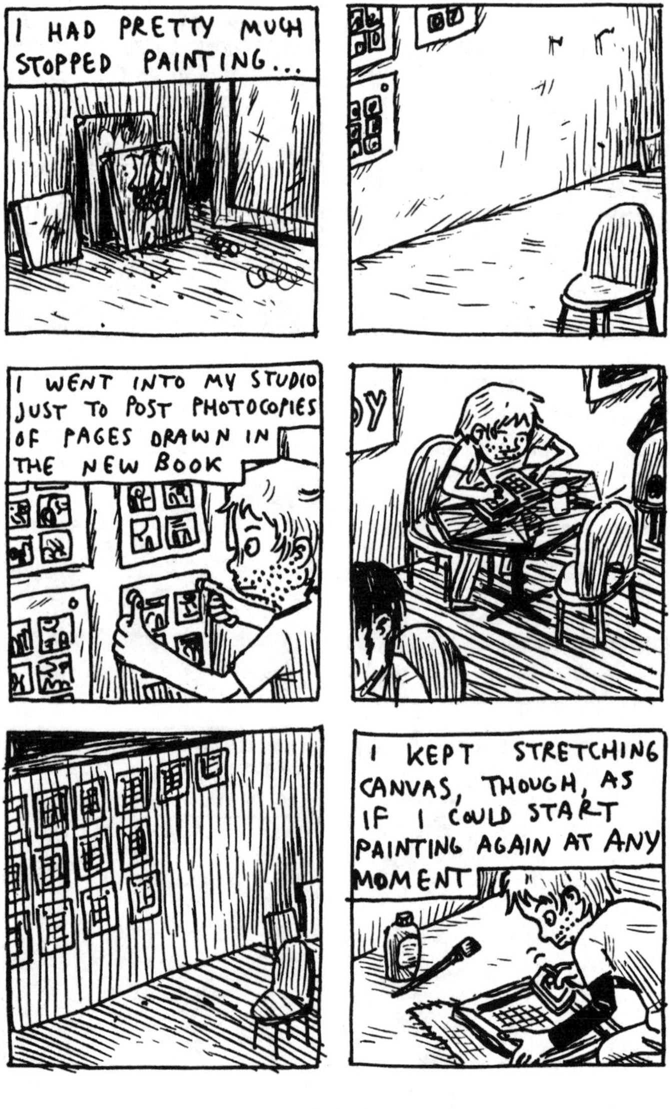
I HAD PRETTY MUCH STOPPED PAINTING...
I WENT INTO MY STUDIO JUST TO POST PHOTOCOPIES OF PAGES DRAWN IN THE NEW BOOK
I KEPT STRETCHING CANVAS, THOUGH, AS IF I COULD START PAINTING AGAIN AT ANY MOMENT

THE PAINTING FACULTY SEEMED UNSURE OF HOW TO HELP ME WITH THE COMICS

I READ YOUR BOOK.

THE LINES OF THE WOOD FLOOR HERE...

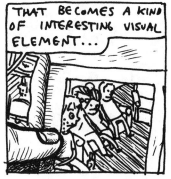

THAT BECOMES A KIND OF INTERESTING VISUAL ELEMENT...

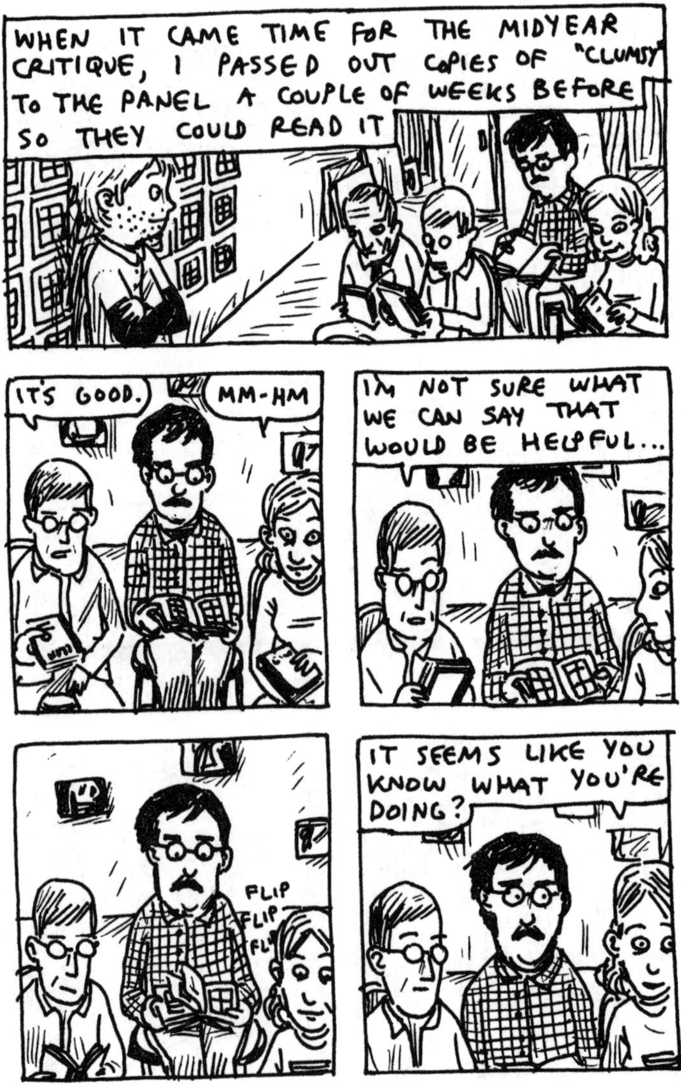
WHEN IT CAME TIME FOR THE MIDYEAR CRITIQUE, I PASSED OUT COPIES OF "CLUMSY" TO THE PANEL A COUPLE OF WEEKS BEFORE SO THEY COULD READ IT
IT'S GOOD.
MM-HM
I'M NOT SURE WHAT WE CAN SAY THAT WOULD BE HELPFUL...
FLIP
FLIP
FL
IT SEEMS LIKE YOU KNOW WHAT YOU'RE DOING?

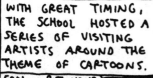

WITH GREAT TIMING, THE SCHOOL HOSTED A SERIES OF VISITING ARTISTS AROUND THE THEME OF CARTOONS.

COOL... BUT NONE OF THESE ARTISTS ARE ANIMATORS?

ATTACK OF THE KILLER ANIMATION SERIES

ALI · HERRERA · CHARLES · SHIMOM...

ONLY ONE OF THE ARTISTS WAS AN ACTUAL CARTOONIST

JOE SACCO?

I'M JEFF. I'LL TAKE YOU TO THE THEATER FOR YOUR PRESENTATION

HI

THE OTHER ARTISTS IN THE SERIES HAD CONNECTIONS TO CARTOONING THAT WERE A BIT OF A STRETCH.

THERE WAS ONE OTHER ARTIST WHO VISITED WITH A TENUOUS CONNECTION TO COMICS.

MY BOOKS ARE ALL FUNDED BY ART MUSEUMS.

HE HAD DONE A SERIES OF ART PROJECTS THAT MIMICKED THE COMIC BOOK FORMAT

SELF-PUBLISHING IS VANITY PUBLISHING.

299

I STARTED TO GET RESPONSES FROM THE PUBLISHERS I SENT "CLUMSY" TO.

SOME DIDN'T RESPOND

must have a signed ???
If you'd live us to revie
submission, please sign ?
and return it to my at?

The Legal Department w
keep your submittal mat
on file for one month.
receive a signed SUB
?reement from you be
?e will forward your ?
?epartment for review
?ither (1) retu
??diss

SOME SENT FORM LETTERS

Dear Creator:

First of all, let me apologize for such a dreaded and impersonal th as a form letter. How ?s we receive a great ma? submissions, and there ?s just no way ?o respon? ?ever

SOME EMAILS ?rld o
melancho? ?ound your
At first I found style crude an
drawing I'll tell ya, it rea
But i'll tell ya? This is
grew on me.

To be quite honest t
given the economic s
of the industry (19
our schedule is saf
i can't see us picki
?or publicati
??or ??of wo?

CHRIS STAROS FROM TOP SHELF DID FOLLOW UP WITH A PHONE CALL

Mm-hm. No... I understand...

BUT THE BOTTOM LINE WAS ALWAYS THE SAME

Subject Clumsy Parts ≣ Messag

NOT FOR PUBLI

Hey Jeffrey,

Thanks for send?

300

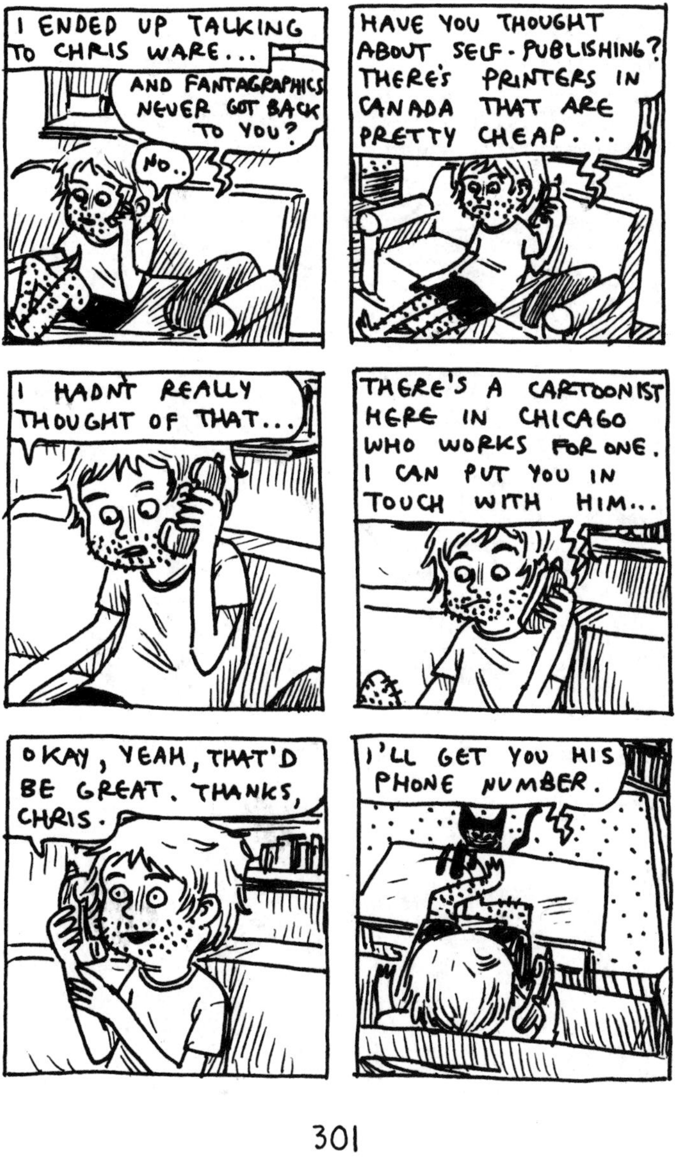
I ENDED UP TALKING TO CHRIS WARE...
AND FANTAGRAPHICS NEVER GOT BACK TO YOU?
NO..
HAVE YOU THOUGHT ABOUT SELF-PUBLISHING? THERE'S PRINTERS IN CANADA THAT ARE PRETTY CHEAP...
I HADNT REALLY THOUGHT OF THAT...
THERE'S A CARTOONIST HERE IN CHICAGO WHO WORKS FOR ONE. I CAN PUT YOU IN TOUCH WITH HIM...
OKAY, YEAH, THAT'D BE GREAT. THANKS, CHRIS.
I'LL GET YOU HIS PHONE NUMBER.

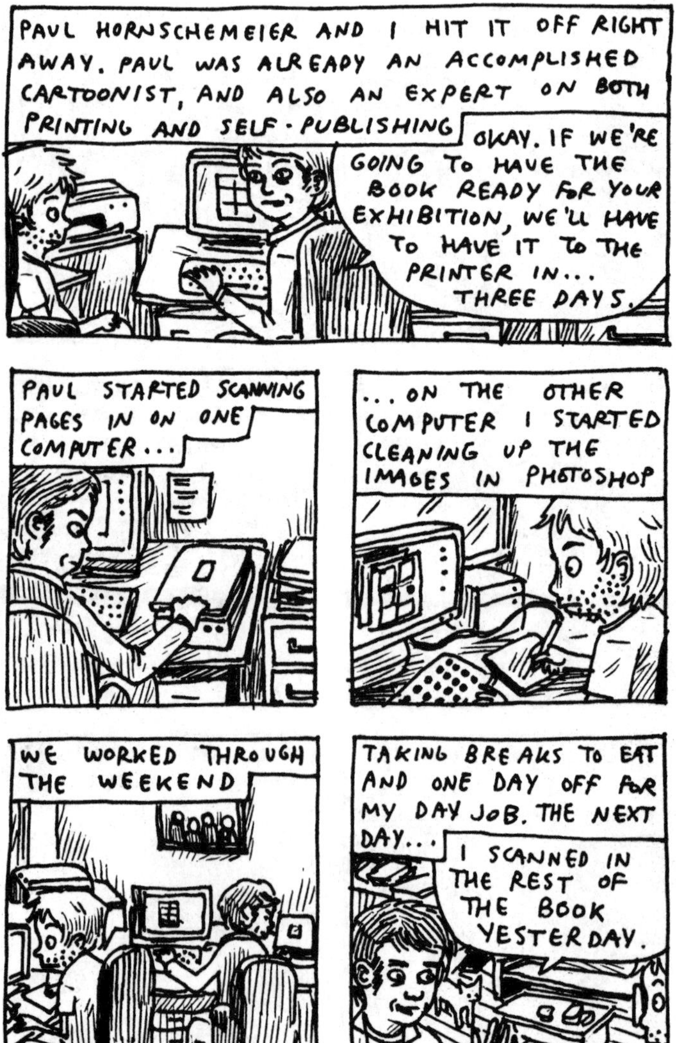
PAUL HORNSCHEMEIER AND I HIT IT OFF RIGHT AWAY. PAUL WAS ALREADY AN ACCOMPLISHED CARTOONIST, AND ALSO AN EXPERT ON BOTH PRINTING AND SELF-PUBLISHING
OKAY. IF WE'RE GOING TO HAVE THE BOOK READY FOR YOUR EXHIBITION, WE'LL HAVE TO HAVE IT TO THE PRINTER IN... THREE DAYS.
PAUL STARTED SCANNING PAGES IN ON ONE COMPUTER...
...ON THE OTHER COMPUTER I STARTED CLEANING UP THE IMAGES IN PHOTOSHOP
WE WORKED THROUGH THE WEEKEND
TAKING BREAKS TO EAT AND ONE DAY OFF FOR MY DAY JOB. THE NEXT DAY...
I SCANNED IN THE REST OF THE BOOK YESTERDAY.

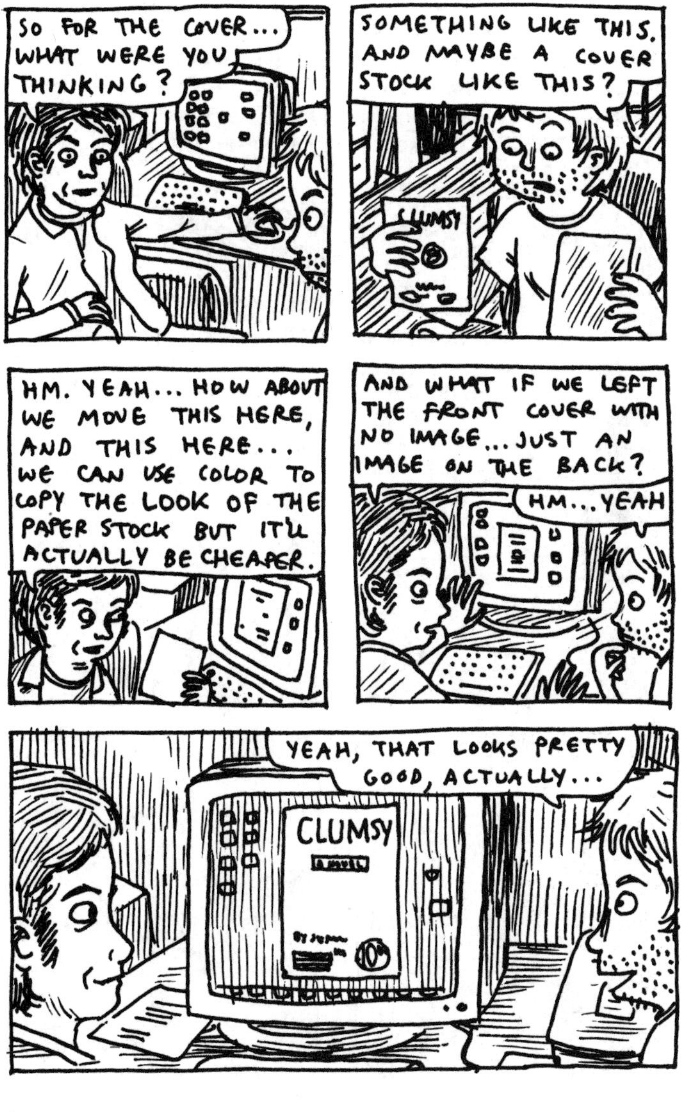
SO FOR THE COVER... WHAT WERE YOU THINKING?
SOMETHING LIKE THIS. AND MAYBE A COVER STOCK LIKE THIS?
CLUMSY
HM. YEAH... HOW ABOUT WE MOVE THIS HERE, AND THIS HERE... WE CAN USE COLOR TO COPY THE LOOK OF THE PAPER STOCK BUT IT'LL ACTUALLY BE CHEAPER.
AND WHAT IF WE LEFT THE FRONT COVER WITH NO IMAGE... JUST AN IMAGE ON THE BACK?
HM... YEAH
YEAH, THAT LOOKS PRETTY GOOD, ACTUALLY...
CLUMSY

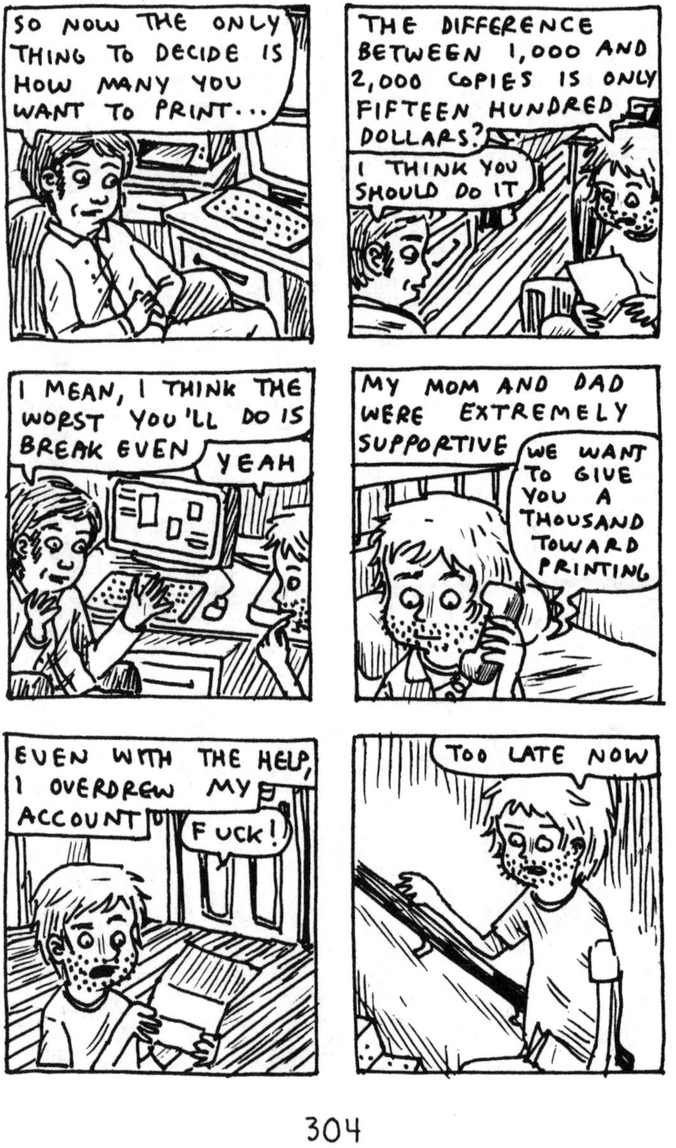
SO NOW THE ONLY THING TO DECIDE IS HOW MANY YOU WANT TO PRINT...
THE DIFFERENCE BETWEEN 1,000 AND 2,000 COPIES IS ONLY FIFTEEN HUNDRED DOLLARS?
I THINK YOU SHOULD DO IT
I MEAN, I THINK THE WORST YOU'LL DO IS BREAK EVEN
YEAH
MY MOM AND DAD WERE EXTREMELY SUPPORTIVE
WE WANT TO GIVE YOU A THOUSAND TOWARD PRINTING
EVEN WITH THE HELP, I OVERDREW MY ACCOUNT
FUCK!
TOO LATE NOW

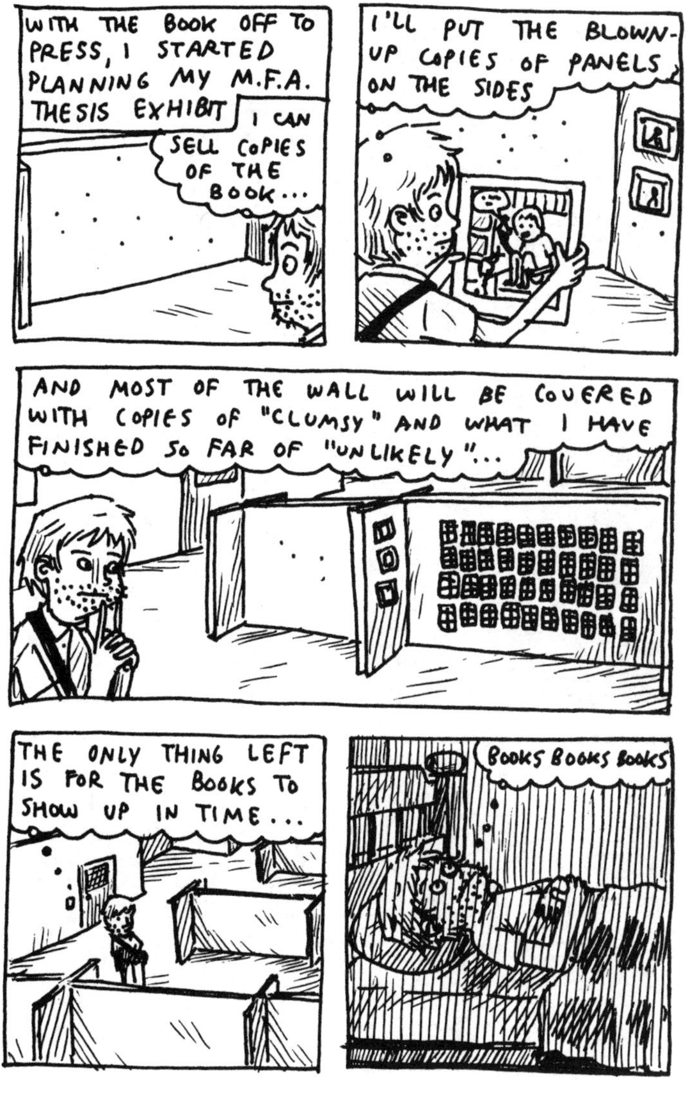
WITH THE BOOK OFF TO PRESS, I STARTED PLANNING MY M.F.A. THESIS EXHIBIT
I CAN SELL COPIES OF THE BOOK...
I'LL PUT THE BLOWN-UP COPIES OF PANELS ON THE SIDES
AND MOST OF THE WALL WILL BE COVERED WITH COPIES OF "CLUMSY" AND WHAT I HAVE FINISHED SO FAR OF "UNLIKELY"...
THE ONLY THING LEFT IS FOR THE BOOKS TO SHOW UP IN TIME...
BOOKS BOOKS BOOKS

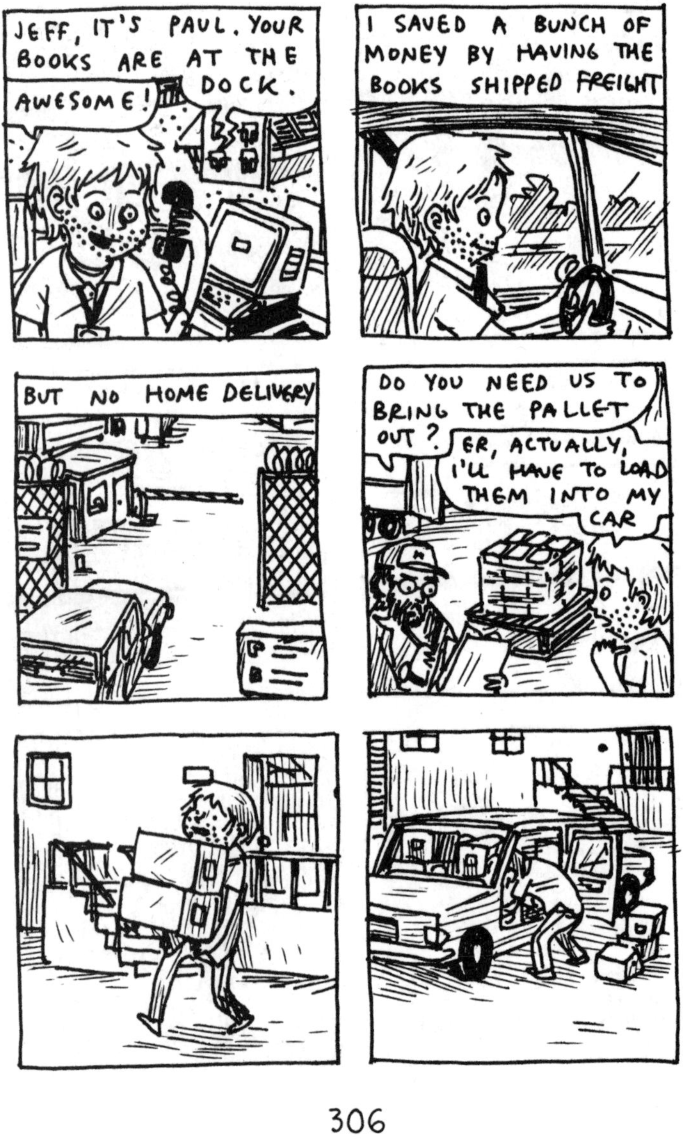
JEFF, IT'S PAUL. YOUR BOOKS ARE AT THE DOCK.
AWESOME!
I SAVED A BUNCH OF MONEY BY HAVING THE BOOKS SHIPPED FREIGHT
BUT NO HOME DELIVERY
DO YOU NEED US TO BRING THE PALLET OUT?
ER, ACTUALLY, I'LL HAVE TO LOAD THEM INTO MY CAR

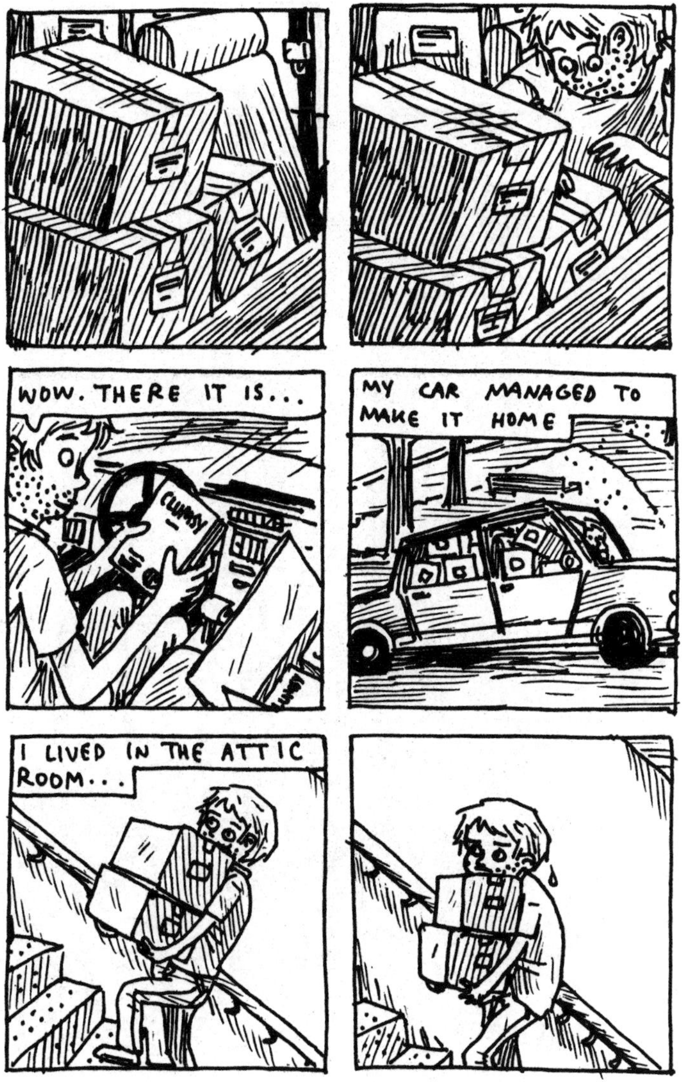
WOW. THERE IT IS...
MY CAR MANAGED TO MAKE IT HOME
I LIVED IN THE ATTIC ROOM...

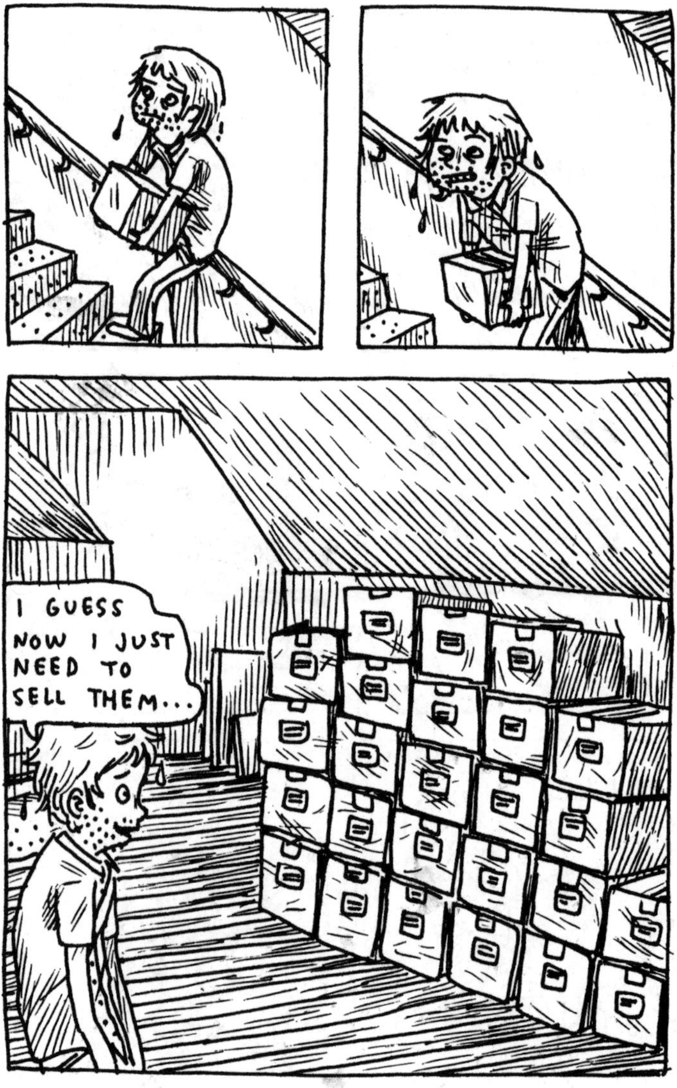
I GUESS NOW I JUST NEED TO SELL THEM...

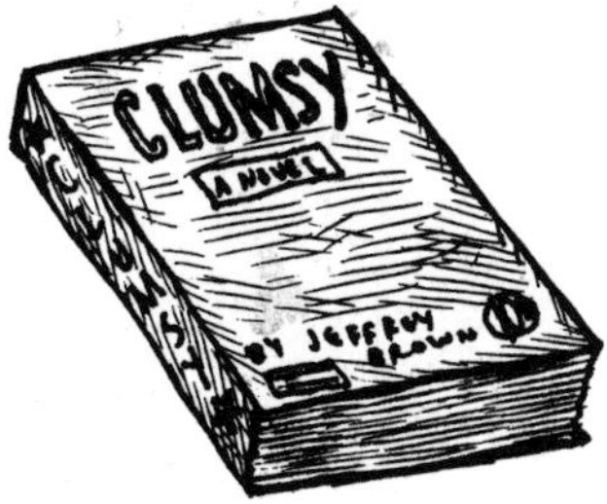
CLUMSY
A NOVEL
BY JEFFREY BROWN

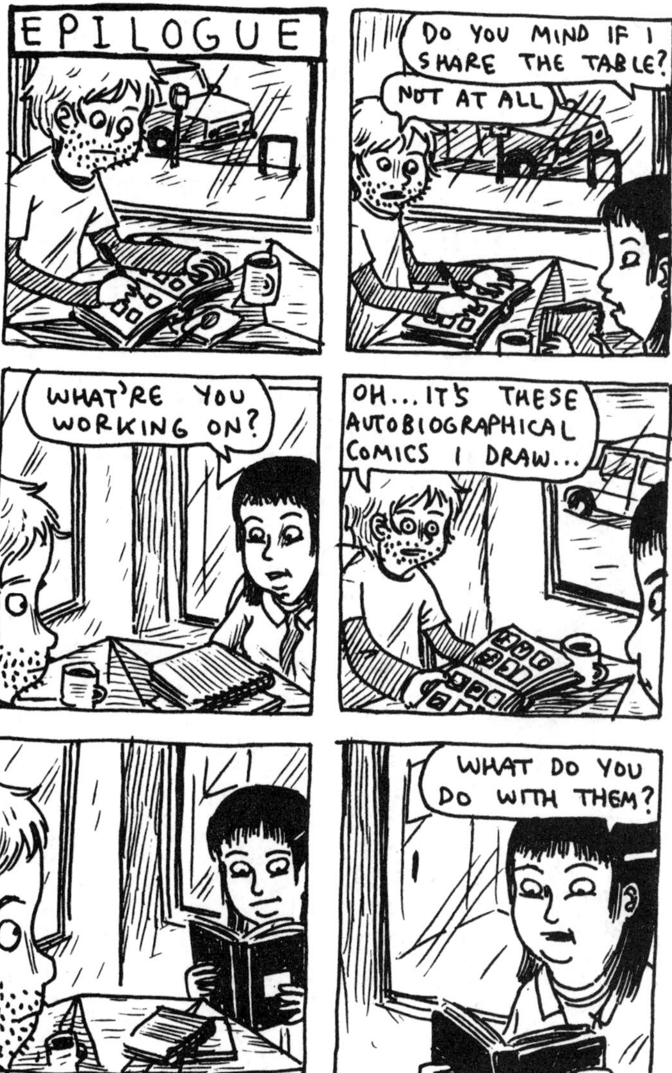
EPILOGUE
DO YOU MIND IF I SHARE THE TABLE?
NOT AT ALL
WHAT'RE YOU WORKING ON?
OH... IT'S THESE AUTOBIOGRAPHICAL COMICS I DRAW...
WHAT DO YOU DO WITH THEM?

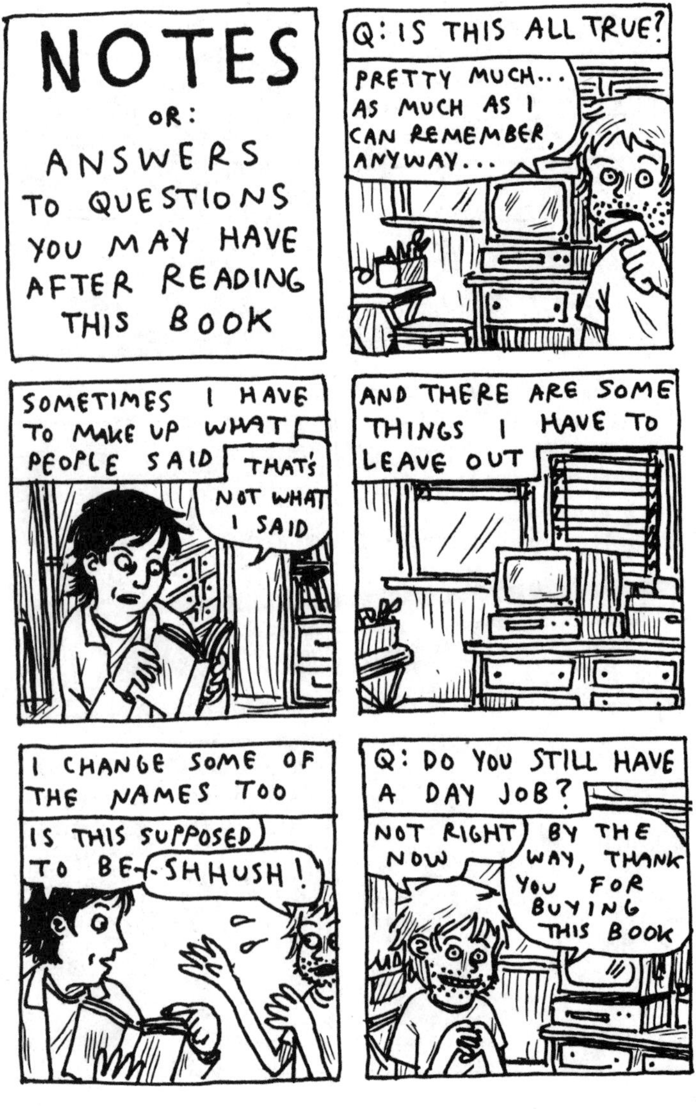
NOTES
OR:
ANSWERS TO QUESTIONS YOU MAY HAVE AFTER READING THIS BOOK
Q: IS THIS ALL TRUE?
PRETTY MUCH... AS MUCH AS I CAN REMEMBER, ANYWAY...
SOMETIMES I HAVE TO MAKE UP WHAT PEOPLE SAID
THAT'S NOT WHAT I SAID
AND THERE ARE SOME THINGS I HAVE TO LEAVE OUT
I CHANGE SOME OF THE NAMES TOO
IS THIS SUPPOSED TO BE-
-SHHUSH!
Q: DO YOU STILL HAVE A DAY JOB?
NOT RIGHT NOW
BY THE WAY, THANK YOU FOR BUYING THIS BOOK

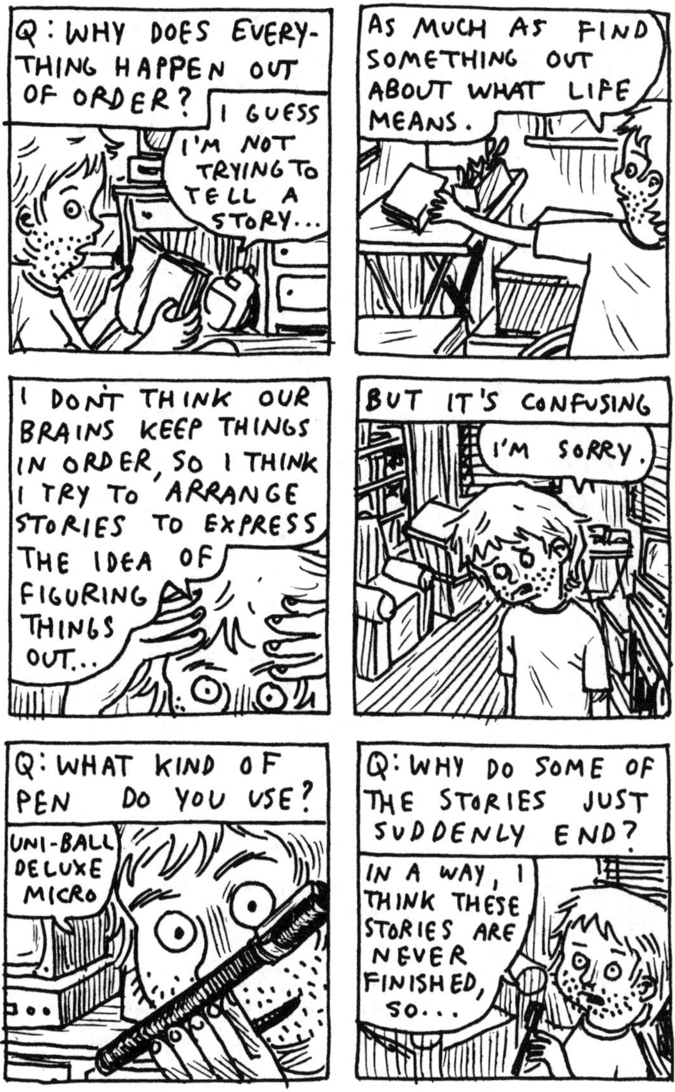

Q: WHY DOES EVERYTHING HAPPEN OUT OF ORDER?
I GUESS I'M NOT TRYING TO TELL A STORY...
AS MUCH AS FIND SOMETHING OUT ABOUT WHAT LIFE MEANS.
I DON'T THINK OUR BRAINS KEEP THINGS IN ORDER, SO I THINK I TRY TO ARRANGE STORIES TO EXPRESS THE IDEA OF FIGURING THINGS OUT...
BUT IT'S CONFUSING
I'M SORRY.
Q: WHAT KIND OF PEN DO YOU USE?
UNI-BALL DELUXE MICRO
Q: WHY DO SOME OF THE STORIES JUST SUDDENLY END?
IN A WAY, I THINK THESE STORIES ARE NEVER FINISHED, SO...

MANY THANKS

TO EVERYONE WHO APPEARS IN THESE
STORIES, EVERYONE WHO READS AND
SUPPORTS MY WORK, AND ALL OF MY
FAMILY AND FRIENDS, ESPECIALLY PAUL,
CHRIS, DANIEL, RYAN, MIKE, BEN, DOUG,
STEVE, MOM, DAD, AND ALSO EVERYONE
WORKING BEHIND THE SCENES TO GET
MY WORK OUT THERE - CHRIS STAROS,
BRETT WARNOCK, STEVE MOCKUS, AMANDA
PATTEN, AND MARC GERALD. THANKS
TO THE COMIC SHOPS THAT HAVE ENABLED
MY COMICS HABIT: COLLECTOR'S CORNER,
APPARITIONS, QUIMBY'S, CHICAGO COMICS,
COMIX REVOLUTION, AND DARK TOWER.
THANKS TO KAVA HOUSE AND EARWAX
(WHERE SOME OF THIS BOOK TAKES
PLACE) AND BEANS & BAGELS (WHERE
MOST OF THIS BOOK WAS DRAWN).
FINALLY, THANKS TO JENNIFER AND
OSCAR FOR ALL THEIR PATIENCE AND
LOVE AND SUPPORT.

THIS BOOK IS DEDICATED TO ALL
THE TEACHERS AND MENTORS WHO
HAVE GUIDED, PUSHED, AND HELPED ME
ON MY WAY TO BEING AN ARTIST...

ABOUT THE AUTHOR

JEFFREY BROWN IS A CARTOONIST BEST KNOWN
FOR HIS HUMOROUS, OCCASIONALLY BITTERSWEET
AUTOBIOGRAPHICAL COMICS. BORN IN GRAND RAPIDS,
MICHIGAN, JEFFREY MOVED IN 2000 TO CHICAGO,
WHERE HE RECEIVED HIS M.F.A. FROM THE SCHOOL
OF THE ART INSTITUTE. HE CURRENTLY LIVES
IN CHICAGO WITH HIS PARTNER, JENNIFER, AND
THEIR SON.
FIND OUT MORE AT:
www.jeffreybrowncomics.com

WRITE TO HIM AT: JEFFREYBROWNRQ@HOTMAIL.COM
OR MORE SLOWLY AT: Jeffrey Brown
P.O. Box 120
Deerfield IL 60015-0120
USA

LITTLE THINGS

A MEMOIR IN SLICES

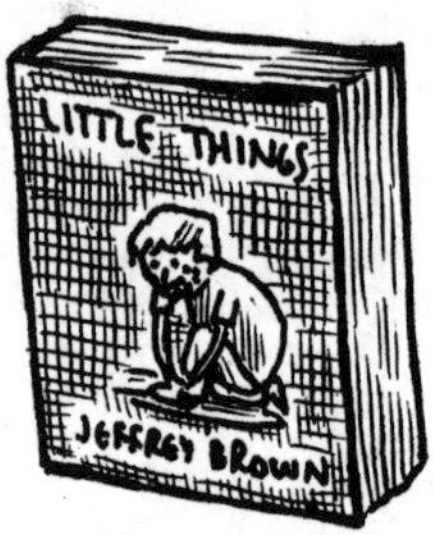
LITTLE THINGS
JEFFREY BROWN

EVOCATIVE GRAPHIC SHORT STORIES DEALING WITH EVERY ASPECT OF DAILY LIFE - FRIENDSHIP, ILLNESS, DEATH, WORK, CRUSHES, LOVE, JEALOUSY AND FATHERHOOD - EACH STORY LOOPS INTO OTHERS, SHOWING HOW THE SMALLEST AND SEEMINGLY MOST INSIGNIFICANT PARTS OF LIFE CAN END UP BECOMING THE MOST MEANINGFUL.

AVAILABLE NOW.

TOUCHSTONE
5"×7" · 352 PAGES
ISBN-13: 978-1-4165-4946-8
ISBN-10: 1-4165-4946-3